PERU

INVESTMENT AND BUSINESS GUIDE

VOLUME 1

STRATEGIC AND PRACTICAL INFORMATION

International Business Publications, USA
Washington DC, USA- Peru

PERU

INVESTMENT AND BUSINESS GUIDE

VOLUME 1 STRATEGIC AND PRACTICAL INFORMATION

UPDATED ANNUALLY

We express our sincere appreciation to all government agencies and international organizations which provided information and other materials for this guide

Cover Design: **International Business Publications, USA**

2019 Edition Updated Reprint International Business Publications, USA
ISBN 0-7397-6290-7 978-0-7397-6290-5

For additional analytical, business and investment opportunities information,
please contact Global Investment & Business Center, USA
at (703) 370-8082. Fax: (703) 370-8083. E-mail: ibpusa3@gmail.com
Global Business and Investment Info Databank - www.ibpus.com

Printed in the USA

For additional analytical, business and investment opportunities information,
please contact Global Investment & Business Center, USA
at (703) 370-8082. Fax: (703) 370-8083. E-mail: ibpusa3@gmail.com
Global Business and Investment Info Databank - www.ibpus.com

PERU

INVESTMENT AND BUSINESS GUIDE

VOLUME 1

STRATEGIC AND PRACTICAL INFORMATION

TABLE OF CONTENTS

STATEGIC AND BUSINESS PROFILES

BASIC INFORMATION

Capital and largest city	Lima 12°2.6'S 77°1.7'W12.0433°S 77.0283°W
Official languages[a]	• Spanish (official) 84.1% • Quechua (official) 13% • Aymara (official) 1.7% (2007 Census)
Ethnic groups (2013)	• 45% Amerindian • 37% Mestizo • 15% White • 2% others
Demonym	Peruvian
Government	Unitary presidential constitutional republic
- President	Ollanta Humala
- Prime Minister	Pedro Cateriano
Legislature	Congress
Independence from the Kingdom of Spain	
- Declared	28 July 1821
- Consolidated	9 December 1824
- Recognized	2 May 1866
Area	
- Total	1,285,216 km^2 (20th) 496,225 sq mi
- Water (%)	0.41
Population	
- 2015 estimate	31,151,643 (41st)
- 2007 census	28,220,764
- Density	23/km^2 (191st) 57/sq mi
GDP (PPP)	2015 estimate
- Total	$403.322 billion
- Per capita	$12,638
GDP (nominal)	2015 estimate
- Total	$217.607 billion
- Per capita	$6,819
Gini	45.3 medium · 35th
HDI	0.737 high · 82nd
Currency	Nuevo sol (PEN)
Time zone	PET (UTC−5)
Date format	dd.mm.yyyy (CE)
Drives on the	right
Calling code	+51
ISO 3166 code	PE

Internet TLD	.pe

Peru officially the **Republic of Peru** (Spanish: *República del Perú*) is a country in western South America. It is bordered in the north by Ecuador and Colombia, in the east by Brazil, in the southeast by Bolivia, in the south by Chile, and in the west by the Pacific Ocean.

Peruvian territory was home to ancient cultures spanning from the Norte Chico civilization, one of the oldest in the world, to the Inca Empire, the largest state in Pre-Columbian America. The Spanish Empire conquered the region in the 16th century and established a Viceroyalty with its capital in Lima, which included most of its South American colonies. After achieving independence in 1821, Peru has undergone periods of political unrest and fiscal crisis as well as periods of stability and economic upswing. Economic cycles have mostly been based on the extraction of raw materials like guano (1840s-1860s) and rubber (ca. 1900).

Peru is a representative democratic republic divided into 25 regions. Its geography varies from the arid plains of the Pacific coast to the peaks of the Andes Mountains and the tropical forests of the Amazon Basin. It is a developing country with a high Human Development Index score and a poverty level around 28.7 percent. Its main economic activities include agriculture, fishing, mining, and manufacturing of products such as textiles.

The Peruvian population, estimated at 30.4 million, is multiethnic, including Amerindians, Europeans, Africans, and Asians. The main spoken language is Spanish, although a significant number of Peruvians speak Quechua or other native languages. This mixture of cultural traditions has resulted in a wide diversity of expressions in fields such as art, cuisine, literature, and music

GEOGRAPHY

Location: Western South America, bordering the South Pacific Ocean, between Chile and Ecuador
Geographic coordinates: 10 00 S, 76 00 W
Map references: South America

Area:
total: 1,285,220 sq km
land: 1.28 million sq km
water: 5,220 sq km

Area—comparative: slightly smaller than Alaska

Land boundaries:
total: 6,940 km
border countries: Bolivia 900 km, Brazil 1,560 km, Chile 160 km, Colombia 2,900 km, Ecuador 1,420 km

Coastline: 2,414 km

Maritime claims:
continental shelf: 200 nm *territorial sea:* 200 nm

Climate: varies from tropical in east to dry desert in west

Boundary representation is not necessarily authoritative
COLOMBIA
ECUADOR
Quito
Manta
Ambato
Guayaquil
Cuenca
Loja
Tumbes
TUMBES
Talara
Sullana
PIURA
Piura
Paita
LORETO
Iquitos
Amazon
Leticia
Benjamin Constant
Yurimaguas
AMAZONAS
Moyobamba
Chachapoyas
Tarapoto
SAN MARTIN
LAMBAYEQUE
CAJAMARCA
Chiclayo
Cajamarca
LA LIBERTAD
BRAZIL
Cruzeiro do Sul
Santa Lucia
Pucallpa
Trujillo
Salaverry
SOUTH PACIFIC OCEAN
Chimbote
ANCASH
Huaraz
Tingo María
HUANUCO
Huánuco
PASCO
UCAYALI
Rio Branco
Goyllarisquizga
Cerro de Pasco
Huacho
JUNIN
Cobija
MADRE DE DIOS
Lima
Callao
LIMA
Huancayo
CUSCO
Huancavelica
HUANCAVELICA
Quillabamba
Ayacucho
Machupicchu (ruins)
Cusco
Puerto Maldonado
Abancay
APURIMAC
Pisco
Ica
AYACUCHO
ICA
PUNO
BOLIVIA
Nazca
Juliaca
Lago Titicaca
Puno
AREQUIPA
Pan American Highway
Arequipa
Desaguadero
La Paz
Guaqui
MOQUEGUA
Matarani
Moquegua
TACNA
Ilo
Tacna
Oruro
Lago Poopó
Arica
CHILE
Peru
International boundary
Department boundary
National capital
Department capital
Railroad
Road
Callao is the capital of the Constitutional Province of Callao which has the status of a department but is too small to be shown on this map.
0 100 200 Kilometers
0 100 200 Miles
Transverse Mercator Projection, CM 71°W
Base 800745 (B01044) 4-91

Terrain: western coastal plain (costa), high and rugged Andes in center (sierra), eastern lowland jungle of Amazon Basin (selva)
Elevation extremes:
lowest point: Pacific Ocean 0 m
highest point: Nevado Huascaran 6,768 m
Natural resources: copper, silver, gold, petroleum, timber, fish, iron ore, coal, phosphate, potash
Land use:
arable land: 3%
permanent crops: 0%
permanent pastures: 21%
forests and woodland: 66% *other:* 10%
Irrigated land: 12,800 sq km
Natural hazards: earthquakes, tsunamis, flooding, landslides, mild volcanic activity

Environment—current issues: deforestation; overgrazing of the slopes of the costa and sierra leading to soil erosion; desertification; air pollution in Lima; pollution of rivers and coastal waters from municipal and mining wastes

Environment—international agreements:
party to: Antarctic-Environmental Protocol, Antarctic Treaty, Biodiversity, Climate Change, Desertification, Endangered Species, Hazardous Wastes, Nuclear Test Ban, Ozone Layer Protection, Ship Pollution, Tropical Timber 83, Tropical Timber 94, Wetlands, Whaling
signed, but not ratified: Climate Change-Kyoto Protocol

Geography—note: shares control of Lago Titicaca, world's highest navigable lake, with Bolivia

PEOPLE

Population: 26,624,582

Age structure:
0-14 years: 35% (male 4,786,048; female 4,637,280)
15-64 years: 60% (male 8,045,747; female 7,939,760)
65 years and over: 5% (male 557,252; female 658,495)

Population growth rate: 1.93%
Birth rate: 26.09 births/1,000 population
Death rate: 5.7 deaths/1,000 population
Net migration rate: -1.13 migrant(s)/1,000 population

Sex ratio:
at birth: 1.05 male(s)/female
under 15 years: 1.03 male(s)/female
15-64 years: 1.01 male(s)/female
65 years and over: 0.85 male(s)/female
total population: 1.01 male(s)/female

Infant mortality rate: 38.97 deaths/1,000 live births

Life expectancy at birth:
total population: 70.38 years

male: 68.08 years
female: 72.78 years

Total fertility rate: 3.23 children born/woman

Nationality:
noun: Peruvian(s)
adjective: Peruvian

Ethnic groups: Amerindian 45%, mestizo (mixed Amerindian and white) 37%, white 15%, black, Japanese, Chinese, and other 3%
Religions: Roman Catholic
Languages: Spanish (official), Quechua (official), Aymara

Literacy:
definition: age 15 and over can read and write
total population: 88.7%
male: 94.5%
female: 83%

GOVERNMENT

Country name:
conventional long form: Republic of Peru
conventional short form: Peru
local long form: Republica del Peru
local short form: Peru

Data code: PE
Government type: republic
Capital: Lima

Administrative divisions: 24 departments (departamentos, singular—departamento) and 1 constitutional province* (provincia constitucional); Amazonas, Ancash, Apurimac, Arequipa, Ayacucho, Cajamarca, Callao*, Cusco, Huancavelica, Huanuco, Ica, Junin, La Libertad, Lambayeque, Lima, Loreto, Madre de Dios, Moquegua, Pasco, Piura, Puno, San Martin, Tacna, Tumbes, Ucayali
note: the 1979 constitution mandated the creation of regions (regiones, singular—region) to function eventually as autonomous economic and administrative entities; so far, 12 regions have been constituted from 23 of the 24 departments—Amazonas (from Loreto), Andres Avelino Caceres (from Huanuco, Pasco, Junin), Arequipa (from Arequipa), Chavin (from Ancash), Grau (from Tumbes, Piura), Inca (from Cusco, Madre de Dios, Apurimac), La Libertad (from La Libertad), Los Libertadores-Huari (from Ica, Ayacucho, Huancavelica), Mariategui (from Moquegua, Tacna, Puno), Nor Oriental del Maranon (from Lambayeque, Cajamarca, Amazonas), San Martin (from San Martin), Ucayali (from Ucayali); formation of another region has been delayed by the reluctance of the constitutional province of Callao to merge with the department of Lima; because of inadequate funding from the central government and organizational and political difficulties, the regions have yet to assume major responsibilities; the 1993 constitution retains the regions but limits their authority; the 1993 constitution also reaffirms the roles of departmental and municipal governments

Independence: 28 July 1821 (from Spain)

National holiday: Independence Day, 28 July (1821)
Constitution: 31 December 1993
Legal system: based on civil law system; has not accepted compulsory ICJ jurisdiction
Suffrage: 18 years of age; universal

Executive branch: *chief of state:*

chief of state: President Pedro Pablo KUCZYNSKI Godard (since 28 July 2016); First Vice President Martin Alberto VIZCARRA Cornejo (since 28 July 2016); Second Vice President Mercedes Rosalba ARAOZ Fernandez (since 28 July 2016); note - the president is both chief of state and head of government

head of government: President Pedro Pablo KUCZYNSKI Godard (since 28 July 2016); First Vice President Martin Alberto VIZCARRA Cornejo (since 28 July 2016); Second Vice President Mercedes Rosalba ARAOZ Fernandez (since 28 July 2016)

cabinet: Council of Ministers appointed by the president

elections/appointments: president directly elected by absolute majority popular vote in 2 rounds if needed for a 5-year term (eligible for nonconsecutive terms); election last held on 10 April 2016 with runoff on 5 June 2016 (next to be held in April 2021)

election results: Pedro Pablo KUCZYNSKI Godard elected president; first round election results from 10 April 2016: percent of vote - Keiko FUJIMORI Higuchi 39.85%, Pedro Pablo KUCZYNSKI Godard 21%, Veronika MENDOZA 18.82%, Alfredo BARNECHEA 6.97%, Alan GARCIA 5.82%; second round election results from 5 June 2016: percent of vote - Pedro Pablo KUCZYNSKI Godard (Peruanos Por el Kambio) 50.1%, Keiko FUJIMORI Higuchi (Fuerza Popular) 49.9%

note: Prime Minister Fernando ZAVALA Lombardi (since 28 July 2016) does not exercise executive power; this power rests with the president

Legislative branch:

description: unicameral Congress of the Republic of Peru or Congreso de la Republica del Peru (130 seats; members directly elected in multi-seat constituencies by closed party list proportional representation vote to serve 5-year terms)

elections: last held on 10 April 2016 with run-off election on 6 June 2016 (next to be held in April 2021)

election results: percent of vote by party - Fuerza Popular 36.34%, PPK 16.47%, Frente Amplio 13.94%, APP 9.23%; APRA 8.31%; AP 7.20%, other 8.51%; seats by party - Fuerza Popular 71, PPK 20, Frente Amplio 20, APP 9; APRA 5; AP 5

Judicial branch: Supreme Court of Justice (Corte Suprema de Justicia), judges are appointed by the National Council of the Judiciary

Political parties and leaders: Change 90-New Majority or C90/NM [Alberto FUJIMORI]; Union for Peru or UPP [Javier PEREZ de CUELLAR]; American Popular Revolutionary Alliance or APRA [Luis ALVA Castro]; Independent Moralizing Front or FIM [Fernando OLIVERA Vega];

Democratic Coordinator or CODE-Pais Posible [Jose BARBA Caballero and Alejandro TOLEDO]; Popular Action Party or AP [Juan DIAZ Leon]; Popular Christian Party or PPC [Luis BEDOYA Reyes]; Renovation Party [Rafael REY Rey]; Civic Works Movement or OBRAS [Ricardo BELMONT]; United Left or IU [leader NA]; Independent Agrarian Movement or MIA [leader NA]

Political pressure groups and leaders: leftist guerrilla groups include Shining Path [Abimael GUZMAN Reynoso (imprisoned), Oscar RAMIREZ Durand (top leader at-large)]; Tupac Amaru Revolutionary Movement or MRTA [Victor POLAY (imprisoned), Hugo AVALLENEDA Valdez (top leader at-large)]

International organization participation: APEC, CAN, CCC, ECLAC, FAO, G-11, G-15, G-19, G-24, G-77, IADB, IAEA, IBRD, ICAO, ICC, ICFTU, ICRM, IDA, IFAD, IFC, IFRCS, IHO, ILO, IMF, IMO, Inmarsat, Intelsat, Interpol, IOC, IOM, ISO (correspondent), ITU, LAES, LAIA, NAM, OAS, OPANAL, OPCW, PCA, RG, UN, UNCTAD, UNESCO, UNIDO, UPU, WCL, WFTU, WHO, WIPO, WMO, WToO, WTrO

Diplomatic representation in the US:

chief of mission: Ambassador Carlos Jose PAREJA Rios (since 16 September 2016)
chancery: 1700 Massachusetts Avenue NW, Washington, DC 20036
telephone: [1] (202) 833-9860 through 9869
FAX: [1] (202) 659-8124
consulate(s) general: Atlanta, Boston, Chicago, Dallas, Denver, Hartford (CT), Houston, Los Angeles, Miami, New York, Paterson (NJ), San Francisco, Washington DC

Diplomatic representation from the US:
chief of mission: Ambassador Krishna R. URS (since 18 October 2017)
embassy: Avenida La Encalada, Cuadra 17 s/n, Surco, Lima 33
mailing address: P. O. Box 1995, Lima 1; American Embassy (Lima), APO AA 34031-5000
telephone: [51] (1) 618-2000
FAX: [51] (1) 618-2397

Flag description: three equal, vertical bands of red (hoist side), white, and red with the coat of arms centered in the white band; the coat of arms features a shield bearing a llama, cinchona tree (the source of quinine), and a yellow cornucopia spilling out gold coins, all framed by a green wreath

ECONOMY

Peru's economy reflects its varied topography - an arid lowland coastal region, the central high sierra of the Andes, and the dense forest of the Amazon. A wide range of important mineral resources are found in the mountainous and coastal areas, and Peru's coastal waters provide excellent fishing grounds. Peru is the world's second largest producer of silver and copper.

The Peruvian economy grew by an average of 5.6% per year from 2009-13 with a stable exchange rate and low inflation. This growth was due partly to high international prices for Peru's metals and minerals exports, which account for 55% of the country's total exports. Growth slipped from 2014 to 2017, due to weaker world prices for these resources. Despite Peru's strong macroeconomic performance, dependence on minerals and metals exports and imported foodstuffs makes the economy vulnerable to fluctuations in world prices.

Peru's rapid expansion coupled with cash transfers and other programs have helped to reduce the national poverty rate by over 35 percentage points since 2004, but inequality persists and continued to pose a challenge for the Ollanta HUMALA administration, which championed a policy of social inclusion and a more equitable distribution of income. Poor infrastructure hinders the spread of growth to Peru's non-coastal areas. The HUMALA administration passed several economic stimulus packages in 2014 to bolster growth, including reforms to environmental regulations in order to spur investment in Peru's lucrative mining sector, a move that was opposed by some environmental groups. However, in 2015, mining investment fell as global commodity prices remained low and social conflicts plagued the sector.

Peru's free trade policy continued under the HUMALA administration; since 2006, Peru has signed trade deals with the US, Canada, Singapore, China, Korea, Mexico, Japan, the EU, the European Free Trade Association, Chile, Thailand, Costa Rica, Panama, Venezuela, Honduras, concluded negotiations with Guatemala and the Trans-Pacific Partnership, and begun trade talks with El Salvador, India, and Turkey. Peru also has signed a trade pact with Chile, Colombia, and Mexico, called the Pacific Alliance, that seeks integration of services, capital, investment and movement of people. Since the US-Peru Trade Promotion Agreement entered into force in February 2009, total trade between Peru and the US has doubled. President Pedro Pablo KUCZYNSKI succeeded HUMALA in July 2016 and is focusing on economic reforms and free market policies aimed at boosting investment in Peru. Mining output increased significantly in 2016-17, which helped Peru attain one of the highest GDP growth rates in Latin America, and Peru should maintain strong growth in 2018. However, economic performance was depressed by delays in infrastructure mega-projects and the start of a corruption scandal associated with a Brazilian firm. Massive flooding in early 2017 also was a drag on growth, offset somewhat by additional public spending aimed at recovery efforts.

GDP (purchasing power parity):

$424.6 billion (2017 est.)
$413.6 billion (2016 est.)
$397.7 billion (2015 est.)
note: data are in 2017 dollars
country comparison to the world: 47

GDP (official exchange rate):
$210 billion (2016 est.)

GDP - real growth rate:
2.7% (2017 est.)
4% (2016 est.)
3.3% (2015 est.)
country comparison to the world: 126

GDP - per capita (PPP):
$13,300 (2017 est.)
$13,100 (2016 est.)
$12,800 (2015 est.)
note: data are in 2017 dollars
country comparison to the world: 118

Gross national saving:

20.5% of GDP (2017 est.)
20.1% of GDP (2016 est.)
19.7% of GDP (2015 est.)
country comparison to the world: 85

GDP - composition, by end use:
household consumption: 65.3%
government consumption: 11.7%
investment in fixed capital: 21.6%
investment in inventories: 0.2%
exports of goods and services: 23.1%
imports of goods and services: -22% (2017 est.)

GDP - composition, by sector of origin:
agriculture: 7.5%
industry: 36.3%
services: 56.1% (2017 est.)

Agriculture - products:
artichokes, asparagus, avocados, blueberries, coffee, cocoa, cotton, sugarcane, rice, potatoes, corn, plantains, grapes, oranges, pineapples, guavas, bananas, apples, lemons, pears, coca, tomatoes, mangoes, barley, medicinal plants, quinoa, palm oil, marigolds, onions, wheat, dry beans; poultry, beef, pork, dairy products; guinea pigs; fish

Industries:
mining and refining of minerals; steel, metal fabrication; petroleum extraction and refining, natural gas and natural gas liquefaction; fishing and fish processing, cement, glass, textiles, clothing, food processing, beer, soft drinks, rubber, machinery, electrical machinery, chemicals, furniture

Industrial production growth rate:
8% (2017 est.)
country comparison to the world: 18

Labor force:
17.03 million
note: individuals older than 14 years of age (2017 est.)
country comparison to the world: 38

Labor force - by occupation:
agriculture: 25.8%
industry: 17.4%
services: 56.8% (2011)

Unemployment rate:
6.7% (2017 est.)
6.7% (2016 est.)
note: data are for metropolitan Lima; widespread underemployment
country comparison to the world: 94

Population below poverty line:
22.7% (2014 est.)
Household income or consumption by percentage share:
lowest 10%: 1.4%

highest 10%: 36.1% (2010 est.)

Distribution of family income - Gini index:
45.3 (2012)
51 (2005)
country comparison to the world: 39

Budget:
revenues: $59.66 billion
expenditures: $65.48 billion (2017 est.)

Taxes and other revenues:
28.4% of GDP (2017 est.)
country comparison to the world: 94

Budget surplus (+) or deficit (-):
-2.8% of GDP (2017 est.)
country comparison to the world: 107

Public debt:
25.7% of GDP (2017 est.)
23.8% of GDP (2016 est.)
note: data cover general government debt, and includes debt instruments issued by government entities other than the treasury; the data exclude treasury debt held by foreign entities; the data include debt issued by subnational entities
country comparison to the world: 176

Fiscal year:
calendar year
Inflation rate (consumer prices):
3.2% (2017 est.)
3.6% (2016 est.)
note: data are for metropolitan Lima, annual average
country comparison to the world: 135

Central bank discount rate:
4.25% (31 December 2016 est.)
5.05% (31 December 2012)
country comparison to the world: 93

Commercial bank prime lending rate:
16.5% (31 December 2017 est.)
16.47% (31 December 2016 est.)
note: domestic currency lending rate, 90 day maturity
country comparison to the world: 30

Stock of narrow money:
$33.83 billion (31 December 2017 est.)
$31.08 billion (31 December 2016 est.)
country comparison to the world: 60

Stock of broad money:
$96.27 billion (31 December 2017 est.)
$84.84 billion (31 December 2016 est.)

country comparison to the world: 57

Stock of domestic credit:
$58.75 billion (31 December 2017 est.)
$52.8 billion (31 December 2016 est.)
country comparison to the world: 63

Market value of publicly traded shares:
$56.56 billion (31 December 2015 est.)
$78.84 billion (31 December 2014 est.)
$80.98 billion (31 December 2013 est.)
country comparison to the world: 47

Current account balance:
-$3.22 billion (2017 est.)
-$5.305 billion (2016 est.)
country comparison to the world: 168

Exports:
$42.47 billion (2017 est.)
$37.02 billion (2016 est.)
country comparison to the world: 53

Exports - commodities:
copper, gold, lead, zinc, tin, iron ore, molybdenum, silver; crude petroleum and petroleum products, natural gas; coffee, asparagus and other vegetables, fruit, apparel and textiles, fishmeal, fish, chemicals, fabricated metal products and machinery, alloys

Exports - partners:
China 23.5%, US 17.3%, Switzerland 7.1%, Canada 4.7% (2016)

Imports:
$38.8 billion (2017 est.)
$35.13 billion (2016 est.)
country comparison to the world: 57

Imports - commodities:
petroleum and petroleum products, chemicals, plastics, machinery, vehicles, TV sets, power shovels, front-end loaders, telephones and telecommunication equipment, iron and steel, wheat, corn, soybean products, paper, cotton, vaccines and medicines

Imports - partners:
China 22.8%, US 20.2%, Brazil 5.8%, Mexico 4.5% (2016)

Reserves of foreign exchange and gold:
$61.34 billion (31 December 2017 est.)
$61.81 billion (31 December 2016 est.)
country comparison to the world: 34

Debt - external:
$70.09 billion (31 December 2017 est.)
$66.76 billion (31 December 2016 est.)
country comparison to the world: 61

Stock of direct foreign investment - at home:
$97.29 billion (31 December 2017 est.)
$91.48 billion (31 December 2016 est.)
country comparison to the world: 47

Stock of direct foreign investment - abroad:
$4.362 billion (31 December 2017 est.)
$4.255 billion (31 December 2016 est.)
country comparison to the world: 74

Exchange rates:
nuevo sol (PEN) per US dollar -
3.265 (2017 est.)
3.3751 (2016 est.)
3.3751 (2015 est.)
3.185 (2014 est.)
2.8383 (2013 est.)

ENERGY

Electricity - production:
38.7 billion kWh (est.)
country comparison to the world: 59

Electricity - consumption:
34.25 billion kWh (est.)
country comparison to the world: 58

Electricity - exports:
0 kWh (est.)
country comparison to the world: 116

Electricity - imports:
6 million kWh (est.)
country comparison to the world: 105

Electricity - installed generating capacity:
7.982 million kW (est.)
country comparison to the world: 63

Electricity - from fossil fuels:
59% of total installed capacity (est.)
country comparison to the world: 138

Electricity - from nuclear fuels:
0% of total installed capacity (est.)
country comparison to the world: 158

Electricity - from hydroelectric plants:
41% of total installed capacity (est.)
country comparison to the world: 55

Electricity - from other renewable sources:
0% of total installed capacity (est.)
country comparison to the world: 172

Crude oil - production:
152,600 bbl/day (est.)
country comparison to the world: 44

Crude oil - exports:
18,880 bbl/day (est.)
country comparison to the world: 53

Crude oil - imports:
99,590 bbl/day (est.)
country comparison to the world: 48

Crude oil - proved reserves:
586.1 million bbl (1 January 2012 est.)
country comparison to the world: 48

Refined petroleum products - production:
173,700 bbl/day (est.)
country comparison to the world: 58

Refined petroleum products - consumption:
172,600 bbl/day (est.)
country comparison to the world: 61

Refined petroleum products - exports:
60,720 bbl/day (est.)
country comparison to the world: 54

Refined petroleum products - imports:
38,390 bbl/day (est.)
country comparison to the world: 77

Natural gas - production:
31.12 billion cu m
country comparison to the world: 28

Natural gas - consumption:
5.41 billion cu m (est.)
country comparison to the world: 56

Natural gas - exports:
3.59 billion cu m (est.)
country comparison to the world: 32

Natural gas - imports:
0 cu m (2011)
country comparison to the world: 114

Natural gas - proved reserves:
352.8 billion cu m (1 January 2012 est.)
country comparison to the world: 37

Carbon dioxide emissions from consumption of energy:
41.88 million Mt (est.)
country comparison to the world: 66

COMMUNICATIONS

Telephones - fixed lines:
total subscriptions: 3.03 million
subscriptions per 100 inhabitants: 10
country comparison to the world: 48

Telephones - mobile cellular:
total: 31.7 million
subscriptions per 100 inhabitants: 105
country comparison to the world: 38

Telephone system:

general assessment: adequate for most requirements; nationwide microwave radio relay system and a domestic satellite system with 12 earth stations
domestic: fixed-line teledensity is only about 12 per 100 persons; mobile-cellular teledensity, spurred by competition among multiple providers, exceeds 100 telephones per 100 persons

international: country code - 51; the South America-1 (SAM-1) and Pan American (PAN-AM) submarine cable systems provide links to parts of Central and South America, the Caribbean, and US; satellite earth stations - 2 Intelsat (Atlantic Ocean) (2010)
Broadcast media:
10 major TV networks of which only one, Television Nacional de Peru, is state owned; multi-channel cable TV services are available; in excess of 2,000 radio stations including a substantial number of indigenous language stations (2010)

Radio broadcast stations:
AM 472, FM 198, shortwave 189

Television broadcast stations:
13 (plus 112 repeaters)
Internet country code: .pe

Internet users:

total: 12.3 million

percent of population: 40.9%
country comparison to the world: 39

TRANSPORTATION

Railways:
total: 2,041 km
standard gauge: 1,726 km 1.435-m gauge
narrow gauge: 315 km 0.914-m gauge

Highways:
total: 72,146 km
paved: 7,353 km
unpaved: 64,793 km

Waterways: 8,600 km of navigable tributaries of Amazon system and 208 km of Lago Titicaca

Pipelines: crude oil 800 km; natural gas and natural gas liquids 64 km

Ports and harbors: Callao, Chimbote, Ilo, Matarani, Paita, Puerto Maldonado, Salaverry, San Martin, Talara, Iquitos, Pucallpa, Yurimaguas
note: Iquitos, Pucallpa, and Yurimaguas are all on the upper reaches of the Amazon and its tributaries

Merchant marine:
total: 7 ships (1,000 GRT or over) totaling 51,518 GRT/75,018 DWT
ships by type: cargo 6, oil tanker 1

Airports: 244

Airports—with paved runways:
total: 44
over 3,047 m: 7
2,438 to 3,047 m: 15
1,524 to 2,437 m: 12
914 to 1,523 m: 8
under 914 m: 2

Airports—with unpaved runways:
total: 200
over 3,047 m: 1
2,438 to 3,047 m: 3
1,524 to 2,437 m: 24
914 to 1,523 m: 73
under 914 m: 99

MILITARY

Military branches:

Peruvian Army (Ejercito Peruano), Peruvian Navy (Marina de Guerra del Peru, MGP; includes naval air, naval infantry, and Coast Guard), Air Force of Peru (Fuerza Aerea del Peru, FAP) (2013)

Military service age and obligation:
18-50 years of age for male and 18-45 years of age for female voluntary military service; no conscription (2012)

Manpower available for military service:
males age 16-49: 7,385,588
females age 16-49: 7,727,623

Manpower fit for military service:
males age 16-49: 5,788,629
females age 16-49: 6,565,097

Manpower reaching militarily significant age annually:
male: 304,094
female: 298,447
Military expenditures:

1.28% of GDP
1.15% of GDP (2011)
1.28% of GDP (2010)

TRANSNATIONAL ISSUES

Disputes - international:

Chile and Ecuador rejected Peru's November 2005 unilateral legislation to shift the axis of their joint treaty-defined maritime boundaries along the parallels of latitude to equidistance lines which favor Peru; organized illegal narcotics operations in Colombia have penetrated Peru's shared border; Peru rejects Bolivia's claim to restore maritime access through a sovereign corridor through Chile along the Peruvian border

Refugees and internally displaced persons:

IDPs: at least 150,000 (civil war from 1980-2000; most IDPs are indigenous peasants in Andean and Amazonian regions; as of 2011, no new information on the situation of these IDPs)

Illicit drugs:

until 1996 the world's largest coca leaf producer, Peru is now the world's second largest producer of coca leaf, though it lags far behind Colombia; cultivation of coca in Peru was estimated at 40,000 hectares in 2009, a slight decrease over 2008; second largest producer of cocaine, estimated at 225 metric tons of potential pure cocaine in 2009; finished cocaine is shipped out from Pacific ports to the international drug market; increasing amounts of base and finished cocaine, however, are being moved to Brazil, Chile, Argentina, and Bolivia for use in the Southern Cone or transshipment to Europe and Africa; increasing domestic drug consumption

IMPORTANT INFORMATION FOR UNDERSTANDING PERU

Official Name: Republic of Peru

PROFILE

OFFICIAL NAME: Republic of Peru

Geography

Area: 1.28 million sq. km. (496,225 sq. mi.). Peru is the third-largest country in South America and is approximately three times the size of California.
Cities: Lima (capital), Arequipa, Chiclayo, Cuzco, Huancayo, Ica, Trujillo, Ayacucho, Piura, Iquitos, Chimbote.
Terrain: Western arid coastal plains, central rugged Andean mountains, and eastern lowlands with tropical forests that are part of the Amazon basin.
Climate: Arid and mild in coastal area, temperate to frigid in the Andes, and warm and humid in the jungle lowlands.

People

Nationality: Peruvian.
Ethnic groups: Indigenous (45%), mixed background ("mestizo") (37%), European (15%), African, Japanese, Chinese, and other (3%).
Population: 27.2 million (2005 census). Approximately 30% of the population lives in the Lima/Callao metropolitan area.
Annual population growth rate (2005 est.): 1.46%.
Religions: Roman Catholic (90%), Seventh Day Adventist (1.4%), other Christian (0.7%).
Languages: Spanish is the principal language. Quechua, Aymara and other indigenous languages also have official status.
Education: *Years compulsory*--11. *Attendance*--92% ages 6-11, and 66% ages 12-16. *Literacy*--95% in urban areas, 77% in rural areas.
Health: *Infant mortality rate* --31.94/1,000. *Life expectancy* --67.77 years male; 71.37 years female.
Unemployment : 9.6%; underemployment : 54.9%.

Government

Type: Constitutional republic.
Independence: July 28, 1821.
Constitution: December 31, 1993.
Branches: *Executive*--President, two Vice Presidents, and a Council of Ministers led by a Prime Minister. *Legislative*--Unicameral Congress. *Judicial*--Four-tier court structure consisting of Supreme Court and lower courts.
Administrative divisions: 25 departments subdivided into 180 provinces and 1,747 districts.
Political parties: Alianza Popular Revolucionaria Americana (APRA), National Unity (UN), Peru Posible (PP), Popular Action (AP), Union for Peru (UPP), Solucion Popular, Somos Peru (SP).
Suffrage: Universal and mandatory for citizens 18 to 70.

PEOPLE

Peru is the fifth most populous country in Latin America (after Brazil, Mexico, Colombia and Argentina). Twenty-one cities have a population of 100,000 or more. Rural migration has increased the urban population from 35.4% of the total population in 1940 to an estimated 73% today.

Most Peruvians are either Spanish-speaking mestizos--a term that usually refers to a mixture of indigenous and European/Caucasian--or Amerindians, largely Quechua-speaking indigenous people. Peruvians of European descent make up about 15% of the population. There also are small numbers of persons of African, Japanese, and Chinese ancestry. Socioeconomic and cultural indicators are increasingly important as identifiers. For example, Peruvians of Amerindian descent who have adopted aspects of Hispanic culture also are considered mestizo. With economic development, access to education, intermarriage, and large-scale migration from rural to urban areas, a more homogeneous national culture is developing, mainly along the relatively more prosperous coast. Peru's distinct geographical regions are mirrored in a socioeconomic divide between the coast's mestizo-Hispanic culture and the more diverse, traditional Andean cultures of the mountains and highlands.

HISTORY, GOVERNMENT, AND POLITICAL CONDITIONS

The Inca Empire and Spanish Conquest

When the Spanish landed in 1531, Peru's territory was the nucleus of the highly developed Inca civilization. Centered at Cuzco, the Incan Empire extended over a vast region from northern Ecuador to central Chile. In search of Inca wealth, the Spanish conqueror Francisco Pizarro, who arrived in the territory after the Incas had fought a debilitating civil war, conquered the weakened people. The Spanish captured the Incan capital at Cuzco by 1533, and consolidated their control by 1542. Gold and silver from the Andes enriched the conquerors, and Peru became the principal source of Spanish wealth and power in South America.

Pizarro founded Lima in 1535. The viceroyalty established at Lima in 1542 initially had jurisdiction over all of the Spanish colonies in South America. By the time of the wars of independence (1820-24), Lima had become one of the most distinguished and aristocratic colonial capital and the chief Spanish stronghold in the Americas.

Independence

Peru's independence movement was led by Jose de San Martin of Argentina and Simon Bolivar of Venezuela. San Martin proclaimed Peruvian independence from Spain on July 28, 1821. Emancipation was completed in December 1824, when Venezuelan General Antonio Jose de Sucre defeated the Spanish troops at Ayacucho, ending Spanish rule in South America. Spain subsequently made futile attempts to regain its former colonies, but in 1879 it finally recognized Peru's independence.

After independence, Peru and its neighbors engaged in intermittent territorial disputes. Chile's victory over Peru and Bolivia in the War of the Pacific (1879-83) resulted in a territorial settlement in which Peru ceded the department of Tarapaca and the provinces of Tacna and Arica to Chile. In 1929, Chile returned Tacna to Peru. Following a clash between Peru and Ecuador in 1941, the Rio Protocol--of which the United States is one of four guarantors (along with Argentina, Brazil and Chile)--sought to establish the boundary between the two countries. Continuing boundary disagreement led to brief armed conflicts in early 1981 and early 1995, but in 1998 the governments of Peru and Ecuador signed an historic peace treaty and demarcated the border. In late 1999, the governments of Peru and Chile likewise implemented the last outstanding article of their 1929 border agreement. Peru and Chile still dispute the sea boundary.

Contemporary History

Military Rule and Return to Democracy (1968-1980)

The military has been prominent in Peruvian history. Coups have repeatedly interrupted civilian constitutional government. The most recent period of military rule (1968-80) began when Gen.

Juan Velasco Alvarado overthrew elected President Fernando Belaunde Terry of the Popular Action Party (AP). As part of what has been called the "first phase" of the military government's nationalist program, Velasco undertook an extensive agrarian reform program and nationalized the fishmeal industry, some petroleum and mining companies, and several banks.

Because of Velasco's economic mismanagement and deteriorating health, he was replaced in 1975 by Gen. Francisco Morales Bermudez. Morales Bermudez tempered the authoritarian abuses of the Velasco administration and began the task of restoring the country's economy. Morales Bermudez presided over the return to civilian government under a new constitution and in the May 1980 elections, President Belaunde Terry was returned to office by an impressive plurality.

Instability in the 1980s (1982-1990)

Nagging economic problems left over from the military government persisted, worsened by an occurrence of the "El Niño" weather phenomenon in 1982-83, which caused widespread flooding in some parts of the country, severe droughts in others, and decimated the fishing industry. The fall in international commodity prices to their lowest levels since the Great Depression combined with the natural disasters to decrease production, depress wages, exacerbate unemployment, and spur inflation. The economic collapse was reflected in worsening living conditions for Peru's poor and provided a breeding ground for social and political discontent. The emergence of the terrorist group Sendero Luminoso (Shining Path) in rural areas in 1980--followed shortly thereafter by the Tupac Amaru Revolutionary Movement (MRTA) in Lima--sent the country further into chaos. The terrorists were financed in part from alliances with narcotraffickers, who had established a stronghold in the Peruvian Andes during this period. Peru and Bolivia became the largest coca producers in the world, accounting for roughly four-fifths of the production in South America.

Amid inflation, economic hardship, and terrorism, the American Popular Revolutionary Alliance (APRA) won the presidential election in 1985, bringing Alan García to office. The transfer of the presidency from Belaunde to García on July 28, 1985, was Peru's first transfer of power from one democratically elected leader to another in 40 years.

The Fujimori Decade (1990-2000)

Economic mismanagement by the García administration led to hyperinflation from 1988 to 1990. Concerned about the economy, the increasing terrorist threat from Sendero Luminoso, and allegations of official corruption, voters chose a relatively unknown mathematician-turned-politician, Alberto Fujimori, as president in 1990. Fujimori felt he had a mandate for radical change. He immediately implemented drastic economic reforms to tackle inflation (which dropped from 7,650% in 1990 to 139% in 1991), but found opposition to further drastic measures, including dealing with the growing insurgency. On April 4, 1992, Fujimori dissolved the Congress in the "auto-coup," revised the constitution, and called new congressional elections. With a more pliant Congress, Fujimori proceeded to govern unimpeded. Large segments of the judiciary, the military and the media were co-opted by Fujimori's security advisor, the shadowy Vladimiro Montesinos. The government unleashed a counterattack against the insurgency that resulted in countless human right abuses and eventually quashed the Shining Path and MRTA. During this time he also privatized state-owned companies, removed investment barriers and significantly improved public finances.

Fujimori's constitutionally questionable decision to seek a third term, and subsequent tainted electoral victory in June 2000, brought political and economic turmoil. A bribery scandal that broke just weeks after he began his third term in July forced Fujimori to call new elections in which he would not run. Fujimori fled the country and resigned from office in November 2000. A caretaker government under Valentin Paniagua presided over new presidential and congressional elections in April 2001. The new elected government, led by President Alejandro Toledo, took office July 28, 2001.

The Toledo Administration (2001-2006)

The Toledo government successfully consolidated Peru's return to democracy, a process that had begun under President Paniagua. The government undertook initiatives to implement the recommendations made by the Truth and Reconciliation Commission (TRC), which had been charged with studying the circumstances surrounding the human rights abuses and violations committed between 1980 and 2000. Criminal charges for corruption and human rights violations were brought against former President Fujimori, who is in Chile fighting efforts to extradite him to Peru. Despite being a frequent target of media criticism, Toledo has maintained strong commitments to freedom of the press.

Under President Toledo, Peru signed a Trade Promotion Agreement (TPA) with the U.S., to replace the Andean Trade Preferences and Drug Eradication Act, which expires in December 2006. Toledo also unveiled the construction of a road that will connect Brazil and Peru's isolated interior to the Pacific coast.

Toledo's strong economic management has led to an impressive economic boom in Peru that remains strong. Poverty reduction has been uneven, however. Although poverty in some areas has decreased by up to 37% over the last five years, nationally it has only decreased by 5% and over half of Peruvians are still considered to be living below the poverty line (living on less than $2 a day). In 2005 the government implemented "Juntos," a program to double the income of people living under extreme poverty (less than $1 a day).

2006 Elections and Transition

Peru held presidential and congressional elections on April 9, 2006, and in a presidential runoff on June 4 between the two top vote-getters, former President Alan Garcia, of the APRA party, defeated Ollanta Humala, of the Union por el Peru (UPP) party, 52% to 47%, respectively. Despite the loss, Humala's UPP will have the largest block in Congress, with 45 seats, followed by Garcia's APRA with 36, the Union Nacional coalition with 17, and four other parties splitting the remaining 22 seats.

Garcia and the members of Congress will be sworn in on July 28, 2006.

Constitution and Political Institutions

The president is popularly elected for a five year term. A constitutional amendment passed in 2000 prevents reelection. The first and second vice presidents also are popularly elected but have no constitutional functions unless the president is unable to discharge his duties. The principal executive body is the Council of Ministers, comprised of 15 members and headed by a prime minister. The president appoints its members, who must be ratified by the Congress. All Executive laws sent to Congress must be approved by the Council of Ministers.

The legislative branch consists of a unicameral Congress of 120 members. In addition to passing laws, Congress ratifies treaties, authorizes government loans, and approves the government budget.

The judicial branch of government is headed by a 16-member Supreme Court. The Constitutional Tribunal interprets the constitution on matters of individual rights. Superior courts in departmental capitals review appeals from decisions by lower courts. Courts of first instance are located in provincial capitals and are divided into civil, penal, and special chambers. The judiciary has created several temporary specialized courts in an attempt to reduce the large backlog of cases pending final court action. In 1996 a human rights Ombudsman's office was created.

Peru is divided into 25 regions. The regions are subdivided into provinces, which are composed of districts. High authorities in the regional and local levels are elected. The country's latest decentralization program is in hiatus after the proposal to merge departments was defeated in a national referendum in October 2005.

Principal Government Officials

Ministry	Current	Since date
President of the Council of Ministers	Fernando Martín Zavala Lombardi	28 July 2016
Minister of Foreign Affairs	Víctor Ricardo Luna Mendoza	28 July 2016
Minister of Defense	Jorge Nieto Montesinos	5 December 2016
Minister of Economy and Finance	Alfredo Eduardo Thorne Vetter	28 July 2016
Minister of the Interior	Carlos Miguel Ramón Basombrío Iglesias	28 July 2016
Minister of Education	Marilú Doris Martens Cortés	18 December 2016
Minister of Health	Patricia Jannet García Funegra	28 July 2016
Minister of Labor and Promotion of Employment	Alfonso Fernando Grados Carraro	28 July 2016
Minister of Agriculture and Irrigation	José Manuel Hernández Calderón	28 July 2016
Minister of Production	Bruno Giuffra Monteverde	28 July 2016
Minister of Foreign Commerce and Tourism	Eduardo Ferreyros Küppers	28 July 2016
Minister of Energy and Mines	Gonzalo Francisco Alberto Tamayo Flores	28 July 2016
Minister of Transportation and Communications	Martín Alberto Vizcarra Cornejo	28 July 2016
Minister of Housing, Construction and Sanitation	Edmer Trujillo Mori	28 July 2016
Minister of Women and Vulnerable Populations	Ana María Romero-Lozada Lauezzari	28 July 2016
Minister of Environment	Elsa Patricia Galarza Contreras	28 July 2016
Minister of Culture	Salvador Alejandro Jorge del Solar Labarthe	5 December 2016
Minister of Justice and Human Rights	María Soledad Pérez Tello de Rodríguez	28 July 2016
Minister of Development and Social Inclusion	Lucía Cayetana Aljovín Gazzani	28 July 2016

Peru maintains an embassy in the United States at 1700 Massachusetts Avenue, NW, Washington, DC 20036 (tel. (202) 833-9860/67, consular section: (202) 462-1084). Peru has consulates in Atlanta, New York, Paterson (NJ), Miami, Chicago, Houston, Denver, Los Angeles, San Francisco, Boston, and Hartford.

ECONOMY

Currency	Peruvian sol (PEN)

Fiscal year	calendar year
	Statistics
GDP	$468 billion (PPP, 2014, est.)
GDP rank	39th (PPP, 2014)
GDP growth	5.9% (2013)
GDP per capita	$ 13,735 (PPP, 2014 est.)
GDP by sector	agriculture: 6.2%; industry: 37.5%; services: 56.3% (2013 est.)
Inflation (CPI)	▼2% (2014 est.)
Population below poverty line	▼25.8%
Gini coefficient	▼ 48.1
Labour force	21.16 million
Labour force by occupation	industry: 17.4%, agriculture: 25.8%, services: 56.8% (2011)
Unemployment	▼3.6%
Main industries	mining and refining of minerals/jewels; steel, metal fabrication; petroleum extraction and refining, natural gas and natural gas liquefaction, fishing and fish processing, cement, glass, textiles, clothing, food processing, beer, soft drinks, rubber, machinery, electrical machinery. chemicals, furniture
Ease-of-doing-business rank	39th
	External
Exports	$73.50 billion (2013 est.)
Export goods	copper, gold, lead, zinc, tin, iron ore, molybdenum, silver, crude petroleum and petroleum products, natural gas, coffee, asparagus, and other vegetables, fruit, apparel and textiles, fishmeal, fish, chemicals, fabricated metal products and machinery, alloys
Main export partners	China 19.5% United States 15.1% Switzerland 7.3% Canada 6.7% Brazil 5.6% Japan 5.2% Chile 4.7% (2014 est.)
Imports	$68 billion (2013 est.)
Import goods	petroleum and petroleum products, chemicals, plastics, machinery, vehicles, color TV sets, power shovels, front-end loaders, telephones and telecommunications equipment, iron and steel, wheat, corn, soybean products, paper, cotton, vaccines and medicines
Main import partners	United States 22.7% China 22.1% Brazil 6.9% Mexico 6.6% Venezuela 4.6% Ecuador 4.2% Colombia 4.2% (2014 est.)
FDI stock	$76.57 billion (31 December 2013 est.)
Gross external debt	$30.15 billion (31 December 2013 est.)
	Public finances
Public debt	10.9% of GDP
Revenues	$70.95 billion
Expenses	$66.42 billion (2012 est.)

Economic aid	$5.250 billion (2012 est.)
Credit rating	• Standard & Poor's: A- (Domestic) BBB+ (Foreign) A (T&C Assessment) Outlook: Stable • Moody's: A3 Outlook: Stable • Fitch: BBB+ Outlook: Positive
Foreign reserves	US$71.22 billion

Peru is classified as *upper middle income* by the World Bank and is the 39th largest in the world by total GDP. Peru is one of the world's fastest-growing economies with a 2012 GDP growth rate of 6.3%.It currently has a high human development index of 0.741 and per capita GDP above $12,000 by PPP.

The core of the current sound economic performance of the country is a combination of:

- Macroeconomic stability
- Prudent fiscal spending
- High international reserve accumulation
- External debt reduction
- Achievement of investment grade status
- Fiscal surpluses

All of these factors have enabled Peru to make great strides in development, with improvement in government finances, poverty reduction and progress in social sectors. Poverty has decreased dramatically in the past decade, from nearly 60% in 2004 to 25.8% in 2012.

Peru is an emerging, social market economy characterized by a high level of foreign trade. The inequality of opportunities has declined: between 1991 and 2012 Peru's rating on The World Bank's Human Opportunity Index improved substantially as increased public investment in water, sanitation and electric power has sustained the downward trend in inequality of opportunities. Its economy is diversified, although commodity exports still make up a significant proportion of economic activity and thus subject the economy to the risks of price volatility in the international markets. Trade and industry are centralized in Lima but agricultural exports have led to development in all the regions.

Peruvian economic performance has been tied to exports, which provide hard currency to finance imports and external debt payments. Peru's main exports are copper, gold, zinc, textiles, chemicals, pharmaceuticals, manufactures, machinery, services and fish meal; its major trade partners are the United States, China, Brazil, European Union and Chile. Although exports have provided substantial revenue, self-sustained growth and a more egalitarian distribution of income have proven elusive.

Services account for 43% of Peruvian gross domestic product, followed by manufacturing (32.3%), extractive industries (15%), and taxes (9.7%).Recent economic growth has been fueled by macroeconomic stability, improved terms of trade, and rising investment and consumption. China has become Peru's largest trading partner following a free trade agreement with the

People´s Republic of China signed on April 28, 2009 additional free trade agreements have being signed with the United States of America (2006) free trade agreement with the United States signed on April 12, 2006, the European Union June 26, 2012.*The EU and Peru Sign Trade Promotion Agreement*, with Japan free trade agreement with the constitutional monarchy of Japan signed on May 31, 2011

Inflation in 2012 was the lowest in Latin America at only 1.8%, but increased in 2013 as oil and commodity prices rose; as of 2014 it stands at 2.5%.The unemployment rate has fallen steadily in recent years, and as of 2012 stands at 3.6%.

Peru's economy is one of the most dynamic in Latin America, showing particularly strong growth over the past five years. During the 1990s, Peru was transformed by market-oriented economic reforms and privatizations, and met many conditions for long-term growth. From 1994 through 1997, the economy recorded robust growth driven by foreign direct investment, but stagnated from 1998 through 2001. Upon taking office in 2001, President Alejandro Toledo maintained largely orthodox economic policies, and took measures to attract investment. GDP grew 6.7% in 2005, 4.8% in 2004, 4.0% in 2003, and 4.9% in 2002. Recent economic expansion has been driven by construction, mining, investment (particularly in the Camisea natural gas project), domestic demand, and exports. Inflation was 1.5% by year-end 2005, and the fiscal deficit fell to 0.6 % of GDP. In 2005 external debt decreased to 41.8% of GDP, and foreign reserves reached a record $14.1 billion by the end of 2005.

Peru's economy is well managed, and better tax collection and growth are increasing revenues, with expenditures keeping pace. Private investment is rising and becoming more broad-based. The government has had success with recent international bond issuances, resulting in ratings upgrades.

Foreign Trade and Balance of Payments
Peru and the U.S. signed the Trade Promotion Agreement on April 12, 2006 in Washington, DC. The Trade Promotion Agreement must still be ratified by both the Peruvian and U.S. Congresses.

Peru registered a $5.2 billion trade surplus in 2005, as exports swelled to $17 billion, up 37% from 2004. Peruvian growth was propelled by high mineral prices, U.S. Andean Trade Promotion and Drug Eradication Act (ATPDEA) benefits and completion of the Camisea gas project. The trade surplus drove up reserves and caused the currency to strengthen 3.4% against the dollar over the year.

Peru's strong economic performance allowed it to buy back $2 billion in debt from the Paris Club in June 2005.

Peru's major trading partners are the U.S., the European Union (EU), China, Chile, and Japan. In 2005, 30.6% of exports went to the U.S. and 17.9% of imports came from the U.S. Exports include gold, copper, fishmeal, petroleum, zinc, textiles, apparel, asparagus and coffee. Imports include machinery, vehicles, processed food, petroleum and steel. Peru belongs to the Andean Community, the Asia-Pacific Economic Cooperation forum (APEC), and the World Trade Organization (WTO).

Foreign Investment
The Peruvian Government actively seeks to attract both foreign and domestic investment in all sectors of the economy. The registered stock of foreign direct investment (FDI) is over $14.3 billion, with the U.S., Spain and Britain the leading investors. FDI is concentrated in telecommunications, mining, manufacturing, finance, and electricity. International investment was

spurred by the significant progress Peru made during the 1990s toward economic, social, and political stability. The Peruvian government's economic stabilization and liberalization program lowered trade barriers, eliminated restrictions on capital flows, and opened the economy to foreign investment, with the result that Peru now has one of the most open investment regimes in the world. Between 1992 and 2001, Peru attracted $10 billion in foreign direct investment, after negligible investment during the 1980s. President Alejandro Toledo has made investment promotion a priority of his government.

The basic legal structure for foreign investment in Peru is formed by the 1993 constitution, the Private Investment Growth Law, and the November 1996 Investment Promotion Law. Although Peru does not have a bilateral investment treaty with the United States, it has signed an agreement (1993) with the Overseas Private Investment Corporation concerning OPIC-financed loans, guarantees, and investments. Peru also has committed itself to arbitration of investment disputes under the auspices of the World Bank's International Center for the Settlement of Investment Disputes (ICSID) or other international or national arbitration tribunals. The Report to Congress on Expropriation Claims and Certain Other Investment Disputes (Section 527) lists 6 active investment disputes in Peru involving U.S. companies for 2005, many of which are either under arbitration or the jurisdiction of the local courts.

Mining and Energy

Peru is a source of both natural gas and petroleum, although the country is a net energy importer. Oil output has been in steady decline since the early 1980s, resulting in Peru running an oil trade deficit since 1992. Crude oil production in 2003 averaged 91,351 barrels per day (bpd), compared to 195,000 in 1982. Recent initiatives by the Peruvian Government have begun to enhance incentives for private sector investment in oil exploration, although several barriers remain in place.

In August 2004, Peru inaugurated operations of the Camisea natural gas project. Camisea gas is fueling an electricity generator and six industrial plans in Lima, with other facilities in the process of switching to gas. In a second phase, liquefied natural gas (LNG) will be exported to the west coast of the United States and Mexico. The gas and condensates from Camisea are equivalent to some 2.4 billion barrels of oil, approximately seven times the size of Peru's proven oil reserves. The Camisea project is expected to gradually transform Peru's economy and catalyze national development. Once the export phase is in place, the project is expected to boost GDP by 1.3% annually for 20 to 40 years, draw over $3 billion in FDI, create thousands of jobs, generate $10 billion in government revenues, and turn Peru into a net energy exporter.

Peru is the world's second-largest producer of silver, sixth-largest producer of gold and copper, and a significant source of the world's zinc and lead. Mineral exports have consistently accounted for the most significant portion of Peru's export revenue, averaging around 50% of total earnings in 1998 to 2005.

Economic Outlook

Under President Toledo, Peru has had one of the best performing economies in Latin America, largely attributable to growth in the mining and export sectors. Solid growth and continued increases in tax revenues, barring severe external shocks, should allow positive macroeconomic trends to continue in 2006.

Despite Peru's macroeconomic success, major challenges remain. The Government of Peru faces strong social pressures to reduce poverty of 52% (under $58/month) and extreme poverty of 19% (under $32/month). One-fourth of children under five are malnourished. Wealth and economic activity are overly concentrated in Lima and other major cities, with rural Andean and jungle areas suffering extreme poverty. Unemployment and underemployment levels total 64.5% nationwide. Growth is barely strong enough to generate employment faster than new entrants come into the labor force. The government lacks revenues for adequate social investment. Boosting long-term growth and reducing poverty will require strengthening the judiciary and other institutions, reducing corruption and completing other reforms to improve the investment climate.

FOREIGN RELATIONS

Peru generally enjoys friendly relations with its neighbors. Peru, however, has expressed concern over recent weapon purchases by Latin American nations, in particular Chile, citing the need to avoid a regional arms race.

In November 1999, Peru and Chile signed three agreements that put to rest the remaining obstacles holding up implementation of the 1929 Border Treaty. (The 1929 Border Treaty officially ended the 1879 War of the Pacific.) However in late 2005, a declaration of maritime borders by Peru's Congress set off a new round of recriminations with Chile, which claims that the maritime borders were agreed to in fishing pacts dating from the early 1950s.

In October 1998, Peru and Ecuador signed a peace accord to resolve once and for all border differences that had sparked violent confrontations. Peru and Ecuador are now jointly coordinating an internationally sponsored border integration project. The U.S. Government, as one of four guarantor states, was actively involved in facilitating the 1998 peace accord between Peru and Ecuador and remains committed to its implementation. The United States has pledged $40 million to the Peru-Ecuador border integration project and another $4 million to support Peruvian and Ecuadorian demining efforts along their common border.

In 1998, Peru became a member of the Asia-Pacific Economic Cooperation (APEC) forum, facilitating closer ties and economic relations between Peru and Asian nations.

Peru has been a member of the United Nations since 1949, and is a member of the Security Council. Peruvian Javier Perez de Cuellar served as UN Secretary General from 1981 to 1991.

Peru maintains 204 troops in peacekeeping operations in Haiti under the UN's MINUSTAH.

U.S.-PERUVIAN RELATIONS

The United States enjoys strong and cooperative relations with Peru. Relations were strained following the tainted re-election of former President Fujimori in June 2000, but improved with the installation of an interim government in November 2000 and the inauguration of the government of Alejandro Toledo in July 2001. The United States continues to promote the strengthening of democratic institutions and human rights safeguards in Peru and the integration of Peru into the world economy.

The United States and Peru cooperate on efforts to interdict the flow of narcotics, particularly cocaine, to the United States. Bilateral programs are now in effect to reduce the flow of drugs on Peru's extensive river system and to perform ground interdiction in tandem with successful law enforcement operations. The United States is considering whether to resume cooperation on an aerial interdiction program. The United States and Peru cooperate on promoting programs of alternative development in coca-growing regions.

U.S. investment and tourism in Peru have grown substantially in recent years. U.S. exports to Peru were valued at $2.1 billion in 2005, accounting for 17.9% of Peru's imports. In the same year, Peru exported $5.2 billion in goods to the United States, accounting for about 30.6% of Peru's exports to the world.

About 200,000 U.S. citizens visit Peru annually for business, tourism, and study. About 16,000 Americans reside in Peru, and more than 400 U.S. companies are represented in the country.

Principal U.S. Embassy Officials

chief of mission: Ambassador Krishna R. URS (since 18 October 2017)

Deputy Chief of Mission--Phyllis Powers
Director, USAID Mission--Hilda Arellano
Counselor for Political Affairs--Alexander H. Margulies
Counselor for Economic Affairs--Timothy M. Stater
Counselor for Narcotics Affairs (NAS)--Susan Keogh
Counselor for Public Affairs--Sam Wunder
Counselor for Management Affairs--Robert Davis
Counselor for Consular Affairs--Ray Baca
Commercial Counselor--Margaret Hanson-Muse
Naval and Defense Attaché--Capt. Lee Rivas
Army Attaché--Col. Kris Cuello
Chief, Military Assistance Advisory Group (MAAG)--Col. Jeffrey Fargo
Consular Agent, Cuzco--Olga Villagarcia

The U.S. Embassy in Peru is located at Avenida Encalada, Cuadra 17 s/n, Monterrico (Surco), Lima 33 (tel. (511) 434-3000; fax. (511) 434-3037. Home page: http://lima.usembassy.gov/

The embassy is open from 8:00 a.m. to 5:00 p.m., Monday-Friday, except U.S. and some Peruvian holidays. The mailing address from the United States is American Embassy Lima, APO AA 34031 (use U.S. domestic postage rates). The American Citizen Services section is open to the public from 8:00 a.m. to 12:00 p.m.

The Consular Agency in Cuzco is located at Anda Tullamayu 125 (tel. (51) (84) 224112 or (51) (84) 239451; fax. (51) (84) 233541). The USAID Building is located at Av. Encalada cdra. 17 s/n, Monterrico (Surco) Lima 33, (tel. (511) 618-1200.

Other Contact Information
U.S. Department of State
Bureau of Western Hemisphere Affairs
Office of Andean Affairs (Room 5906)
2201 C Street NW
Washington, DC 20520-6263
Tel: 202-647-4177
Fax: 202-647-2628
Home Page: http://www.state.gov/

U.S. Department of Commerce
International Trade Administration
Office of Latin America and the Caribbean
14th and Constitution, NW

Washington, DC 20230
Tel: (202) 482-0475
(800) USA-TRADE
Fax: (202) 482-0464
Home Page: http://www.ita.doc.gov/

American Chamber of Commerce of Peru
Avenida Ricardo Palma 836, Miraflores
Lima 18, Peru
Tel: (511) 241-0708
Fax: (511) 241-0709
E-Mail: amcham@amcham.org.pe
Home Page: http://www.amcham.org.pe/

U.S. TRADE IN GOODS WITH PERU

All figures are in millions of U.S. dollars on a nominal basis, not seasonally adjusted unless otherwise specified. Details may not equal totals due to rounding. Table reflects only those months for which there was trade.

Month	Exports	Imports	Balance
January 2016	644.9	447.4	197.5
February 2016	663.5	388.6	274.9
March 2016	644.6	355.2	289.4
April 2016	630.7	357.6	273.1
May 2016	605.5	497.5	107.9
June 2016	705.7	505.6	200.0
July 2016	604.6	511.7	92.9
August 2016	689.3	575.1	114.2
September 2016	733.0	699.2	33.7
October 2016	724.0	608.7	115.3
TOTAL 2016	6,645.7	4,946.8	1,699.0

TRAVEL AND BUSINESS INFORMATION

The U.S. Department of State's Consular Information Program provides Consular Information Sheets, Travel Warnings, and Public Announcements.

Consular Information Sheets exist for all countries and include information on entry requirements, currency regulations, health conditions, areas of instability, crime and security, political disturbances, and the addresses of the U.S. posts in the country.

Travel Warnings are issued when the State Department recommends that Americans avoid travel to a certain country. **Public Announcements** are issued as a means to disseminate information quickly about terrorist threats and other relatively short-term conditions overseas that pose significant risks to the security of American travelers. Free copies of this information are available by calling the Bureau of Consular Affairs at 202-647-5225 or via the fax-on-demand system: 202-647-3000. Consular Information Sheets and Travel Warnings also are available on the Consular Affairs Internet home page: http://travel.state.gov. Consular Affairs Tips for

Travelers publication series, which contain information on obtaining passports and planning a safe trip abroad, are available on the Internet and hard copies can be purchased from the Superintendent of Documents, U.S. Government Printing Office, telephone: 202-512-1800; fax 202-512-2250. Emergency information concerning Americans traveling abroad may be obtained from the Office of Overseas Citizens Services at (202) 647-5225. For after-hours emergencies, Sundays and holidays, call 202-647-4000.

The National Passport Information Center (NPIC) is the U.S. Department of State's single, centralized public contact center for U.S. passport information. Telephone: 1-877-4USA-PPT (1-877-487-2778). Customer service representatives and operators for TDD/TTY are available Monday-Friday, 8:00 a.m. to 8:00 p.m., Eastern Time, excluding federal holidays.

Travelers can check the latest health information with the U.S. Centers for Disease Control and Prevention in Atlanta, Georgia. A hotline at 877-FYI-TRIP (877-394-8747) and a web site at http://www.cdc.gov/travel/index.htm give the most recent health advisories, immunization recommendations or requirements, and advice on food and drinking water safety for regions and countries. A booklet entitled Health Information for International Travel (HHS publication number CDC-95-8280) is available from the U.S. Government Printing Office, Washington, DC 20402, tel. (202) 512-1800.

STRATEGIC INFORMATION FOR DOING BUSINESS[1]

PERU ECONOMY - STRATEGIC INFORMATION AND DEVELOPMENTS

Peru is classified as *upper middle income* by the World Bank and is the 39th largest in the world by total GDP. Peru is one of the world's fastest-growing economies with a 2012 GDP growth rate of 6.3%. It currently has a high human development index of 0.741 and per capita GDP above $12,000 by PPP.

The virtues of today's new multi-polar world for Peru are many. At 30 million people, Peru is neither too small to matter nor so big it is going to be a power in its own right. Midsized states, benefits from a world where it is no longer mandatory to pick a big-power patron.

With expanding ports loading up boats to China on one side, and a new superhighway to Brazil on the other, along with a free trade agreement with the United States in its hip pocket, Peru seems well-positioned to prosper in the coming years. But former President Toledo may not be hyperbolic when he worries the future stability of the state may depend on its willingness to distribute wealth more evenly.

Forecasts for the medium- and long-term remain highly positive. Peru's real GDP growth in 2007 was (8.3%) and largest in Latin America in 2008 was an outstanding 9.8%, the highest in the world. Inflation remained low, at about 3%, while the budget surplus is expected to remain at about 1% of GDP.

Private investment should keep growing at a rate of 15% a year Exports and imports are expected to keep rising The unemployment and underemployment indexes (5.2% and 34%, respectively, in Lima) should keep coming down as the economy grows other cities in Peru like Cajamarca, Ica, Cuzco and Trujillo are starting to show less unemployment nowadays. The country is likely to attract future domestic and foreign investment in tourism, agriculture, mining, petroleum and natural gas, power industries and financial institutions. According to the IMF and the World Bank, Peruvian GDP economic growth between 2007 and 2013 was:

In 2007 at 8.9%, in 2008 at 9.7%, in 2009 at 0.9%, in 2010 at 8.6%, in 2011 at 6.0%, in 2012 at 6,3% and in 2013 at 5.3%.

Therefore, Peruvian GDP grew in the 2007-2013 6 years period an outstanding net growth of 45.7% or a 7.61% yearly average. The IMF forecast for Peru's economic growth for the next 6 years 2013-2019 is a 7% yearly growth.

In FY 2011 for the first time since 1991 the size of the Peruvian economy surpassed the Chilean economy. Peru now is the fifth major economy in South America and is expected to become the fourth South American economy in 2018 by surpassing Venezuela.

Private investment reached 25% of the GDP in 2007, and has remained stable through 2010; and inflation is under control at an average 2% per year for the next 5 years. International Debt will reach 25% of the GDP by 2010, down from 35% in 2006, and will be only 12% of the GDP by

[1] Government of Peru and WTO materials

2015. The International Monetary Reserves of the National Reserve Bank (Dollar, Euro, Yen, Gold, and other currencies) reached US$27 billion by the end of 2007, and US$31 billion at the end of 2008. Currently reserves are at a US $73 billion level for end of FY 2013, which more than doubles the total foreign debt of Peru which is US$30 billion at the end of FY 2013.

Exports are growing at a pace of 25% and reached US$28 billion at the end of 2007 and US$30 billion at the end of 2010. In FY 2012 Peruvian exports reached a total of US$46 billion.

High technological investment is growing fast in Peru, and will be 10% of the GDP by 2010.

The core of the current sound economic performance of the country is a combination of:

- Macroeconomic stability
- Prudent fiscal spending
- High international reserve accumulation
- External debt reduction
- Achievement of investment grade status
- Fiscal surpluses

All of these factors have enabled Peru to make great strides in development, with improvement in government finances, poverty reduction and progress in social sectors. Poverty has decreased dramatically in the past decade, from nearly 60% in 2004 to 25.8% in 2012.

Peru is an emerging, social market economy characterized by a high level of foreign trade. The inequality of opportunities has declined: between 1991 and 2012 Peru's rating on The World Bank's Human Opportunity Index improved substantially as increased public investment in water, sanitation and electric power has sustained the downward trend in inequality of opportunities. Its economy is diversified, although commodity exports still make up a significant proportion of economic activity and thus subject the economy to the risks of price volatility in the international markets. Trade and industry are centralized in Lima but agricultural exports have led to development in all the regions.

Peruvian economic performance has been tied to exports, which provide hard currency to finance imports and external debt payments. Peru's main exports are copper, gold, zinc, textiles, chemicals, pharmaceuticals, manufactures, machinery, services and fish meal; its major trade partners are the United States, China, Brazil, European Union and Chile. Although exports have provided substantial revenue, self-sustained growth and a more egalitarian distribution of income have proven elusive.

Services account for 43% of Peruvian gross domestic product, followed by manufacturing (32.3%), extractive industries (15%), and taxes (9.7%). Recent economic growth has been fueled by macroeconomic stability, improved terms of trade, and rising investment and consumption. China has become Peru's largest trading partner following a free trade agreement with the People´s Republic of China signed on April 28, 2009 additional free trade agreements have being signed with the United States of America free trade agreement with the United States signed on April 12, 2006, the European Union June 26, 2012.*The EU and Peru Sign Trade Promotion Agreement*, with Japan free trade agreement with the constitutional monarchy of Japan signed on May 31, 2011

Inflation in 2012 was the lowest in Latin America at only 1.8%, but increased in 2013 as oil and commodity prices rose; as of 2014 it stands at 2.5%. The unemployment rate has fallen steadily in recent years, and as of 2012 stands at 3.6%.

Peru has a relatively open and diversified economy that depends increasingly on international trade. Its trade (exports plus imports) to GDP ratio grew from 27% in 2002 to nearly 50% in 2012[1], and the rapid expansion of merchandise trade has gone hand-in-hand with changes in its composition and direction. The share of traditional exports (basically goods obtained from the extraction and processing of natural resources) has increased significantly, reflecting rising prices among oil and petroleum products during much of the review period, as well as in products such as coffee, copper and gold. While the United States, China and the European Union remain Peru's leading trading partners, China's share has grown substantially (section 1.3.1) .

The services sector is the leading economic activity, accounting for nearly half of the country's GDP and employment (Table 1.1), and is followed by the manufacturing sector, which contributes 14% of real GDP, absorbs 16% of employment and represents 12% of total goods exports. Agriculture and fishing also continue to make major contributions to real GDP, employment and merchandise exports (section 4.1) . Peru's natural resource wealth makes it one of the world's leading mineral producers (the third largest producer of silver, copper, zinc and tin; fourth producer of lead, molybdenum and mercury; and the sixth largest gold producer) .[2] Mining as a whole contributes 4.7% of real GDP and generates about 60% of merchandise export earnings

The authorities expect Peru to remain the region's most dynamic and stable economy, with real GDP growth of between 6% and 6.5% during the period 2012-2015 – provided there is no global crisis similar to that of 2008, and assuming private investment grows by around 11% per year and a number of projects come on-stream, including mining projects which would raise copper production by about 90% between now and 2016. On that basis, private investment would amount to 25% of GDP in 2015, and total investment (private and public) would represent 30% of GDP.

Despite a major improvement in Peru's infrastructure in recent years, the amount of capital invested in infrastructure and access to basic services remain insufficient, particularly outside Lima. This is reflected in the competitiveness index published by the World Economic Forum, which ranks Peru 111th out of 144 countries in terms of overall infrastructure quality (74th in airport infrastructure, 97th in terms of the quality of its roads, 111th in relation to port infrastructure, 74th in electricity supply, 87th in fixed telephone lines, and 58th in mobile telephone subscriptions) .[22] Consequently, one of the main challenges for Peru to continue growing at relatively high rates in the long term is to reduce its "infrastructure gap" (difference between infrastructure supply and demand), which is calculated at around 30% of GDP.[23]

Among the components of the calculated infrastructure deficit, the transport sector requires the largest investment, accounting for 37% of the total shortfall (US$13,961 million)[24], as a result of delays in project execution and insufficient public investment in the past. The electricity and natural gas sector accounts for 31.9% of the overall investment gap, owing to growing demand for electric energy in the wake of economic expansion. The health sector represents 16.7% of the total shortfall, and the telecommunications sector accounts for 14.4%.

1.29. To close the infrastructure gap, Peru is adopting measures to promote public-private partnerships (section 2.4), encourage technological innovation, improve human capital, diversify production and enhance the quality of public investment expenditure. These measures are included in Peru's various development plans (section 2.2) .

The Peruvian economy has performed very strongly both in regional terms and by historical standards, with real GDP growing at an average annual rate of 6.9% between 2007 and 2012 (compared to 4.8% between 2000 and 2006) . This has been the result of sound macroeconomic fundamentals, robust domestic demand and a strong export performance, particularly in the case of raw materials. Peru was also able to overcome the global economic crisis in 2009-2010, thanks partly to a countercyclical fiscal policy that included a public expenditure stimulus equivalent to 1.25% of GDP in 2009, which was later phased out as economic activity recovered.

The rapid economic growth recorded during the review period underpinned a continuous recovery of per capita GDP in dollar terms, which grew from US$3,772 in 2007 to US$6,623 in 2012, together with lower unemployment, which dropped from 8.4% to 6.8% during the period, and reductions in both total and extreme poverty (Table 1.1) . Nonetheless, major disparities persist across the country, particularly between rural and urban areas.[4] Peru's Human Development Index ranks it 77th out of 187 countries.[5]

Between 2007 and 2012, Peru also kept inflation at relatively low levels, improved its fiscal position, reduced the public debt and strengthened its external accounts. All of this reflects prudent macroeconomic management and the continuation of its structural reforms which have encouraged investment growth (section 1.3.3) .[6]

Since 1991, the domestic currency has been the nuevo sol (S/.) . Peru does not apply foreign exchange restrictions. The Central Reserve Bank of Peru (BCRP), which is responsible for formulating monetary and foreign exchange policy, operates a managed floating exchange rate system. The average nominal exchange rate against the United States dollar (S/. per US$) fell from 3.13 in 2007 to 2.64 in 2012. The real exchange rate, measured in terms of the basket of currencies of Peru's 20 main trading partners, appreciated in 2007 and 2012, partly reflecting the terms-of-trade improvement that occurred in those years; but it then depreciated in the period 2008-2011, basically owing to uncertainty surrounding the local electoral process and the problematic global financial situation.

ECONOMIC TRENDS

From 1994 through 1998, under the government of Alberto Fujimori, the economy recorded robust growth driven by foreign direct investment, almost 46% of which was related to the privatization program. The government invested heavily on the country's infrastructure, which became a solid foundation for the future of the Peruvian economy. The economy stagnated from 1998 through 2001, the result of the century's strongest El Niño weather phenomenon, global financial turmoil, political instability, a stalled privatization program, increased government intervention in markets and worsening terms of trade. President Alejandro Toledo implemented a recovery program after taking office, maintained largely orthodox economic policies, and took measures to attract investment, including restarting the privatization program. Nonetheless, political uncertainty led to GDP growth of 0.2% in 2001. The Lima Stock Exchange general index fell 34.5% in 2000 and 0.2% in 2001. Inflation remained at record lows, registering 3.7% in 2000

The year 2001 saw deflation of 0.1%. The government's overall budget deficit rose sharply in 1999 and 2000 to 3.2% of GDP, the result of hikes in government salaries, expenditures related to the 2000 election campaign, higher foreign debt service payments, and lower tax revenues

The government brought the deficit down to 2.5% of GDP in 2001, and set a target of 1.9% of GDP for 2002. Peru's stability brought about a substantial reduction in underemployment, from an average of 74% from the late 1980s through 1994 to 43% in the 1995-96 period, but the rates began climbing again in 1997-2002 to over half the working population. The poverty rate remained at 54% in 2001, with 24% of Peruvians living in extreme poverty. In 2005, 18% of Peruvians were living in extreme poverty and a poverty rate at 39%.

As of 2010, around 30% of its total population is poor

NARCOTICS

Coca has a long history of cultivation in the Andes, and has always been a traditional part of Peruvian life. However, the narcotic properties of coca were known only locally until 1786, when Lamarck listed the leaf in his botanical encyclopedia.

After the arrival of the Spanish, coca cultivation increased and its use became more common and widespread. Since 1543, coca has been internationally recognized for its trading value, and regulations imposed upon it have attached increasing economic importance to the plant. Exchange of the coca leaf between consumers in the highlands and growers in the low-lying hills has gone on for at least the last millennium, strengthening local economic ties. Between 1884 and 1900, coca and cocaine grew in popularity for medical purposes and mass consumption in the United States. From 1905 to 1922, anti-cocaine sentiments in the US resulted in criminalization of both coca and cocaine. It was not until the 1920s that US diplomats began to extend drug prohibitions internationally.

CURRENT TRENDS

The Peruvian coca and cocaine industry is as huge as it is today because of advanced industrial nations' demand for drugs. This high demand has created a framework of dependence on "coca-dollars" and on US drug policy. Money from cocaine trafficking feeds local economies, supports inflation, and even causes social changes such as cocaine smoking among indigenous Peruvians.

Coca farming today is still a significant source of income for peasants, as it accounts for 48% of total net family income in the high coca-growing Apurímac River region. In an effort to reduce drug use in America, for the past 50 years the US government together with the United Nations have been waging a war on drugs.

The US Drug Control Program maintains that "eliminating the cultivation of illicit coca and opium is the best approach to combating cocaine and heroin availability in the US."

With US government cooperation, the Peruvian Government installed the National Plan for the Prevention and Control of Drugs in 1995. This government prohibition of narcotics trafficking in Peru has resulted in a 70% reduction of coca leaf cultivation since 1995. However the reduction in cultivation may not have actual effects on cocaine production, as recent advances in coca growing and more efficient processing methods allow for greater cocaine yield.

The size of the narcotics industry as a part of the national economy is difficult to measure, but estimates range from $300–$600 million. An estimated 200,000 Peruvian households have economies based on the production, refining, or distribution of coca.

Many economists believe that large flows of dollars into the banking system contribute to the traditional depression of the dollar exchange rate vis-a-vis the sol The Central Bank engages in open market activities to prevent the price of the sol from rising to levels that would cause Peruvian exports to become prohibitively expensive.

Hurt economically by Peruvian Air Force interdiction efforts in the mid-1990s, drug traffickers are now using land and river routes as well as aircraft to transport cocaine paste and, increasingly, refined cocaine to consumers around and out of the country. The Air Bridge Denial program was suspended in April 2001 after the Peruvian Air Force and strength of the U.S. DEA misidentified a civilian aircraft as a drug trafficker and shot it down, killing two American citizens on board. Peru continues to arrest drug traffickers and seize drugs and precursor chemicals, destroy coca labs, disable clandestine airstrips, and prosecute officials involved in narcotics corruption.

Working with limited aid of the U.S. Agency for International Development (USAID), the Peruvian Government carries out alternative development programs in the leading coca-growing areas in an effort to convince coca farmers not to grow that crop. Although the government previously eradicated only coca seed beds, in 1998 and 1999 it began to eradicate mature coca being grown in national parks and elsewhere in the main coca growing valleys. In 1999 the government eradicated more than 150 km^2 of coca; this figure declined to 65 km^2 in 2000, due largely to political instability. The government agency "Contradrogas", founded in 1996, facilitates coordination among Peruvian Government agencies working on counter-narcotics issues. Alternative crops, however, are not economically comparable to coca. 2004 prices indicate an annual income per hectare of $600 for coffee and $1000 for cocoa, versus up to $7500 for a hectare of coca.

Effect on Family Economies

The anti-coca policies imposed in 1995 have had adverse effects on Peruvian's household economies. Many families dependent on coca farming have been forced to send their children to work as eradication of crops has decreased their household income. In states where coca is grown, child labour increased by 18% in 1997 and 40% in 2000. Work hours and domestic work increased as well, with girls taking on 28% more domestic work with boys doing 13% more. Wage work for adults also increased since 1995. As such, it can be inferred that the increase in child labour since eradication policies have come into effect is caused by children filling in for working parents.

However, the issue of child labour in coca production is still present in Peru as reported in 2013 in the U.S. Department of Labor's report *Findings on the Worst Forms of Child Labor* and in December 2014, in the Bureau of International Labor Affairs's *List of Goods Produced by Child Labor or Forced Labor.*

CORRUPTION

Peru is the 72nd least corrupt country in the world according to Transparency International's Corruption Perceptions Index.

The Peruvian organization *"Ciudadanos al Dia"* has started to measure and compare transparency, costs, and efficiency in different government departments in Peru. It annually awards the best practices which has received widespread media attention. This has created competition among government agencies in order to improve. A last case of corruption was the 2008 Peru oil scandal.

BALANCE OF PAYMENTS

Except in 2007, the current account of the balance of payments was in deficit throughout the review period, mainly owing to the growing negative balance of factor income (Table 1.3) . In relation to GDP, the current account moved from a surplus of 1.4% in 2007 to a deficit of 3.6% of GDP in 2012, and the IMF is forecasting a deficit of 4.9% for 2013.[16]

The trade account surplus shrank considerably in 2008-2009, and also in 2012, owing to the deterioration in the terms of trade in those years as a result of the global economic crisis.[17] This caused merchandise export earnings to fall steeply in 2009, and again slightly in 2012 compared to their 2011 level. Goods imports also retreated sharply in 2009, but they have since recovered thanks to the buoyancy of the Peruvian economy.

In 2011, Peru was ranked 41st and 40th among global merchandise exporters and importers, respectively, (considering European Union countries as one and excluding trade between them) . In services trade, Peru was the 49th largest exporter and 47th largest importer.[18] Traditionally, its services trade has generated a deficit (section 1.3.2) .

The negative balance on the income account largely reflects an increase in private outflows – mainly remittances of profits to other countries and undistributed earnings by firms with foreign ownership. Remittances received from Peruvians living abroad are a major source of income on the current account and remained relatively stable throughout the review period. Nonetheless, in relative terms, they declined from 2% of GDP in 2007 to 1.4% in 2012 (Table 1.2) .

The financial account has been in surplus during the review period, thanks mainly to the large inflows of foreign direct investment (FDI) received by Peru in the last few years (section 1.3.3) . The net capital inflow enabled Peru to accumulate international reserves over the period 2007-2012, the balance of which stood at almost US$64 billion in 2012 (Table 1.2), equivalent to 32% of GDP.

TRENDS IN TRADE AND INVESTMENT

Trade in goods

Peru has a relatively diversified merchandise export basket. Nonetheless, as one of the world's leading producers of raw materials, it is sensitive to changes in the respective prices. According to the World Bank, a 10% fall in raw material prices reduces export earnings by 3.5% (about 0.7% of GDP) .[19]Although Peru exports a variety of minerals, over the last few years, it has been relying increasingly on copper and gold, which in 2012 accounted for about 80% of its mineral exports (mostly sent to the Chinese market) and 10% of GDP.

The share of agricultural products in total merchandise exports grew from 14.9% to 16.8% in the period 2007-2012, while minerals accounted for between 26% and 32% of the total during the period, excluding gold and gold products, whose share rose from 14.9% in 2007 to 21.2% in 2012. Meanwhile, the export share of manufactures, mainly textiles and chemical products, fluctuated between 11% and 13% in the period 2007-2012 (Table A1.1 and Chart 1.1) . There was a sharp increase in fuel exports, particularly liquefied natural gas as from 2010.

On the import side, manufactured products accounted for almost three quarters of all goods sourced from abroad in 2012 (65.4% in 2007), the vast majority corresponding to transport machinery and equipment and chemical products (Table A1.2 and Chart 1.1) . The share of fuels in total goods imports declined from 18.8% in 2007 to 14.4% in 2012. Agricultural products accounted for about 11%-12% of total imports during the period, led by wheat, maize, oilseed cake and soya oil.

In terms of destinations, China, the European Union and the United States between them absorbed 48.3% of Peru's total goods exports in 2012, very close to the 48.7% recorded in 2007 (Table A1.3 and Chart 1.2) . Nonetheless, China increased its share significantly during the period (from 10.8% to 17.1%), while that of the United States declined from 19.9% to 14.2%, despite the trade promotion agreement that entered into force between the United States and Peru in 2009. Other countries that have negotiated regional trade agreements with Peru, such as Canada, the Republic of Korea and Switzerland/Liechtenstein, have gained increasing proportions of its total exports. The Andean Community's share in Peru's total merchandise exports grew from 4.4% in 2007 to 5.2% in 2012.

The United States, China and the European Union are also the main sources of Peru's goods imports, jointly supplying 49.2% of the total in 2012, compared to 41.2% in 2007 (Table A1.4 and Chart 1.2) . Imports from the United States increased from 17.6% of the total in 2007 to 18.8% in 2012, while China's share grew from 12.1% in 2007 to 18.5% in 2012. In contrast, the Andean Community's share in Peru's total imports shrank from 12.9% to 9.7% in the period.

Trade in services

The deficit in Peru's services trade, which in 2007-2012 averaged around US$2 billion per year, largely reflects a growing negative balance in freight transport services, which widened from US$1,198 million in 2007 to US$1,630 million in 2012, owing to the vigorous growth of merchandise trade during the period. Insurance services were also in deficit, but travel services generated a surplus, which grew from US$755 million to US$1,168 million in the period 2007-2012 (Table 1.4) .

FOREIGN DIRECT INVESTMENT

According to BCRP figures, the annual flow of FDI in Peru averaged around US$7.9 billion in 2007-2012 (way above the average of US$2 billion recorded in the period 2000-2006) . FDI stock in Peru amounted to US$63,448 million in 2012 (Table 1.5) . This growth was largely the result of the positive performance of the Peruvian economy in the period. Nonetheless, efforts to attract larger FDI flows have been hindered by a number of factors, particularly the lack of adequate infrastructure (section 1.4) .

The balance of foreign investment in the form of capital contributions (including share reductions and transfers) stood at US$22,674 million in late 2012.[20] The main source countries for these capital contributions were Spain (20.5%), the United Kingdom (19.8%) and the United States (14%) . The contributions were mainly concentrated in the following sectors: mining (23.9%), finance (18.5%), communications (17.3%), industry (13.7%) and energy (13.5%) .

PERU - UNITED STATES TRADE PROMOTION AGREEMENT

Main article: United States – Peru Trade Promotion Agreement
The *United States – Peru Trade Promotion Agreement* (Spanish: *Tratado de Libre Comercio Perú – Estados Unidos*) is a bilateral free trade agreement, whose objectives are eliminating obstacles to trade, consolidating access to goods and services and fostering private investment in and between the United States and Peru. Besides commercial issues, it incorporates economic, institutional, intellectual property, labor and environmental policies, among others. The agreement was signed on April 12, 2006; ratified by the Peruvian Congress on June 28, 2006; by the U.S. House of Representatives on November 2, 2007 and by the U.S. Senate on December 4, 2007. The agreement was implemented on February 1, 2009. Peru looks to the agreement are to:

- Consolidate and extend the trade preferences under ATPDEA
- Attract foreign investment
- Generate employment
- Enhance the country's competitiveness within the region
- Increase workers' income
- Curb poverty levels
- Create and export sugar cane ethanol

The United States looks to the agreement to:

- Improve access to goods and services
- Strengthen its investments
- Promote security and democracy
- Fight against drug trafficking

The U.S.-Peru agreement has faced criticism. In Peru, the treaty was championed by Toledo, and supported to different extents by former President Alan García and candidates Lourdes Flores and Valentín Paniagua. Current President Ollanta Humala has been its most vocal critic. Humala's Union for Peru won 45 of 120 seats in Congress in 2006, the largest share by a single party, prompting debate on ratification of the agreement before the new legislature was sworn in. Some Congressmen-elect interrupted the debate after forcibly entering Congress in an attempt to stop the agreement ratification.

One controversial element of the agreement relates to land resources. Laura Carlsen, of the Center for International Policy, who is also a contributor to Foreign Policy in Focus notes that "Indigenous organizations warn that this ruling effectively opens up 45 million hectares to foreign investment and timber, oil, and mining exploitation."

However, most of the criticism of the agreement has focused on its potential impact on Peru's agricultural sector. By planting crops to similar to those subsidized by the U.S., Peru faced a competitive disadvantage in the production of agricultural products because poor farming families with inadequate tools, technology and techniques may not be able to produce crops at low enough prices to export. In response to these concerns, Peruvian lawmakers created a Compensation Fund which directed $34 million per year to cotton, maize/corn, and wheat producers for a five-year period to help them adjust to the new competitive pressures.

Toledo is therefore a market-oriented politician who continued to globalize Peru's economy and is rumored to be getting ready for another run for president. Toledo says bluntly that unless the poorest in the country are better educated, better paid, housed, and fed, the Peruvian economic miracle will stall.

ACUERDO NACIONAL

In November 2001, Toledo opened talks which concluded in the National Accord of July 22, 2002. In the accord, seven political parties and seven social organizations agreed upon a framework that would guide policy for the next twenty years. The accord set forth twenty-four policy goals divided into four categories: democracy and the rule of law, equity and social justice, economic competitiveness, and an institutional framework of efficiency, transparency, and decentralization. Initially, the accord opened up dialogue in Peru's political arena, but within a year, the public considered it to be less effective than had been hoped.

Maria Elena García calls the years of Toledo's presidency a transition rife with new opportunities for indigenous people, noting the "reframed state-indigenous interactions", "increase in NGO projects and social movements", and "proliferation of indigenous organizations." Toledo created and first lady Eliane Karp headed a new agency for indigenous and Afro-Peruvian affairs, CONOPA (Commission for Amazonian, Andean, and Afro-Peruvian Peoples). The agency was meant to establish a development agenda for indigenous communities, provide representation of indigenous interests within the government, and lead the way for multicultural constitutional reforms. Some critics viewed these actions as a state co-optation of indigenous identity, mockingly dubbing the agency the "Karp Commission".However, Oxfam's Martin Scurrah points out the agency's good work, noting that in addition to promoting a chapter on indigenous rights in the new constitution, Eliane Karp has "intervened on numerous occasions in support of or in defense of indigenous initiatives."

Toledo also brought serious attention to bilingual education in indigenous schools, creating a new and well-staffed division within the Ministry of Education devoted to the issue. This effort gives advocates greater autonomy and opportunity to influence policy and work toward institutionalizing bilingual education.

Toledo's efforts at decentralization sought to give indigenous groups greater influence upon policy-making on a regional level. The first regional and local elections, held in November 2002, required that 15% of the candidates in regions with an indigenous presence must have indigenous backgrounds. However, decentralization has been viewed critically by some, who claim that in dividing up regions, administrators have at times ignored the distinctive cultural and historical factors that define different areas.

In a speech to the Human Rights of Indigenous Peoples in Latin America conference, Toledo expressed disappointment at the growing disparity between the incomes of indigenous people and other citizens. Despite the growth achieved by the Peruvian economy, the poverty gap has widened between the upper and lower classes. Toledo mentions the reintegration of the indigenous populations into the Peruvian social and political system as a key to sustainability and economic growth.

Advocates of indigenous rights have also criticized some of Toledo's efforts to jump-start the economy through investments, such as his support for the Camisea natural gas project and other projects that involved exploring or developing natural resources. These critics claim that companies buy land at unreasonable prices, force indigenous people off of land that is historically theirs, and exploit natural resources in ways that are harmful to communities and the environment. Peru is one of the largest producers of gold, silver, and zinc in Latin America, and some critics complain about the priority the Peruvian government gives to mining as opposed to industries like fishing and agriculture, with which indigenous peoples are more familiar. They note that mining companies may bring new jobs to rural areas, but that they are not jobs for which natives are well qualified.

Despite unprecedented, strong, and consistent economic growth under his leadership, Toledo dealt with much labor unrest during his presidency as workers demanded higher wages and the fulfillment of campaign promises. The crisis underlined a basic flaw in Peru's economy as pointed out by *The Economist*, which noted that "some 70% of output falls within the grey or *informal*" economy, and thus escapes tax. Tax-collections, at below 12.1% of GDP, are stagnant, with most coming from a handful of large, formal companies. Evasion is widespread, particularly among better-paid independent professionals." Tax collections by Toledo's government could simply not cover the wages that had been promised to civil servants.

Even as the Peruvian government was taking in too little money to pay civil servants, the country saw its cost of living increase dramatically during the early years of Toledo's administration. These hardships, combined with increasing unemployment and stagnant wages caused the general public to doubt that Toledo was living up to lofty campaign promises. By 2003, Toledo's approval rating had fallen below 10%, the lowest of any South American president at the time.

Toledo did implement some of his plans for investment in social infrastructure and institutions. The amount of paved roads increased by 20% during his presidency; medical attention to the poor doubled in rural areas, and public sector salaries increased (school teachers' pay rose by 87%) and over 100,000 new homes were built for poor Peruvians.

By 2004, Peru had a far-reaching social safety net that included food programs serving 35 percent of the population, and work programs offering temporary employment to unskilled workers. The Cooperative Fund for Social Development funded projects to construct and improve schools, health clinics, rural roads, water and sanitation systems, and electric grids. Toledo placed food and infrastructure programs under the Ministry for Women and Social Development and urged that municipalities implement decentralization. Social safety-net spending in Peru remained well below the Latin American average under Toledo even as it covered a larger percentage of the population, which means that outlays were insufficient to lift many people up out of poverty.

Toledo also attempted to improve access to healthcare in the most remote places. His Juntos program awarded a monthly benefit to poor families who agreed to get vaccinations and screenings, attend school, and obtain birth registration documents. The Toledo administration also provided financial incentives to young doctors who were willing to spend the first few years of their practices in remote areas.

Peru faced a major housing deficit in 2001, with the majority of its urban population living in slums. Toledo's administration sought to improve access to affordable housing through subsidies, loans, down payments, land titling, and encouraging financial institutions to reach further down-market. Most of these efforts were grouped under the Fondo Mivivienda, which was program started in 1999.

Under Toledo's predecessor, Fujimori, the governing authority in Peru was condensed and centralized. A Fujimori-dominated congress passed a new constitution in 1993, which consolidated the bicameral legislature into a unicameral legislature with a single national district. Under Fujimori local governments retained minimal legal authority including fees for utilities, basic civil registries, and management of public spaces and markets.

Decentralization was among Toledo's most successful institutional reforms. In addition to announcing regional elections upon his inauguration, he charged a Decentralization and Regionalization Commission with developing proposals. In 2002, a constitutional amendment was approved which established three levels of government: local, regional, and national. Over the next few years, the congress gradually passed on resources and responsibilities to the regional and municipal governments including food programs, social development projects, and health and education programs.

He divided the single district up, called for regional elections, and eliminated the centralist Ministry of the Presidency that had been instituted under Fujimori.

However, when Peru Possible's rival political party APRA made significant gains in regional elections, the Toledo administration halted its decentralization program by withholding power in the areas of revenue and expenditure. This left many regionally elected governors confused as to how far their authority extended. Without strong fiscal plans to support his new policy of centralization, Toledo had to continue decentralizing power and recognizing more regions. Toledo continued to assert control of regional governments, however, by withholding funding.

Toledo's plan for decentralization enjoyed widespread popular support. Most of the opposition to his program came from, and most of the difficulty in implementing his proposals was owing to, politicians and bureaucratic agencies who were accustomed to a centralized form of government.

The Toledo administration held freetrade agreement talks with Singapore and Thailand, came to an agreement with Thailand on air transport, and signed an extradition treaty with South Korea. Foreign Minister García-Sayan visited China and discussed support for multilateralism and strengthening the UN. In 2004 China declared Peru an official tourist destination, and in 2005 the countries concluded several trade agreements.

In conducting Peru's relations with Brazil, Toledo's goal was to reorient Peru from the Andean Community, toward the more economically active Brazil and MERCOSUR. In August 2003, Toledo met with President Lula. They committed to increased political and economic cooperation under the Initiative for Integration of Regional Infrastructure in South America which invests in large-scale, debt-heavy projects, aimed at developing 10 economic axes or hubs throughout South America. Construction projects, including roads, discussed. President Lula also agreed to allow Peru access to two surveillance systems which Brazil had developed in the Amazon Basin to target legal and illegal activity.

While Peru and Ecuador had been at peace for years, President Toledo worked to solidify and build upon that peace. During a 2001 visit to Ecuador, Toledo expressed support for the Brasília Accords, agreed to the demilitarization of the two countries' common border, advocated reduced military spending, and agreed to greater energy, transportation, and police cooperation. Toledo joined Ecuadorian President Noboa at the International Advisory Committee of the Binational Development Plan, where they called for greater investment in their region, with Toledo putting forth a detailed program for international assistance. Economic activity in the region subsequently improved as the demining of the border continued, construction projects were completed, and military forces were reduced. By 2006, investment in the area had reached $1.2 billion.

President Toledo worked hard throughout his presidency on what became a very productive relationship with the U.S., and what Toledo described as a personal friendship with President Bush. He received lavish praise from the American president for his economic and domestic security policies. During a visit to Peru, Bush announced the establishment of an Andean Center of Excellence for Teacher Training, with a base in Peru, and a fellowship program to give Andean professionals access to education in information technology. In June 2002, the U.S. agreed to forgive $14 million of Peru's debt in exchange for a promise to invest $12 million in conservation projects. In September, Toledo secured a $300 million commitment from Bush to fund alternative-crop development in coca-producing areas. In 2003, the Peace Corps returned to Peru. Peru opposed U.S. efforts most visibly in the War in Iraq, refusing to support the intervention in any international arena.

In an attempt to increase remittances from Peruvians abroad, the Ministry of Foreign Affairs under Toledo sought to strengthen the link between Peruvian migrants and their homeland through the creation of advisory councils. The issue is especially important for a country which experienced a massive emigration of professionals under Fujimori and which still has 10% of its population living abroad. The councils were also part of an effort by the first Minister of Foreign Affairs, García Sayan, to professionalize the foreign service.

THE PERUVIAN MIRACLE

The Peruvian economy has undergone considerable free market reforms, from legalizing parts of the informal sector to significant privatization in the mining, electricity and telecommunications industries. Thanks to strong foreign investment and the cooperation between the Fujimori government and the International Monetary Fund and World Bank, growth was strong in 1994-97 and inflation was brought under control. In 1998, El Niño's impact on agriculture, the financial crisis in Asia, and instability in Brazilian markets undercut growth. 1999 was another lean year for Peru, with the aftermath of El Niño and the Asian financial crisis working its way through the economy. Lima did manage to complete negotiations for an Extended Fund Facility with the IMF in June 1999, although it subsequently had to renegotiate the targets.

Peru's exponential per-capita growth rates has been standard the last quarter century. Peru's GDP per capita is now FY 2013 at $12.000 USD PPP. By the end of 2006 the government had enacted measures that allowed the economy to improve by increasing investments, expanding production and exports. Raw materials and agroindustrial products represent half of exports with the other half being non-traditional exports such as clothing, electronics, machinery and services. By the end of the decade of 2014, investment is expected to total US$65 billion for mining activities, US$20 billion in energy and petroleum, US$12 billion for commerce, US$18 billion for agricultural industries, and US$15 billion for tourism. Thanks to the discovery and exploitation of large petroleum and natural gas reserves in southern Peru in the Cusco and Madre de Dios regions by Consorcio Camisea, Peru is expected to become an important exporter of hydrocarbons by 2015, after being a net importer for decades.

Positive results have begun to appear after 15 years, reflecting an expanding global economy; according to figures provided by the INEI, in 2007 the gross national product grew by 8.99%, exports grew by over 35% (reaching US$27.8 billion), private and public investments accounted for 21% of the GDP (24.4% in 2008), net international reserves (including gold) reached US$35.1 billion, state income from taxation increased by 33%, national debt with respect to GNP was reduced from 50% in 2000 to 34% in 2006; finally, the national budget has grown by 50% in the five years before 2007.

In 2007, the Peruvian economy experienced a growth rate of 9%, the highest in Latin America, and this repeated in 2008 with a 9.8% rate; in 2006 and 2007, the Lima Stock Exchange grew by 185.24% and 168.3%, respectively. However, in the wake of the 2008 global crisis, growth for 2009 was only 0.9 percent, but rebounded to 8.8 percent the following year. The pro-market policies enacted by Fujimori, were continued by presidents Alejandro Toledo and Alan Garcia, While poverty of Lima is 8.5%, the national average is 25.8%, while the unemployment rate is 6.5% and 74% are employed formally.

AGRICULTURE

Peru is a country with many climates and geographical zones that make it a very important agricultural nation. Peru agricultural exports are highly appreciated and include artichokes, grapes, avocados, mangoes, peppers, sugarcane, organic coffee and premium-quality cotton.

INDUSTRY AND SERVICES

EXTRACTION

Fishing: Peru is an international leader in fishing, producing nearly 10 percent of the world's fish catch.

Mining in Peru: Peru ranks fifth worldwide in gold production (first in Latin America), second in copper, and is among the top 5 producers of lead and zinc.

MANUFACTURING

Peru has developed a medium manufacturing sector. The sector now represents 23 percent of GDP and is tied heavily to mining, fishing, agriculture, construction and textiles. Manufacturing is mainly devoted to processing to gain a value-added advantage. The most promising sector is textiles, metal mechanics, food industry, agricultural industry, manufactures, chemicals, pharmaceuticals, machinery and services.

SERVICES

Tourism has represented a new growth industry in Peru since the early 1990s, with the government and private sector dedicating considerable energies to boosting the country's tourist destinations both to Peruvians and foreigners.

NATURAL RESOURCES

Peru's natural resources are copper, silver, gold, timber, fish, iron ore, coal, phosphate, potash, and natural gas.

EXTERNAL TRADE AND INVESTMENT

FOREIGN INVESTMENT AND BALANCE OF PAYMENTS

In 2001 the current account deficit dropped to about 2.2% of GDP (US$1.17 billion)--from 3.1% in 2000—while the trade balance registered a small deficit. Exports dropped slightly to $7.11 billion, while imports fell 2.1% to $7.20 billion. After being hit hard by El Niño in 1998, fisheries exports have recovered, and minerals and metals exports recorded large gains in 2001 and 2002, mostly as a result of the opening of the Antamina copper-zinc mine. By mid-2002, most sectors of the economy were showing gains. After several years of substantial growth, foreign direct investment not related to privatization fell dramatically in 2000 and 2001, as well as in the first half of 2002. Net international reserves at the end of May 2002 stood at $9.16 billion, up from $8.6 billion (2001), $17 billion at the end of 2006, over $20 billion in 2007, and over $35 billion in May 2008. Peru has signed a number of free trade agreements, including the 2007 United States-Peru Trade Promotion Agreement, and agreements with Chile, Canada, Singapore, Thailand and China.Under President Alan Garcia administration Peru achieved a bilateral Trade agreement with U.S. since 2010 to improve exports for its country and reach in August 2011 its pick in exports of more than 4,700 MM.

FOREIGN INVESTMENT

The Peruvian government actively seeks to attract both foreign and domestic investment in all sectors of the economy. International investment was spurred by the significant progress Peru made during the 1990s toward economic, social, and political stability, but it slowed again after the government delayed privatizations and as political uncertainty increased in 2000. President Alejandro Toledo has made investment promotion a priority of his government. While Peru was previously marked by terrorism, hyperinflation, and government intervention in the economy, the Government of Peru under former President Alberto Fujimori took the steps necessary to bring those problems under control. Democratic institutions, however, and especially the judiciary, remain weak.

The Government of Peru's economic stabilization and liberalization program lowered trade barriers, eliminated restrictions on capital flows, and opened the economy to foreign investment, with the result that Peru now has one of the most open investment regimes in the world. Between 1992 and 2001, Peru attracted almost $17 billion in foreign direct investment in Peru, after negligible investment until 1991, mainly from Spain (32.35%),the United States (17.51%), Switzerland (6.99%), Chile (6.63%), and Mexico (5.53%). The basic legal structure for foreign investment in Peru is formed by the 1993 constitution, the Private Investment Growth Law, and the November 1996 Investment Promotion Law. Although Peru does not have a bilateral investment treaty with the United States, it has signed an agreement (1993) with the Overseas Private Investment Corporation (OPIC) concerning OPIC-financed loans, guarantees, and investments. Peru also has committed itself to arbitration of investment disputes under the auspices of ICSID (the World Bank'sInternational Center for the Settlement of Investment Disputes) or other international or national arbitration tribunals.

CURRENCY

The nuevo sol (commonly referred to simply as "sol") is the currency of Peru. The exchange rate as of October 15, 2015 is 3.2330 soles to the US dollar and 3.6971 soles to the Euro. It was instated in 1991, when the Peruvian government abandoned the inti due to hyperinflation of the currency; the nuevo sol has since maintained the lowest inflation rate in Latin America. the nuevo sol replaced the inti at a rate of 1 nuevo sol = 1,000,000 intis. The inti itself replaced another inflated currency, the sol, which was used between 1863 and 1985. The name *sol* comes from the Latin *solidus*, and is also the Spanish word for "sun", which the ancient Inca civilization worshiped as the god Inti.

The nuevo sol currently enjoys a low inflation rate of 2.5%. Since it was put into use, the nuevo sol's exchange rate with the United States dollar has stayed mostly between 2.80 and 3.30 to 1. Out of all the currencies of the Latin American region, the nuevo sol is the most stable and reliable, being the least affected by the downturn in the value of the US dollar; during late 2007 and early 2008, the exchange rate fell to 2.69 to 1, which had not been seen since 1997. The exchange rate is set on a daily basis by the *Banco Central de Reserva del Perú* (Central Reserve Bank of Peru).

The nuevo sol is divided into 100 céntimos. The highest-denomination banknote is the 200 nuevos soles note; the lowest-denomination coin is the rarely used 5 céntimos coin.

TRADE AND INVESTMENT REGIME

GENERAL FRAMEWORK

The general institutional framework for the formulation of Peru's trade and investment policy has remained virtually unchanged since the country's previous trade policy review in 2007.[26] The structure of the Peruvian State is laid out in its 1993 Political Constitution, which entered into force on 1 January 1994. The Government of Peru is unitary, representative and decentralized. In accordance with the principle of the separation of powers, it is divided into executive, legislative and judicial branches.

There are three levels of Government: national, regional and local. The national Government is composed of the Office of the President of the Republic, the Ministries and public entities making up the executive branch.[27] Each region has a regional government made up of a regional council, a regional presidency and a regional coordinating council. Local governments comprise provincial and district municipalities.

The Head of State is the President of the Republic elected by direct suffrage along with two Vice-Presidents for a term of five years. Consecutive re-election is not permitted. The last presidential election took place in June 2011. Under the Constitution, the President is authorized to direct overall government policy, direct foreign policy and conclude and ratify treaties, enact extraordinary economic and financial measures by issuing emergency decrees having the force of law when such measures are in the national interest and Congress is accordingly informed, and to regulate tariffs, amongst other things. The President of the Republic is empowered to appoint and dismiss the President of the Council of Ministers, whose responsibilities include coordinating the functions of the other ministers and signing off on the regulations provided for in the Constitution.

Legislative functions are incumbent on a single-chamber Congress composed of 130 representatives who are elected by direct proportional vote on a regional basis. All congressional seats come up for re-election every five years. Congress drafts and passes laws and oversees the actions of the Executive. The Constitution takes precedence over all other laws, decrees, resolutions and directives (Table 2.1)[28], which are published in the Official Journal *El Peruano*.[29]

Regulations

Legal instrument	Definition
Law	Instrument adopted by the Congress in the exercise of its legislative powers and in accordance with the procedure stipulated in the Constitution.
Legislative decree	Instrument with the status and force of law emanating from express authorization and power delegated by the Congress; it is limited to the specific matter at hand and must be issued within the time-frame specified by the authoritative law concerned.
Decree law	Instrument with the status of law adopted de facto by the governments.
Emergency decree	Instrument with the status and force of law laying down extraordinary economic and financial measures, except in tax matters; it is issued when required by the national interest and is based on the urgency of regulating extraordinary and unpredictable situations.
Supreme decree	Instrument of a general nature that governs instruments with the status of law or regulates sectoral or multisectoral activity at the national level.
Supreme resolution	Specific decision signed by the President of the Republic and endorsed by one or more Ministers within whose remit it falls, and published in the cases stipulated by law when it is regulatory in nature.
Legislative resolution	Acts of Parliament which generally govern cases in a specific and

	concrete manner. They have the force of law pursuant to Article 102:1 of the Constitution.
Ministerial resolution	Instrument adopted by a Minister of State concerning, inter alia, the domestic and sectoral policies within his purview.
Vice-Ministerial resolution	Legal instrument adopted by a Vice-Minister within his sphere of competence.
Directorial resolution	Instrument adopted by the Directors of Departments of the Public Administration in the exercise of their functions.
Directive	Its purpose is to specify policies and determine procedures or actions that are to be executed in fulfilment of legal provisions in force.

Source: Information provided by the Peruvian authorities.

International treaties that entail administrative changes and affect national sovereignty, financial obligations or taxes, including WTO Agreements and some regional accords, must be approved by Congress and ratified by the President before they can enter into force.[30] The Congress is not empowered to alter a treaty that has been submitted to the Executive for approval and signed by it. International treaties that are approved and in force become part of Peruvian legislation and have the status of law. The provisions of international treaties can therefore be invoked before national courts.

The Judiciary is headed by the Supreme Court of the Republic. Superior courts form the second level of the hierarchy, with jurisdiction over an entire Judicial District.[31] The third level is made up of courts of first instance, whose jurisdictions roughly coincide with the provinces. Finally, there are district magistrates' courts. Arbitral and military tribunals also exercise judicial functions in exceptional cases.

TRADE POLICY OBJECTIVES

The main objective of Peru's trade policy is to achieve sustained growth of trade with an emphasis on exports from non-traditional sectors, consolidate Peru's image as an exporter of competitive goods and services, and boost trade and investment flows between Peru and the rest of the world. Trade policy is formulated at the national level and takes account of international commitments. The President of the Republic is empowered to regulate foreign trade.[32]

The Ministry of Foreign Trade and Tourism (MINCETUR) is responsible for setting, directing, implementing, coordinating and supervising foreign trade and tourism policy.[33] MINCETUR conducts international trade negotiations in coordination with the Ministry of Foreign Affairs, the Ministry of the Economy and Finance (MEF) and other branches of the Government in the areas falling within their purview. The MEF directs and controls tariff and customs policy, coordinating tariff policy with other Ministries.[34]

Since its last review in 2007, Peru has continued to liberalize its trade regime unilaterally, including tariff reduction (section 3.1.4), and has implemented an ambitious agenda of regional trade agreement negotiations, leading to the entry into force of 14 new agreements. Peru currently has 17 regional trade agreements in force with 52 countries (section 2.3.2) . At the same time Peru has remained active at the multilateral level, convinced that the multilateral trading system is an important means of securing greater trading advantages in multilateral negotiations and of defending its interests through the dispute settlement mechanism. Peru also considers the regulatory implications of its multilateral and regional negotiations to be complementary.

Under Peru's various development plans such as the National Strategic Development Plan 2021, the Multi-Annual Strategic Sector Plan (PESEM) for Foreign Trade and Tourism 2012-2016 and the National Strategic Export Plan (PENX) 2003-2013 , trade policy aims to further promote exports, in particular non-traditional exports, increase value added, improve product quality, enhance the competitiveness of the economy and derive greater benefit from international markets. It is planned, by 2016, to double total exports (to US$86 billion), triple non-traditional exports (US$23 billion), double the number of exporting companies to 15,600 (versus 7,840 in 2011), reach a level of 95% for non-traditional exports linked to trade agreements, and to have 25 regional trade agreements in force.

To formulate foreign trade policy, the Government holds regular consultations with the private sector through professional associations and trade unions. The private sector participates on an *ad hoc*basis in coordination meetings on trade issues with the relevant ministries and agencies.

Main trade and investment legislation

Area	Legislation
Customs	General Customs Law (Legislative Decree No. 1053 and amendments thereto) and its implementing regulations (Supreme Decree No. 010-2009-EF and amendments thereto)
Anti-dumping and countervailing measures	Supreme Decree governing rules laid down in the Agreement on Implementation of Article VI of the GATT 1994, the Agreement on Subsidies and Countervailing Measures and the Agreement on Agriculture (Supreme Decree No. 006-2003-PCM and amendments thereto); Regulations on Dumping and Subsidies for non-WTO Members (Supreme Decree No. 133-1991-EF and amendments thereto);
Safeguards	Supreme Decree adopting regulatory provisions of the WTO Agreements on Safeguards and Textiles and Clothing (Supreme Decree No. 023-2003-MINCETUR); Supreme Decree regulating transitional safeguards under the rules and commitments accepted by WTO Members (Supreme Decree No. 023-2003-MINCETUR); Supreme Decree adopting procedures for implementing bilateral safeguards and safeguards relating to textiles pursuant to the integration agreements and international trade agreements signed by Peru (Supreme Decree No. 008-2009-MINCETUR)
Technical regulations and standards	Law on National Standardization and Accreditation Systems (Legislative Decree No. 1030) and its implementing regulations (Supreme Decree No. 081-2008-PCM); Andean system of standardization, accreditation, testing, certification, technical regulations and metrology (Andean Community Decision No. 419); Guidelines for the preparation, adoption and application of technical regulations (Andean Community Decision No. 562); Measures to ensure the freedom of foreign/domestic trade (Legislative Decrees Nos. 668 and 682); Measures establishing the mandatory endorsement by the MEF of measures aimed at restricting the free flow of goods imports and exports (Decree-Law No. 25629 and Decree-Law No. 25909); Remit of the MEF regarding formalities or requirements affecting free domestic marketing or exportation or importation, and the National Public Investment System (Supreme Decree No. 149-2005-EF)

Sanitary and phytosanitary measures	General Law on Agrarian Health (Legislative Decree No. 1059) and its implementing regulations (Supreme Decree No. 018-2008-AG); General Health Law (Law No. 26842); Regulation on sanitary surveillance and control of food and beverages (Supreme Decree No. 007-98 SA); Law on the National Fisheries Health Service (Law No. 28559); Law on Food Safety (Legislative Decree No. 1062) and its implementing regulations (Supreme Decree No. 034-2008-AG)
Government procurement	Government Procurement Law (Legislative Decree No. 1017), as amended by Law No. 29873 and its implementing regulations (Supreme Decree No. 184-2008-EF)
Investment	Framework Law on Public-Private Partnerships (Legislative Decree No. 1012); Law on Harmonization with the WTO TRIMs Agreement (Legislative Decree No. 1035); Law on Foreign Investment (Legislative Decree No. 662); Framework Law for the Growth of Private Investment (Legislative Decree No. 757); Law on the Promotion of Private Investment in Public Infrastructure Works and Public Services (Supreme Decree No. 059-96-PCM)

Source: Information provided by the Peruvian authorities.

INTERNATIONAL TRADE RELATIONS

WTO

Peru became a founding Member of the WTO on 1 January 1995.[40] The WTO Agreements form part of Peru's national legislation and may be invoked in national courts. MINCETUR and the Ministry of Foreign Affairs are Peru's accredited representatives to the WTO. Both Ministries perform that function in a coordinated manner. Peru has made use of the transition periods available to developing countries under the various WTO Agreements. Peru provides, as a minimum, most-favoured-nation treatment to both Members and non-Members of the WTO.

The country took part in the negotiations on telecommunications and financial services subsequent to the Uruguay Round. Its commitments in the area of telecommunications are set out in the Fourth Protocol to the General Agreement on Trade in Services; its commitments in regard to financial services are contained in the Fifth Protocol. Peru is neither a party to the WTO Plurilateral Agreement on Government Procurement nor is it an observer in the WTO Committee on Government Procurement. Peru has been a participant in the WTO Information Technology Agreement since 18 February 2009.[41]

Peru has made several notifications in fulfilment of its WTO commitments (Table A2.1) . It does, however, have some notifications pending for submission to the Committee on Agriculture in particular (section 4.1.3) .

Peru was not involved as a complainant in any case before the WTO Dispute Settlement Body during the review period but was involved once as a defendant.[42] Peru also took part in six cases as a third party.[43] Since the creation of the WTO, Peru has been three times a complainant, five times a defendant and 14 times a third party.[44]

Peru participates actively in the work of the WTO and in the Doha Round negotiations. It recognizes the importance of concluding these negotiations and improving the WTO disciplines so as to ensure the effectiveness of the multilateral system. In the framework of the negotiations, Peru has submitted several proposals individually or jointly with other WTO Members, in fields such as special and differential treatment; agriculture; fisheries subsidies; market access;

biodiversity, traditional knowledge and genetic resources; trade facilitation; environmental goods and services and services.

Regional agreements

At the time of the preceding trade policy review in 2007, there were regional trade agreements in force between Peru and the other Andean Community member countries, the MERCOSUR countries, as well as other member countries of the Latin American Integration Association (LAIA) .[46] Since then it has signed 14 new trade agreements, which are already in force, with Canada, Chile, China, Costa Rica, the European Free Trade Association (EFTA), the European Union, Japan, the Republic of Korea, Mexico, Panama, Singapore, Thailand, the United States and the Bolivarian Republic of Venezuela (Table A2.2) .

Peru has also has signed a trade agreement (not yet in force) with Guatemala, and others are being negotiated with Chile, Colombia, El-Salvador, Honduras, Mexico and Thailand[47], in the context of the Pacific Alliance[48] and the Trans-Pacific Partnership (TPP) .[49]

Peru has 17 regional trade agreements in force covering 52 countries altogether. In 2012, 73.9% of Peru's total exports went to trading partners with which regional agreements were in force and 76.2% of its total imports came from those partners.

Given their importance to Peru, the Andean Community and the Trade Promotion Agreement with the United States are described below.

Andean Community

Peru is a signatory to the Andean Subregional Integration Agreement of 1969, known as the Cartagena Agreement, which laid the groundwork for the Andean Community. This integration process or Andean Pact was notified to the GATT in 1990 under the Enabling Clause[50], and has evolved into what is now the Andean Community (CAN) . The Andean Council of Ministers of Foreign Affairs and the Andean Community Commission are the bodies of the Andean Integration System charged with formulating a community strategy for deepening regional integration.[51] The CAN has a free trade area for all goods produced in the region and has developed common rules governing trade relations amongst member countries and harmonizing domestic legislation in areas such as customs, tariff nomenclature, services, agricultural health, technical regulations, trade defence measures and intellectual property.

Although a Common External Tariff (CET) is one of the objectives of the Andean integration process, this instrument is under evaluation given the current tariff policy of the member countries. The CET is not mandatory at this time and its application has been suspended until 31 December 2014.[52] Peru therefore applies its national tariff (section 3.1.4) .

The Andean free trade area was fully constituted on 1 January 2006 when, pursuant to Decision No. 414, Peru successfully completed the gradual tariff reduction process it had been pursuing since 1997. Peru also applies the commitments under Andean regulations pertaining to the liberalization of trade in services. The establishment of a common market allowing for the free movement of services, capital and people is still pending.

The CAN member countries may negotiate trade agreements with third parties on a community, individual or joint basis.[53] The purpose of the trade negotiations authorized through this Decision "can be the establishment of free trade areas and may refer to topics other than the liberalization in the trade of goods".[54] Members that negotiate trade agreements individually with third countries must abide by guidelines requiring them to: "preserve the Andean legal system in relations between member countries of the Andean Community; take into account the commercial sensitivities of other Andean partners in trade liberalization offers; and maintain an adequate exchange of information and consultations in the course of the negotiations, within a framework of transparency and solidarity".[55]

In 2010, the Andean Council of Foreign Ministers, meeting in a session extended to include the CAN Commission, approved the guiding principles for giving direction to the Andean integration process and the Andean Strategic Agenda containing 12 focal points of consensus: Andean citizen participation through integration; common external policy; trade integration and economic complementarity, promotion of sustainable production, trade and consumption; physical integration and border development; social development; the environment; tourism; security; culture; cooperation; energy integration and natural resources; and the institutional development of the CAN.

In 2011, the Andean leaders laid down the main policy guidelines for the CAN, giving priority to three topics: (i) strengthening and vitalizing the Andean integration process, promoting the "re-engineering" of the Andean Integration System; (ii) fomenting the process of convergence and dialogue between the various regional and subregional integration mechanisms, in particular MERCOSUR, the Union of South American Nations (UNASUR)[57] and LAIA; and (iii) promoting regional energy integration.

US AND PERU TRADE AGREEMENT

The Trade Promotion Agreement between the United States and Peru was signed on 12 April 2006 and took effect on 1 February 2009. It is Peru's first regional agreement covering trade in both goods and services and including a chapter on investment[58] and which has served as a reference for subsequent agreements negotiated by Peru. It comprises 23 chapters and annexes. The measures pertaining to trade in goods figure mainly in Chapters Two to Eight. Trade in services includes modes of supply 1 (cross-border trade), 2 (consumption abroad) and 4 (presence of natural persons) of the WTO General Agreement on Trade in Services (GATS); its liberalization is governed mainly by the provisions of Chapter Eleven regarding cross-border trade in services. The provisions on investment, including all measures relating to GATS mode 3 (commercial presence), are governed by Chapter Ten on investment, by Articles 11.4, 11.7 and 11.8 and the chapters on financial services and telecommunications. There are also provisions on competition policy, labour and environment policy, e-commerce and dispute settlement.

After negotiating the Trade Promotion Agreement with the United States and in order to derive greater benefit from all its regional agreements, Peru made major changes to its trade policies and practices by enacting new laws on customs (section 3.2.1), government procurement (section 3.3.5) and intellectual property rights (section 3.3.6) . To that same end, Peru also amended its domestic legislation on competitiveness, investment and employment promotion, institution building and administrative simplification. Peru applies all these changes on an MFN basis.

The tariff elimination commitments are spread over a 17-year period (2009-2025); most other commitments in respect of both goods and services have applied fully since 1 February 2009. On that date, 53.3% of Peru's tariff and 36.4% of that of the United States were already duty free on an MFN basis. With the entry into force of the Agreement, Peru liberalized a further 32.7% of its lines in favour of US products, whilst an additional 61.5% of the United States tariff was duty free for Peruvian products.[60]Under the Trade Promotion Agreement between the United States and

Peru, both the *ad valorem* and specific components were eliminated for products subject to Peru's price band system (section 3.1.5) .

The United States is Peru's biggest trading partner when it comes to imports and ranks third in terms of the destination of Peruvian exports (section 1.3.1) . In 2012, 18.8% of Peru's goods imports came from the United States (a percentage very similar to the 18.9% recorded in 2008, before the effective date of the Agreement), whilst 14.2% of Peru's goods exports went to the United States (18.7% in 2008) .

Other agreements

Since 1998, Peru has been a participant in the Asia-Pacific Economic Cooperation Forum (APEC), in which the commitment was made to realize the Bogor Goals concerning the liberalization and facilitation of trade and investment by 2020.[61] Peru's participation in APEC also enables it to coordinate joint positions on WTO issues and launch bilateral negotiations with other members. Peru hosted the main APEC meetings in 2008 and will again do so in 2016.

Peru qualifies for preferences granted under the Generalized System of Preferences (GSP) by, *inter alia*, Australia, Belarus, the European Union, New Zealand, the Russian Federation and Turkey.[62] In 2012, 27.4% of all certificates of origin issued were for Peruvian exports meant to benefit from GSP preferences.

Peru takes part in the Global System of Trade Preferences among Developing Countries (GSTP) – comprising 43 countries – under which it grants tariff preferences for a group of 22 products.

FOREIGN INVESTMENT REGIME

The MEF is still responsible for formulating foreign investment policy. The Private Investment Promotion Agency (PROINVERSIÓN) implements national policy for the promotion of private investment in accordance with the general policy guidelines established by the MEF. PROINVERSIÓN also oversees investors' compliance with the investment commitments they have assumed, in cases where this task has not been assigned to any other regulatory agency.

2.36. The legal framework relating specifically to foreign investment includes Article 63 of the Constitution, the Foreign Investment Law (Legislative Decree No. 662), the Framework Law for the Growth of Private Investment (Legislative Decree No. 757), the Law on the Promotion of Private Investment in Public Infrastructure Works and Public Services (Supreme Decree No. 059-96-PCM), and the Framework Law on Public-Private Partnerships for the Generation of Productive Employment (Legislative Decree No. 1012, which also establishes regulations on the streamlining of private investment promotion processes), which was enacted largely as a result of the Trade Promotion Agreement between the United States and Peru. This Decree is designed to promote private-sector participation in the development of public infrastructure and the provision of public services, to which end it lays down, *inter alia*, the requirements for the classification of projects into two types (self-sustaining and co-financed) and includes arbitration as a dispute settlement mechanism.[63]

Legislative Decree No. 1035 was enacted on 25 June 2008 approving the Law on Harmonization with the WTO Agreement on Trade-Related Investment Measures (TRIMs), which eliminates: (i) the condition that primary products produced in the Amazon region (products of domestic origin) be used in order to obtain tax benefits (Law No. 27037 on the Promotion of Investment in the Amazon Region); (ii) the condition that products of domestic origin or sourced domestically be used in order to obtain tax and labour-related benefits (Law No. 27360 adopting the rules for the promotion of the agricultural sector); (iii) the ban on imports of powdered milk, fatty anhydride and other dairy inputs used for reconstitution and recombination in the manufacture of dairy products (Legislative Decree No. 653, Law on the Promotion of Investment in the Agricultural Sector); and (iv) the awarding, by the State, of additional bonus points in bids and tenders for concessions/privatizations to companies that commit (in the tender and the contract) to purchasing domestic goods and undertaking works in the country (Law No. 28242 supplementing Law No. 27143 on Promotion of the Development of National Production) .

Domestic and foreign investment are generally subject to the same conditions. The Foreign Investment Law automatically authorizes foreign investments in the country, and once undertaken, they must be registered with PROINVERSIÓN. Foreign investors are guaranteed the right to transfer all their capital, dividends or profits derived from their investments out of the country in freely convertible currencies, once the statutory taxes have been paid.

Foreign investment is restricted in the following cases:

i. Foreigners may not acquire or possess, under any title whatsoever, mines, land, forests, bodies of water, fuels or energy sources located within 50 km of the country's borders, either directly or indirectly, as individuals or as corporations, on pain of surrendering their ownership rights to the State[64] ;

ii. foreign ownership of air transport services is limited to a 49% interest at the start-up of operations by national airlines; the share of foreign ownership may be increased to as much as 70% after the enterprise has been in operation for six months (section 4.5.4); and

iii. commercial cabotage is reserved exclusively to Peruvian flagged vessels owned by a national ship owner or national shipping enterprise or leased under a financial lease or a bareboat charter with an obligatory purchase option. The owner of a national vessel or shipping company must be an individual of Peruvian nationality or a corporate body in which at least 51% of the equity is held by Peruvian citizens (section 4.5.5) .

Private investment, whether national or foreign, is not permitted in protected nature reserves, although the regulated development and use of such areas may be permitted subject to the applicable laws.

The Constitution also provides that the law may, for reasons of national security only, place temporary restrictions and specific prohibitions on the acquisition, possession, utilization and transfer of certain goods. The authorities have noted that this provision has not been applied, given the existence of the ordinary expropriation regime set forth in Article 70 of the Constitution. The Constitution also provides that publicly owned assets[65] are inalienable and imprescriptible but may be assigned on concession to private parties in accordance with the applicable legal provisions for their economic use. Recourse may be had to the courts in order to contest the property value set by the State in the course of expropriation proceedings.

Peru provides guarantees of legal stability to Peruvian and foreign investors and to the companies in which they invest, by means of agreements in the form of "contracts with force of law" *(contratos-ley)*, which are subject to the provisions of the Civil Code.[66] The agreements are valid for ten years. In the case of concessions, they cover the term of the concession. Disputes are settled by arbitral tribunals.[67] Between 2007 and 2012 Peru signed 140 legal stability agreements with Peruvian and foreign investors worth US$7 billion.[68]

In addition to the legal stability agreements, holders of mining concessions may enter into tax stability agreements with the State under the provisions of the General Law on Mining (section 4.3) .

Since 2007 there has been a change in the negotiation of investment protection mechanisms with the inclusion of a chapter on investment in the preferential trade agreements now in force with Canada, Chile, China, Costa Rica, the Republic of Korea, Mexico, Panama, Singapore and the United States, in that which is about to take effect with Guatemala and in those being negotiated with El Salvador and Honduras, and in the context of the Pacific Alliance and the TPP.

Under the Andean Community's Common Investment Regime approved by Andean Community Decision No. 291, subregional investments are guaranteed national treatment, while the treatment of other foreign investments is determined by the national laws of each member country. In addition, by its Decision No. 578, the Andean Community approved the Regime for the Avoidance of Double Taxation and Prevention of Tax Evasion among the Andean countries.

Peru has concluded reciprocal investment promotion and protection agreements with 33 countries, 31 of which are in effect.[69] Peru is a member of the International Centre for Settlement of Investment Disputes (ICSID) and the Multilateral Investment Guarantee Agency (MIGA) .

Peru has three agreements in force for the avoidance of double taxation and the prevention of tax evasion with Brazil, Canada and Chile. In the context of the Andean Community, Peru has an agreement of this kind in force with the Plurinational State of Bolivia, Colombia and Ecuador. Peru has also signed agreements for the avoidance of double taxation and the prevention of tax evasion with the Republic of Korea, Mexico, Portugal and Switzerland, though they are not in force. The country has also started negotiations on the subject with France, Italy, Qatar, Singapore, Spain, Sweden, the United Kingdom and Thailand.

MEASURES AFFECTING IMPORTS

CUSTOMS PROCEDURES

In Peru, customs procedures are mainly governed by the General Customs Law, the Regulations implementing the General Customs Law and amending regulations.[71] The National Customs and Tax Administration Supervisory Authority (SUNAT), through the Customs Administration, remains the authority responsible for applying customs legislation and collecting customs duties and other import taxes.

The customs regime to be followed is specified at the time the goods are declared. In addition to the import for consumption regime, Peru has other customs regimes or procedures such as import into zones for special customs treatment; reimport in the same state; temporary admission for re-export in the same state; customs transit; transhipment; reloading; and special or exceptional customs regimes.[72]

Importers generally have to be registered with SUNAT and be in possession of a valid single taxpayers' registration number (RUC) before they can import. Goods may be imported without an RUC, simply using a national identity document (DNI) in the case of Peruvians or a foreign identity card, passport or safe-conduct in the case of foreigners, provided that the goods are only imported occasionally (a maximum of three times a year) and are valued at less than US$1,000 f.o.b.; or are single imports whose f.o.b. value is US$1,000 to US$3,000; or the importers are Peruvian or foreign diplomats or international civil servants.[73]

SUNAT may grant certification as an Authorized Economic Operator (OEA) to foreign trade operators with a proper accounting and logistics system that enables operations to be verified, provided that their financial solvency and capital adequacy have been duly established and that their level of security is satisfactory. OEAs are eligible for streamlined customs procedures and controls, for example, they are not required to provide the same amount of information in their customs declarations.[74]

In general terms, the following documents have to be submitted to the SUNAT for processing: the bill of lading, the air waybill or freight bill, depending on the mode of transport; the invoice or equivalent document and/or the sworn declaration of value according to the mode of import; proof of payment; a power of attorney for streamlined clearance if this is to be done by a third person acting on behalf of the importer, owner or consignee; together with the other documents required. The latter applies mainly to restricted goods, which may only be imported if they have the requisite authorization from the competent bodies corresponding to the nature of the goods.[75] An import declaration has to be submitted together with the aforementioned documents, and this may be a simplified import declaration (DSI) or customs declaration of goods (DAM), as applicable. The DSI is used when importing samples of no commercial value, gifts whose value does not exceed US$1,000 or goods not exceeding US$2,000.

The services of a customs broker are required for clearance of goods under the import for consumption regime, and this may be the owner, the consignee, an official broker or a customs agent.[76]

Before arrival of the mode of transport, the carrier or its representative in Peru must forward the cargo manifest and other documents to SUNAT electronically, within the time-limit laid down in the regulations implementing the General Customs Law. Customs declarations may be corrected either ex officio or at the request of a party.[77]

Imports under the regimes regulating import for consumption, temporary admission for inward processing, temporary admission for re-export in the same state, customs warehouse, customs transit or transhipment, are eligible for advance customs clearance. For this purpose, the goods must arrive within the prescribed time-limit. Advance clearance offers several advantages that help to facilitate trade, including the following: release of the goods within 48 hours (with a prior guarantee); examination of the documents prior to arrival; inspection by scanner, which may replace the physical inspection of the goods; and the opportunity for prior acceptance and electronic release of the goods (without the need to submit a hard copy of the DAM) .

There are also other forms of clearance, for example, urgent clearance depending on the type of goods and exceptional clearance, used for goods that require special treatment, or goods imported in cases of disaster or emergency. The import requirements applicable to any of the various forms of clearance are virtually the same: a duly endorsed or guaranteed DAM (prior guarantee) is always required, together with an authenticated photocopy or the original copy of the invoice or equivalent document (including those generated or printed electronically), an authenticated photocopy of the transport documents and an authenticated photocopy of the control document, except for those documents processed through the single window for foreign trade (VUCE) .

Once the cargo manifest has been forwarded and the customs taxes and other charges applicable have been paid, the DAM is assigned to a channel using risk management techniques. There is no examination of documents or physical inspection for goods assigned to the green channel. Nevertheless, the customs broker has to keep the original documents so that SUNAT may examine them if necessary. For goods assigned to the amber channel, the documents are examined, and for those assigned to the red channel there is a physical inspection.[78] The customs broker and the importer are informed of the control channel electronically. The percentage of goods which entered Peru through the maritime customs at Callao and were processed through the green channel increased from 67% in 2007 to 82% in 2012.[79]

The VUCE was created in 2006 as an integrated system to facilitate trade, allow parties engaged in foreign trade and international transport to submit electronically the documents required by the competent control authorities for the transit, entry or exit of goods in Peru.[80] The VUCE started operating in July 2010 and now has three components: restricted goods, port services, and origin. The restricted goods component allows users to carry out formalities electronically in order to obtain permits, certificates, licences and other authorizations required by the competent authorities for the entry, transit or exit of goods. All formalities required for the arrival, stay and clearance of ships in ports can be carried out electronically through the port component. The origin component allows administrative formalities and procedures related to eligibility and issue of certificates of origin to be carried out, involving producers, exporters and the competent authority.[81]

CUSTOMS VALUATION

The customs valuation system is governed by the Regulations on the valuation of goods in accordance with the WTO Agreement on Customs Valuation and amendments thereto[83]; decisions and resolutions of the Andean Community (CAN)[84]; decisions of the WTO Committee on Customs Valuation; and the instruments of the Technical Committee on Customs Valuation (Brussels) . There are also special procedures for determining the customs value of media with digital content and used vehicles.[85]

In Peru, the customs value of imported goods is determined according to the valuation methods set out in the WTO Agreement on Customs Valuation. SUNAT remains the authority responsible for verifying and determining the customs value of goods imported into Peru.[86] The importer must furnish the necessary documents and information to ensure that the value declared corresponds to the transaction value; if this is not the case, SUNAT employs the other valuation methods determined in the Agreement in order to verify the declared value.

For the DSI, if the importer so requests, the customs value can be determined according to the list of reference values published on SUNAT's website.[87]

The importer may declare a provisional value when submitting the DAM if the price negotiated has not been finally determined.[88] In such cases, the Customs allows delivery of the goods subject to payment of the import taxes corresponding to the provisional value declared and the deposit of security. The importer has 12 months, which may be extended by six months, to regularize the declared value and pay any taxes due.

If the Customs Administration has any reason to doubt the declared value or the exactitude of the documents submitted as proof of the declaration, it may request the importer to provide additional explanations or to substantiate the declaration with documents or other evidence proving that the value declared represents the total amount actually paid or payable for the goods imported, adjusted as applicable. Once the additional information has been received, if the Customs Administration still entertains reasonable doubts regarding the exactitude of the declared value, it may employ the other methods of valuation successively and in order. If the Customs Administration needs more time to resolve the reasonable doubts, bearing in mind the risk indicators, it may attribute a provisional value to the goods. Once the value has been determined, the Customs Administration informs the importer of the reasons for doubting the accuracy or exactitude of the information or documents submitted and its rejection of use of the transaction value as the valuation method. If the importer disagrees with the procedures, he may begin proceedings against SUNAT.

RULES OF ORIGIN

During the review period, Peru informed the WTO of changes in the preferential rules of origin applied under the preferential agreements signed within the LAIA framework and the new preferential agreements it had signed from 2007 onwards.[89] For most of the preferential agreements, the basic criterion used to determine origin continues to be a change in tariff classification or, alternatively, the regional content value (Table 3.1) . The agreements signed by Peru also lay down specific requirements of origin.

Non-preferential rules of origin are used in Peru to determine the origin of imported products subject to provisional or definitive anti-dumping and/or countervailing duties. In 2011, Peru established a new regulatory framework for non-preferential rules of origin.[90] This mainly concerns the minimum information to be provided by the importer in order to determine the origin of goods.[91] Up to 2011, a certificate of origin was required, but since then an importer has only had to give the Customs Authority a sworn signed declaration of origin.[92]

The Ministry of Foreign Trade and Tourism (MINCETUR) determines the non-preferential criteria of origin, which have to be approved by ministerial resolution (Table 3.1)[93] and specifies the special format required for certificates of origin.[94]

Non-preferential criteria of origin

Product	Legislation	Validity
Zippers and parts thereof	Ministerial Resolution No. 339-2005-MINCETUR/DM; Ministerial Resolution No. 338-2005-MINCETUR/DM	Entry into force: 2 November 2005 Entry into force: 2 November 2005
Fabrics	Ministerial Resolution No. 076-2006-MINCETUR/DM	Entry into force: 28 February 2006
Footwear	Ministerial Resolution No. 074-2007-MINCETUR/DM	Entry into force: 29 March 2007
Ceramic dishes	Ministerial Resolution No. 339-2005-MINCETUR/DM; Ministerial Resolution No. 338-2005-MINCETUR/DM	Entry into force: 2 November 2005 Until: 13 October 2009[a]
Iron hinges	Ministerial Resolution No. 075-2006-MINCETUR/DM	Entry into force: 28 February 2006 Until: 12 May 2009[b]

TARIFFS

Peru's customs tariff is based on the Common Tariff Nomenclature of the Member Countries of the Andean Community (NANDINA), approved by Decision No. 766 of the Commission of the CAN, which incorporates the various amendments to the Harmonized Commodity Description and Coding System (HS) .[95] Peru usually only applies *ad valorem* tariffs, although 47 tariff lines in the 2013 tariff schedule (0.6% of the tariff universe) are subject to a price band system involving two components: one *ad valorem* and the other specific. The price band system applies to imports of certain agricultural products, namely, rice, sugar, maize and dairy produce.

Ad valorem import tariffs are calculated according to the c.i.f. value of the goods, whereas tariffs under the price band system are determined according to an *ad valorem* component and another, specific component, which may be a reduction or an increase in the MFN *ad valorem* rate. The specific component is calculated according to the international price compared to the "band" composed of "floor" and "ceiling" prices fixed on the basis of historical international prices in the reference markets.[96] When the price on the international reference market is below the "floor", a tariff surcharge is imposed and when it rises above the "ceiling", a reduction on the MFN *ad valorem* tariff is applied. If the reference price lies within the "band", the corresponding MFN *ad valorem* tariff applies, with no surcharges or reductions (section 4.1.2) .

In 2013, Peru's tariff contained 7,554 tariff lines at the ten-digit level of the 2012 HS. There has been an increase in the number of tariff lines since the previous trade policy review in 2007 (7,370 lines) following the transposition of the nomenclature. During the period under review, Peru continued to lower its tariffs unilaterally, with the average applied MFN tariff declining from 8% to 3.2%, one of the lowest rates on the continent (Table 3.2) .

MFN tariff structure,(%)

	2007	2013[a]	2013[b]
Total number of lines	7,370	7,554	7,554
Non-ad valorem tariffs (% of all tariff lines)	0.6	0.6	0.6
Non-ad valorem tariffs without any ad valorem equivalents (% of all tariff lines)	6	0.6	0.0
Tariff quotas (% of all tariff lines)	0.0	0.0	0.0
Duty-free tariff lines (% of all tariff lines)	43.6	55.9	55.3
Average of lines exceeding zero (%)	14.1	7.2	7.2
Simple average (%)	8.0	3.2	3.2
Agricultural products	12.9	3.9	4.3
Non-agricultural products (including petroleum)	7.2	3.1	3.1
Raw materials	9.6	2.9	2.9
Semi-processed products	7.1	3.0	3.1
Finished products	8.2	3.3	3.4
National tariff peaks (% of all tariff lines)[c]	0.0	10.5	10.8
International tariff peaks (% of all tariff lines)[d]	15.1	0.0	0.1
Overall standard deviation of applied rates	7.5	3.8	3.9
Bound tariff lines (% of all tariff lines)	100.0	100.0	100.0

Source: WTO Secretariat estimates based on data provided by the authorities.

In 2013, Peru's tariff schedule comprised three rates: 0%, 6% and 11%, excluding tariffs that might apply as a result of the price band. In 2007, the tariff also comprised three rates, but these were 0%, 12% and 20%. One of the most important changes in Peru's tariff structure has been the decrease in the maximum rate applied, from 20% to 11%, and the 6 percentage points reduction in the 12% rate applied in 2007, which is now 6%. Likewise, the percentage of lines with a zero rate increased from 43.6% to 55.9% over the period under review (Chart 3.1) . The highest rate of 11% applies first and foremost to products such as textiles and clothing. If the tariffs resulting from application of the price band are taken into account, however, Peru's tariff has rates of over 20% on sugar and some dairy produce, and up to 55.7% for some milk products. According to the authorities, no tariff surcharges resulting from the price band system were applied during most of the period 2007-2012.

The protection given to agricultural products (WTO definition), which was 12.9% in 2007, fell sharply to 3.9% in 2013. Protection for non-agricultural products (3.1%) is still lower than for agricultural products, although the gap has narrowed following the tariff reduction which abolished the 20% rate that applied principally to agricultural products such as meat, dairy products, fruit and vegetables, cereals and food preparations in 2007. Taking into account the tariff resulting from application of the *ad valorem*equivalent of the specific price band duty when calculating the average tariff would increase the protection given to agricultural products from 3.9% to 4.3% (Table 3.2) .[97]

3.25. In 2013, Peru's applied tariffs rose in line with the level of processing of the goods, whereas in 2007 raw materials received more protection than semi-processed or finished products (Table 3.2) . A similar trend exists as regards tariff protection for capital goods (0%), intermediate goods (3.2%) and consumer goods, which enjoy a slightly higher level of protection (5.6%) (Table 3.3) . Peru has had a policy of tariff reduction for capital and intermediate goods since 2007, in line with its economic policy, as it considers trade to be a cornerstone for development and growth. Accordingly, the purpose of the tariff reduction is to make the country more competitive, not only by increasing and diversifying the exportable offer (particularly in the mining sector), but also by facilitating trade, *inter alia* by upgrading the infrastructure, for which capital goods are necessary (section 4) .

BINDINGS

Peru has bound all its tariffs at three levels: 0%, 30% and 68%. The lines bound at 68% concern agricultural products: dairy produce; cereals such as wheat, maize and rice; sugar; and pasta. Some of these, for example, dairy produce, maize, rice and sugar, are also subject to the price band. When comparing the bindings made by Peru in the Uruguay Round and the applied MFN tariff in 2013, without taking into account the tariffs resulting from application of the price band, it can be seen that the MFN tariffs are below the bindings. If the MFN tariff turns out to be higher than the bound rate because of application of the price band, the bound rate applies.[98]

Tariff quotas

Peru does not apply tariff quotas to MFN imports. It has negotiated preferential tariff quotas under agreements with Canada, Costa Rica, the European Free Trade Association (EFTA) (only Switzerland), the European Union, Mexico, Panama and the United States. A rate of 0% applies to in-quota imports under the preferential tariff quotas and the MFN or preferential rate, depending on the agreement, to out-of-quota imports. For tariff quotas applicable to products subject to the price band, both the *ad valorem* and the specific components have been liberalized. Little and in most cases no use was made of quotas in 2012 (Table A3.2) .

Preferential tariffs

Peru grants preferential treatment to imports from countries with which it has signed agreements within the LAIA framework (Chapter 2 and Table A2.2) . In the CAN, Peru gives preferential treatment to imports from the Plurinational State of Bolivia, Colombia and Ecuador. Peru has signed 14 new trade agreements since 2007 and those with the following have already come into force: Canada; Chile; China; Costa Rica; EFTA; the European Union; Japan; the Republic of

Korea; Mexico; Panama; Singapore; Thailand (Early Harvest Protocol); the United States; and the Bolivarian Republic of Venezuela.[99] The lowest average preferential tariffs apply under the agreements with Canada and the United States, followed by the preferences given to EFTA member countries. In most cases, the average preferential tariff applicable to agricultural products is higher than that for non-agricultural products (Table 3.4) .

TARIFF CONCESSIONS

The temporary admission procedure for re-export in the same state allows goods destined for export without being modified, except for "normal wear and tear", to be imported without payment of customs duty or any other taxes applicable to imports for consumption. In 2012, imports amounting to US$2 billion entered under this procedure.

3.30. Some foreign goods may enter Peruvian customs territory under the temporary admission for inward processing procedure[100], which allows suspension of payment of customs duty and any other taxes applicable to imports for consumption, as well as other charges, and the goods must be exported within a specified period after having been processed in some way.[101] In 2012, imports under the temporary admission for inward processing procedure amounted to US$7,513 million.

Imports for certain institutions or for certain uses are still exempt from payment of customs duty (Box 3.1) .[102] These include medicines and inputs for treating cancer, HIV/AIDS and diabetes, which remain exempt from customs duty, the general sales tax (IGV) and the selective consumption tax (ISC) .[103]

Imports exempt from payment of customs duty

Samples of no commercial value;
Prizes awarded abroad to Peruvians or foreigners resident in Peru officially representing Peru at exhibitions, competitions or contests;
Coffins or urns containing human bodies or remains;
Special vehicles or prostheses for the exclusive use of disabled persons;
Donations approved by ministerial resolution given to government sector bodies, except for companies that are part of the State's business activities; as well as to foreign bodies or institutions engaged in international cooperation (ENIEX), non-governmental national development organizations (ONGD-PERU), and private non-profit-making institutions receiving donations for assistance or education (IPREDAS) listed in the register of the Peruvian International Cooperation Agency (APCI);
Donations to religious institutions, and to legally established foundations whose statutes provide for one or more of the following purposes: education, culture, science, charity, social welfare or hospital care (Article 19 of Peru's Political Constitution);
Imports of goods intended solely for teaching purposes by universities, higher education institutes and educational centres;
Medicines and/or inputs used for the manufacture of therapeutic equivalents in Peru for the treatment of cancer, HIV/AIDS or diabetes;
Travel and household articles belonging to Peruvians who died outside Peru;
Repatriation of goods that are part of the nation's cultural heritage;
Mail for the personal and sole use of the addressee;
Express courier mail under normal conditions consisting of correspondence, documents, newspapers or periodicals, not for commercial purposes, or goods up to a value of US$200.

Source: General Customs Law and amendments thereto.

From 2010 onwards, the import of some capital goods to be used for "production" activities in the High Andean regions has been exempt from the IGV and tariffs.[104]

OTHER CHARGES

The additional 5% tariff which applied to 392 ten-digit tariff lines in early 2007 was removed the same year.

The customs clearance charge for processing the DAM for the import for consumption or customs warehouse regimes still applies to goods whose declared customs value exceeds three times the tax unit in effect at the time the declaration is submitted.[105] Its rate has not changed since 2007 and is still 2.35% of the UIT for imports for consumption or the customs warehouse.[106] The customs clearance charge does not apply to procedures involving a DSI or special operations or uses.

As is the case for domestic production, imports are subject to the IGV at 16% (formerly 17%)the municipal promotion tax (IPM) of 2%; and also the ISC and/or other special customs taxes in certain cases.

The IGV applies to imports of all goods, except for some agricultural products and fertilizers; wool, cotton and other fibres; gold; and some used vehicles or vehicles for diplomatic use.[108] The tax base for the IGV is the c.i.f. customs value plus the tariffs and other taxes on imports. Imported goods to which the IGV applies are also subject to the IPM, whose tax base is the same as that for the IGV (Table 3.5) .

The ISC applies to the import of certain goods such as fuels, spirits, new and used vehicles, aerated beverages and cigarettes (Table 3.5) . Since May 2013, some alcoholic beverages that were previously subject to an *ad valorem* rate of 20% became classified according to their degree of alcohol and the ISC is calculated alternatively using three methods: specific (fixed amount), on the value, or on the value according to the retail selling price. The ISC payable is the highest amount obtained by applying the three methods (Table 3.6) .

Import taxes, 2007-2013

Tax	Type of tax	Rate	Tax base	Comments
General sales tax (IGV)	Ad valorem	16%	Customs value plus tariffs and other import taxes.	The goods listed in Appendix I to the Single Harmonized Text on Tax are exempt from the IGV.
Municipal promotion tax (IPM)	Ad valorem	2%	Customs value plus tariffs and other import taxes, except for the IGV.	This tax is imposed on goods subject to the IGV.
Selective Consumption Tax (ISC)				

Products subject to the value system

	Ad valorem	0% 10% 17% 20%[a] 30% 50%	Customs value plus the applicable import taxes.	Certain goods such as new or used motor vehicles; mineral waters; wine and other spirits; cigars and cheroots, tobacco and cigarettes are taxed.

Products subject to application of a fixed amount

	Specific	Amount in nuevos soles: from S/.0.007 to S/.2.30	Per unit, litre, tonne, gallon or kilogram.	Certain goods such as pisco, cigarettes of dark or blond tobacco, gasoline for engines, kerosene, gasoil, and liquefied petroleum gas are taxed.

Products subject to the retail selling price scheme

	Ad valorem	27.80% (beer)[b] 30% (cigarettes)[c]	The retail selling price suggested by the producer or importer multiplied by 0.840.	Only beer and cigarettes of dark or blond tobacco are taxed.

a The goods subject to the 20% rate were modified in 2013 by Supreme Decree No. 092-2013-EF of 13 May 2013.

b Abolished as of 13 May 2013 by Supreme Decree No. 092-2013-EF of 13 May 2013.

c Abolished as of 15 January 2010 by Article 2 of Supreme Decree No. 004-2010-EF of 14 January 2010.

Source: Ministry of the Economy and Finance (2011), Text of the Law on the General Sales Tax and the Selective Consumption Tax, Lima (Supreme Decree No. 055-99-EF); Payments and Guarantees: Customs Taxation. Information viewed online at: http://www.sunat.gob.pe/orientacionaduanera/pagosgarantias/; and Appendices to the Single Harmonized Tax of the Law on the IGV and the ISC. Information viewed online at:http://www.sunat.gob.pe/legislacion/igv/ley/apendice.htm#acla4b[16/05/2013].

The tax on the sale of pounded rice (IVAP) imposed on the sale of pounded rice in Peru also applies to the import of pounded and other types of rice.[109] The IVAP is an *ad valorem* tax of 4% imposed on the first sale of pounded rice in Peru and on the customs value, including other import duties and taxes, and on imports of pounded rice and other types of rice.

RESTRICTIONS, CONTROLS AND LICENCES

The import of certain goods may be prohibited or require an authorization or registration for reasons of public health or morals, and also to protect the environment, national security or to comply with the commitments undertaken in international agreements signed by Peru.

Peru has notified the WTO that no licences are required for imports and no quantitative restrictions are applied.

There have been no changes as regards the products prohibited since the previous review in 2007 (Table 3.7) . Nevertheless, some of these goods may be imported, for example, used engines, components and spare parts for vehicles that are not on the road in Peru but are to be used in production.[111]

Prohibited imports, 2013

Product	Reason	Legislation[a]
Toy known as "Yoyo loco"	Health protection	Supreme Decree No. 003-2004-SA of 19 February 2004
Foreign alcoholic beverages whose description includes the word "Pisco"	Protected appellation of origin	Law No. 26426 of 1 January 1995
Used tyres	Public health, safety and environmental protection	Supreme Decree No. 003-2001-SA of 8 February 2001
Used clothing and footwear "for commercial purposes"	Public health	Law No. 28514 of 25 May 2005
Used engines, components and spare parts for road vehicles	Safety	Supreme Decree No. 053-2010-MTC of 11 November 2010
Ban on the import of used goods, machinery or equipment that uses radioactive sources	Safety	Law No. 27757 of 19 June 2002 Supreme Decree No. 001-2004-EM of 25 March 2004

In order to boost private investment and make the dairy industry more competitive, since 2008 Peru has once again allowed the import of powdered milk, fatty anhydride and other dairy inputs used for reconstitution and recombination in the manufacture of dairy products[112], which had previously been prohibited.[113]

ANTI-DUMPING AND COUNTERVAILING MEASURES

The principal domestic legislation on anti-dumping and countervailing measures consists of Supreme Decree No. 006-2003-PCM, the Regulations on Dumping and Subsidies, as amended by Supreme Decree No. 004-2009-PCM[114], which introduces amendments regarding the calculation of the normal value and the dumping margin in special cases; the period for imposition of anti-dumping or countervailing duties; the time-limit and the procedure for requesting the refund of wrongfully imposed provisional duties or the excess amounts paid; and the procedure for reviewing the expiry of anti-dumping duties (sunset review) . New provisions have also been added concerning the administrative procedure for contesting the payment of anti-dumping or countervailing duties and their refund.[115] Supreme Decree No. 133-91-EF, as amended by Supreme Decree No. 051-92-EF, still applies to non-WTO Members.[116]

The Dumping and Subsidies Commission (CFD) of the National Institute for the Defence of Competition and the Protection of Intellectual Property (INDECOPI) remains the authority responsible for applying trade defence instruments in order to avoid or, where applicable repair, injury that may be caused in the market by dumping or subsidization. The CFD is the administrative authority of first instance with powers to initiate and conduct dumping or subsidies investigations. It also acts as the investigating authority in proceedings for the imposition of safeguard measures.[117] Appeals may be lodged with the INDECOPI Tribunal against decisions by the CFD, and the latter's decisions can be appealed directly to Peru's Supreme Court.

Peruvian producers who consider that they have suffered injury or threat of injury as a result of the import of like goods that have allegedly been subsidized or imported at dumped prices may request the CFD to initiate an investigation to determine whether or not dumping or subsidization has occurred. Both dumping and subsidy investigations are administrative procedures through which it is determined whether the goods have been imported at a price lower than their normal value or have been subsidized, and if this has caused injury, or threatens to cause injury or retardation, in a domestic industry over a particular period (Box 3.2) .

Procedure for dumping or subsidy investigations and review of definitive duties, 2013

1. An application is submitted for initiation of an anti-dumping or subsidy investigation or the review of definitive duties, identifying the applicant, giving details of its domicile and economic activity, and attaching copies of documents proving the applicant's existence and, where applicable, that of its legal representative.
2. A questionnaire duly completed by the applicant, which must include the following information:
A. For companies that are producers and request the initiation of an investigation into dumping or subsidization: -Proof that the applicant is representative of the domestic industry or has the support of domestic producers that are not applicants. A complete description of the dumped or subsidized product and the like product produced domestically. -The country of export and of origin. -The identity of each known producer or foreign exporter. -The list of importers, proof of the price at which the product is sold in the country of origin (at a comparable level, i.e. the same level of trade) . -Proof of the existence of dumping (invoices, computed value) or subsidization (legal text, etc.) . -Data on the trend in the volume of imports. -Effect of these imports on the price of the like product on the domestic market. -Impact of the imports on the domestic industry (production, sales, inventories, use of plant capacity, etc.) and other information. The quantitative data must be submitted in writing and on magnetic media.
B. For exporting or importing companies or domestic producers requesting the review of definitive duties: -Data on the price at which the product that is the subject of the application for definitive duties is sold in the country of origin (at a comparable level, i.e. at the same level of trade) . -Trend in the volume of imports. -Effect of these imports on the price of the like product on the domestic market. -Impact of the imports on the domestic industry (production, sales, etc.) and other information. The quantitative data must be submitted in writing and on magnetic media.
3. In order to request that certain information remain confidential, the applicant must explain the reasons why the information should remain confidential and provide a non-confidential summary thereof.
4. Copies for all the parties mentioned in the application or, in the case of review of definitive duties, for the number of parties that participated in the investigation leading to application of such duties.
5. Proof of payment of the tax corresponding to one UIT. Payment of 40% must be made when the application is submitted and the balance paid via a refund solely if the Commission orders the initiation of the investigation or the review of definitive duties.

Source: Single Text of Administrative Procedures (TUPA) . Information viewed online at:http://www.indecopi.gob.pe/repositorioaps/0/0/jer/datgentupa1/Tupa/CFD.pdf.

During the review period, 38 anti-dumping investigations were initiated, compared to 40 between January 2000 and December 2006. Of these 38 investigations, only eight corresponded to initial investigations and the others were procedures for the review of anti-dumping duties previously imposed (Table 3.8) . During the period 2007-2012, five definitive anti-dumping measures were imposed on imports of biodiesel (United States), footwear (Viet Nam), white cement (Mexico) and textiles (India) .[118]According to the notification to the WTO, at 31 December 2012 Peru had 11 anti-dumping measures in effect, of which seven concerned China and the others India, Pakistan, the United States and Viet Nam. Five measures have been in effect for over ten years. Most of the measures applied to textiles and footwear.[119]

Between 2007 and 2012, Peru conducted four subsidy investigations, of which only two led to the imposition of countervailing duties (Table 3.8) . The imports concerned were olive oil from Spain and Italy and biodiesel from the United States.[120] The measures imposed on imports of olive oil were repealed in 2013.

Safeguards

Peru's domestic legislation on WTO safeguards is still Supreme Decree No. 020-1998-ITINCI. It also has legislation establishing the procedures for implementing the bilateral safeguards provided in the regional agreements it has signed.[121]

3.49. Safeguard investigations can be initiated at the request of a party with a legitimate interest or ex officio. INDECOPI, through the CFD, is responsible for deciding whether to initiate a safeguard investigation within the WTO framework. If it is decided to initiate an investigation, the proceedings must be conducted within six months calculated from the date of publication of the notice of initiation in the Official Journal *El Peruano*. After the investigation has been concluded, the CFD has to issue a technical report containing its recommendation on whether or not the safeguard measure requested needs to be applied. In critical circumstances where delay would cause damage to the domestic industry which it would be difficult to repair and if so requested by the applicant, INDECOPI draws up a preliminary technical report during the course of the investigation to assess whether it is necessary to impose provisional measures. The decision on whether or not to apply the definitive or provisional safeguard measures requested, however, lies with a multisectoral commission composed of the Ministers of Foreign Trade and Tourism (MINCETUR), the Economy and Finance (MINEF), and the sector to which the domestic industry affected belongs. Box 3.3 describes the procedure for initiating a safeguard investigation.

Procedure for safeguard measures, 2013

1. An application is submitted for initiation of an investigation or extension of a safeguard measure, identifying the applicant, giving details of its domicile and economic activity, and attaching copies of documents proving the applicant's existence and, where applicable, that of its legal representative.
2. A questionnaire duly completed by applicant producers, which must include the following information: -Complete description of the imported product.

-Tariff heading. -Applicable tariff. -Description of the like or directly competitive domestic product. -Data on imports and on domestic production for the previous three calendar years (by month) . -Quantitative data indicating the degree of serious injury or threat thereof. -The causal link. Quantitative data must be submitted in writing and on magnetic media.
3. In order to request that certain information remain confidential, the applicant must explain the reasons why the information should remain confidential and provide a non-confidential summary thereof.
4. Proof of payment of the tax corresponding to one UIT. Payment of 40% must be made when the application is submitted and the balance paid via a refund solely if the Commission orders the initiation of the investigation or the review of definitive duties.

Source: TUPA. Information viewed online at:http://www.indecopi.gob.pe/repositorioaps/0/0/jer/datgentupa1/Tupa/CFD.pdf.

3.50. During the review period, Peru initiated only one investigation, in 2009, with a view to the application of a general safeguard measure to imports of cotton yarn (HS 5205 and 5206)[122], although this ended without any measure being applied.[123]

A corrective *ad valorem* tax of 29% on the c.i.f. value applies to imports of fats (NANDINA 1511.90.00, 1516.20.00 and 1517.90.00) from Colombia and the Bolivarian Republic of Venezuela.[124]

TECHNICAL REGULATIONS AND STANDARDS

3.52. Peru's legal framework governing standardization is composed of both domestic legislation and international and supranational rules (Table 3.9) .

Legal framework governing Peru's standardization system

Legal instrument	Description
International agreements:	
Legislative Resolution No. 26407	Approves the Agreement establishing the WTO and the multilateral trade agreements contained in the Final Act of the Uruguay Round (December 1994) .
ISO 59:2008	Code of Good Practice for Standardization.
Supranational rules:	
CAN Decision No. 376	Andean system of standardization, accreditation, testing, certification, technical regulations and metrology.
CAN Decision No. 419	Amendment to Decision No. 376 and establishing the

	Andean system of standardization, accreditation, testing, certification, technical regulations and metrology.
CAN Decision No. 615	Notification information and technical regulation system of the CAN.
CAN Decision No. 562	Guidelines for the preparation, adoption and application of technical regulations in member countries of the CAN and at the Community level.
CAN Resolution No. 313	Updates the regulations of the Andean Standardization Network.
Domestic legal rules:	
Legislative Decree No. 1033	Law on the Organization and Functions of INDECOPI (Article 28) .
Legislative Decree No. 1030	Law on National Standardization and Accreditation Systems.
Legislative Decrees Nos. 668 and 682	Measures to ensure the freedom of foreign/domestic trade (September 1991) .
Supreme Decree No. 149-2005-EF	Regulatory provisions for the WTO Agreement on Technical Barriers to Trade in relation to goods and the General Agreement on Trade in Services in relation to services.
Supreme Decree No. 081-2008-PCM	Regulations implementing the Law on National Standardization and Accreditation Systems.
Regulations of the Commission:	
Resolution No. 048-2008/INDECOPI-CNB	Regulations on the preparation and approval of Peruvian technical standards.
Resolution No. 048-2008/INDECOPI-CNB	Regulations of technical standardization committees.
Standardization guidelines:	
GP 001:1995	Guidelines for the drafting, format and presentation of Peruvian technical standards.
GP 002:1995	Guidelines for the presentation of printed texts of outlines, drafts and Peruvian technical standards.
GP-ISO/IEC 2:2013	Standardization and related activities: General glossary.
GP-ISO/IEC 21-1:2013	Regional or national adoption of international standards and other outcomes of international standardization, Part 1: Adoption of international standards.
GP-ISO/IEC 21-2:2008	Regional or national adoption of international standards and other outcomes of international standardization, Part 2: Adoption of other documents arising from international standardization other than international standards.

Source: Online information from INDECOPI, viewed at: http://www.indecopi.gob.pe/0/modulos/JER/JER_Interna.aspx?ARE=0&PFL=6&JER=421.

INDECOPI's Committee for the Harmonization and Regulation of Non-Tariff Barriers to Trade (CNB)[125], created in 2008, is the standardization agency responsible for approving Peruvian technical standards (NTP) for all sectors[126] and these are voluntary[127]; they are public documents that may be consulted, referenced and used by any person who so wishes.

NTPs are drawn up by technical standardization committees, which first prepare a technical document called a "draft technical standard" (Box 3.4) and then finalize it in collaboration with representatives of producers, consumers and academic circles. The technical committees, the Commission or entities interested in the topic such as trade unions or ministries may request that the standardization procedure be applied to any subject matter. In June 2013, there were 125 technical committees, of which 102 were operating.[128]

Standardization procedure

The standardization procedure consists of the following stages:
Proposal: the drafting or revision of an NTP is proposed for inclusion in the technical committee's plan of work.
Preparation: the technical committee and the CNB, when it is acting ex officio, prepare a preliminary working document entitled "Outline or preliminary draft of a technical standard".
Review by the committee: the outline or preliminary draft of the technical standard is reviewed by the technical committee and subsequently approved as a draft NTP and is then forwarded to the CNB for approval.
Public discussion: the draft NTP is put before interested parties for review in order to guarantee the transparency and impartiality of the standardization procedure. The procedure is published in El Peruano.
Deadlines are set for submitting comments on the draft NTP, which run from the first day of publication until the time-limit expires. There are three systems with different deadlines:
System 1 or adoption: publication for one month (30 days) to allow interested parties to submit comments. System 2 or regular system: publication for two months (60 days) to allow interested parties to submit comments. This system is followed, inter alia, when there are no international standards or, because of climatic or geographical factors, these are considered insufficient. System 3 or emergency system: publication determined by the Commission. This system is only followed when there is a substantiated request to resolve a situation urgently.
Approval: the NTP has to be approved by a resolution by the CNB, published in El Peruano.
Editing: period that runs from approval as an NTP to final publication.
Dissemination: the NTP is disseminated through electronic communication channels, forums and meetings. This is done jointly by INDECOPI and the committees.

Source: Online information from INDECOPI, "Normalización", viewed at:http://www.indecopi.gob.pe/0/modulos/JER/JER_Interna.aspx?ARE=0&PFL=6&JER=405.

In June 2013, 4,248 NTPs had been approved by INDECOPI[129], of which 686 were identical to international standards.[130] The competent authorities converted 111 of these into technical regulations (RT), making them mandatory.

RTs have to be applied and they are prepared by various ministries in the Central Government according to their spheres of competence. When drawing up a draft RT, the ministries must base themselves on the available scientific and technical information. The draft then has to be published in *El Peruano,* on the websites of the ministries concerned or in any other medium for a minimum of 30 calendar days in order to receive comments before it is officially published, not forgetting the notification which MINCETUR has to send to the WTO and the CAN. The lapse of time between publication of the definitive RT and its entry into force may not be less than six months. The RT must be approved by a Supreme Decree and endorsed by MINEF, which ensures before, during and after the publication and notification procedure, *inter alia,* that the draft RT does not contain measures that unnecessarily restrict trade, either internally or externally. When approving an RT that is based on an NTP or refers to one, for reasons of transparency INDECOPI publishes the regulation on its website under the heading "Peruvian Mandatory Technical Regulations", indicating the RT that is being made mandatory.[132]

Technical regulations are published on the Peruvian Technical Regulations website created in 2009.[133] The Peruvian authorities have indicated that, during the period under review (2007-2012), 18 technical regulations were approved, of which four are the same as international standards and the others are based on them. Through MINCETUR, Peru submitted 38 notifications concerning the drafting or adoption of technical regulations between 2007 and May 2013. Most of these measures were adopted in order to protect human health and safety and to provide consumers with accurate information. The products concerned by such measures are for the most part pharmaceuticals, medical devices, sanitary products, food and beverages.[134]

Peru's legislative texts on the adoption of technical regulations (Table 3.9) also cover the adoption of emergency technical regulations, which may be adopted without having to consult various trading partners, although they must be notified within 24 hours of their publication. Such regulations can only be adopted when there are, or there is a risk of, problems of national security, health or protection of the environment. Emergency technical regulations are valid for one year and may be extended by a maximum of six months. When it is in the national interest and the circumstances so warrant, however, an emergency technical regulation may be converted into an RT before one of these time-limits expires, after having undergone the required approval procedure. During the period under review, ten emergency RTs concerning various products were issued.[135]

Products subject to RTs must have a certificate issued by the specialized public or private institutions designated by the ministries.

Importers and domestic manufacturers of goods governed by a technical regulation must apply to the competent ministries for a "Statement of Compliance", which is valid for one year and may be renewed for further one-year periods. Importers may use this statement for all customs clearance procedures and it must be forwarded to the Customs before inward clearance of the goods.[136] The operations needed for compliance with the RT's requirements may be carried out while the goods to be imported are stored prior to clearance.

Peru has notified that the Vice-Ministry of Foreign Trade in MINCETUR is the body designated to act as the National Enquiry Point for mandatory technical regulations and conformity assessment procedures and INDECOPI'S CNB is the body designated to act as the National Enquiry Point for voluntary standards and conformity assessment procedures.[137]

INDECOPI, through the CNB, represents Peru in various international standardization bodies such as ISO and the International Electrotechnical Commission, as well as at the regional level in the CAN's Andean Standardization Network; the Pan American Standards Commission (COPANT); the Sub-Committee on Standards and Conformance of the Asia-Pacific Economic Cooperation Forum (APEC); and the Pacific Area Standards Congress (PASC) .[138]

Sanitary and phytosanitary measures

Peru has three national authorities with competence for sanitary and phytosanitary matters and they are responsible for issuing and implementing regulations in their respective spheres of competence. The National Agrarian Health Service (SENASA) at the Ministry of Agriculture (MINAG) deals with animal and plant health and the safety of agricultural and livestock food products at the production and primary processing stages; the National Fisheries Health Service/Production Technology Institute (SANIPES/ITP) at the Ministry of Production (PRODUCE) inspects and monitors fishing and aquaculture and the processing of fisheries products; and the Directorate-General of Environmental Health (DIGESA) at the Ministry of Health (MINSA) is responsible for sanitary monitoring and control of industrially processed foods. Although they have different responsibilities, these three bodies cooperate closely and, as far as food safety is concerned, there is a Standing Multisectoral Commission on Food Safety (COMPIAL), attached to and chaired by MINSA, in which SENASA, DIGESA and SANIPES/ITP participate.

Peru considers that agrarian health is a public asset that makes an important contribution to protecting consumers' health and promoting competition among domestic producers inasmuch as it limits the losses caused by the introduction and spreading of pests and diseases, as well as the risk of not having access to foreign markets because of sanitary factors.[140] Accordingly, and bearing in mind the updated international regulations and the treaties and agreements Peru has signed, since 2007 Peru has issued new rules and updated those already existing in order to raise the level of competitiveness of products and sanitary services (Table 3.10) . One of the most important rules is the General Law on Agrarian Health, which lays down the legal framework for providing official animal and plant health services essential for the protection of human, animal and plant health.[141]

The sanitary and phytosanitary regulations issued by the three institutions responsible are based on international standards, guidelines and recommendations drawn up by the competent international organizations, namely, the International Plant Protection Convention (IPPC), the World Organisation for Animal Health (OIE) and the Codex Alimentarius

SENASA lays down animal health requirements for imports (RZI) to prevent the introduction of diseases into Peru and these are in addition to the animal health import permit (PZI) .[143] An importer may request SENASA's Subdirectorate of Animal Quarantine to draw up RZIs if none exist. The Subdirectorate examines the sanitary information available in the country of origin or source, including a risk analysis where necessary, and determines whether it is feasible to issue such requirements. If that is the case, the requirements are forwarded to the competent official authority in the exporting country so that they can be harmonized and receive final approval. Once harmonized, the RZIs are published and the corresponding animal health import permit is issued.

SENASA has defined five risk categories for livestock goods depending on their capacity to transmit pathogens that present a risk for public or animal health, their level of processing, or their form of presentation or use.[145] The action taken by SENASA depends on the risk category of the product to be imported (Box 3.5) .

Risk categories

Risk category 1: Products and byproducts of animal origin that have undergone one or more chemical or physical treatments, resulting in a high degree of transformation from their natural state, eliminating the possibility of carriage of pathogens of quarantine importance. No sanitary import permit or sanitary export certificate is required, and they do not have to undergo sanitary inspection at the point of entry into Peru.

Risk category 2: Products and byproducts of animal origin that have undergone one or more chemical or physical treatments in the course of their production, lessening the possibility of carriage of pathogens of quarantine importance. No sanitary import permit for entry into Peru is required, but they must have an original sanitary export certificate that complies with the sanitary requirements laid down and they are inspected at the point of entry.
Risk category 3: Products and byproducts of animal origin whose production or industrialization process does not guarantee the destruction of pathogens of quarantine importance. A sanitary import permit and an original sanitary export certificate are required for entry into Peru and an inspection is carried out at the point of entry.
Risk category 4: Primary products of animal origin, used directly or without processing. A sanitary import permit and an original sanitary export certificate are required for entry into Peru, and an inspection is carried out at the point of entry.
Risk category 5: This category includes animals, materials for reproduction or other products of animal origin deemed to pose a higher sanitary risk of introducing pathogens. A sanitary import permit and an original sanitary export certificate are required for entry into Peru, and an inspection is carried out at the point of entry.

Source: Directorate Resolution No. 004-2013-AG-SENASA-DSA of 14 March 2013.

Any facility manufacturing products of animal origin to be exported to Peru must be approved by SENASA. The procedure is initiated with the official animal health authority in the exporting country, which has to forward an official request to SENASA in Peru.[146] The latter decides whether the facility complies with the requirements and, depending on the result of its evaluation, an *in situ* inspection of the facility is conducted, at the expense of the interested party. After this inspection, SENASA decides whether or not to approve the facility. If it considers it appropriate, it may grant approval after examining the documents alone.

Through its Plant Health Directorate, SENASA also determines phytosanitary requirements according to the product, its country of origin and/or source and its proposed use, after carrying out a pest risk analysis.[147] The analysis may be carried out on the basis of the requests and technical information furnished by national phytosanitary protection organizations (ONPF) in the countries of origin or by importers or exporters, and also using the relevant databases.[148]

In accordance with the regulations on plant quarantine[149], a PFI is the official document issued by SENASA authorizing the import of plants, plant products and other items that are regulated, and is a mandatory requirement before such products may enter Peru.[150] This document has to be issued and certified officially in the country of origin and/or source before the products are shipped to Peru. It is valid for a single shipment and for 90 calendar days calculated as of its date of issue. Products to be shipped to Peru must be inspected by SENASA at authorized border control points (PCCE) .[151] The Plant Quarantine Inspector takes the necessary precautionary measures if a phytosanitary problem is detected and, if the shipment does not comply with the information in the documents, he may withhold it and give a time-limit for remedying the situation. Plant material for propagation may also be subject to post-entry quarantine for a specified period in order to eliminate the presence of any potential pests which, in general, appear during the cultivar's active growth cycle.[152]

The aim of the Law on Food Safety is to guarantee the safety of foods for human consumption in order to protect human life and health, with a precautionary and comprehensive approach throughout the food chain, which also includes animal feed.

3.72. In order to be sold on the domestic market, locally produced and imported processed foods require an official document issued by DIGESA, which is processed through the VUCE, confirming sanitary registration for food and beverages for human consumption.[153] Imported processed foods also need a certificate of sanitary registration of an imported product.[154] In order to obtain this registration/certificate, the food or beverages must have been produced in a facility with sanitary approval. To obtain such approval, it is verified that the facility meets all the sanitary requirements and criteria specified for the manufacture of food and beverages and that it applies the HACCP system.[155] In addition, the food or beverages are inspected and analysed by taking samples.

DIGESA also monitors the storage and distribution of food for human consumption in order to ensure that the products are in conformity and comply with the sanitary requirements.

Between 2007 and May 2013, Peru submitted 339 notifications on the adoption of SPS measures through SENASA (Table 3.11) . Most of these were adopted to protect plants. There were no notifications in respect of food safety or the protection of human health. The majority were regular notifications, with only five emergency measures notified in relation to animal health and adopted to prevent the entry of diseases such as foot-and-mouth disease or avian influenza into Peru.

MEASURES AFFECTING EXPORTS

REGISTRATION AND DOCUMENTATION

Export procedures have varied little since 2007. The most noteworthy change has been the streamlining and computerization of procedures. In general, in Peru natural or legal persons in possession of an RUC may export although, in special cases, natural persons who are not obliged to have an RUC[156] may export using a personal identification document such as a DNI or foreign identity card or passport.

As is the case for imports, exports must be placed under a particular customs regime or procedure, which may be: definitive export, temporary export for reimport in the same state or temporary export for outward processing (Box 3.6) .

EXPORT REGIMES OR PROCEDURES

Definitive export Customs regime that allows Peruvian goods or goods that have been inward cleared to leave the customs territory for use or definitive consumption abroad.
Temporary export for reimport in the same state Customs procedure allowing the temporary exit (for 12 months) from the customs territory of Peruvian goods or goods that have been inward cleared with the intent of reimporting them within a specified time-frame, without having undergone any modification, except for normal wear and tear. Goods exported under this customs procedure are not subject to the payment of tariffs or other taxes on imports for consumption or the corresponding surcharges when they are reimported.
Temporary export for outward processing Customs procedure under which Peruvian goods or goods that have been inward cleared are allowed to leave the customs territory to be transformed, processed or repaired and are then reimported as compensating products within a specified time-frame.

Source: General Customs Law.

In order to facilitate trade and boost exports, (definitive) export procedures were computerized in Peru from 2007 onwards. The DAM and other export-related documents can now be processed electronically or through a customs broker. Exports whose f.o.b. value is less than US$5,000 are processed by means of a streamlined export declaration (DSE)[157], which can be done electronically through SUNAT's website or directly in its offices. The documents required to substantiate export are the same in both cases: a copy or photocopy of the transport document; a copy of proof of payment (invoice or sales slip); and special authorizations or other certificates depending on the nature of the goods (for example, certificates of origin or sanitary certificates) . Export formalities can now be completed in full using digital media, whereas up until 2009 all DAMs and other documents had to be submitted to SUNAT in hard copy.

SUNAT, using risk management techniques, decides to which declarations the amber channel will apply and which the red channel. The amber channel applies to most declarations and they are automatically regularized solely through acceptance of the digitalized information indicating that the goods have been shipped. For goods assigned to the red channel, the documents are examined and there is also a physical inspection. Currently, only 4% of goods go through the red channel.[158]

All goods for export, with a few exceptions, must be placed under the authority of the Customs and therefore stored in a temporary warehouse. Perishable goods requiring special storage and live animals are exempt from this requirement, together with dangerous goods, heavy and/or large machines and products to be exported in bulk in any state. In these cases, after the DAM has been processed, the customs broker has to forward the request for direct loading from the warehouse designated by the exporter.[159]

RESTRICTIONS, CONTROLS AND LICENCES

Exports of goods or services are not subject to any tax, including the IGV.

Peru prohibits or restricts some exports for reasons of public health, morals, to protect the environment, or to comply with commitments in international agreements and treaties it has signed, for example, the Convention on International Trade in Wild Species of Fauna and Flora (CITES) .

Peru still bans the export of wild species, vicunas and guanacos and hybrids; skins and leather articles made from wild animals protected by the MAG; cedar and mahogany; maca in the natural state; specimens of camu camu berries (*Myrciaria dubia*); specimens of cats' claw (*Uncaria tomentosa* and*Uncaria guianensis*); pijuayo; some organic chemicals; works of art, copies and books over 100 years' old.[161]

MAG continues to set annual quotas for the export of alpacas and llamas in order to foster economic, social and environmental sustainability in the Andean and High Andean regions and among farming communities and agricultural firms involved in this activity. Peru does not use export licences.

EXPORTS SUPPORT

Peru has notified the WTO that during the period 2007-2011 it did not grant any export subsidies for agricultural products.[163]

The duty drawback scheme is still in effect in Peru. It gives producers and exporters of goods total or partial refund of the tariffs paid on the inputs imported for production, and the goods produced using imported inputs or raw materials purchased from local suppliers, provided that the c.i.f. value of the imported inputs used does not exceed 50% of the f.o.b. value of the product exported.

This scheme allows the refund of a percentage of the f.o.b. value of exports if they do not exceed US$20 million annually, by tariff heading and by unrelated exporter.[165] The duty drawback may not exceed 50% of the cost of producing the exports. Moreover, certain products are excluded from the scheme.

3.88. During the period 2007-2009, the rate remained 5%. In response to a negative situation in overseas markets caused by the international crisis, however, the rate rose to 8% in the first half of 2010, falling to 6.5% in the second half of the year and returning to 5% as of January 2011.[166]

The goods not covered by the drawback scheme (some 279 ten-digit tariff lines) include some of Peru's key traditional exports: copper ore and its concentrates: raw gold; fresh edible offal of bovine species and fish waste; coffee and oilseed cake.[167] The drawback scheme does not apply either to exports which: incorporate inputs that have entered under the temporary admission and/or import procedures; have been the subject of inward clearance under the replacement of duty-free goods regime; have been the subject of inward clearance with tariff exemption; or are duty free under regional agreements.

FINANCING AND INSURANCE

The Development Finance Corporation S.A. (COFIDE S.A.) still acts as Peru's only development bank. It has programmes and lines of credit to finance all stages of the investment process and foreign trade operations by Peruvian companies, including micro and small enterprises (MSEs) . The credit lines and programmes administered by COFIDE are channelled through intermediate financial institutions (IFI) . COFIDE does not finance entrepreneurs directly. The interest rates for the various programmes are set by common agreement between the IFIs and the financial beneficiary, and not by COFIDE.

Through the integral financing programme for the export sector (FIEX), COFIDE continues to provide support for Peru's export growth by financing investment, working capital and foreign trade operations in general. Beneficiaries must be domiciled in Peru and must directly or indirectly export at least 30% of their production or prove that the resources sought are to be used to finance their exports, which may include capital goods, durable consumer goods or engineering and assembly services. The programme has three components: pre- and post-shipment (FIEX-PPE), working capital (FIEX-CT) and investment (FIEX-INV) and the interest rates are fixed by negotiations between the IFI and the sub-borrower, as is the case for the other programmes financed by COFIDE.

SMEs are, in general, eligible for all the financing programmes and credit lines administered by the Corporation, but to facilitate access to financing and liquidity for MSEs, which accounted for 99% of the country's economic units and employed 66% of the economically active population[168] in 2012, COFIDE has a series of programmes specifically designed for them such as Comex Exportación, MICROGLOBAL and PROPEM.[169] Through Comex Exportación, COFIDE offers natural and legal persons domiciled in Peru financing of up to 100% of the capital needed for both pre- and post-shipment of exports of goods and services of Peruvian origin. These funds may not be used to finance the export of arms or foreign trade operations with Cuba or Haiti. In 2009, as a temporary measure, the Business Guarantee Fund (FOGEM) was created, to be administered by COFIDE, in order to guarantee loans for working capital and fixed assets to exporting SMEs.[170] By March 2013, guarantees covering over S/.330 million had been granted.

COFIDE still administers the export credit insurance scheme for SMEs (SEPYMEX), created in 2002. Under this programme, exporting SMEs are given easier access to credit through a credit insurance policy granted to firms in the national financial system as security for preshipment loans with Peruvian or foreign operators, without prior authorization to operate in Peru being required in the latter case. By October 2012, Peruvian financing companies had disbursed over US$1.7 billion in loans.

The Commission for the Promotion of Peru's Exports and Tourism (PROMPERU), within MINCETUR, is responsible for promoting exports of goods and services according to sectoral policies and objectives. It carries out its activities in coordination with other relevant government authorities and in collaboration with the private sector. Peru's trade bureaux abroad are in charge of promoting trade, tourism and investment.

INCENTIVES

Sectoral support programmes

In 2007, Peru established a special procedure for the advance refund of the IGV, which consists of refunding the IGV on the purchase of new capital and intermediate goods and construction services, whether imported and/or purchased locally, used during the pre-production stage of economic activities subject to the IGV or for export.[171]

In 2012, Peru notified to the WTO two programmes for promoting aquaculture and small-scale fishing.[172] Beneficiaries of the aquaculture promotion and development programme are eligible for a preferential 15% rate of income tax rate up to 31 December 2013.[173] Moreover, through the National Fisheries Development Fund (FONDEPES), natural or legal persons engaged in aquaculture or small-scale maritime or continental fishing may obtain loans and financial support at preferential rates, which in 2013 ranged from 3% to 7% depending on the fishing activity and the amount of the loan.[174]

In its latest notification on domestic support for the period 1999-2003, Peru notified, *inter alia,* the National Programme for Managing Catchment Areas and Soil Conservation (PRONAMACHCS), the Southern Sierra Natural Resources Management Programme (MARENASS) and the Special Project to Promote the Use of Fertilizer from Seabirds (PROABONOS), which were merged into a single programme entitled AGRORURAL in 2008.[175] Other programmes in this notification such as that on "payment documents", which concerned the payment of taxes on the import and sale of fertilizer, agricultural chemicals, mechanized irrigation, and breeding animals, were abolished in 2004.[176]

Farmers also receive a preferential rate for income tax and advance refund of the IGV.[177] Since 2008, the tax concessions granted to agricultural producers have no longer been conditional upon the use of products of domestic origin (section 4.4) .[178]

As a second-tier development bank, COFIDE also offers credit lines and programmes to finance various sectors.Peru continues to implement programmes in support of other sectors such as mining (section 4.3), manufacturing (section 4.4) and the merchant marine (section 4.5.5) .

Support for micro and small enterprises (MSEs)

In 2012, the MSEs sector accounted for 99.2% of Peru's economic units and employed 66% of the economically active population.[179] The State promotes all aspects of this sector and, pursuant to the Constitution, one of the State's functions is to boost sectors suffering from any inequality.[180] Since 2003, Peru has promoted the formalization and development of MSEs in order to raise productivity, employment and tax collection, as well as this sector's share of the domestic market, government procurement and exports.[181] PRODUCE, through the National Council for the Development of Micro and Small Enterprises (CODEMYPE), defines national policies on the promotion of MSEs and coordinates the consistency and complementarity of sectoral policies with public and private sector bodies.

The tools used to promote the development and competitiveness of MSEs include mechanisms for access to financial services and their promotion. COFIDE is responsible for promoting the decentralization and expansion of the offer of financial services and capital for MSEs. It channels financial resources to those MSEs which produce or use products manufactured or transformed in Peru.

COFIDE allocates a percentage of the financial resources it manages to financing MSEs as some of the resources given to the financial institutions specializing in micro and small enterprises (IFIE) go to the guarantee funds for MSEs. COFIDE also has training and technical assistance activities designed to reinforce the development of the financial sector specializing in financing MSEs, such as the Subordinate Credit Programme. Efforts are also made through COFIDE to increase the assets of IFIEs.[183]

The overall aim of the credit support programme for small and microenterprises (PAME), implemented by the Cooperation for Social Development Fund (FONCODES), is to assist the development and consolidation of the financial credit services market for MSEs in rural areas and underprivileged urban areas in Peru that have no access to the financial system.[184] The PAME has two components: (i) the Loan Fund (with two types of lines, one for rural areas and the other for underprivileged urban areas) intended to finance production by microenterprises; and (ii) the Training and Technical Assistance Fund.

REGIONAL DEVELOPMENT PROGRAMS

Zones receiving special treatment were created in Peru in order to reinforce regional socio-economic development through national and foreign private investment, the creation of more jobs and export growth. This regime was notified to the WTO and does not appear to have changed much since 2007.[185] Each special treatment zone (or Export, Processing, Industry, Marketing and Service Centre (CETICOS)) has been established by a special law which specifies the concessions and the activities that may be conducted in each of them. Currently, there are the following special treatment zones or CETICOS: Ilo[186], Loreto, Matarani, Paita[187] and Tumbes, the ZOFRATACNA[188] and the Puno Economic Zone (ZEEDEPUNO) .[189] The Tumbes CETICOS was created in 2011.[190]

MINCETUR remains responsible for overseeing the special treatment zones.[191] Any foreign trade operation may be carried out from these zones as they include logistics operators and SUNAT offices. In the case of ZOFRATACNA, foreign goods may go to third countries through any national customs post upon presentation of a transfer request. Exports originating in other special zones may go to third countries using a transfer request, but have to proceed through specific customs posts. Goods must be eligible for the transit regime in order to be exported through any customs post.

The tax concessions given to users of free zones or CETICOS have been extended up until 31 December 2022 in the case of the Ilo, Matarani and Palta CETICOS, until 2042 for the Tumbes CETICOS and up until 2041 for the ZOFRATACNA (Box 3.7) .[192] Products exported to Peruvian territory from the special zones pay the lowest tariff negotiated by Peru in a trade agreement and products definitively exported from Peruvian territory to a special zone are eligible for the drawback regime and refund of the IGV.

The activities usually carried out in the special zones include: manufacturing or transformation; maquila (in-bond assembly) or assembly; agricultural industries; storage; services such as packaging, wrapping, labelling, classification of goods and repair of machinery and equipment. The activities that may or may not be conducted in each of the free zones are specifically stipulated in the laws creating each of the zones.[193]

Tax concessions in special treatment zones

Exemption from import tax
Exemption from income tax
Exemption from the general sales tax
Exemption from the municipal promotion tax
Exemption from the selective consumption tax
Exemption from payment of the ad valorem customs tariff on the entry of goods Exemption from any other tax imposed by the Central Government or regional or municipal governments.

Source: Information compiled by the Secretariat.

The programme on the promotion of investment in the Amazon region dates back to 1999 and is still in force.[194] Its purpose is to promote sustainable and overall development of the Amazon region through public and private investment. The tax concessions provided are only available to companies located in this area.[195] They are granted for 50 years as of 1999 and have not changed to any major extent since 2007. Taxpayers living in the Amazon region are given income tax exemption or reduction, depending on their activity; exemption from the IGV on sales in the area for consumption there; exemption for services provided in the region and on construction contracts or the first sale of real estate by constructors in the region; and exemption from the IGV and the ISC on sales to dealers and final consumers of petroleum, natural gas and their byproducts.

Since 2010, in order to alleviate poverty in the High Andean regions through production activities that generate value added, Peru has granted waivers and/or exemptions from income tax to natural persons, MSEs, cooperative associations, communal and multicommunal companies which have their tax domicile, place of business and production centre in Andean regions at an altitude of 2,500 m or more above sea level, and companies in general established at an altitude of 3,200 m or more above sea level and engaged in any of the following activities: fish farming, aquaculture, meat processing, forestry plantations for commercial or industrial purposes, milk production, breeding of South American camelids and ovine animals and processing of their fibres and fleeces, agribusiness, crafts and textiles.[197] The concessions, which include exemption from income tax, tariffs and the IGV on imports of capital goods, will remain in effect until 31 December 2021.[198] As of the second year, the income tax exemption is only granted to companies which increase value added, and for this they must comply with the production/sales ratio determined annually by MINEF.[199]

COMPETITION POLICY

Peru's competition policy is mainly governed by the Constitution and, since 2008, also by the Law on the Suppression of Anti-Competitive Conduct[200], which repealed Legislative Decree No. 701 of 1991.[201] In addition to these general legislative texts, Peru also has provisions regulating business concentration operations in particular sectors, such as electricity.[202] There have been no notable changes to these special provisions since the previous review in 2007.

Peru's Political Constitution prohibits and punishes anti-competitive conduct with the aim of boosting economic efficiency in markets.[203] Pursuant to the Constitution, the State must facilitate and monitor free competition, and also combat any restrictive practices or abuse of a dominant or monopolistic position. Consequently, authorization and creation of monopolies by law or by concerted action are not allowed in Peru. Abuse of a dominant position and horizontal or vertical collusion in any sector are punishable[204], while prior control of business mergers is only required in the electric power sector. Conduct that has an anti-competitive effect throughout Peru or in any part of the country is punished, even if the act originated abroad.

INDECOPI is in charge of implementing competition policy in all sectors, except for the public telecommunications services market, for which the Supervisory Authority for Private Investment in Telecommunications (OSIPTEL) is responsible (section 4) .[205] INDECOPI's role is to promote and oversee free competition so as to boost economic efficiency in markets and raise the level of well-being.

INDECOPI's Free Competition Commission (CLC) is the collegiate body responsible for ensuring compliance with the competition laws[206] and for settling proceedings concerning anti-competitive conduct at the first administrative level.[207] The Technical Secretariat is a technically autonomous body which initiates investigation proceedings, punishes anti-competitive conduct and issues opinions on whether or not the offence investigated has been committed.[208] Lastly, INDECOPI's Chamber for the Defence of Competition is responsible for reviewing challenges to rulings issued by the Commission or the Secretariat at the second and last instances (Box 3.8) .

Responsibilities of the institutions

Free Competition Commission (CLC)
The CLC's responsibilities include: Declaring the existence of anti-competitive conduct and imposing the penalty applicable. Determining precautionary measures. Determining remedial measures concerning anti-competitive conduct. Issuing guidelines to enable market operators to interpret competition policy-related rules correctly. Proposing and recommending the implementation of measures to promote free competition.
Technical Secretariat of the Commission
The Technical Secretariat's responsibilities include:

Conducting preliminary investigations. Initiating investigation procedures ex officio and punishing anti-competitive conduct. Deciding whether to conduct an investigation and punish anti-competitive conduct following a complaint by a party, declaring the complaint out of order or unfounded where appropriate.
Requesting the Commission to order a precautionary measure.
Undertaking training activities and propagating the implementation of the rules on free competition.

Source: INDECOPI.

Investigations may be initiated at the instigation of the Technical Secretariat or following a complaint made to INDECOPI.[209] Over the period 2008 to 2012, 31 proceedings were initiated following a complaint by a party and 15 ex officio. At the beginning of the proceedings, the Technical Secretariat may publish a note so that interested parties are apprised of the proceedings and may attend in person or provide information for the investigation. This note is published on INDECOPI's website, in *El Peruano* and in one of the leading national newspapers.

The authorities have indicated that, since the previous trade policy review, the CLC has reinforced its work on investigations and the punishment of anti-competitive conduct, with the result that the number of proceedings initiated ex officio doubled from 2008 to 2012 (15) compared to 2003 to 2007 (8) and fines also increased from 305.60 UIT to 12,213.79 UIT between these two periods.[211]

3.117. Over the period 2008-2012, the CLC initiated 46 proceedings in various sectors, including the following: dairy produce and fuels; and financial, transport, health and construction services. During this period, 42% of the proceedings which concluded with penalties were initiated following a complaint by a party and the remainder ex officio.

3.118. The CLC (or the Tribunal) punishes anti-competitive conduct on the basis of the UIT[212]; fines vary depending on the seriousness of the offence (Table 3.12) . Repeat of the offence is deemed to be an aggravating circumstance and the penalty applicable may not be less than the previous penalty. In addition to penalties imposed for offences, the CLC may order remedial measures to restore competition.[213] Any offender that fails to comply with a precautionary or remedial measure imposed by the Commission or the Tribunal automatically incurs a fine. If non-compliance persists, the Commission may impose a new, coercive fine, doubling the previous coercive fines imposed successively until the remedial measure ordered is implemented, with a limit of 16 times the amount of the coercive fine originally imposed.

Types of violation of competition

Classification of the offence[a]	Penalty
Minor violation	Fine of up to 500 UIT, provided that it does not exceed 8% of the sales or gross income received by the offender or its economic group, derived from all economic activities during the fiscal year immediately preceding the issuance of the Commission's ruling.
Serious violation	Fine of up to 1,000 UIT, provided that it does not exceed 10% of the sales or gross income received by the offender or its economic group, derived from all economic activities during the fiscal year

	immediately preceding the issuance of the Commission's ruling.
Extremely serious violation	Fine of over 1,000 UIT, provided that it does not exceed 12% of the sales or gross income received by the offender or its economic group, derived from all economic activities during the fiscal year immediately preceding the issuance of the Commission's ruling.

a The criteria used to define the seriousness of the violation and the scale of the fine are defined in Article 44 of Legislative Decree No. 1034.
Source: Legislative Decree No. 1034 of 25 June 2008.

Appeals against the CLC's final ruling may be made to the Tribunal by the accused, by the party making the complaint or by third parties attending the proceedings, within a period of 15 working days. The Technical Secretariat may also appeal against a ruling acquitting those investigated and against the fine imposed. If necessary and if all administrative channels at INDECOPI or OSIPTEL have been exhausted, an appeal may be made to the courts through the relevant administrative dispute procedure.

In 2008, in addition to the legislative texts regulating competition policy, the Law on the Suppression of Unfair Competition was also implemented, prohibiting and punishing acts of unfair competition, and violations of the rules governing commercial advertising.[214] This Law applies to all natural or legal persons offering or requesting goods or services or engaged in other economic activities in the market and applies to any act that has effect in Peru, even if it originated abroad.

INDECOPI's Commission on the Control of Unfair Competition is empowered to implement this Law. It also issues guidelines in order to give guidance to economic operators and promote the proper functioning of the market so that fair competition generates well-being for all.[216] The Commission has a Technical Secretariat, which is responsible for conducting investigations and, when necessary, for punishing acts of unfair competition.[217] INDECOPI's Chamber for the Defence of Competition is responsible for reviewing challenges to rulings issued by the Commission or the Technical Secretariat at the second and last instances. The Tribunal may act ex officio.

The following are some of the acts of unfair competition punished by the Commission: deception, confusion, taking undue advantage of another's reputation, vilification, undue comparison or assimilation, violation of business secrets, violation of rules and commercial sabotage.[219]

During the review period, the Commission on the Control of Unfair Competition and its Technical Secretariat initiated 826 proceedings ex officio, of which 93% were deemed to be founded, and imposed penalties and/or the necessary remedial measures to restore competition. In 2012, the majority of cases (60%) concerned the alcoholic beverages industry and the health, tourism and education sectors.[220] The outcome of the investigations is notified in an INDECOPI ruling.[221] Over the same period, the Commission dealt with 740 complaints by parties, mostly relating to the food and pharmaceutical industries, and the telecommunications and transport sectors. The Commission declared 42% of these to be founded.

The penalties determined by the Commission depend on the practical impact of an act on the market, according to which the seriousness of the violation is measured (Table 3.13) . In addition to the penalty imposed as a result of unfair competition, the Commission or Tribunal may determine remedial measures to restore fair competition in the market.[222] If these are not observed, coercive fines are imposed.

Types of unfair competition violation

Classification of the offence[a]	Penalty
Minor violation that has no practical impact on the market	Warning
Minor violation	Fine of up to 50 UIT, which may not exceed 10% of the offender's gross income, derived from all economic activities during the fiscal year immediately preceding the issuance of the Commission's ruling.
Serious violation	Fine of up to 250 UIT, which may not exceed 10% of the offender's gross income, derived from all economic activities during the fiscal year immediately preceding the issuance of the Commission's ruling.
Extremely serious violation	Fine of up to 700 UIT, which may not exceed 10% of the offender's gross income, derived from all economic activities during the fiscal year immediately preceding the issuance of the Commission's ruling.

a The criteria used to define the seriousness of the violation and the scale of the fine are defined in Article 52 of Legislative Decree No. 1044.
Source: Legislative Decree No. 1044 of 26 June 2008.

PROTECTION OF CONSUMERS

Special attention has been paid to protecting consumers since 2007 and this is reflected in the number of legal texts adopted by Peru governing this area, for example, the Code for the Protection and Defence of Consumers (Box 3.9) .[223] The Code applies to any consumer relations occurring throughout Peru.

Legal instruments regulating protection of consumers

Legislation
Law No. 29571 Code for the Protection and Defence of Consumers
Law No. 28587 Law supplementing the Consumer Protection Law in relation to financial services
Decrees
Legislative Decree No. 1045 Law supplementing the Consumer Protection System
Supreme Decrees Supreme Decree No. 046-2011-PCM Regulations on the consumer arbitration system referred to in Articles 137 to 144 of Law No. 29571, Code for the Protection and Defence of Consumers.
Supreme Decree No. 030-2011-PCM Regulations on judicial proceedings to protect the collective interests of consumers and the Special Fund for Financing and Disseminating Consumers' Rights.
Supreme Decree No. 031-2011-PCM Regulations establishing the mechanisms for proposing and appointing representatives of bodies and trade unions on the National Consumer Protection Council.
Supreme Decree No. 032-2011-PCM Regulations on criteria for using the funds for operation of consumers' associations.
Supreme Decree No. 029-2011-PCM Regulations on registration of violations and penalties set forth in the Code for the Protection and

Defence of Consumers.
Supreme Decree No. 011-2011-PCM Regulations on the complaints book of the Code for the Protection and Defence of Consumers.
Supreme Decree No. 110-2010-PCM Incorporation of summary proceedings for consumer protection in INDECOPI's TUPA.
Supreme Decree No. 006-2009-PCM Single Harmonized Text of the Law on the Consumer Protection System.
Supreme Decree No. 039-2000-ITINCI Single Harmonized Text of Legislative Decree No. 716, Consumer Protection Law.
Directives
Directive No. 005-2010/DIR-COD-INDECOPI Rules on the decentralized competence of the commissions attached to regional offices and other INDECOPI offices.
Directive No. 004-2010/DIR-COD-INDECOPI Supplementary rules applicable to summary proceedings relating to consumer protection.

Source: INDECOPI.

INDECOPI has primary responsibility for dealing with alleged violations of the provisions contained in the legislative texts protecting consumers, and for imposing the administrative penalties and remedial measures laid down in the regulations. For this task, it has the Commission for Consumer Protection (CPC) . INDECOPI may, on its own initiative, commence penalty proceedings to protect consumers. It also supervises and oversees compliance with the legal obligations in order to guarantee the protection and defence of consumers.

INDECOPI is not empowered to resolve complaints and disputes arising between users and operators of public services: telecommunications, electricity, drinking water, sewage or transport services. The operator always intervenes in the first instance in these cases and, at second instance depending on the service concerned, OSIPTEL, the Supervisory Authority for Investment in Energy and Mining (OSINERGMIN), the National Supervisory Authority for Sanitation Services (SUNASS), or the Supervisory Authority for Investment in Public Transport Infrastructure (OSITRAN) .

In order to reverse the effects of violations or prevent such conduct from recurring in the future, the CPC is empowered, *inter alia,* to seize and destroy goods, containers, wrapping and labels; to request temporary closure of the establishment for a maximum period of six months if the offence is extremely serious or is a repeat offence; to require payment of costs incurred by the consumer to alleviate the violation; to require the replacement or repair of products; to oblige the supplier to comply with commitments and/or to reimburse the consumer if the product delivered or the service provided does not correspond to what has been expressly agreed by the parties.

PRICE CONTROL

Peru does not in general impose price controls or price margins for goods. The rates for public telecommunications, energy, sanitation and infrastructure services, however, are still controlled by special regulatory agencies. In addition, the rate for transporting LPG by pipeline is determined according to the regulations approved by the Ministry of Energy and Mining[224] and for reasons of national interest and public necessity the State may fix minimum and maximum rates for national or international air transport.[225]

The Price Stabilization Fund for petroleum-based fuels was created in 2004 to prevent sharp fluctuations in the international price of oil and its byproducts from being passed on to consumers in the domestic market.[226] Because of the sustained increase in the average international price of oil, this mechanism gradually built up sizeable obligations towards fuel producers and importers, which the State had to fulfil. Consequently, from 2012 onwards, in order to mitigate the impact of the Fund's debts on the treasury, measures were taken to steer the Fund's benefits to the sectors most affected by the volatility of international fuel prices. Certain products were therefore excluded from the Fund's list. Some products such as LPG also received differential treatment so as to help the poorest sectors of the population, which use LPG in bottles with a net content of up to 10 kg.[227]

The 1991 Law on the Promotion of Investment in the Agricultural Sector provides for the creation of a price stabilization mechanism to promote efficient production and correct distortions in the supply of imported like products that have been subsidized in their countries of origin[228] , although the mechanism has never been set up.[229]

STATE TRADING, STATE-OWNED ENTERPRISES AND PRIVATIZATION

During the period 2005-2012, Peru did not have any State-trading enterprises within the meaning of Article XVII of the GATT 1994 and paragraph 1 of the Understanding on the Interpretation of Article XVII.[230]

The State's presence in business activities in Peru has continued to decline. At the end of 2012, 14 State-owned enterprises were being wound up or had been merged or privatized.[231] In 2012, the State had holdings in 31 enterprises, most of them in the electricity sector (Table A3.3) .

GOVERNMENT PROCUREMENT

The legal framework for government procurement is mainly covered by Peru's Political Constitution and the Government Procurement Law of 2009, its implementing Regulations, and amendments thereto, the latest in 2012.[232] The Constitution stipulates that works, the purchase of supplies and the purchase or disposal of goods using public funds must be the subject of a procurement or public bidding procedure.[233]The Government Procurement Law applies to procurement by government agencies in order to obtain goods, services or works. There are nevertheless exceptions to this Law, which does not apply to the procurement of certain services such as audits, legal or financial advice or the services of public notaries; banking or financial contracts; or the procurement of legal services required for the State's defence in international investment disputes in arbitral or judicial forums.[234] Procurement with a value ranging between S/.0 and 3 UIT also remains outside the scope of the Law. In addition, there are special laws regulating government procurement in certain areas and procurement by entities or companies such as PETROPERÚ[235] , PROINVERSIÓN[236] and Peru's Municipal Savings and Loan Funds.[237]

MINEF still lays down the rules and guidelines for government procurement, taking into account the overall objectives of government procurement policy, which include achieving a better quality-price ratio, encouraging competition, and reinforcing control mechanisms.[238] The Supervisory Authority for Government Procurement (OSCE), created in 2009[239] , oversees and supervises (selectively and/or randomly) procurement processes and issues directives pursuant to the Government Procurement Law. It is also responsible for replying to queries and furnishing information on government procurement procedures; administering the National Register of Suppliers (RNP) and the Electronic Government Procurement System (SEACE); and settling disputes arising during selection procedures, dealing with complaints and imposing sanctions. The Government Procurement Tribunal is a body with decisional power that forms part of the

OSCE's administrative structure and enjoys full autonomy and independence in the exercise of its functions. It is in charge of settling disputes arising between agencies, participants and bidders during the selection process and applying temporary or definitive ineligibility sanctions to suppliers, participants, bidders, contractors, arbitrators or independent experts, as the case may be.

In order to take part as a bidder or contractor in government procurement in Peru, the candidate must be registered as a government supplier in the RNP, which is published on the OSCE's website. Both Peruvians and foreigners may register. Bidders or contractors for public works are given a maximum procurement capacity calculated according to their registered paid-up capital in Peru and their experience. Legal persons not established in Peru and with no registered capital in the country are given a maximum procurement capacity according to the amount of capital actually deposited in a Peruvian financial entity. This requirement does not apply to foreign companies registered in countries with which Peru has signed an international treaty that includes provisions on government procurement or to MSEs.[241]

The new Government Procurement Law determines the procedures for selection according to specific thresholds (Chart 3.2) . The procedures are as follows: public bidding, public competition, direct award of a contract or small contract award, which may involve corporate procurement or selection criteria for reverse auctions or framework agreements.[242]

The Government Procurement Law allows for certain exceptions to enable government authorities to procure goods, services and works without the need to go through a selection procedure. The exceptions are: contracts between government authorities; when supplies are short or there is an emergency; when there is a single supplier of goods or services that is impossible to replace; procurement by the Armed Forces or of a secret nature; and services provided by natural persons, with due objective substantiation.[243]

Procurement of goods or services or the execution of works may not be split up in order to avoid any type of selection procedure or application of the rules by awarding contracts for less than three UIT (or S/.11,100) . The Law does not consider procurement to be divided up in the case of stages, tranches, packages or lots when this is possible because of the nature of the subject matter, or when a contract is broken down in order to encourage the participation of MSEs in those economic sectors where there is a competitive offer.

Practices that affect any contest and/or competition in procurement are also prohibited, notably agreements not to take part or not to present proposals in procurement procedures.[244] If the Government Procurement Tribunal identifies any conduct that might constitute an anti-competitive practice, it informs INDECOPI accordingly so that the latter, through its competent bodies and when appropriate, can initiate the corresponding penalty proceedings and determine where responsibility lies. If INDECOPI finds that there has been a violation, the OSCE enters the offenders in the register of those ineligible for government procurement.

Since 2012, State bodies have been required to use the electronic government procurement system (SEACE) . Procurement using the small contract award procedure must be carried out electronically through the SEACE for the procurement of services (optional for the procurement of goods); however, the bodies concerned have to register their procurement for amounts of one to three UIT each month.[245]

Despite the global financial crisis, government procurement over the past three years has ranged from S/.29,000 to S/.34 billion, corresponding to 6.4% of GDP in 2012 (Chart 3.3) .

Peru still applies certain preferences and special government procurement schemes for the benefit of local or regional producers and SMES. Pursuant to the Regulations implementing the Government Procurement Law, for procurement of works or services to be executed or supplied outside the provinces of Lima and Callao with contracts awarded according to the ADS and small contract (AMC) procedures, a preference of 10% is given on the amount of the technical and economic proposal of bidders domiciled in the province where the work is to be carried out or the service supplied, or in neighbouring provinces.[246]

All social support and food security programmes implemented by the State follow a streamlined procedure for the procurement of local or regional food products from individual producers and/or agribusiness SMEs which use inputs produced in the zone.[247]

There is also a preference scheme for MSEs. If bids using the ADS or AMC procedures are equal, an order of preference is established for awarding the contract, giving priority to: (i) MSEs composed of disabled persons or associations composed entirely of such enterprises; (ii) MSEs in general or associations composed entirely of such enterprises; and (iii) other enterprises. For regular contracts for the supply of goods or services, and for contracts for carrying out works or consultancy services for works, MSEs may deposit security of 10% of the contract, which is held by the government authority, instead of presenting a letter of guarantee for the amount. Government institutions must also plan for no less than 40% of their procurement to be awarded to MSEs and give preference to regional or local MSEs in the place where the goods are procured.[248] According to the authorities, the above is not provided for in the Government Procurement Law, which repeals the other regulations that conflict with its provisions.

Special programmes have also been put in place to promote the participation of SMEs in government procurement, for example, the "Compras a MYPErú" programme, implemented by FONCODES, which encourages the purchase by the State of footwear, textiles and clothing made by MSEs in various regions of Peru.[249] For 2012, this programme had a budget of S/.381.5 million to finance the production and purchase of school uniforms, track suits and footwear for pre-school and primary school pupils, as well as uniforms, clothing and various accessories for the National Police Force, the Army, the Air Force and the Navy.[250]

TRADE-RELATED INTELLECTUAL PROPERTY RIGHTS

INDECOPI is responsible for implementing the legal texts designed to protect intellectual property rights.[251] It currently has three directorates to perform this task: the Copyright Directorate (DDA) for matters relating to copyright and related rights[252]; the Distinctive Signs Directorate (DSD) for matters relating to trademarks, trade names and slogans, collective marks, certification marks and appellations of origin; and the Inventions and New Technologies Directorate (DIN) for matters relating to patents, utility models, industrial designs, protected plant varieties, traditional knowledge and other new technologies.[253]

The DDA, DSD and DIN coordinate the application of, and monitor compliance with, the national and international commitments on intellectual property rights within their spheres of competence. These Directorates are the first administrative instance for dispute or other proceedings brought following a complaint by a party or ex officio. The administrative rulings implemented by these INDECOPI Directorates cover opposition (to use or registration); annulment of registration for non-use or dissemination, or because the subject matter is well known to the public or its registration is invalid; proceedings for unfair competition relating to registered distinctive signs; and proceedings for infringement of industrial property rights. Appeals may be made against rulings by these Directorates to the Special Intellectual Property Chamber of the INDECOPI Tribunal, which is a body independent of the DDA, DSD and DIN, and is the second and final administrative instance of appeal for intellectual property matters. The Chamber may establish precedents that must be followed, by means of rulings and administrative decisions, but it is not a judicial authority and appeals against its decisions may be made to the courts.

The Fiscal Police Directorate, through the Division for Investigation of Offences against Intellectual Property Rights, has the task of combating offences against copyright and related rights and against industrial property when goods are produced making unauthorized use of patents or reproduction of industrial designs, or a trademark is imitated or unlawfully used.[254] SUNAT applies border measures such as suspension of clearance of goods allegedly counterfeited, pirated or misleadingly similar, pursuant to the legislation on protection of copyright and related rights and trademark rights.

Legal framework

Peru's legal framework for intellectual property comprises its domestic legislation, multilateral and CAN legal texts and the preferential agreements Peru has signed. The Agreement on Trade-Related Aspects of Intellectual Property Rights (TRIPS), together with other WTO Agreements, has been incorporated into Peru's domestic legislation and may be invoked before its courts. CAN's legal texts are also directly applicable and are supranational in Peru.

Peru's legislation covers all types of intellectual property rights mentioned in the TRIPS Agreement and contains provisions on enforcement. During the period under review, several legal texts concerning various types of intellectual property rights and enforcement were adopted or amended.[255] Peru attaches great importance to the protection of traditional knowledge, access to genetic resources and the protection of biological diversity. These requirements have been incorporated into Peru's legislation since 1996, and into CAN legislation, through Decision No. 391, which establishes a common regime for access to genetic resources, and Decision No. 486.[256] Peru also has provisions to prevent anti-competitive practices in contractual licences concerning intellectual property rights. In some cases, for example, copyright and related rights and industrial property, Peru grants a level of protection that is higher than that specified in the multilateral texts; this is partly attributable to the amendments introduced into domestic legislation following the signature of certain regional agreements (see below) .

PARTICIPATION IN THE WTO

Peru provided information on its domestic enforcement system in 2000.[257] The TRIPS Council reviewed this legislation in 2001.[258] In 2010, Peru notified the WTO of many of the legal texts on intellectual property adopted or amended in recent years.[259] Peru has not yet accepted the Protocol amending the TRIPS Agreement, intended to confirm the decision taken by Members in 2003 to establish the system provided for by paragraph 6 of the Doha Declaration on the TRIPS Agreement and Public Health. According to the authorities, however, the draft instrument of ratification is being processed for approval and enactment by the President of the Republic.

In the Doha Round, Peru was one of the main sponsors of various reforms relating to the protection of intellectual property rights. Together with other Members, it put forward proposals on issues such as the patent system, in order to incorporate the requirement to disclose the origin of genetic resources and traditional knowledge.[260] For Peru, protection of biodiversity under the patent regime in the TRIPS Agreement is a priority issue and it has therefore sought to demonstrate that the current regime does not allow proper protection of its genetic resources and the traditional knowledge of its indigenous communities.[261] In this connection, Peru considers that a legal obligation establishing a mandatory disclosure requirement for patent applications would help to prevent both misappropriation of genetic resources and the wrongful grant of patents and would also enhance transparency regarding the utilization of genetic resources and/or associated traditional knowledge.[262] In the international sphere, Peru has also presented proposals on the need to link the patent system to the regime for access to genetic resources and protection of traditional knowledge in the Convention on Biological Diversity (CBD), WIPO and in other forums (including regional processes) .[263]

PARTICIPATION IN OTHER INTERNATIONAL INITIATIVES

Peru has signed 15 of the treaties administered by the World Intellectual Property Organization (WIPO) .[264] Since the previous trade policy review in 2007, Peru has acceded to four of these treaties: the Budapest Treaty (October 2008), the Patent Cooperation Treaty (March 2009), the Trademark Law Treaty (August 2009) and the UPOV Convention (July 2011) . In June 2012, Peru signed the Beijing Treaty on Audiovisual Performances and, according to information provided by the authorities, it is being ratified.

Peru has also undertaken commitments to protect intellectual property in the regional agreements it has signed since 2007 (Table A2.2) . One of the most important of these agreements is that of the CAN, which establishes a common regime for different forms of intellectual property rights and constitutes an essential framework of reference for the regime on the protection of such rights in Peru. The CAN nonetheless allows its members to adopt their own internal legislation on the protection of industrial property[265], which is why Peru adopted internal legislation during the review period amending certain aspects of its industrial property regime.

The commitments made by Peru in its Trade Promotion Agreement with the United States were the reason for many of the changes in Peru's intellectual property regime during the review period.[266] These include reforms concerning infringement of intellectual property rights, copyright and related rights, manufacturers' marks or trademarks, patents and protection of test data, and the application of border measures. Further to the agreement with the United States, Peru also undertook to accede to several of the treaties administered by WIPO.

The trade agreement between Colombia and Peru and the European Union also contains several provisions on intellectual property, some of them related to public health. One distinctive feature of this agreement is that it covers geographical indications, traditional knowledge and genetic resources; the lists annexed to the agreement include four geographical indications for Peru and 115 for the European Union.[267] The agreements with China, Costa Rica, EFTA, Japan, the Republic of Korea, Mexico, Panama and Singapore also include provisions on intellectual property rights. The provisions vary depending on the agreement, but generally include substantive rules for all categories of intellectual property and enforcement procedures; they also determine a level of intellectual property protection that is higher than that in the TRIPS Agreement.

PERU MINING SECTOR: STRATEGIC INFORMATION AND OPPORTUNITIES

In 2009, Peru occupied a leading position in the global production of the following mineral commodities: arsenic trioxide (fourth after China, Chile, and Morocco), bismuth (third after China and Mexico), copper (second after Chile), gold (sixth after China, Australia, South Africa and the United States, and Russia), lead (fourth after China, Australia, and the United States), molybdenum (fourth after China, the United States, and Chile), rhenium (fourth after Chile, Kazakhstan, and the United States), silver (first followed by China and Mexico), tin (third after China and Indonesia), and zinc (second after China). In Latin America, Peru was first in the production of bismuth, gold, lead, silver, tellurium, tin, and zinc, and second in the production of cadmium, copper, molybdenum, and selenium (Brooks, 2010a, b; Carlin, 2010a, b; Edelstein, 2010; George, 2010; Guberman, 2010; Ministerio de Energía y Minas, 2010a, p. 18; Polyak, 2010a, b; Tolcin, 2010).

PERU: RESERVES OF MAJOR MINERALS

(Thousand metric tons unless otherwise specified)

Commodity		Reserves
Coal, all types		**1,100,000**
Copper		**90,815**
Gold	metric tons	**1,970**
Iron ore		**12,482**
Lead		**7,863**
Molybdenum		**450**
Natural gas	billion cubic meters	**881**
Natural gas liquids	million barrels	**1,337**
Petroleum crude	do.	**5,810**
Phosphate rock		**820**
Salt		**100,000**
Silver	metric tons	**120,532**
Sulfur		**150,000**
Tin		**307**
Uranium		**100**
Zinc		**22,258**

[e]Estimated; estimated data are rounded to no more than three significant digits; the amounts are proven reserves.
[1]2009 and 2010 "Anuario de la Minería del Perú" Ministerio de Energía y Minas, except for natural gas and petroleum crude; U.S. Geological Survey Mineral Commodity Summaries 2010; U.S. Energy Information Administration, 2010; Perúpetro S.A., 2010; BP Statistical Review of World Energy, June 2009.
[2]Excludes metal in placer deposits.
[3]Recoverable at prices of $100 or less per kilogram of uranium.

Peru occupies a leading position in the global production of the following mineral commodities: arsenic trioxide (fourth after China, Chile, and Morocco), bismuth (third after China and Mexico), copper (third after Chile and the United States), gold (fifth after South Africa, Australia, the United States, and China), lead (fourth after China, Australia, and the United States), molybdenum(fourth after the United States, China, and Chile), rhenium (fourth after Chile, Kazakhstan, and the United States), silver (first followed by Mexico and China), tin (third after China and Indonesia), and zinc (third after China and Australia). In Latin America, Peru was the first ranked producer of, in order of value, gold, silver, zinc, lead, tin, and tellurium and the second ranked producer of copper and molybdenum (after Chile), and bismuth (after Mexico).

Peru's economy benefited from high prices for mineral commodities. To date, the Government has privatized 220 state-owned firms via joint ventures and consortia in the mining and fuels industries. The firms have generated $9.2 billion, with an additional committed capital flow of about $11.4 billion, representing 17% and 21% of Peru's GDP, respectively. Privatizations and concessions generated a committed investment of $6.9 billion (2006-2010) by mining companies such as Perú Copper Inc. forToromocho copper project ($2.5 billion), Xstrata plc. for Las Bambas

($1 billion), Phelps Dodge for expansion of Cerro Verdecopper mine ($850 million), Monterrico Metals Inc. for Rio Blanco base metals project ($800 million), Rio Tinto Limited for La Granja copper project ($700 million), Southern Copper Corporation for expansion of Ilo smelter ($400 million), Goldfields Ltd. forCerro Corona copper-gold project ($350 million), and Companhia Vale do Rio Doce for the Bayovar phosphate project ($300 million). The Ministerio de Energía y Minas reported that of the committed investment in 2006, Peru received $1 billion for gas and $200 million for petroleum.

Petróleos del Perú (PETROPERU S.A.) was created on July 24, 1969 (law No.17753) as a state-owned entity, dedicated sequentially to transportation, refining, and commercialization of refined products and other derivatives of petroleum. The Peruvian Congress on June 2, 2004 (law No.28244) excluded PETROPERU S.A. from the privatization process and authorized its participation in the exploration and production of hydrocarbons. The state agency Perupetro S.A. was created on November 18, 1993 (law No. 26221) to be responsible for promoting investments for hydrocarbon exploration and production in the country. Perupetro negotiates, signs, and administers hydrocarbon contracts, for which PETROPERU must compete with private firms as well. In 2006, PETROPERU invested $4.5 billion in the hydrocarbon sector

RESERVES AND RESOURCES

Table lists the Peruvian reserves of major minerals, such as copper, gold, iron ore, lead, molybdenum, silver, and zinc, as of about January 1, 2010. Data are shown in terms of metal contained in ore for the base and precious metals or recoverable quantities of other mineral commodities, which included industrial minerals and mineral fuels. These mineral reserves represent “proven” (measured) and “probable” (indicated) categories and exclude quantities reported as “possible” (inferred). Reserves are defined as being well delineated and economically recoverable volumes of crude oil and natural gas from wells and minable ore from mines committed to production (U.S. Bureau of Mines and U.S. Geological Survey, 1980; Ministerio de Energía y Minas, 2010d).

According to the Anuario Minero 2009, Peru’s economy is committed to trade integration through 36 investment agreements with investors from Australia, Brazil, Canada, China, the European Union, Mexico, Switzerland, the United States, and others. In spite of the global economic crisis, Peru’s legal framework is expected to continue to be favorable to foreign investment in the fields of energy, mining, and related industries and to attract capital flows by way of joint ventures and consortia, privatizations, and direct acquisitions. Continued privatization in the mineral sector and investment in every sector of the Peruvian economy, particularly in the mineral and energy industries, are expected to generate additional investments. Peru is likely to continue to be the world’s leading producer of silver and the second ranked producer of copper and zinc, as well as Latin America’s leading producer of, in order of value, silver, gold, zinc, tin, bismuth, and lead and the second ranked producer of copper and molybdenum.

The country has high potential for nonmetallic production as well, such as bentonite, borates, diatomite, phosphate rock, and travertine. Increased demand for copper, gold, iron ore, natural gas, and silver is likely to encourage investors to expand and modernize their operations. The liquefaction of Camisea’s natural gas for export to China, member countries of the Mercado Comun del Cono Sur (MERCOSUR) (the second largest trade association in the Americas), member countries of the North America Free Trade Agreement (the largest trade association in the Americas), and other markets and trading partners is expected to increase Peru's mineral exports further (Banco Central de Reserva del Perú, 2010, p. 34-35; Camisea Project, 2010; Ministerio de Energía y Minas, 2010a, p. 51, 2010d; ProInversión—Private Investment Promotion Agency in Peru, 2010a; 2010b, p. 12-13).

In 2009, Peru's gross domestic product (GDP) grew at a real rate of 0.9% compared with 9.8% in 2008. Peru's net international reserves increased to $33.1 billion compared with $31.2 billion in 2008, exports exceeded imports by $5.7 billion, and foreign direct investment (FDI) amounted to $4.1 billion. Private investment in Peru continued to be significant, increasing to $37 billion in 2009 from $27.3 billion in 2008 and $19.5 billion in 2007. The mining investment in the country amounted almost $2.8 billion in 2009 compared with more than $1.7 billion in 2008, which was an increase of almost 65% (Banco Central de Reserva del Perú, 2010, p. 8-9; Ministerio de Energía y Minas, 2010a, p. 44-47; ProInversión—Private Investment Promotion Agency in Peru, 2010a; 2010b, p. 10, 32).

In 2009, several mining companies invested in the Peruvian mining sector–Southern Peru Copper Corp. (a subsidiary of Grupo Mexico, S.A. de C.V.) invested $434.8 million in the expansion of the Ilo smelter by 2012; Xstrata Tintaya S.A. (a subsidiary of Xstrata plc of Switzerland) invested $332.1 million in the Tintaya copper mine, which was to start operations by 2014; Cia. Minera Miski Mayo S.A. invested $257.6 million in the Bayovar phosphate project; Cia. de Minas Buenaventura S.A.A. invested $251.1 million in the Brepampa and the Titiminas gold projects in the Department of Ayacucho; Votorantim Metais Cajamarquilla S.A. invested $155.4 million in the expansion of its Cajamarquilla refinery; Minera Yanacocha S.R.L. invested $146.7 million in the initiation of the Conga gold mine; and others invested $842 million in diverse expansions for base-metal and iron ore mines (Luna, 2010, p. 111-112; Ministerio de Energía y Minas, 2010a, p. 48-49).

The stability of the Peruvian judicial framework was fundamental to encouraging investments in the mining sector. The total committed investment in the mining sector for the period 2009-16 was $35.5 billion. Of leading investors, Xstrata Perú S.A. (a subsidiary of Xstrata) committed to invest $3.6 billion in Las Bambas copper project, which is located in the Apurimac Region and was to start operations by 2014; Jinzhao Mining Perú S.A. (a subsidiary of Nanjinzhao Group Co. Ltd., Zibo of China) committed to invest $3.3 billion in the Pampa de Pongo iron project, which is located in the Arequipa Region and was to start operations by 2012; Anglo American Quellaveco S.A. (a subsidiary of Anglo American plc. of the United Kingdom) committed to invest $3.0 billion in the Quellaveco copper project, which is located in the Moquegua Region and was to start operations by 2014; Lumina Copper S.A.C. (a subsidiary of Minmetals Jiangxi Copper Co. of China) committed to invest $2.5 billion in the Galeno copper project, which is located in the Cajamarca Region and was to start operations by 2012; Minera Chinalco Perú S.A. (a subsidiary of Chinalco-Aluminum Corp. of China) committed to invest $2.2 billion in the Toromocho copper project, which is located in the Junin Region and was to start operations by 2012; and Anglo American Michiquillay S.A. committed to invest $700 million in the Michiquillay copper project, which is located in the Cajamarca Region and was to start operations by 2016. Other investors were Rio Blanco Copper S.A. and Zijin Mining Group of China, which each committed to invest $1.44 billion in the Rio Blanco copper project, which was to start operations by 2012; Rio

Tinto Ltd. of Australia, which committed to invest $1 billion in La Granja copper project, which was to start operations by 2014; and Sociedad Minera Cerro Verde S.A. (a consortium formed by the U.S company Freeport-McMoRan Copper Inc.), which invested $1 billion for expansion of the Cerro Verde copper mine by 2012 (Banco Central de Reserva del Perú, 2010, p. 34; Ministerio de Energía y Minas, 2010a, p. 51).

Petróleos del Perú S.A. (Petroperú), which was a state-owned company, was involved in the transportation, refining, and marketing of refined products and other derivatives of petroleum. Petroperú was excluded from the privatization process but was authorized to participate in the exploration for and production of hydrocarbons (law No. 28244 of June 2, 2004). The state agency Perúpetro S.A. was created on November 18, 1993 (law No. 26221) to be responsible for promoting investments in the Peruvian hydrocarbon sector. Perúpetro negotiates, signs, and administers hydrocarbon contracts for which Petroperú must compete with the private sector. Private investment in Peru continued to increase owing to the country's macroeconomic stability and the involvement of operating companies with the communities where they operate. The Peruvian Government made the country's legal framework, for both the Mines and the Hydrocarbon Divisions of the mineral industry investor-friendly, and Peru's national economy continued to attract foreign investment (Ministerio de Energía y Minas, 2010a-c).

In 2009, Perúpetro attracted investment of more than $3.4 billion to the hydrocarbon sector. The Camisea Natural Gas Project received an investment of $1.3 billion, and investment in Camisea was expected to increase to $3.0 billion by 2013. PERU LNG, which was Camisea's liquefied natural gas (LNG) project, was a partnership of Hunt Oil Co. of Dallas, Texas (50%), Repsol YPF, S.A. of Spain and SK Energy Co. Ltd. of the Republic of Korea (20% each), and Marubeni Corp. of Japan (10%). Construction of the PERU LNG plant, which would have the capacity to produce 4.4 million metric tons per year (Mt/yr) of LNG, continued on schedule, with initial delivery of LNG projected for mid-2010. The total project cost was estimated to be about $3.8 billion, which included financing costs (Camisea Project, 2010; ProInversión—Private Investment Promotion Agency in Peru, 2010b, p. 2, 10, 32).

MINERALS IN THE NATIONAL ECONOMY

The mining and hydrocarbon sectors registered a small growth of 0.6% in 2009 compared with 7.6% in 2008. The mining and mineral processing industries registered a negative growth of 1.4% of the GDP in 2009 compared with 7.3% of the GDP in 2008 owing to decreases of certain mineral commodity prices (except small price increases for copper, gold, and silver) as a result of the world financial crisis. In 2009, hydrocarbon production in Camisea (Lot 56 of the Pagoreni deposit and Lot 88 of the Cashiriari deposit) started in September 2008; as a result, the hydrocarbon sector's output increased by 16.1% in 2009 compared with 10.3% in 2008. The mineral sector employed 125,603 people in 2009 compared with 127,232 in 2008; this did not include the nearly 60,000 active informal miners (Banco Central de Reserva del Perú, 2010, p. 28; Ministerio de Energía y Minas, 2010a, p. 70-73; U.S. Central Intelligence Agency, 2010).

GOVERNMENT POLICIES AND PROGRAMS

Peru's legal framework regarding domestic and foreign investors is governed by such constitutional mandates as Legislative Decree No. 662 (promotion of foreign investment), which allows investors unrestricted access to all economic sectors; Legislative Decree No. 757 (framework for the development of private investment), which pertains to private investment growth; and Legislative Decree law No. 868 of May 1996 (Texto Unico Oficial) as approved by Supreme Decree No. 059-96-PCM, which promotes private investment in public infrastructure and utility works. Within the framework of Decree law No. 708 of November 1991 (promotion of investment in mining), Legislative Decree law No. 818 of April 1996 (incentives for investing in natural resources), and Supreme Decree law No. 162-92-EF of October 1992 (rules guaranteeing foreign investment), more than 250 domestic stability and guarantee contracts had been signed since 1993 (Banco Central de Reserva del Perú, 2010, p. 97; Ministerio de Energía y Minas, 2010a, p. 44-69; 2010b).

Supreme Decree law No. 014-92-EM of June 1992 (the general mining law) and the Texto Unico Oficial provide guaranteed protections to mining ventures and contracts under the Peruvian Civil Code. Consequently, such ventures and contracts are immune from unilateral changes by any governmental authority in Peru without an appropriate legal or administrative remedy or arbitration by the Convenio Constitutivo del Centro Internacional de Arreglo de Diferencias Relativas a Inversiones [Formal Consent of the International Center for Settlement of Relative Differences on Investments] (Banco Central de Reserva del Perú, 2010, p. 95, 97).

Peru enacted Supreme Decree law No. 047-2002-EF of April 2002 (import duties for capital goods) to reduce the duties paid to 7% from 20% and 12% on capital goods to be used in exploration and production of certain minerals, such as oil and gas in the Amazon region. Law No. 27623-EF was enacted in January 2002 to eliminate the 18% sales tax on capital, goods, and services for mineral exploration. Supreme Decree law No. 015-2004-PGM of January 2004 (legal framework for decentralization) was established to use revenues from mineral production to maximize the well-being of the local communities through economic growth, environmental protection, and social development in a sustainable way. Supreme Decree law No. 066-2005-EM of May 2006 (legal framework for creation of the Dirección de Gestión Social) was established to administer the Corporate Social Responsibility program in the mining sector (Banco Central de Reserva del Perú, 2010, p. 95; Ministerio de Energía y Minas, 2010a, p. 78-81).

The Peruvian Constitution establishes equal protection for domestic and foreign investors who enter into agreements with the Government. Hydrocarbon law No. 26844 of May 1997 eliminated the exclusive rights of state-owned Petroperú to control the secondary recovery of crude oil, refining, and imports and subsequent resale of petroleum and byproducts. The Peruvian laws have attempted to ensure more-favorable minerals and crude oil and gas exploration and production contract terms for investors (Ministerio de Energía y Minas, 2010a, p. 12-17; 2010b; ProInversión—Private Investment Promotion Agency in Peru, 2010b, p. 2).

Legal procedures to obtain mining rights were made easier by the enactment of complementary legislation Supreme Decree law No. 018 of July 9, 1992. The

Government relinquished its exclusive management of exploration, mining, smelting, and refining of metals and fuel minerals. Individuals and private companies are allowed to hold mining permits in Peru. In the legal framework for investment and taxation, no distinction is made among domestic and foreign investors, and consortia, corporations, and joint ventures formed in Peru or abroad. Municipalities and Regional governments in areas where mineral resources (metals and industrial minerals) are exploited will receive 50% of the taxes collected to be invested in education and social programs (health, housing, and others) in conformance with the Canon Minero (Ministry Resolution No. 266-2002-EF/15 of May 1, 2002). The remittance of depreciation, dividends, and royalties abroad has no restrictions. Contracts can be signed by investors, and the Government guarantees the stability of legal commitments and taxes. To increase protection of investors' interests, Peru signed agreements with the World Bank's Multilateral Investment Guarantee Agency in April 1991, which was authorized by Legislative Decree law No. 25312, and with the Overseas Private Investment Corporation in December 2002, which was authorized by Legislative Decree law No. 25809 (Ministerio de Energía y Minas, 2010b, c; ProInversión—Private Investment Promotion Agency in Peru, 2010b, p. 10).

The Dirección General de Asuntos Ambientales (DGAA) of the Ministerio de Energía y Minas (MEM) has the responsibility to address environmental problems that result from energy and mining activities and is mandated to implement the laws and regulations of the environmental legal framework, such as Legislative Decree No. 613 of September 1990 (the environmental code) and Supreme Decree No. 016-93-EM of April 28, 1993 (the environmental regulation). The sustainable development model for the mining and energy sectors began in 1993 with regulations and procedures for the gradual reduction of pollution, which include economic development policies and environmental protection. The mining industry must comply by adjusting its ongoing operations to permissible effluent levels and its new operations by using cleaner technologies. The DGAA evaluates and proposes the environmental regulations for the mining and energy sectors, which include the maximum emission levels that are compatible with the internationally accepted limits set by the United Nations and the World Bank, approves environmental impact assessments for new operations and environmental adjustment and management programs for ongoing ones, and administers the national environmental information system. The MEM is authorized to manage environmental affairs in the mineral sector, such as by establishing the environmental protection policy and maximum allowable levels for effluents, signing environmental administrative stability agreements, overseeing the impact of operations, determining responsibilities, and imposing administrative sanctions. The oil companies, in particular, were under pressure because the number of operations in the Amazon Rain Forest—one of the world's most sensitive ecosystems—was increasing (Ministerio de Energía y Minas, 2010b, c; ProInversión—Private Investment Promotion Agency in Peru, 2010b, p. 9, 14).

PRODUCTION

In 2009, the effect of the global financial crisis generated increases and decreases in the international prices of Peru's leading mineral commodities, including an increase in the price of gold and decreases in the prices of copper, iron, lead, silver, and zinc. The global financial crisis caused companies in the Peruvian base-metals sector to initiate cost-reduction programs to offset their lower prices. In 2009, slight increases in mineral production were led by silver (4.6%), gold (1.4%), and copper (0.6%); decreases in mineral production included lead (12.4%), zinc (5.8%), and tin (3.9%); and significant decreases took place in refined products led by lead (77.2%), antimony (72.7%), indium (66.7%), silver (62.6%), bismuth (60.1%), zinc (21.5%), and copper (10%). The hydrocarbon sector's output increased owing to the increased extraction of natural gas mostly at Camisea. Crude oil output decreased by 7.5%; it was, however, expected to increase in the near future as a result of the 25 new oil exploration and long-term production contracts signed in 2007 (table 1; Banco Central de Reserva del Perú, 2010, p. 28; Ministerio de Energía y Minas, 2010a, p. 20, 35; 2010d, p. 5).

STRUCTURE OF THE MINERAL INDUSTRY

The structure of the Peruvian mineral industry continued to change owing to the establishment of consortia in such deregulated industries as petroleum and natural gas, and joint ventures in energy and mining projects. Peruvian laws ensure equitable treatment of domestic and foreign investors involved in mineral, crude oil, and natural gas exploration and production. Because of these laws, an increased number of domestic and foreign companies had expressed interest in participating in prospecting, exploration, production, and distribution of natural gas and petroleum contracts with Perúpetro and mineral properties with the state agency Centromín Perú S.A. Some of these companies included Anglo American and BHP Billiton plc of the United Kingdom; Sulliden Gold Corp. Ltd. and Teck Cominco Ltd. of Canada; Hunt Oil Co. and Newmont Mining Corp. of the United States; Marubeni Corp., Mitsubishi Corp. and Mitsui & Co., Ltd. of Japan; Shougang Corp. and Zijin Mining Group of China; Peñoles S.A. of Mexico; SK Energy Co. Ltd. of the Republic of Korea; Repsol YPF, S.A. of Spain; Vale S.A. and Votorantim Metais of Brazil; and Xstrata plc of Switzerland (table 2; Ministerio de Energía y Minas, 2010a, p. 50-51; 2010b, c; ProInversión—Private Investment Promotion Agency in Peru, 2010a; 2010b, p. 15-17).

Private domestic interests owned most of the medium- and small-sized mining operations. More than 300 foreign mining companies had been established in Peru since 1990. Crude oil was transported through the country's 1,754 kilometers (km) of pipeline; natural gas and natural gas liquids, through 983 km of dual pipeline; and refined products, through 13 km of pipeline. Ports that were important to the mineral industry included Callao, Chimbote, Ilo, Matarani, Paita, Puerto Maldonado, Salaverry, San Martin, San Nicolas, and Talara on the Pacific Ocean, and Iquitos Pucallpa and Yurimaguas on the Amazon River and its tributaries. Peru had an installed electricity-generating capacity of 5,050 megawatts (MW), about 90% of which was in hydroelectric plants. The energy mix, by source, was hydroelectric (79%), fossil fuel (20%), and others (1%) (Ministerio de Energía y Minas, 2010a, p. 82-83; 2010c, d; U.S. Central Intelligence Agency, 2010).

MINERAL TRADE

Peru's mining sector accounted for about 61% ($16.4 billion) of total export revenues of about $26.9 billion in 2009 compared with about 59.4% ($18.7 billion) of total export revenues of about $31.5 billion in 2008. In 2009, Peru's total trade balance recorded a surplus of almost $5.9 billion compared with $3.1 billion in 2008, which indicates that the country imported goods valued at $21 billion in 2009 compared with $28.4 billion in 2008. Peru's petroleum and derivatives sector accounted for about 7.1% ($1.9 billion) of total export revenues compared with about 8.6% ($2.7 billion) of total export revenues in 2008. Peru's imported crude oil and lubricants amounted to $2.9 billion in 2009 compared with $5.2 billion in 2008. Peru's mineral sector had a trade surplus of $15.3 billion in 2009 compared with $16.1 billion in 2008 (Banco Central de Reserva del Perú, 2010, p. 60-61; Luna, 2010, p. 91; Ministerio de Energía y Minas, 2010a, p. 8-9).

In 2009, the leading destination markets of Peruvian exports as a percent of total exports were the United States (17.4%), China (15.3%), Switzerland (14.9%), Canada (8.7%), Japan (5.1%), Germany (3.9%), Chile (2.8%), and others (31.9%). Peru's leading import partners were the United States (19.7%), China (15.0%), Brazil (7.6%), Ecuador (4.9%), Chile (4.7%), Colombia (4.3%), Japan (4.1%), and others (39.7%). The United States, China, Brazil, Japan, and Chile, in order of value, were the main importers of gold, copper, and molybdenum. Peru sold about 5% of its exports to other members of the Mercado Común Andino (ANCOM), whose members were Bolivia, Colombia, Ecuador, Peru, and Venezuela; about 4.7% to the Mercado Común del Cono Sur (MERCOSUR) countries of Argentina, Brazil, Paraguay, and Uruguay and associate members Bolivia and Chile; and 12% to other Latin American countries (Banco Central de Reserva del Perú, 2010, p. 58-59; Ministerio de Energía y Minas, 2010a, p. 6-7).

METALS

Copper.—Peru's copper output (Cu content) in 2009 was about the same level as that of 2008, or 1.1 million metric tons (Mt). The country's copper metal exports in 2009 totaled about 1.25 Mt valued at about $5.9 billion compared with 1.24 Mt valued at more than $7.7 billion in 2008; this value decreased by about 23.4% compared with that of 2008 owing to the copper price decrease to $2.14 per pound of copper in 2009 from $2.85 per pound in 2008 (Banco Central de Reserva del Perú, 2010, p. 61; Ministerio de Energía y Minas, 2010a, p. 21-22, 35).

Owing to China's increased demand for copper, the Chinese firm Chinalco was planning to develop the Toromocho deposit, which contains 1.4 billion metric tons (Gt) of proven and probable reserves at a grade of 0.71% copper equivalent, and to produce 275,000 metric tons per year (t/yr) of copper metal by 2012. Consorcio Xiamen Zijin Tongguan Investment Development Co. Ltd. (Zijin Mining Group) was also planning to develop the Rio Blanco copper project, which is located in the Department of Piura and contains 1.3 Gt of proven and probable reserves at a grade of 0.57% copper equivalent, to produce 25 Mt/yr of copper ore by 2012 (Ministerio de Energía y Minas, 2010a, p. 51).

In 2009, Peru's planned investments of about $35.5 billion included mineral projects with advanced exploration, feasibility studies, and expansion work, such as Las Bambas ($3.6 billion) and Los Chancas ($1.2 billion) copper deposits, which are located in the Department of Apurimac and were owned by Xstrata and Southern Copper, respectively (Banco Central de Reserva del Peru, 2010, p. 63; Ministerio de Energía y Minas, 2010a, p. 51). Other investments in copper deposits included the partnership of China Minmetals Corp. and Jiangxi Copper Co., Ltd., which had acquired 93.9% interest in Northern Perú S.A.'s Galeno copper project in Celendin, Department of Cajamarca. The estimated investment in the Galeno copper project (which has reserves of 803 Mt at a grade of 0.63% equivalent copper) was $2.5 billion to produce copper metal by 2012. Southern Copper was planning to invest $600 million in additional exploration and to improve efficiencies at the Cuajone and the Toquepala copper mines by 2012 and to invest $950 million in its Tia María copper project, which is located in the Department of Arequipa, to produce 120,000 t/yr of copper metal by 2012. Other investments included Rio Tinto's La Granja copper deposit in Cajamarca; Xstrata Copper's investment of $1.3 billion in the Antapaccay copper deposit in Cusco; and an investment of almost $15 billion to explore 13 additional copper deposits located in the Departments of Ancash, Arequipa, Apurimac, Cajamarca, Cusco, Huancavelica, La Libertad, Lambayeque, and Moquegua between 2011 and 2016 (Ministerio de Energía y Minas, 2010a, p. 51).

Gold.—In 2009, gold output was almost 182.4 metric tons (t) compared with 180 t in 2008, which was an increase of about 1.3%. Peru's gold exports in 2009 totaled about 218 t (7.01 million troy ounces) valued at about $6.8 billion compared with about 200 t (6.42 million troy ounces) valued at about $5.6 billion in 2008, which was an increase in value of more than 21.4%. In 2009, Peru's planned investments of about $23 billion were expected to include mineral projects with advanced exploration and environmental assessment work for gold, such as Minera Yanacocha's Pita cianuration plant at Yanacocha Mine ($270 million), its project at Chaquicocha ($400 million), and its Minas Conga project ($1.1 billion) in the Department of Cajamarca, which was expected to be completed by 2014; Buenaventura's Tantahuatay gold deposit ($56 million), which was expected to be completed by 2011; and Sulliden's Shahuindo gold deposit ($90 million), which was expected to be completed by 2012; the latter two deposits are located in the Department of Cajamarca (Banco Central de Reserva del Perú, 2010, p. 61; Ministerio de Energía y Minas, 2010a, p. 23-24, 35, 51).

From the total gold output in 2009, large- medium- and small-scale producers reported 156.1 t of gold and an unknown number of gold placers and informal individual miners reported 26.3 t of gold. Placers accounted for more than 14% of the gold produced in the country. The southeastern Andes have well-known gold placers on the Inambari River and its tributaries. Placer gold was produced mostly in the Inca and the Mariategui Regions and from rivers and streams throughout the jungle (Ministerio de Energía y Minas, 2010a, p. 24, 51).

Iron Ore.—Shougang Hierro Perú S.A.A. (a subsidiary of China's Shougang Corp.) continued to be Peru's sole iron ore producer (exclusively from the Marcona iron ore mine in the Department of Ica). Mine output decreased to almost 4.5 Mt of iron content in 2009 from more than 5.2 Mt in 2008. In 2009, iron ore exports remained at about the same level as in 2008 (7 Mt) with a value of $299 million compared with $385 million in 2008, or a decrease of more than 22%. This iron ore value decrease was in response to lower prices ($44 per metric ton in 2009 compared with $56 per metric ton in 2008). According to the Ministerio de Energía y Minas, besides China's Nanjinzhao Group commitment to the Pampa de Pongo iron project, Strike Resources Inc. of Australia was exploring the Apurimac iron ore deposit and was planning to invest $2.3 billion to start operations there by 2015, and Cuervo Resources Inc. of Canada was exploring the Cerro Ccopane and the Huillque iron ore deposits, which are located in the Department of Cusco (Banco Central de Reserva del Perú, 2010, p. 61; Ministerio de Energía y Minas, 2010a, p. 29, 51).

Lead, Silver, and Zinc.—The Peruvian zinc industry produced more than 1.5 Mt of zinc in concentrates in 2009 compared with about 1.6 Mt in 2008. The country's total silver content output increased to 3,854 t from 3,686 t in 2008. Peru surpassed China's and Mexico's silver output of 3,000 t and 2,500 t, respectively, in 2009. Companies that produced silver, such as Aruntani S.A.C., Compañía de Minas Buenaventura S.A.A., Sociedad Minera El Brocal S.A., and Volcan Compañía Minera S.A.A., were more active in 2009, and silver production was higher than in 2008 because Minera Yanacocha S.R.L. and medium-sized gold-silver mines exceeded their initial production goals. Yanacocha increased its output mainly as a result of technological innovations in its gold-silver recovery process. Lower international prices of $14 per troy ounce in 2009 compared with $15 per troy ounce in 2008 did not affect the medium-sized mines and small-scale producers that mined lower grade ores. Peru produced 302,412 t of lead in concentrates compared with 345,109 t in 2008. Exports of lead amounted to 680,000 t valued at $1.14 billion in 2009 compared with 525,000 t valued at $1.11 billion in 2008; prices decreased to $0.720 per pound in 2009 from $1.002 per pound in 2008. The export value of silver amounted to $214 million in 2009 compared with $595 million in 2008; prices decreased to $14 per troy ounce in 2009 from $15 per troy ounce in 2008. The value of exports of zinc amounted to more than $1.2 billion in 2009 compared with almost $1.5 billion in 2008; prices decreased to $0.390 per pound in 2009 from $0.472 per pound in 2008 (Banco Central de Reserva del Perú, 2010, p. 61; Ministerio de Energía y Minas, 2010a, p. 25-29, 35, 51).

Tin.—Production from Minsur's San Rafael Mine, which is located in the Mariategui Region, was 37,503 t in concentrate in 2009 compared with 39,037 t in 2008. Minsur's tin smelting and refining operations, which are located in Pisco, south of Lima, produced 34,503 t of metal in 2009 compared with 38,865 t in 2008. Peru continued to be the leading tin producer in Latin America followed by Bolivia and Brazil. Minsur, which was the only fully integrated tin supplier in Peru, produced more than 11% of the world's output and exported 38,000 t valued at $476 million in 2009 compared with 39,760 t valued at $695 million in 2008 (Banco Central de Reserva del Perú, 2010a, p. 60; Carlin, 2010b; Ministerio de Energía y Minas, 2010a, p. 29, 35).

INDUSTRIAL MINERALS

Phosphate Rock.—Empresa Minera Regional Grau Bayóvar S.A.'s phosphate deposits (Bayovar project) produced about 38,000 t of phosphate rock, which was about the same level as that of 2008. The 90,000-t/yr phosphate plant that was operated by Grau Bayóvar produced an estimated 17,100 t of phosphate (P_2O_5) in 2009. Vale owned the Bayovar phosphate project located in the Sechura desert in the Department of Piura. The Bayovar project comprised 150,000 hectares of phosphate and brine. The planned Bayovar open pit contained a reserve base of 238 Mt of phosphate with a nominal production capacity of 3.9 Mt/yr of phosphate concentrate with a minimum grade of 29% P_2O_5, which is used mostly in fertilizers. The approximately $600 million project was expected to enter into production by mid-2010 and would have an estimated life of 27 years. Vale had already started construction of the concentrating plant, which was to be completed by 2010 (Ministerio de Energía y Minas, 2010a, p. 30; Vale S.A., 2010).

MINERAL FUELS

Coal.—Peru's largest coal deposits are located at Alto Chicama in La Libertad Department. Other known coal deposits occur in the Cuenca del Santa in the Marañon Region and the coal basins of Goyllarisquizga and Hatun Huasi in the Caceres Region of central Peru. In 2009, Peru's recoverable coal reserves were estimated to be 1.1 Gt, and coal production was 156,371 t compared with 142,021 t in 2008; the estimated consumption of coal was more than 1.3 Mt/yr and imports were about 1.2 Mt/yr and came mostly from Colombia (tables 1, 3; Ministerio de Energía y Minas, 2010a, p. 30-31; U.S. Energy Information Administration, 2010).

Natural Gas and Petroleum.—In 2009, Peru's recoverable (proven and probable) and possible resources of crude oil were estimated to be 5,810 million barrels (Mbbl); of LNG, 1,337 Mbbl; and of natural gas, 881 billion cubic meters. The leading gasfields were the Aguaytia, which is located about 41 km west-northwest of Pucallpa, Ucayali Department, and had proven reserves of 8.5 billion cubic meters of gas and 9 Mbbl of natural gas liquids (NGL) and the Camisea gasfields in the Ucayali Basin, Cusco Department, which had proven reserves of 250 billion cubic meters of gas and 411 Mbbl of NGL. Natural gas production increased to 3,474 million cubic meters in 2009 from 3,387 million cubic meters in 2008 and was produced by Pluspetrol S.A. (81.7%), Aguaytia S.A. (10.1%), Petróleo Brasileiro S.A. (Petrobrás) (3.1%), and others (5.1%) (Camisea Project, 2010; Ministerio de Energía y Minas, 2010d; U.S. Energy Information Administration, 2010).

The Camisea Project encompasses three segments—Upstream, Transportation, and Distribution of natural gas from the Camisea field—and is located in the Ucayali Basin in the Department of Cusco. Peru had received an investment of $1.1 billion to implement the above segments in 2009. Pluspetrol was planning to invest about $3.0 billion in Camisea's natural gas project by 2013 (Camisea Project, 2010; Ministerio de Energía y Minas, 2010d).

In 2009, crude oil production decreased to about 71,000 barrels per day (bbl/d) from 76,500 bbl/d in 2008. Production of petroleum derivatives decreased to about 168,500 bbl/d from 173,200 bbl/d in 2008. Peru imported an average of 10,600 bbl/d of crude oil and petroleum products to satisfy its internal consumption of 157,000 bbl/d. Peru's total crude oil production of 26 Mbbl in 2009 came from Pluspetrol (42.3%), Petrobrás (18.8%), Petrotech (15.7%), and others (23.2%) (table 1; Banco Central de Reserva del Perú, 2010, p. 28; Ministerio de Energía y Minas, 2009d; U.S. Energy Information Administration, 2010).

In 2009, the largest oil refinery in Peru continued to be La Pampilla, which had a designed capacity of about 110,000 bbl/d. The second largest oil refinery was Talara, which had a designed capacity of about 62,000 bbl/d. Other refineries had the following designed capacities: Conchan, 15,500 bbl/d; Iquitos, 10,500 bbl/d; Pucallpa, 3,300 bbl/d; and El Milagro, 1,700 bbl/d. Pluspetrol was planning to build the 5,200 bbl/d-capacity

Shiviyacu petroleum refinery, which would be located in the Department of Loreto, by 2013. In 2009, refinery production came from La Pampilla (44.3%), Talara (34.9%), Conchan (14.4%), Iquitos (4.3%), Pucallpa (1.1%), and Milagro (1.0%) (Ministerio de Energía y Minas, 2010d).

PRACTICAL INFORMATION FOR CONDUCTING BUSINESS[2]

Peru offers foreign investors a wide-freedom climate and rights guaranteeing juridical stability.

Foreign investments to be made in the country in any economic activity are not required from prior authorization. There is no restriction as to the amount of investment and transfer of shares.

Foreign investment, made in freely convertible currency, shall be channelled through the National Financial System. The full amount of profits is allowed to be remitted abroad by foreign investors, without restrictions.

This booklet includes general guidelines to set up a company in Peru. The main procedures are also herein indicated.

INVESTMENT AND BUSINESS CLIMATE - STRATEGIC INFORMATION AND CONTACTS FOR STARTING BUSINESS

Peru has been one of the fastest growing Latin American economies over the past decade. Between 2003 and 2013 the Peruvian economy grew an average of 6% per year. Though the trend did not continue in 2014, Peru's 2.35% growth was still higher than the 2.0% average growth in Latin America. The government's counter-cyclical stimulus spending, consumption, and private investment are the main driving forces of this growth. Investment grew by 8.3% year-on-year to a value of USD 33.5 billion in 2013. The Ministry of Economy and Finance set a target of 30% growth in public investment, and pledged a total of USD 30 billion over the next five years to address Peru's infrastructure gap, estimated at USD 80 billion. As the economy has grown, poverty in Peru has steadily decreased falling by half from 56% in 2005 to 23.9% in 2013 according to the World Bank. HSBC describes Peru could eventually "be a bigger economy than Chile, Colombia, or even South Africa in the long term."

The steady economic growth began with the pro-market policies enacted by former President Alberto Fujimori in the 1990s. All subsequent governments have continued these policies, including the current administration inaugurated in July 2011 for a five-year term. President Ollanta Humala pledged to encourage private and public investment in infrastructure projects in transportation, telecommunications, energy, sanitation, airports, and maritime ports. Congruent with his other campaign goals to reduce poverty and narrow the nation's socioeconomic gap, President Humala has increased social spending and raised taxes on mining companies.

Peru's local currency, the Nuevo Sol (PEN), has been among the least volatile within Latin American over the past few years. In 2014, it did depreciate close to 10% in comparison to the USD. Since the mid-1990's, the PEN's exchange rate with the USD has fluctuated between 1.25 and 3.55 per USD. The exchange rate, as of March 16, 2015, was PEN 3.097 per USD.

The Government of Peru (GOP) has encouraged integration with the global economy by signing a number of free trade agreements, including the United States-Peru Trade Promotion Agreement (PTPA), which entered into force in February 2009. In 2014, trade between the United States and Peru totaled USD 16.1 billion up from USD 9.1 billion in 2009 the first year of entry into force. From 2009 to 2014, Peruvian exports to the United States jumped from USD 4.2 billion to USD

[2] This section based in part on materials of the US Department of Commerce www.export.gov

6.1 billion (a 45% increase) while U.S. exports to Peru jumped from USD 4.9 billion to USD 10.1 billion (a 106% increase). Peru has preferential trade agreements with 49 countries and unions, including the United States, Argentina, Brazil, Uruguay, Paraguay, Bolivia, Colombia, Ecuador, Canada, Chile, China, Mexico, Japan, Singapore, South Korea, Norway, Iceland, Liechtenstein, Switzerland, Thailand, Panama, and the European Union.

In the 2015 World Bank's Ease of Doing Business report, Peru ranked 35 out of 189.

1. OPENNESS TO, AND RESTRICTIONS UPON, FOREIGN INVESTMENT

Attitude toward Foreign Direct Investment

The GOP seeks to attract investment -- both foreign and domestic -- in nearly all sectors of the economy. Several high level Peruvian officials, including President Ollanta Humala, the Minister of Economy and Finance, and the Central Bank President, attended global business conferences and toured several countries in 2014 in an effort to attract foreign investment. Some of these tours were organized and sponsored by In Peru, a private industry organization (**http://inperu.pe**). Peruvians and Americans benefit from the United States-Peru Trade Promotion Agreement (PTPA) which entered into force on February 1, 2009. Since entry into force, total trade (exports and imports) between Peru and the United States expanded significantly from USD 9.1 billion to USD 16.1 billion. The PTPA establishes a secure, predictable legal framework for U.S. investors operating in Peru. The PTPA protects all forms of investment. U.S. investors enjoy in almost all circumstances the right to establish, acquire and operate investments in Peru on an equal footing with local investors.

Other Investment Policy Reviews

Peru aspires to become a member of the Organization for Economic Cooperation and Development (OECD). On February 5, 2015 the GOP announced the start of an 18-month study to identify economic, social, and political "bottle necks" that could hamper Peru's OECD membership aspirations. The government noted that the study would act as a "roadmap" for Peru's goal to achieve membership by 2021 and highlighted education as an example of a key area that Peru must improve. According to the OECD, Peru dedicates only 2.8% of GDP towards education compared to the OECD average of 5.6% of GDP. As a result, Peruvian 15 year olds achieve education results equivalent to 12 year olds in OECD member countries. The result of this lack of investment in education is a chronic shortage of skilled labor in Peru.

Laws/Regulations of Foreign Direct Investment

The 1993 Constitution grants national treatment for foreign investors and permits foreign investment in almost all economic sectors. Under the Constitution, foreign investors have the same rights as national investors to benefit from any investment incentives, such as tax exemptions. In addition to the 1993 Constitution, Peru has several laws governing foreign direct investment (FDI) including the Foreign Investment Promotion Law (Legislative Decree (DL) 662 of September 1991) and the Framework Law for Private Investment Growth (DL 757 of November 1991). Other important laws include the Private Investment in State-Owned Enterprises Promotion Law (DL 674), the Private Investment in Public Services Infrastructure Promotion Law (DL 758), and specific laws related to agriculture, fisheries and aquaculture, forestry, mining, oil and gas, and electricity. Article 6 of Supreme Decree No. 162-92-EF (the implementing regulations of DLs 662 and 757) authorizes private investors to enter all industries except investments in natural protected areas and manufacturing of weapons.

The GOP has passed several laws and related implementing regulations aimed at encouraging more private investment, such as two important decrees in 2008. The first was a legislative decree containing the Law on Public-Private Partnerships (PPPs). The second decree presents a priority list of projects for PPPs. Congress passed a law to reform regulations that would make PPPs less bureaucratic and more transparent, thus more attractive to foreign companies, in March 2014. Among these public-private partnerships are major infrastructure projects of national importance and upgrades to existing projects: Salaverry maritime port project, Quillabamba thermal power plant (Cusco region), liquid petroleum gas (LPG) transport system (from Pisco to Callao), lines three and four of the Lima and Callao Metro system, water supply to Lima and related headwater works, distribution system of natural gas via pipeline networks (Apurimac, Ayacucho, Huancavelica, Junin, Cusco, Puno, and Ucayali regions), rural broadband installation (optical fiber transportation networks and access networks), and connections to three existing 220 kV power transmission lines. Project opportunities are available on ProInversion's Project Portfolio page, available at: **http://www.proyectosapp.pe/modulos/JER/PlantillaProyectoEstadoSector.aspx?are=1&prf=2&jer=5892&sec=30**.

Although all Peruvian administrations since the 1990s have vowed to support private investment and abide by Peruvian laws, the GOP occasionally has passed measures that some observers have regarded as contravening legal principles. For example, the Garcia Administration in 2011 rescinded a Canadian company's rights to operate a silver mining project in Puno after violent protests opposing the project. The Canadian company delivered to the Peruvian Minister of Economy and Finance a Notice of Intent to submit a claim to arbitration under the terms of the Canada-Peru Free Trade Agreement in February 2014. Furthermore, President Ollanta Humala signed into law a 10-year moratorium on the entry into Peru of live genetically-modified organisms (GMOs) to be used for cultivation in December 2011. Peru also has implemented two inconsistent sets of rules for importing pesticides, one for "regular" importers, which is extremely restrictive and requires importers to file a full dossier with technical information, and another for farmers, which is rather loose and only requires a written affidavit.

The GOP created the Private Investment Promotion Agency, ProInversion, in 2002, based on an existing similar agency. ProInversion has completed both privatizations and concessions of state-owned enterprises and natural resource-based industries. Major recent concession areas include ports, power generation facilities, electrical transmission lines, oil and gas distribution, and telecommunications. In July 2014 the Peruvian Congress passed legislation to reform the public-private concessions process and require more oversight by the Ministry of Economy and Finance. The Ministry of Economy and Finance is working on the implementing regulations, and expects a final draft before the end of 2015.

Industrial Promotion

ProInversion also aims to attract investment in the following sectors: agricultural, construction, ground transportation, energy and mining, finance, health technologies, telecommunications, and travel. Information can be found on ProInversion's website: **http://www.proyectosapp.pe/modulos/JER/PlantillaProyectoEstadoSector.aspx?are=0&prf=2&jer=5351&sec=22**.

Limits on Foreign Control

The Constitution (Article 6 under Supreme Decree No. 162-92-EF) authorizes foreign investors to carry out any economic activity provided investors comply with all constitutional precepts, laws and treaties. Exceptions exist, including exclusion on foreign investment activities in natural protected reserves and manufacturing of war weapons, pursuant to Article 6 of Legislative Decree No. 757. While long-term concessions are granted, the law states Peruvians must maintain majority ownership in certain strategic sectors: media; air, land and maritime transportation infrastructure; and private security surveillance services.

Prior approval is required in the banking (for regulatory reasons, and also applies to domestic investment) and defense-related sectors. Foreigners are also legally prohibited from owning a majority interest in radio and television stations in Peru; nevertheless, foreigners have in practice owned controlling interests in such companies. Under the Constitution, foreign interests cannot "acquire or possess under any title, mines, lands, forests, waters, or fuel or energy sources" within 50 kilometers of Peru's international borders. However, foreigners can obtain concessions and rights within the restricted areas with the authorization of a supreme resolution approved by the Cabinet and the Joint Command of the Armed Forces.

Privatization Program

The GOP initiated an extensive, but not yet complete, privatization program in 1991 in which foreign investors were encouraged to participate. Since 2000, the GOP has promoted multi-year concessions as a means of attracting investment in major projects. In 2000, the government granted a 30-year concession to a private group (Lima Airport Partners) to operate the Lima airport. In 2006, the government granted a 30-year concession to Dubai Ports to build and operate a new container terminal in the Port of Callao. The terminal's first phase became operational in May 2010. In 2006, the Swiss-Spanish-Peruvian consortium Swissport received a 25-year concession to manage nine of Peru's northern airports. In 2011, the GOP awarded the Argentine-Peruvian consortium Aeropuertos Andinos a 25-year concession to manage six of Peru's southern airports. Also in 2011, the government granted a 30-year concession to a Danish-Peruvian consortium led by the Danish-based A.P. Moller-Maersk Group to operate and modernize the multipurpose northern terminal at the Port of Callao. On June 30, 2014 the GOP awarded a multi-billion USD concession for the Southern Gas Pipeline to a consortium led by Brazilian company Odebrecht. The GOP continues to award multi-year concessions for various energy, natural gas, hydro-energy and irrigation, telecommunications, ports, sanitation, roads, and tourism projects.

The concessions process is challenging for U.S. and other international companies interested in bidding on projects. ProInversion, the government agency responsible for drawing up and competing public-private-partnership (P3) concession projects, has come under considerable criticism for its bidding process, deadlines, and ambitious timetables. As a result, U.S. and other international companies have shown limited interest in Peruvian P3 projects.

Screening of FDI

The GOP does not screen, review, or approve foreign direct investment outside of those sectors that require a governmental waiver (see Limits on Foreign Control).

Competition Law

The Institute for the Protection of Intellectual Property, Consumer Protection, and Competition (INDECOPI) is the GOP agency responsible for reviewing competition-related concerns of a domestic nature.

Investment Trends

Peru has made significant strides in various rankings within the World Bank's Doing Business report, including reformed procedures on starting a business, securing construction permits, registering property, and closing a business. Although Peru's efforts to reform business start-up procedures has made significant strides, according to the 2011 report, Peru declined by three places in the World Bank's business start-up ranking from 60th in 2013 to 63rd in 2014. At the same time, Peru lowered the average amount of time it takes to start a business from 41 days (in 2010) to 25 days (in 2014). Although the 2013 report noted Peru's efforts to strengthen investor protections through a new law regulating the approval of related-party transactions and making it easier to sue directors when such transactions are prejudicial, the 2014 does not show any relevant legal modifications for Peru.

Table 1

Measure	Year	Index or Rank	Website Address
TI Corruption Perceptions index	2014	85 of 175	transparency.org/cpi2014/results
World Bank's Doing Business Report "Ease of Doing Business"	2015	35 of 189	doingbusiness.org/rankings
Global Innovation Index	2014	73 of 143	globalinnovationindex.org/content.aspx?page=data-analysis
World Bank GNI per capita	2013	USD 6,270	data.worldbank.org/indicator/NY.GNP.PCAP.CD

Millennium Challenge Corporation Country Scorecard

In 2008, Peru received USD 35.6 million from the Millennium Challenge Corporation Threshold funding for health and anti-corruption programs. In 2009 Peru reached upper-middle income country status and is officially ineligible for further Millennium Challenge Corporation assistance.

2. CONVERSION AND TRANSFER POLICIES

Foreign Exchange

There are no reported difficulties in obtaining foreign exchange. Under Article 64 of the 1993 Constitution, the GOP guarantees the freedom to hold and dispose of foreign currency. The GOP has eliminated all restrictions on remittances of profits, dividends, royalties, and capital, although foreign investors are advised to register their investments with ProInversion to ensure these guarantees. Exporters and importers are not required to channel foreign exchange transactions through the Central Reserve Bank of Peru (BCR) and can conduct transactions freely on the open market. Anyone may open and maintain foreign currency accounts in Peruvian commercial banks. U.S. firms have reported no problems or delays in transferring funds or remitting capital, earnings, loan repayments or lease payments since Peru's economic reforms of the early 1990s. Under the PTPA, portfolio managers in the United States are able to provide portfolio management services to both mutual funds and pension funds in Peru, including funds that manage Peru's privatized social security accounts.

The 1993 Constitution guarantees free convertibility of currency. However, limited capital controls still exist as private pension fund managers (AFPs) are constrained by how much of their portfolio can be invested in foreign securities. The maximum limit is set by law (currently 50% since July

2011), but the BCR sets the operating limit AFPs can invest abroad. Over the years, the BCR has gradually increased the operating limit, which reached 40% in July 2014. Several additional increases were made between October 2014 and January 2015, bringing the current operating limit up to 42 percent.

The BCR is an independent institution, free to manage monetary policy to maintain financial stability. The BCR's primary goal is to maintain price stability, via inflation targeting. Inflation at year-end in Peru reached 3.9% in 2007, 6.7% in 2008, 0.3% in 2009, 2.1% in 2010, 4.7% in 2011, 2.7% in 2012, 2.8% in 2013, and 3.2% in 2014.

The GOP has implemented policies to de-dollarize the economy, but in the last few years market forces have been more effective in reducing dollarization as the Peruvian Nuevo Sol had trended (until 2014) to appreciate vis-à-vis the U.S. dollar. U.S. dollars account for a decreasing share of banking system transactions, according to the Peruvian Banking Superintendence (SBS). In 2001, U.S. dollars accounted for 82% of loans and 73% of deposits. As of February 2015, U.S. dollars accounted for 42.6% of loans.

The foreign exchange market operates freely, for the most part. To quell "extreme variations" of the exchange rate, the BCR intervenes through purchases and sales in the open market without imposing controls on exchange rates or transactions. In the last few years, the BCR has consistently purchased U.S. dollars to mitigate the risk that spillover from expansionary U.S. monetary policy might result in over-valuation of the Peruvian Nuevo Sol relative to the U.S. dollar. This policy is likely to continue for the foreseeable future, until U.S. economic recovery begins to tighten credit conditions.

Remittance Policies

Peru is neither a major regional financial center nor an offshore financial center. Currently, businesses involved in the transfer of funds only need prior authorization by the Peruvian Banking Authority (SBS) while cash couriers need a signed agreement with the Ministry of Transportation and Communication. The GOP's Financial Intelligence Unit (FIU) is an independent agency that monitors and investigates financial institutions and cash transfers (physical and electronic for money laundering and other financial crimes.

Peru's cash-based and heavily-dollarized economy, large informal sector (estimated to be 70% of GDP), and deficient regulatory supervision of designated non-financial businesses and professions (DNFBPs), such as informal money exchanges and wire transfer services, make the economy vulnerable to money laundering and other financial crimes. The informal remittance businesses remain unsupervised and vulnerable to money laundering, including travel agencies and small wire transfer businesses. Peru would benefit from expanded supervision and regulation of financial institutions and DNFBPs. Progress was made in monitoring and regulating notaries, pawn shops, and exchange houses. Peru is a member of the Financial Action Task Force on Money Laundering in South America (GAFILAT).

A U.S. company complained to the Embassy that their pension plans, issued in the United States and registered under the Texas Commissioner, have been excluded by the SBS from being used by their clients to demonstrate provisional coverage within the funds transfer abroad procedure, despite the company having certified compliance with the coverage requirements. This is notwithstanding the AFPs (pension funds) accepting private voluntary plans from other countries.

3. EXPROPRIATION AND COMPENSATION

The Peruvian Constitution states that the GOP can only expropriate private property on the bases of public interest, such as public works projects or for national security. In order to expropriate Congress is required to pass a decree. The Government of Peru has expressed its intention to comply with international standards concerning expropriations. On January 12, 2012, Congress approved legislation to expropriate a number of homes and other real estate adjacent to the Lima Airport for an airport expansion project. Compensation for expropriations is based on fair market value. Notably, concessionaires have complained that the government has been extremely slow in implementing expropriations, which have caused delays to their investment commitments.

4. DISPUTE SETTLEMENT

Legal System, Specialized Courts, Judicial Independence, Judgments of Foreign Courts

The PTPA includes a chapter on dispute settlement, which applies to implementation of the Agreement's core obligations, including labor and environment provisions. Dispute panel procedures set high standards of openness and transparency through the following measures: open public hearings; public release of legal submissions by parties, enlisting special labor or environment expertise for disputes in these areas, and opportunities for interested third parties to submit views. The Agreement emphasizes compliance through consultation and trade-enhancing remedies. The Agreement also encourages arbitration and other alternative dispute resolution measures for disputes between private parties.

Peru is a party to the 1958 Convention on the Recognition and Enforcement of Foreign Arbitral Awards (New York Convention) and to the International Center for the Settlement of Investment Disputes (ICSID convention). Disputes between foreign investors and the GOP regarding pre-existing contracts must still enter national courts, unless otherwise permitted, such as through provisions found in the PTPA. In addition, investors who enter into a juridical stability agreement may submit disputes with the government to national or international arbitration if stipulated in the agreement. Several private organizations -- including the American Chamber of Commerce, the Lima Chamber of Commerce, and Universidad Catolica – operate private arbitration centers. The quality of such centers varies, however, and investors should choose arbitration venues carefully.

Bankruptcy

Peru has a creditor rights hierarchy similar to that established under U.S. bankruptcy law, and monetary judgments are usually made in the currency stipulated in the contract. However, administrative bankruptcy procedures under INDECOPI (the Antitrust, Unfair Competition, Intellectual Property Protection, Consumer Protection, Dumping, Standards and Elimination of Bureaucratic Barriers Agency) have proven to be slow and subject to judicial intervention. Compounding this difficulty are occasional laws passed to protect specific debtors from action by creditors that would force them into bankruptcy or liquidation.

Investment Disputes

The 1993 Constitution allows disputes among foreign investors and the government or state-controlled enterprises to be submitted to international arbitration. In 2005, in order to reinforce the constitution, the Supreme Court ruled that all arbitration awards are final and are not subject to appeal.

International Arbitration

The Constitution permits international arbitration of disputes between foreign investors and the government or state-controlled enterprises. Although Peruvian law stipulates the GOP must accept binding arbitration, parastatal companies and government ministries disregarded unfavorable judgments several times over the past three years. Previously, the Government of Peru turned these arbitration cases over to the judiciary, where they were bureaucratically delayed until the companies conceded the cases. Peru's Supreme Court ruled that effective July 2005 all arbitration findings and awards are final and not subject to appeal.

Peru is a party to the 1958 Convention on the Recognition and Enforcement of Foreign Arbitral Awards (New York Convention), and to the 1965 International Center for the Settlement of Investment Disputes (ICSID convention). Disputes between foreign investors and the GOP regarding pre-existing contracts must still enter national courts. However, investors who conclude a juridical stability agreement for additional investments may submit disputes with the government to national or international arbitration if stipulated in the agreement. Several private organizations -- including the Universidad Catolica, the Lima Chamber of Commerce and the American Chamber of Commerce -- operate private arbitration centers. The quality of these centers varies, and investors should choose arbitration venues carefully.

ICSID Convention and New York Convention

Peru became a signatory to the Convention on the Settlement of Investment Disputes between States and Nationals of Other States (ICSID Convention) since September 4, 1991. Peru ratified the 1958 New York Convention on the Recognition and Enforcement of Foreign Arbitral Awards on July 7, 1988.

Duration of Dispute Resolution

Dispute settlement remains problematic in Peru; although in 2004 the GOP took steps to improve the dispute settlement process by establishing commercial courts to rule on investment disputes, including two courts of appeal. Prior to the existence of the commercial courts, it took an average of two years to resolve a commercial case through the civil court system. With their specialized judges, these courts have reduced the amount of time to resolve a case to just two months. The appeals level resolves most of these cases.

The criminal and civil courts of first instance and appeal are heard at the provincial level. The Supreme Court is located in Lima. In principle, Peruvian law recognizes secured interests in property, both movable and immovable. With the exception of the commercial courts, the judicial system is extremely slow to hear cases and to issue decisions. A large backlog of cases further complicates decision-making. Court rulings and the degree of enforcement have been difficult to predict. The competence of individual judges varies, and allegations of corruption, political interference, and outside interference in the judicial system are common. Frequent use of appellate processes as a delay tactic leads to the belief among foreign investors that contracts can be difficult to enforce in Peru. The 1997 Law of Conciliation (DL 26872) requires disputants in many types of civil and commercial matters to consider conciliation before a judge can accept a dispute for litigation. Private parties often resort to arbitration to resolve business disputes, avoiding involvement in judicial processes.

Peru has a creditor rights hierarchy similar to that established under U.S. bankruptcy law, and monetary judgments are usually made in the currency stipulated in the contract. However, administrative bankruptcy procedures under INDECOPI (the National Institute for the Defense of Free Competition and the Protection of Intellectual Property) have proven to be slow and subject to judicial intervention. Compounding this difficulty are occasional laws passed to protect specific debtors from action by creditors that would force them into bankruptcy or liquidation.

The 1993 Constitution permits international arbitration of disputes between foreign investors and the government or state-controlled enterprises. Previously, the Government of Peru appealed arbitration cases to the judiciary, where they were typically delayed until the international companies conceded the cases. To reinforce Peruvian law, the Supreme Court ruled that effective July 2005, all arbitration findings and awards are final and not subject to appeal.

5. PERFORMANCE REQUIREMENTS AND INVESTMENT INCENTIVES

WTO/TRIMS

The PTPA has resulted in benefits to U.S. enterprises seeking to invest in Peru. Under the PTPA, Peru has made concessions beyond its commitments to the World Trade Organization (WTO) eliminating investment barriers, such as the requirement for U.S. firms to hire nationals rather than U.S. professionals, and measures requiring the purchase of local goods.

Investment Incentives

Peru offers both foreign and national investors legal and tax stability agreements to stimulate private investment. These agreements guarantee that the statutes on income taxes, remittances, export promotion regimes (such as drawbacks, or refunds of duties), administrative procedures, and labor hiring regimes in effect at the time of the investment contract will remain unchanged for that investment for 10 years. To qualify, an investment must exceed USD 10 million in the mining and hydrocarbons sectors or USD 5 million within two years in other sectors. An agreement to acquire more than 50% of a company's shares in the privatization process may also qualify an investor for a legal or tax stability agreement, provided that the added investment will expand the installed capacity of the company or enhance its technological development.

Research and Development

Promoting science, innovation, and technology and improving Peru's education system remain priorities for the Humala Administration. Peru ranked last out of 65 surveyed countries in the OECD's 2013 Program for International Student Assessment (PISA). The OECD noted the high inequity of quality between urban and rural schools and low levels of Peruvian students meeting PISA standards in mathematics, science, and reading. The Humala Administration increased spending on education for 2015, including USD 1 billion to build and renovate schools and USD 450 million to hire more teachers. In 2014, the GOP launched an ambitious national plan to promote innovation, science, and technology jobs.

Performance Requirements

There are no performance requirements that apply exclusively to foreign investors. Peruvian civil law applies to legal stability agreements, which means the GOP cannot unilaterally alter agreements. Notwithstanding these protections, investors should be aware that government officials have delivered negative remarks to the press regarding companies exercising their contractual rights and obligations.

Laws specific to investment in the petroleum and mining sectors provide assurances to investors in those sectors. However, a history of tightening of benefits has occurred in these industries. In

2000, the government modified the General Mining Law, reducing some benefits to investors in that sector. Among the changes were reductions in the term concessionaires are granted to achieve the minimum annual production, increases in fees for holding non-productive concessions, increases in fines for not achieving minimum production within the allotted time, reductions in the maximum allowable annual accelerated depreciation, and revocation of the income tax exemption for reinvested profits.

After a growing number of local communities demanded a share of mining profits from operations in their areas, the incoming Garcia Administration and mining companies agreed in 2006 to a voluntary contribution system whereby companies agreed to provide funding to the government (in addition to the regular corporate income tax) for community infrastructure projects. This voluntary contribution averted adoption of exacting taxes. The agreement allowed mining companies to control where their contributions were invested and did not apply if the prices of metals or minerals drop below certain levels. As the voluntary contribution agreement was to expire at the end of 2011 during a period of windfall profits for extractive industries, the incoming Humala Administration and mining companies agreed in August 2011 to replace it with a new tax regime on mining profits called the "gravamen minero." It produced tax revenues (including the royalty tax) of USD 1.97 billion in 2012; but with declining metals prices the contribution in the January-November tax 2013 period was USD 1.48 billion.

With regard to licensing arrangements, private parties may freely negotiate contractual conditions related to licensing arrangements and other aspects of technology transfer, needing no prior governmental authorization. Registration of a technology transfer agreement with INDECOPI is required for a payment of royalties to be counted against taxes.

Current law limits foreign employees to 20% of the total number of employees in a local company (whether owned by foreign or national interests). The combined salaries of foreign employees are limited to no more than 30% of the total company payroll. However, DL 689 from November 1991 provides a variety of exceptions to these limits. For example, a foreigner is not counted against a company's total if he or she holds an immigrant visa, has a certain amount invested in the company (approximately USD 4,000), or is a national of a country that has a reciprocal labor or dual nationality agreement with Peru. The United States and Peru tolerate dual nationality, but do not have a formal agreement. Furthermore, the law exempts foreign banks, and international transportation companies from these hiring limits, as well as all firms located in free trade zones. Companies may apply for exemption from the limitations for managerial or technical personnel.

The GOP does not maintain any measures that are inconsistent with Trade-Related Investment Measure (TRIM) requirements, according to a WTO Committee on Trade-Related Investment Measure notification dated August 19, 2010.

Although there are no discriminatory or onerous visa requirements, residence, or works permit requirements that inhibit foreign investors' mobility, the application and approval process can be cumbersome and lengthy.

Data Storage

Peru adopted the Personal Data Protection Law (N° 29733) in July 2011 and went into effect on March 22, 2013. The Law is available here in English: **http://web.ita.doc.gov/ITI/itiHome.nsf/1dd3c7c4faeeff0585256ccb00657bab/112a1a2f4d01989c85257a78004dd2ec/$FILE/Peru%20Data%20Protection%20Law%20July%2028_EN.pdf**.

The implementing regulations are available in Spanish here: **http://spij.minjus.gob.pe/normas/textos/220313T.pdf**.

A data controller who processes personal data must notify the National Authority for Personal Data Protection (ANPDP for its Spanish acronym), which keeps a public register of data processors and the type of data they collect. Personal data is defined by the Law as any information on an individual which identifies or makes him/her identifiable through means that may be reasonably used. Sensitive personal data means any of the following: biometric data, data concerning the racial and ethnic origin; political, religion, philosophical or moral opinions or convictions, personal habits, union membership and information related to health or sexual life. Unless otherwise exempted by statute, data controllers are generally required to obtain the consent of data subjects for the processing of their personal data. Consent must be prior, informed, expressed, and unequivocal. In the case of sensitive personal data, consent must also be given in writing, which may be done digitally. Even without the consent of the subject, sensitive data may be processed when authorized by law, provided that it in in the public interest.

Data controllers may process personal data without consent:

When the personal data are compiled or transferred for public entities in control of the personal data and in the performance of its duties;

When personal data is accessible to the public or is intended to be accessible to the public;

To comply with other laws related to financial solvency and credit;

In the case of a law for the promotion of competition in regulated markets under certain circumstances;

When necessary to perform a contract to which the data subject is a party;

For personal data related to health, under certain circumstances;

When processing is carried out by non-profit organizations with political, religious or union purposes, under certain circumstances; or

In an anonymization or disassociation procedure.

A data controller may transfer personal data to places outside of Peru only if the recipients have adequate protection measures. The ANPDP supervises compliance with this requirement. That provision does not apply in the following cases:

When the data subject has given his/her prior, informed, express and unequivocal consent;

Agreements under international treaties to which Peru is a party;

International judicial cooperation;

International cooperation between intelligence agencies for the fight against terrorism, illegal drug trafficking, money laundering, corruption, human trafficking and other forms of organized crime;

When necessary to implement a contract to which the data subject is a party;

To comply with laws concerning the transfer of bank or stock exchanges; or

When the transfer is for the prevention, diagnosis or medical or surgical treatment of the data subject; or when necessary to carry out epidemiological or similar studies (provided that adequate disassociation procedures are applied).

Data controllers must adopt technical, organization and legal measures to guarantee the security of personal data and avoid their alteration, loss, unauthorized processing or access. Peru's law does not require any notifications to any data subject or any other entity upon a breach. Peru does not mandate special regulations be enacted for the processing of personal data of minors. The ANPDP is responsible for enforcement and can issue the following administrative sanctions/fines based upon whether the violation is mild, serious or very serious. The law provides a "Principle for availability of recourse for the data subject" stating that any data subject must have the administrative and/or jurisdictional channel necessary to claim and enforce his rights when they are violated by the processing of his personal data.A

6. RIGHT TO PRIVATE OWNERSHIP AND ESTABLISHMENT

Peruvian law generally grants foreign and domestic entities the right to establish and own business enterprises and to engage in most forms of remunerative activity. Subject to the restrictions listed earlier in this document, both foreign and domestic entities may invest in any legal economic activity -- including foreign direct investment, portfolio investment, and in real estate. Private entities may generally freely establish, acquire, and dispose of interests in business enterprises. In the case of some privatized companies deemed important by the government, the privatization agency ProInversion has included a so-called "golden share" clause in the sales contract, which allows the government to veto a potential future purchaser of the privatized assets.

7. PROTECTION OF PROPERTY RIGHTS

Real Property

The GOP recognizes and enforces secured interests in property, both movable and immovable. The GOP is working on improving the registry of those rights, which will further enable the government's enforcement capabilities.

Peru's legal framework provides for easy registration of trademarks, and inventors have been able to patent their inventions since 1994. Peru's 1996 Industrial Property Rights Law provides an effective term of protection for patents and prohibits devices that decode encrypted satellite signals, along with other improvements. Peruvian law does not provide pipeline protection for patents or protection from parallel imports. Peru's Copyright Law is generally consistent with the TRIPS Agreement.

Intellectual Property Rights

While the legal framework for protection of intellectual property (IP) in Peru has improved over the past decade, including the law enacted in 2011 to criminalize the sale of counterfeit medicines, enforcement mechanisms remain weak. However, Peru has remained on USTR's Section 301

"Watch List" since 1992 because of continued high piracy rates, inadequate enforcement of IP laws, and weak or unenforced penalties for IP violators.

Under the PTPA, Peruvian law should treat U.S. companies at least as well as Peruvian companies in all IP categories. The PTPA provides for improved IP protection on a broad range of intellectual property rights. Such improvements include protections for digital products such as U.S. software, music, text, and video; protection for U.S. patents, trademarks and pharmaceutical and agrochemical test data; legal penalties to deter piracy; and an electronic system to register and maintain trademarks.

Despite PTPA implementation and recent legal code amendments creating stricter penalties for some types of IP theft, the judicial branch has failed to impose sentences that adequately deter future IP theft. Prosecutors do not pursue piracy cases through the entire process to final judgment. Furthermore, the Peruvian public lacks motivation to change perceptions regarding IP theft. The public continues to purchase pirated software, CDs, DVDs, pharmaceutical products, and books from vendors in public. The purchases continue openly since most Peruvians realize their government will not prosecute this theft.

Some GOP institutions, sometimes with the support of the U.S. Embassy in Lima, sponsor public awareness campaigns to raise awareness about the damage that IP theft causes the Peruvian economy and Peruvians consumers. Peruvian newspapers complain about piracy, including pirated versions of Peru's Nobel Laureate Mario Vargas Llosa's books. While the GOP occasionally has carried out raids against small-time vendors of pirated goods, piracy remains a significant problem for legitimate owners of copyrights in Peru.

The International Intellectual Property Alliance (IIPA) estimates that the piracy level in Peru for recorded music is at 98% and 100% for video content and books. The Business Software Alliance estimates that software piracy level is at 65%, costing the industry USD 60 million in 2014.

The U.S. pharmaceutical industry advises that the GOP fails to provide data exclusivity protection for all pharmaceutical products and does not provide patent linkage or "second use" medical patents. The pharmaceutical industry also advises that the GOP does not offer any extension of the patent term for pharmaceutical products to compensate for processing delays at the patent office. There has also been at least one instance of GOP initiatives creating a backdoor for domestic companies to avoid complying with IP laws. This backdoor can be seen in the pharmaceutical sector in the registration of biosimilar products of biologics, drugs made from organic material that infringe upon patented U.S. biological products.

The GOP agency charged with promoting and defending intellectual property rights is the Antitrust, Unfair Competition, Intellectual Property Protection, Consumer Protection, Dumping, Standards and Elimination of Bureaucratic Barriers Agency (INDECOPI, www.indecopi.gob.pe), established in 1992. Peru belongs to the World Trade Organization (WTO) and the World Intellectual Property Organization (WIPO). It is also a signatory to the Paris Convention on Industrial Property, Geneva Convention for the Protection of Sound Recordings, Bern Convention for the Protection of Literary and Artistic Works, Brussels Convention on the Distribution of Satellite Signals, Phonograms Convention, Satellites Convention, Universal Copyright Convention, the World Copyright Treaty, and the World Performances and Phonographs Treaty and the Film Register Treaty. In December 1994, the Peruvian Congress ratified the World Trade Organization's Agreement on Trade-Related Aspects of Intellectual Property (TRIPs).

Pursuant to the terms of the PTPA, Peru has ratified or acceded to the following agreements: the Convention Relating to the Distribution of Program-Carrying Signals Transmitted by Satellite; the

Budapest Treaty on the International Recognition of the Deposit of Microorganisms for the Purposes of Patent Procedure; the WIPO Copyright Treaty; the WIPO Performances and Phonograms Treaty; the Patent Cooperation Treaty; the Trademark Law Treaty; and, the International Convention for the Protection of New Varieties of Plants (UPOV Convention). Although Peru has ratified or acceded to several of the above agreements as part of its implementation of the PTPA, it has not yet fulfilled its PTPA commitments by ratifying or acceding to the following agreements: the Patent Law Treaty; the Hague Agreement Concerning the International Registration of Industrial Designs; and, the Protocol Relating to the Madrid Agreement Concerning the International Registration of Marks.

The GOP does not have a single database that tracks seized counterfeit goods. Moreover, the various Peruvian agencies/ministries do not share information, which results in conflicting and/or an imperfect survey. This information is not available to the public.

Customs officials have the authority to seize counterfeit goods. There is a process of rights holders to be notified for an inspection of the seized goods, but implementation of the process is inconsistent.

Piracy remains a prevalent problem in Peru. GOP officials recognize that the country will not achieve its full economic potential if IPR laws are not implemented more robustly to protect legitimate owners of trademarks, copyrights, and patents. Even Peruvian businesses complain that piracy is biting into their bottom lines, and are joining U.S. and foreign companies to engage the GOP on the economic costs of IPR violations. The World Economic Forum ranked Peru 119 out of 144 countries in its Global Competitiveness Index 2014-2015 (an improvement of one point from last year), significantly behind fellow Pacific Alliance members Chile (56), Mexico (82), and Colombia (96).

INDECOPI reports that hundreds of millions of dollars-worth of pirated goods are sold with impunity in notorious markets like “Polvos Azules,” “El Hueco,” and “Fronteras Unidas” in Lima. For example, El Hueco is full of shoppers buying the latest pirated movies even though it is located just a few blocks away from the national PNP headquarters. In the outer Andean and Amazon regions, notorious markets for pirated goods operate even more openly with little fear of interference from law enforcement (ref B).

Piracy is so common that notorious markets have fragmented into specializations. For instance, Lima’s “Capon Center Mall” specializes in selling low-priced counterfeit medicines. During a July 2014 raid, PNP and SUNAT agents discovered that over 50% of all medicines sold at Capon were counterfeit. Gamarra, a district in Lima, is home to large notorious markets (“Galeria Azul,” “Galeria Santa Lucia,” “Galeria San Miguel,” “Galeria Markata,” and “Galeria Senor de Chacos”) that specialize in counterfeit clothing. Even upscale districts in Lima like La Molina and Miraflores are home to well-known notorious markets like “La Esquina” and “La Quinta” where hawkers sell fake Gucci, Louis Vuitton, and other high-end merchandise.

GOP and private sector interlocutors note that piracy groups are utilizing internet tools to expand their business. Notorious markets are becoming more adept at using social media to promote and sell their goods, with Facebook being the social media of choice. For instance, “Fronteras Unidas’” Facebook page (**http://www.facebook.com/pages/galeria-fronteras-unidas-grau/173545512699294**) promotes the latest sales and discounts for new merchandise, looking as professional as legitimate companies that use Facebook. MINSA is concerned over the growth of counterfeit medicine moving towards online distribution and sales. One MINSA interlocutor noted that her office has insufficient resources to adequately monitor the ever growing number of unregistered websites offering deeply discounted and counterfeit medicines to the public.

Piracy in Peru is most rampant in software, music, and video content. The International Intellectual Property Alliance estimates that the piracy level for music is around 98% and nearly 100% for video content. The Software Business Alliance estimates that the piracy level for software is 65%, costing copyright holders an estimated USD 60 million in 2014. The Peruvian market is so saturated with pirated movies that there is no legitimate rental market for movies and few legitimate venues to buy legal DVDs of music and movies. Pirated movies sell for three to five Peruvian Nuevo Soles (PEN) (USD 1.00-1.65) per DVD while pirated books sell for less than a third of the price of licensed editions. Novels by noted Peruvian author Mario Vargas Llosa sell in stores for PEN 70 (USD 23.00) while illegal book venders sell it for PEN 25 Soles (USD 8.30). Customers can even use their cell phones to pay for downloading pirated movies. For example, PeliculaSONL (www.peliculasonl.com) allows customers to pay for weekly subscriptions through their Claro and Movistar (the two largest and legitimate cellular network providers) accounts to pay for illegal video downloads.

Resources for Rights Holders

Contact at Mission:

Benjamin Yates
Economic Officer
+51-1-618-2414
YatesBA@state.gov

A list of lawyers can be requested from the Embassy's Commercial Service Office (**Office.Lima@trade.gov**).

Country/Economy resources:

The American Chamber of Commerce in Peru can be contacted via this link:**http://www.amcham.org.pe/contactenos/escribanos.php**.

8. TRANSPARENCY OF THE REGULATORY SYSTEM

Regulatory transparency and independence have become central issues for foreign investors in Peru. Although many of the central government regulators related to foreign investment have relatively transparent and predictable procedures, delays and the lack of predictability in the rulings of these institutions, have been impediments to doing business in Peru.

The Securities Market Superintendence (SMV) maintains the company registry and supervises the securities market. ProInversion handles privatization and most concessions. INDECOPI handles competition policy, bankruptcy, and intellectual property matters. The Superintendence of Banking and Insurance (SBS) regulates banks, insurance companies, and private pension funds, including determination of whether potential market entrants qualify to operate in Peru.

When the GOP privatized state-owned monopolies in the areas of telecommunications, energy, and the hydrocarbons sector in the late 1990s, it also established regulatory institutions to oversee the new private sectors – among them OSIPTEL for telecom, and OSINERGMIN for energy, mining and hydrocarbons – the GOP created the Environmental Enforcement Organism (OEFA) in 2008 which is progressively taking over the environmental enforcement functions previously held by OSINERGMIN and other agencies.

In 2010, OSIPTEL established a "glide path" plan to continuously lower the mobile termination rates for all carriers by October 2013. This created a more favorable and competitive environment for the smaller carriers. In July 2014, OSIPTEL introduced number portability—which allows consumers to keep their mobile phone number despite changing service providers—and cut interconnection fees by 68% to spur competition and facilitate new entrants into the market. OSIPTEL also lowered costs for rural operators to facilitate mobile penetration. Since these changes, over 200,000 Peruvian consumers have switched providers.

U.S. and other non-Peruvian firms and investors have complained about the reinterpretation of rules and the imposition of disproportionate fines coupled with usurious interest charges on unpaid taxes or fines by the Peruvian tax agency, SUNAT. U.S. firms and other investors allege SUNAT's capricious behavior and reinterpretation of tax laws are often contrary to the spirit of the law and intent of government policies, thereby complicating and making normal business operations costlier. This situation may be at least be partly explained by the fact that the remuneration of SUNAT employees is partially determined by the theoretical tax liability they assess in audits. The U.S. Embassy continues to hear that this perverse incentive leads to overzealous tax collection practices.

Businesses point out that SUNAT's retroactive reinterpretation of regulations and laws, levying of disproportionate fines, usurious interest rates on the alleged assessments and below market interest rates on payable tax rebates, lengthy resolution processes, and initiation of full company audits when companies request a refund or legal revaluation of assets for depreciation purposes, create additional investment and trade barriers. In one case, a U.S. firm requested, by clerical mistake, an improper drawback of USD 1,345, only to face SUNAT fines of USD 645,000. Although the case was resolved, legislation now allows for an independent tax tribunal to serve as a check on alleged abuses by SUNAT. However, when SUNAT exercises its right of appeal against unfavorable tax tribunal rulings, the disputed assessments and liabilities on companies' balance sheets are prolonged. As a balance to this tendency, a tax ombudsman must approve SUNAT's request to appeal adverse tax tribunal decisions. At times, the ombudsman has also acted to end unwarranted litigation of disputed assessments. For example, in 2005, a U.S. company won long-standing tax cases against SUNAT as a result of these improvements. Nevertheless, the U.S. Embassy has heard of cases of companies deciding to pay long-disputed assessments in order to eliminate liabilities from their books. A conspicuous case was that of a Canadian bank, which in late-February 2014 decided to pay under protest approximately USD 170 million in tax liabilities, most of it accumulated interest. In recent years a number of companies have opened international arbitration cases against the GOP.

Businesses also complain about high health insurance and pension tax rates, and state that these tax policies hinder investment capital flows. The lack of a U.S.-Peru treaty on double taxation is also a disincentive to foreign investment.

9. EFFICIENT CAPITAL MARKETS AND PORTFOLIO INVESTMENT

Credit is allocated on market terms and the banking industry in Peru is generally considered competitive in offering services to business customers. Private pension funds have keenly competed in recent years with financial companies for bonds issued locally by companies and the GOP. These entities compete because the supply of local securities is insufficient given the small size of the market. Under the PTPA, U.S. financial service suppliers have full rights to establish subsidiaries or branches for banks and insurance companies.

The private sector has access to a variety of credit instruments. In 2013, firms placed USD 1.75 billion on the local bond market, 3.7% below the year earlier. Mutual funds managed USD 5.9

billion in December 2013, a large 16.3% decrease from the December 2013 level. Private pension funds managed a total of USD 36.2 billion in December 2013. (Full 2014 Statistics are not yet available.)

The Securities Market Superintendence (SMV) is the GOP entity charged with regulating the securities and commodities markets. Following the IMF's recommendations, the GOP passed a law reforming the SMV's predecessor, CONASEV (the National Commission for the Supervision of Companies, Securities and Exchanges). SMV's mandate includes controlling securities market participants, maintaining a transparent and orderly market, setting accounting standards, and publishing financial information about covered companies. SMV requires stock issuers to report events that may affect the stock, the company, or any public offerings. This requirement promotes market transparency, and aims to prevent fraud. Trading on insider information is a crime, with some reported prosecutions in past years. One case at the end of 2010 involved three (government-owned health care provider) ESSALUD employees, a stock brokerage firm and an employee of the stock brokerage firm. CONASEV fined these individuals and the stock brokerage firm, and their cases are moving through the Peruvian court system. SMV must vet all firms listed on the Lima Stock Exchange (Bolsa de Valores de Lima) or the Public Registry of Securities. SMV also maintains the Public Registry of Securities and Stock Brokers. SMV is studying ways to improve the regulatory system to encourage and facilitate portfolio investment.

Money and Banking System, Hostile Takeovers

The banking system is considered generally sound, thanks to lessons learned during the 1997-1998 Asian crises, and continues to revamp operations, increase capitalization, and reduce costs. Under the SBS's conservative criteria, non-performing loans rose in the last two years, to 2.14% of total loans as of December 2013, yet down from a high of 11% in early 2001. Able bank supervision and strong GDP growth over the last decade through 2014 also helped banks weather the 2008-2009 global financial crises with little trouble.

Economic opening since the 1990s, coupled with competition, has led to banking sector consolidation. Sixteen commercial banks comprise the system, with assets accounting for 88.9% of Peru's financial system. Three banks account for 73% of local loans and deposits among commercial banks. Of USD 93.2 billion in total banking assets at the end of December 2013, assets of the three largest commercial banks amounted to USD 67.3 billion. As of December 2013, foreigners had significant shares in thirteen banks, of which they were majority owners of eleven (including one of the country's largest ones) and operator of one of the largest commercial banks. Notably, two of the four banks that are majority-owned by residents account for 45.1% of commercial banks' assets.

Peru's financial system has 12 specialized institutions ("financieras"), 31 thriving micro-lenders and savings banks (although several large banks also lend to small enterprises), two leasing institutions, two state-owned banks, and one state-owned development bank. In 2013, the Economist Intelligence Unit again ranked Peru number one worldwide on microfinance business environment for the sixth consecutive year because of its sophisticated legal and regulatory framework and competitive microfinance sector. Nevertheless, Peru's over 150 savings and loan cooperatives operate in an environment almost devoid of government oversight.

Peruvian law and regulations do not authorize or encourage private firms to adopt articles of incorporation or association to limit or restrict foreign participation. There are no private or public sector efforts to restrict foreign participation in industry standards-setting organizations. However, larger private firms often use "cross-shareholding" and "stable shareholder" arrangements to restrict investment by outsiders -- not necessarily foreigners -- in their firms. As close families or associates generally control ownership of Peruvian corporations, hostile takeovers are practically non-existent. In the past few years, several companies from the region, China, North America, and Europe have actively been buying local companies in power transmission, retail trade, fishmeal production, and other industries.

10. COMPETITION FROM STATE-OWNED ENTERPRISES

Several electricity, water and sewage, bank, and oil companies remain state-owned and state-operated. The most notable area of SOE activity pertains to the petroleum sector, where the state-owned petroleum company PetroPeru is an oil refiner and operator of an underutilized oil pipeline. Congress passed several laws since which purport to strengthen PetroPeru and free it from bureaucratic controls, so that it can enter into all stages of the petroleum and petrochemical sectors, especially upstream. In 2008, PetroPeru took center stage in a corruption scandal related to oil and gas concessions. The scandal led to the resignation of the Minister of Energy and Mines and the PetroPeru President and forced the GOP to implement a number of changes in PetroPeru's management. Over the last two decades, PetroPeru has experienced significant attrition in managerial and technical expertise. This, coupled with its limited financial resources, cast into doubt the company's ability to implement its long-held plans to expand and upgrade its aging Talara refinery – which continues to produce dirty gasoline and diesel fuel, a situation the government permits by not enforcing regulatory standards. Limited resources and expertise also downplay expectations following repeated announcements from its leadership regarding entrance to upstream, and participation in a proposed gas pipeline and petrochemical complex in southern Peru. Up until recently, PetroPeru's leadership's plans even included a return to oil production through participation in tenders of oil producing blocks that the GOP was set to auction in 2013, with a requirement to partner with PetroPeru. Limited or no interest shown by oil companies in that auction and in several exploration blocs' pending auctions, have left those plans up in the air.

Significant SOEs have audited accounts that are made public. In addition, the accounts are monitored by a board of directors. The majority of the country's SOEs is corporately managed by FONAFE and is listed on FONAFE's website along with their audited accounts (**http://www.fonafe.gob.pe/portal/empresas?accion=transparenciaNew&m=6&Contenidoid=32**). Petroperu, which is managed independently from FONAFE, publishes a report that includes the audited financial statements of the company, such as those of comprehensive income, changes in equity, and cash flows, as well as a summary of significant accounting policies and other explanatory notes included in Petroperu's financial statements. The report is produced annually and is publicly available on Petroperu's website (**http://www.petroperu.com.pe/transparencia/ley27806.asp**).

11. CORPORATE SOCIAL RESPONSIBILITY

Peruvian businesses participate in Corporate Social Responsibility (CSR) programs, primarily on a voluntary basis. For the energy and mining sector, certain regulations do exist to promote social responsibility. Supreme Decree No. 042-2003-EM promotes social responsibility within the mining sector, encouraging local employment opportunities, support to communities' projects, development activities, and purchase of local goods and services. The decree requires mining companies to publish an annual report on sustainable development activities. The Ministry of Energy and Mines has prepared a guidebook for community relations, as well as public information on social measures related to the mining and energy sectors. In February 2011, INDECOPI adopted the Peruvian Technical Regulation of Social Responsibility ISO 26000 that serves as a voluntary guide to CSR activities.

On February 15, 2012, Peru was listed as a compliant country under the Extractive Industries Transparency Initiative (EITI), as the GOP and extractive industries openly publish all company payments and government revenues from oil, gas, and mining. Peru is the only EITI-compliant country in Latin America.

Peru continues to implement its 2013-2017 National Strategy to Combat Forced Labor, which emphasizes the state's role to protect and promote labor rights. The plan simultaneously prioritizes building capacity and empowering vulnerable groups to transform their environment and enforce their rights. The plan addresses both medium and long-term multi-sector plans to eliminate or reduce conditions that enable forced labor. Despite these efforts, the government did not effectively enforce labor laws in all cases. Child labor, particularly in informal sectors, forced labor, and employers engaging in antiunion practices remain significant problems.

12. POLITICAL VIOLENCE

Although political violence against investors is rare, protests, sometimes violent, have taken place in or near communities with extractive industry operations. Environmental concerns were often the cited pretext. Protestors often object to the fact that environmental impact assessments are reviewed by the Ministry of Energy and Mines, rather than the Ministry of Environment, when in fact, the Ministry of Environment along with other national agencies do participate in assessment reviews. In many cases, protestors sought public services not provided by the government. Ideological opposition to foreign mining firms, not opposition to mining itself, often leads to protest in communities incited by NGOs. In some cases, organizers from outside the local community are brought in to foment protests against the companies. Groups blocked roads and an airport in 2014 to protest extractive industry operations; hydroelectric projects; restrictions on informal gold mining, gas exports, and the Government's coca eradication policies. In several of these protests, police and civilians were injured or killed. As of February 2015, the Ombudsperson's Office reported 211 conflicts in Peru; 67% of these conflicts involve socio-economic concerns, usually linked to extractive industries.

Politically motivated movements at times have opposed large extractive projects. In some cases, these movements have been successful in delaying large investments, as occurred in the USD 4.8 billion Conga mine project in Cajamarca in August 2012. In other cases, protests have stopped such investments entirely.

The National Office of Dialogue and Sustainability is actively engaged in mitigating social conflict connected to the extractive industry in Peru. This office addresses conflict in a broader community development context, rather than only responding to social conflicts after they have already erupted. To this end, the government is providing more education, infrastructure, and health care services in areas where extractive industry projects are planned or under development, which will increase government presence and reduce potential for conflict in those (historically underserved and often remote) areas. Peru's Prior Consultation Law was signed in 2011, and its implementing regulations were approved in 2012. The law requires the GOP to consult with indigenous communities before enacting any legislation, administrative measures, or development projects that could affect communities' rights of territorial demarcation. There have been several successful prior consultation processes related to the extractive industry, but the law remains controversial. Critics believe it creates burdensome processes and results in delays. The industry association Peruvian Society of Hydrocarbons alleges that work on 30 oil exploration blocks is paralyzed due to lengthy permit processing. The National Society of Mining, Electricity and Petroleum (SNMPE) and the government have become involved in assisting local governments to access the extractive industry "canon" (tax revenue-sharing scheme with funding for public works projects) as a way to both stimulate local development and prevent conflicts.

Although these efforts have been effective in some mining regions, in others, conflicts have continued or expanded.

Violence remains a concern in coca-growing regions. The government reported that through October 2014, the Shining Path conducted 18 terrorist acts, resulting in the death of two soldiers and two civilians, as well as injuries to six soldiers, seven civilians, and one police officer in the Apurimac, Ene, and Mantaro River Valleys (VRAEM) emergency zone, which includes parts of Ayacucho, Cusco, Huancavelica, Huanuco, and Junin regions. A separate emergency zone in the Upper Huallaga Valley (UHV) includes parts of San Martin and Ucayali regions. There were reports that the Shining Path abducted children to work for the terrorist organization during the year. The Humala government continues the longstanding practice of authorizing separate 60-day states of emergency in two areas where the Shining Path operates – the Apurimac, Ene, and Mantaro River Valleys (VRAEM) and the Upper Huallaga Valley. On September 11, 2014 the GOP declared a new emergency zone in the Loreto region due to drug trafficking activity. The state of emergency authorization suspends some civil liberties and gives the security forces additional authority to maintain public order.

There is little government presence in the remote coca-growing zones of the VRAEM and Upper Huallaga Valley, although significant ramp-up of government presence and programs is underway. The U.S. Embassy in Lima restricts visits by official personnel to these areas because of the threat of violence by narcotics traffickers and columns of the Shining Path. Information about insecure areas and recommended personal security practices can be found at **http://www.osac.gov** or**http://travel.state.gov**.

13. CORRUPTION

It is illegal in Peru for a public official or employee to accept any type of outside remuneration for the performance of his or her official duties. Peru has ratified both the UN Convention against Corruption and the Organization of American States Inter-American Convention against Corruption. Peru is not a member of the Organization of Economic Cooperation and Development (OECD), but it signed a Country Program agreement in December 2014 to provide an anchor for policy reforms aimed at meeting OECD standards and practices. It has not signed the OECD Convention on Combating Bribery, although it has participated as an observer in the Working Group. The Contraloría General is the responsible government agency for overseeing proper procedures in public administration, thus ends up being responsible in combating corruption.

U.S. firms have reported problems resulting from corruption, usually in government procurement processes and in the judicial sector, with defense and police procurement generally considered among the most problematic in spite of PTPA's stipulations and of Peru's Government Procurement Law (Legislative Decree No. 1017, DL 1017, one of several laws passed with the specific intention to implement PTPA). Transparency International ranked Peru 85th out of 175 countries in its 2014 Corruption Perceptions Index, two points lower than 2013.

At the end of 2014, three former regional presidents – roughly equivalent to U.S. state governors – were in jail awaiting trial on corruption charges while a fourth was a fugitive from justice. Three newly elected regional presidents – sworn into office January 1, 2015 – were facing legal problems: two had been sentenced to jail for crimes they committed prior to assuming office but remained at their posts while they appealed; the third was barred from assuming office for failure to pay a USD 333,000 fine associated with a prior bribery conviction. A study published in May of 2014 by the office of the anti-corruption solicitor reported that 92 percent of the over 1,800 district-level mayors in office between 2011 and 2014 had been investigated for criminal activity.

Ten percent of sitting members of congress had been suspended for ethical violations since taking office in 2011.

The Peruvian armed forces and national police continue to prefer to execute government-to-government procurements (i.e., purchases by a GOP agency from a foreign government agency or government-owned company). This practice has impeded the participation of U.S. companies in GOP procurement, mainly with the Ministries of Defense and Interior. The Embassy is currently trying to reach an agreement with the Ministry of Interior that could be acceptable for both parties. In July 2012, the Government Procurement Supervisory Agency ruled that government-to-government procurements do not fall under the government procurement law (DL 1017). An article in the 2013 Budget Law also specified that procurements by the GOP from another state are not under the scope of DL 1017. Since then, there have been a number of local media reports of overvalued prices in several government-to-government purchases, of goods or services for the police or the armed forces. Cases include purchases of a satellite, planes, helicopters, and technical assistance training. Overvaluation has apparently occurred even in the case of open tenders, as in the notorious recent case of the purchase of 591 binoculars by the Interior Ministry for the National Police in December 2013. El Comercio, Peru's paper-of-record, published a report in January 2014 alleging the Interior Ministry bought 591 binoculars at a price more than ten times the market rate. In early-March 2014, local media reported that the Public Prosecutor's Office would investigate a technical assistance-training procurement made in 2009 by the Armed Forces Joint Command. This probe comes after the Comptroller General found irregularities and circumstantial evidence of collusion, embezzlement and other crimes. During 2014, the press published articles alleging that Peruvian Air Force officers had accepted kickbacks for illegally selling fuel on the open market.

UN Anticorruption Convention, OECD Convention on Combatting Bribery

Peru signed the UN Anticorruption Convention on December 10, 2003 and ratified it on November 16, 2004.

Peru is not a participating country of the OECD Convention on Combating Bribery of Foreign Public Officials in International Business Transactions.

Resources to Report Corruption

Contact at government agency or agencies are responsible for combating corruption:

Sara Arobes
a.i Technical Secretary
High Commission to Fight Corruption (CAN)
Jr. Carabaya Cdra. 1 S/N - Lima,
(51) (1) 219-7000, ext. 7202
sarobes@pcm.gob.pe

Soraya Altabas
Officer of Technical Cooperation
General Comptroller's Office
Jr. Camilo Carrillo 114, Jesus Maria, Lima
(51) (1) 330-3000, ext.
faltabas@contraloria.gob.pe

Contact at "watchdog" organization (international, regional, local or nongovernmental organization operating in the country/economy that monitors corruption, such as Transparency International):

Samuel Rotta
a.i Executive Director
ProEtica, the Peruvian chapter of Transparency International
Calle Manco Capac 816, Miraflores, Lima
(51) (1) 446-8581, 446-8941, 446-8943
srotta@proetica.org.pe

14. BILATERAL INVESTMENT AGREEMENTS

The United States-Peru Trade Promotion Agreement (PTPA) eliminated the need for a bilateral investment agreement between the United States and Peru. Peru also has free trade agreements with Canada, Chile, China, Colombia, Costa Rica, the European Free Trade Association (which includes Iceland, Liechtenstein, Norway and Switzerland), Japan, Mexico, Panama, Singapore, South Korea, and Thailand. It has Framework Agreements with MERCOSUR countries (Argentina, Brazil, Paraguay, Uruguay, and Venezuela). It has a partial preferential agreement with Cuba. More agreements have been signed and are awaiting full implementation, including with Guatemala, and the Pacific Alliance (Mexico, Colombia, Chile, and Costa Rica).

Peru has bilateral investment agreements in force with Argentina, Bolivia, Canada, Chile, China, Colombia, Costa Rica, Czech Republic, Denmark, Ecuador, El Salvador, Finland, Italy, Korea, Netherlands, Norway, Paraguay, Portugal, Romania, Spain, Sweden, Switzerland, Thailand, United Kingdom, Venezuela, and the European Union.

Bilateral Taxation Treaties

Peru does not have a bilateral taxation treaty with the U.S.

15. OPIC AND OTHER INVESTMENT INSURANCE PROGRAMS

The Overseas Private Investment Corporation (OPIC), an independent U.S. Government agency, offers medium-to-long-term financing and political risk insurance. From 2010 thru 2014, OPIC supported solar power plants, consumer lending, operation and expansion of retail stores, microfinance, installation/operation of stereotactic radiosurgery equipment, consulting services, export services, import-export logistical services, and portfolio expansion of SME, micro-credit and consumer loans, in the form of commitments totaling more than USD 21 million.

Because of the free convertibility of currency, the U.S. Embassy purchases Peruvian currency for expenses on an as-needed basis at the market exchange rate. The USD averaged PEN 2.84/USD in 2014. Peru is a member of the Multilateral Investment Guarantee Agency.

It is unlikely that the GOP would either devalue or revalue the Nuevo Sol. The foreign exchange market mostly operates freely. However, the Peruvian BCR intervenes in the foreign exchange market to prevent significant exchange rate variations – at times day after day. To many observers, this regime has succeeded in avoiding traumatic foreign exchange adjustments to the economy.

16. LABOR

Labor is abundant, although several large investment projects in recent years led to localized shortages of highly skilled workers in some fields. While the legal framework to uphold international labor standards is well-defined, the government did not effectively enforce the law in all cases.

Mining sector contacts praise the technical knowledge and professional dedication of Peruvian engineering graduates. Since the 1960s, the number of jobs created by the Peruvian economy was consistently below the number of new entrants to the labor market. The situation meant underemployment or seeking work in the informal economy. According to the National Bureau for Statistics (INEI), 74.3% of the labor force is informal.

The statutory monthly minimum wage is PEN 750/month (approximately USD 242). INEI estimated the poverty line to be PEN 292/month (USD 92) per person, although it varied by region due to different living costs. The Ministry of Labor (MOL) enforces the minimum wage only in the formal sector. Many workers in the unregulated informal sector, most of them self-employed, make less than the minimum wage. Wages are sometimes higher than U.S. wages in the mining sector for management positions and consulting services. Workers in Peru are paid by the month, not by the year. Some workers, like formal miners, are highly paid and also (per statute) receive a share of company profits up to a maximum total annual amount of 18 times their base monthly salary. Current labor law provides for a 48-hour work week and one day of rest, and requires companies to pay overtime for more than eight hours of work per day and additional compensation for work at night. Noncompliance with the law is a punishable infraction. There is no prohibition on excessive compulsory overtime. Micro-enterprise workers are entitled to social security and pensions.

Peruvian labor law requires that employees provide advance notice to the MOL before holding a strike, with the new legislation not being as permissive as before. According to the MOL, 95 strikes took place in the private sector in 2014, just 1.1% above 2013, but person-hours lost almost doubled, for a total of 3.153 million work hours. Unions in what the government determines are "essential public services" are permitted to call a strike but must provide 10 working days' notice, receive the approval of the MOL, be approved by a simple majority of workers, and provide a sufficient number of workers during a strike to maintain operations, as jointly determined by the union and labor authorities on an annual basis. As of September 2014, the MOL registered 53 total strikes during 2014, 48 of which were declared illegal. According to labor leaders permission to strike was difficult to obtain. The MOL justified its decisions by citing failure of unions to fulfill the legal requirements necessary to strike.

The labor procedure (No.29497) law requires that labor conflicts be resolved in less than six months, allows unions or their representatives to appear in court on behalf of workers, requires proceedings to be conducted orally and video-recorded, and relieves the employee from the burden of proving an employer-employee relationship. At year's end, the labor procedure law was in effect in at least 25 of the 31 judicial districts in Peru.

July 2014 labor reforms to the Occupational Safety and Health (OSH) Law and inspection law allow employers to outsource the management of health and safety to third-party service providers. Employers are now responsible for conducting one health exam every two years, rather than every year, which labor NGOs and unions were concerned leaves short-term contracted workers exposed to industrial illness. These reforms narrow the justification for a criminal penalty to only those cases where employers have "deliberately" violated safety and health laws and where labor authorities have previously notified employers who have chosen not to adopt measures in response to a repeated infraction. Labor experts and NGOs expressed concern about what they considered an unreasonably high threshold for holding employers accountable for workplace injuries and for not maintaining health and safety standards. The law reduces the sentence for employers found guilty of health and safety violations from four-to-eight years' to one-to-four years' imprisonment. In the case of a serious or fatal accident where a worker is found to be solely responsible for noncompliance with OSH rules, the employer is exempted from responsibility.

Six percent of the labor force in the private sector was organized in 2014, with unionization highest in electricity, water, construction, and mining (from 39% to 22%) and generally low in the rest of economy. Unemployment in Lima officially stood at 6.9%% during the first quarter of 2014. A 2012 GOP survey showed that 41.1% of Lima's labor force was underemployed in the same period (versus 58.3% in the same period of 2011). The average nominal monthly salary increased 8.0% year-on-year in the fourth quarter of 2013, INEI reported. The ILO's Global Wage Report 2012/2013 released in December 2012 stated that average real wages in Peru grew at over 3% per annum between 2004 and 2011.

The law forbids businesses from hiring subcontracted workers as a simple provision of personnel, requires businesses to monitor their contractors with respect to labor rights, and imposes liability on businesses for the actions of their contractors, and created a national registry of contracting companies. The PTPA requires Peru to adopt and maintain fundamental labor rights as stated in the ILO Declaration on Fundamental Principles and Rights at Work. In January 2010, the GOP and U.S. Government established the bilateral Labor Affairs Council as mandated in Article 17.5 of the PTPA.

According to labor leaders, the current labor law has weakened unions in part because companies create competing unions that are seen as more favorable to management. Workers in probation status or on short-term contracts are not eligible for union membership. Bargaining agreements are considered contractual agreements, valid only for the life of the contract. Productivity provisions must be included in any collective bargaining agreement. The amount of time union officials may devote to union work is limited to 30 days per year. Unless there is a pre-existing labor contract covering an occupation or industry as a whole, unions must negotiate with each company individually.

The government did not effectively enforce the law in all cases. Penalties for violations of freedom of association and collective bargaining exist, but were rarely enforced. Workers faced prolonged judicial processes and lack of enforcement following trade union activity-related dismissals. For instance, NGOs reported that emblematic cases of labor arbitration dating from 2013 remained in limbo, with the implementation of arbitrators' decisions delayed by ongoing judicial appeals processes.

In practice, workers faced some challenges in exercising their rights of freedom of association and collective bargaining. Unions were generally independent of government and political parties. Employers continued to dismiss workers for exercising the right to strike. Dismissal of striking workers and delays in reinstatement of these workers, in both legal and illegal strikes, was the main tactic used by employers to dissuade workers from going on strike. Labor leaders and the ILO argue that current labor laws erode labor protections and encourage outsourcing in ways that undercut union activity.

Either unions or management can request binding arbitration in contract negotiations. Strikes can be called only after approval by a majority of all workers (union and non-union), voting by secret ballot, and only in defense of labor rights. Unions in essential public services, as determined by the government, must provide a sufficient number of workers during a strike to maintain operations.

The government created in April 2014 the National Labor Superintendence (SUNAFIL, for its Spanish acronym) and opened nine regional offices to represent the labor inspectorate nationally.

All labor in the (very small) export processing zones (EPZs) is subcontracted. With the exception of enjoying greater flexibility in hiring temporary labor, there are no special laws or exemptions from regular labor laws in EPZs.

Foreign employees may not comprise more than 20% of the total number of employees of a local company (whether owned by foreign or Peruvian persons) or more than 30% of the total company payroll. However, under the PTPA, Peru has agreed not to apply most of its nationality-based hiring requirements to U.S. professionals and specialty personnel. Peru also has bilateral agreements with Spain and Argentina, for example, so that Spaniards and Argentines working in Peru do not count as foreigners and vice versa.

17. FOREIGN TRADE ZONES/FREE PORTS/TRADE FACILITATION

Peruvian law currently covers two types of trade zones: export, transformation, industry, trade and services zones (CETICOS), and a free trade zone (ZOFRATACNA) in Tacna. The rules and tax benefits applying to these zones are the same for foreign and national investors. These zones have failed to attract any sizeable investment, and their importance for Peru's economy is negligible.

CETICOS exist at Ilo, Matarani and Paita. One CETICO is authorized in Loreto department, but is not operational. There is concern that the GOP does not have the proper WTO waivers to validate the CETICOS export requirement. The U.S. automotive industry has expressed a specific concern that U.S. brands are unable to compete with used Japanese vehicles that enter the Peruvian market duty-free through the CETICOS. The Ministry of Transportation and Communications banned the importation of right-hand drive vehicles in 2013, citing environmental and safety concerns. Imports of used cars more than five years old and used buses and trucks more than two years old are prohibited.

18. FOREIGN DIRECT INVESTMENT AND FOREIGN PORTFOLIO INVESTMENT STATISTICS

The stock of foreign direct investment in Peru stood at USD 73.6 billion in December 2013 according to the BCR, up from USD 63.4 billion at the end of 2012. According to the most recent data from the BCR, the largest investors in Peru are the United States, Canada, Spain, and Chile. By industry, the main investment destinations are mining (29%), services (24%), oil and gas (17%), manufacturing (10%), finance (13%), and energy (6%).

U.S. foreign direct investment in Peru amounted to USD 10.9 billion in 2012, a 21.4% increase from 2011, according to the U.S. Department of Commerce Bureau of Economic Analysis. Of that sum, USD 4.1 billion was invested in mining, USD 1 billion in manufacturing, and USD 319 million in wholesale trade.

Major foreign direct investments included Xstrata (Switzerland), Hunt Oil (U.S.), Newmont Mining Corporation (U.S.), BHP Billiton (Australia), Cencosud Internacional Limitada (Chile), Endesa Latinoamericana (Spain), Freeport-McMoRan (U.S.), Golds Fields Corona (South Africa), SN Power Peru (Norway), Compania Minera Latino-Americana (Chile), Sempra Energy (U.S.), Citibank (U.S.), Southern Peru Copper (Mexico), Pluspetrol (Argentina), Scotiabank (Canada), Telefonica (Spain), Repsol (Spain), Gerdau (Brazil), Anglo American (United Kingdom), Invercale (Chile), Asa Iberoamerica (Spain), Fraport AG Frankfurt Airport Services Worldwide (Germany),

Aeropuertos Andinos del Peru (Argentina), Odebrecht (Brazil), and the Falabella Group (Chile). When completed, Glencore-Xstrata's USD 5.2 billion Las Bambas copper mine project in Apurimac will rank as Peru's largest foreign direct investment ever. The multi-year Hunt Oil-led investment is part of a consortium that invested USD 3.8 billion to develop a natural gas liquefaction plant, maritime terminal, and pipeline in southern Peru.

Peru's direct investment abroad amounts to USD 2.1 billion, according to the BCR. Peruvian investment in Chile, Brazil, the United States, and Bolivia comprised the vast majority of Peru's direct investment abroad.

Table 2: Key Macroeconomic Data, U.S. FDI in Host Country/Economy

	Host Country Statistical source*		USG or international statistical source		USG or International Source of Data: BEA; IMF; Eurostat; UNCTAD, Other
Economic Data	Year	Amount	Year	Amount	
Host Country Gross Domestic Product (GDP) ($M USD)	2013	193,214	2013	202,350	www.worldbank.org/en/country
Foreign Direct Investment	Host Country Statistical source*		USG or international statistical source		USG or international Source of data: BEA; IMF; Eurostat; UNCTAD, Other
U.S. FDI in partner country ($M USD, stock positions)	2013	No data	2013	10,061	BEA data available at http://www.bea.gov/iTable/iTable.cfm?ReqID=2&step=1#reqid=2&step=7&isuri=1&202 1&203=30&204=10&205=1,2&200=1&201=1
Host country's FDI in the United States ($M USD, stock positions)	2013	No data	2013	100	BEA data available at http://www.bea.gov/iTable/iTable.cfm?ReqID=2&step=1#reqid=2&step=7&isuri=1&202 1&203=22&204=10&205=1,2&200=2&201=1
Total inbound stock of FDI as % host GDP	2014	No data	2014	No data	N/A

*Peruvian statistical sources: **http://www.mef.gob.pe/index.php?option=com_content&view=article&id=1116&Itemid=100233&lang=es**; **http://elibrary-**

data.imf.org/DataReport.aspx?c=11666795&d=33061&e=171392; http://www.bea.gov/international/di1usdbal.htm

Table 3: Sources and Destination of FDI

(The chart does not reflect committed investment yet to be executed, for example China Minmetals' Las Bambas project.)

Direct Investment from/in Counterpart Economy Data					
From Top Five Sources/To Top Five Destinations (US Dollars, Millions)					
Inward Direct Investment			Outward Direct Investment		
Total Inward	38,841	100%	Total Outward	1,239	100%
United States	9,199	24%	Chile	367	30%
Canada	4,710	12%	United States	267	22%
Spain	3,700	10%	Panama	212	17%
Panama	2,803	7%	Jamaica	194	16%
Cayman Islands	2,590	7%	Bolivia	116	9%
"0" reflects amounts rounded to +/- USD 500,000.					

Source: IMF Coordinated Direct Investment Survey

STARTING AND DOING BUSINESS IN PERU - BASIC INFORMATION AND REGULATIONS

MARKET OVERVIEW

Peru has been one of the fastest growing Latin American economies over the past decade. Between 2003 and 2013 the Peruvian economy grew an average of 6% per year. Though the trend did not continue in 2014, Peru's 2.35% growth was still higher than the 2.0% average growth in Latin America. The government's counter-cyclical stimulus spending, consumption, and private investment are the main driving forces of this growth. Investment grew by 8.3% year-on-year to a value of USD 33.5 billion in 2014. The Ministry of Economy and Finance set a target of 30% growth in public investment, and pledged a total of USD 30 billion over the next five years to address Peru's infrastructure gap, estimated at USD 80 billion. As the economy has grown, poverty in Peru has steadily decreased, falling by half from 56% in 2005 to 23.9% in 2013 according to the World Bank.

Peru's steady economic growth began with the pro-market policies enacted by former President Alberto Fujimori in the 1990's. All subsequent governments have continued these policies, including the current administration inaugurated in July 2011 for a five-year term. President Ollanta Humala pledged to encourage private and public investment in infrastructure projects in transportation, telecommunications, energy, sanitation, airports, and maritime ports. Congruent with his other campaign goals to reduce poverty and narrow the nation's socioeconomic gap, President Humala has increased social spending and raised taxes on mining companies.

Peru's currency, the "Nuevo Sol" (PEN), has been among the least volatile of all Latin American currencies in the past few years, but has depreciated by almost 10% against the USD over 2014.

Since the mid-1990's, the PEN's exchange rate with the USD has fluctuated between 1.25 and 3.55 per USD. The exchange rate, as of June 24, 2015, was 3.15 PEN per USD.

The Government of Peru (GOP) has encouraged integration with the global economy by signing 17 free trade agreements with 52 economies, including the United States-Peru Trade Promotion Agreement (PTPA), which entered into force in February 2009. In 2014, trade between the United States and Peru totaled USD 16.1 billion, up from USD 9.1 billion in 2009 the first year of entry into force. From 2009 to 2014, Peruvian exports to the United States jumped from USD 4.2 billion to USD 6.1 billion (a 45% increase) while U.S. exports to Peru jumped from USD 4.9 billion to USD 10.1 billion (a 106% increase). Peru has preferential trade agreements with 52 countries and unions, including Argentina, Brazil, Bolivia, Chile, China, Colombia, Ecuador, the European Union, Iceland, Japan, South Korea, Lichtenstein, Mexico, Norway, Panama, Paraguay, Singapore, Switzerland, Thailand, the United States, and Uruguay.

In its Doing Business 2015 publication, the World Bank ranked Peru 35th among 189 countries surveyed in terms of ease of doing business. The report rates the ease of processes like starting a business, dealing with construction permits, registering property, and obtaining credit (http://www.doingbusiness.org/data/exploreeconomies/peru/).

MARKET CHALLENGES

Over the past couple of years, Embassy Lima has received multiple complaints from U.S. firms on cumbersome and inconvenient government procurement processes. Furthermore, some ministers within the GOP are more frequently using a government-to-government (G2G) procurement method in both non-defense and defense-related procurements. This presents a challenge for U.S. exporters trying to comply with all of the tender requirements.

Dispute settlement generally remains problematic in Peru. In 2004, the Peruvian Government established commercial courts to rule on business disputes. With their specialized judges, these courts have reduced the amount of time to resolve a case from an average of two years to just two months. The appeals process resolves most of these cases. However, with the exception of the commercial courts, the judicial system is often extremely slow to hear cases and to issue decisions. A large backlog of cases further complicates businesses' operations.

Court rulings and the degree of enforcement are often inconsistent and highly unpredictable. Allegations of political corruption and outside interference in the judicial system are common, a situation that analysts think leads to the judiciary receiving low approval rates in public opinion polls. Frequent use of appellate processes as a delay tactic leads to the belief among foreign investors that contracts can be difficult to enforce in Peru.

While the legal framework for protection of intellectual property (IP) in Peru has improved over the past decade, enforcement mechanisms remain weak. Despite PTPA implementation and recent changes in laws, which created stricter penalties for some types of IP theft, the judicial branch still has yet to vigorously pursue investigations, convictions and stiff penalties for IP violations.

Both domestic and foreign firms continue to identify cumbersome bureaucratic procedures as impediments to doing business in Peru. For example, shipments are regularly held up for various reasons, including typographical errors on shipping documents. Firms operating in Peru also note difficulties in securing legal solutions to commercial disputes or enforcing arbitration awards.

MARKET OPPORTUNITIES

The best prospects for U.S. exports of non-agricultural products to Peru include the following sectors:

- Construction Equipment
- Electronic Commerce
- Food Processing & Packaging Equipment
- Industrial Chemicals
- Medical Equipment
- Mining Industry Equipment
- Plastic Resins
- Security & Safety Equipment

The best prospects for U.S. agricultural products include:

- Beef and Offal
- Biofuels (Ethanol)
- Cotton
- Dairy Products (Whey, Cheese)
- Forest Products
- Hard Wheat
- Pet Food
- Soybean Meal
- Yellow Corn

MARKET ENTRY STRATEGY

U.S. companies often find it convenient to appoint local representatives to investigate market opportunities and establish sales networks. Retention of local legal counsel is often required to successfully navigate Peru's business practices and bureaucracy. U.S. exporters, especially those targeting government agencies, are encouraged to contact the Commercial Service (U.S. Department of Commerce) at the U.S. Embassy in Lima to obtain a market briefing and assistance in arranging appointments during a business trip to Peru, and to learn how the Advocacy Center can support their efforts competing in government tenders. For more information on these services, please refer to http://export.gov/peru/ .

The Foreign Agricultural Service (FAS) (http://www.usdaperu.org.pe/) and U.S. Department of State Economic Section (http://lima.usembassy.gov/econ.html/) can also provide briefings on the economic, financial, and investment climate in Peru.

NEW COMPANIES OR BRANCHES:

Foreign investors and/or companies shall decide if they will operate either through new companies, branches or joint ventures.

Peruvian Legislation recognizes various entrepreneurial forms. Some of them are as follows: corporation, limited liability company, general partnership, noncommercial limited company, limited partnership issuing shares, partnerships and branches.

The Corporation and Branches of foreign companies are the most common form used in Peru, because of the advantages it grants.

A. CORPORATION:

1. Business Name

Corporations may adopt any name; nevertheless, they must include the terms Sociedad Anónima (Corporation) or the main letters S.A.

2. Capital

Capital stock is represented by registered stocks and formed by the shareholders' contributions, who do not support, by themselves, the corporation debts.

Incorporation requires that the capital stock be fully underwritten, and paid up, at least in 25%. There is no minimum capital amount.

3.Shareholders

Shareholders must be at least three individuals or juridical persons, residents or nonresidents.

4.Incorporation

There are two types of incorporation: By one action (Direct Creation) or by successive creation (Public Subscription). In both cases, a Notary is required. Also in both cases, the company's founder shareholders must supply the Notary with the documents necessary to start the incorporation (shareholder's identification documents and a deposit of the capital equity in a peruvian bank)

a) Direct Creation:

The capital stock must be deposited in an account opened with a Peruvian Financial Institution. Once the money has been deposited, the shareholders will draw up the Incorporation Papers, which must be duly countersigned by an attorney; and then submit them to the Notary, who will make a Public Deed for the registration thereof with the Commercial Registry corresponding to the place where it is incorporated.

b) Public Subscription:

The founder shareholders shall draw up a foundation program, which will be submitted to the notary, for the authentication of their signatures. Once the signatures have been certified, the program must be deposited in the Commercial Registry to be further published in order to find potential subscribers. A meeting of subscribers must be held within six months as from the date in which the program was deposited in the Commercial Registry. Within the thirty days following the meeting, the appointed person or persons shall provide for the company's Incorporation Public Deed, which shall be registered with the Commercial Registry where the company is addressed.

5. Setup Costs:

The expenditures involved in the incorporation are the following:

- Notary's expenses, calculated on the total capital stock and the length of the Public Deed.

- Registration Expenses, the rate to be paid is the 3/1000 of the capital stock.

- Other expenses, include the registration of the appointment of Directors and attorney's fees, etc.

6. Corporation's Term

Unless otherwise specified in the articles of association, the corporation term is unlimited.

7.Contributions

These can be made in national and/or foreign currency; or, in physical or tangible goods. It is also allowed intangible technological contributions, which can adopt the form of physical goods, technical papers and instructions, in order to be appraised. Non-money contribution shall be duly evaluated.

8. Company's Bodies:

8.1. General Meeting of Shareholders, is the meeting duly called to decide on inherent matters thereof. This body decides by majority, taking into consideration the proportion to the total capital equity. This is the maximum body of the company.

Meetings may be Special or Regular.

8.2. Board of Directors, it is elected by the General Meeting of Shareholders. This appointment must be registered with the Commercial Registry of the place where the company is domiciled. To become a Director, it is not necessary to be shareholder, unless the by-laws specify so. There is no residence or nationality requirement. The number of directors shall be fixed by the by-laws, or, otherwise, by the General Meeting. The Board of Directors is empowered with legal and management representation, necessary for the administration of the company, within its purpose.

The Board of Directors must prepare, in a maximum term of 180 days, counted as from the end of the fiscal year, the balance sheet with the profit and loss account, proposal of profit allocation and the annual report. The aforementioned documents shall establish, in a clear and exactly way, the partnership assets, gained profits or suffered losses and the state of its business.

8.3. Management: The manager is appointed by the Board of Directors, except the by-laws empower the General Meeting therefor. More than one manager may exist, if the by-laws or the General Meeting establish so. The term of post is unlimited, except the by-laws establish otherwise or the appointment has been made for specific term. Manager's duties are set forth in the by-laws, or at the time of the appointment; otherwise, it is assumed that the manager is empowered to perform acts and execute contracts inherent to the corporate business.

9. Accounting Requirements

Companies shall keep accounting books, considered as main books, which shall be in Spanish and in national currency, unless the company is expressly authorized to keep it in foreign currency, because it receives or makes foreign investments; provided that the company contracts with the State or with Public
Enterprises or Institutions. The taxable base shall be determined in foreign currency; nevertheless, the payment of the corresponding taxes shall be made in national currency at the current exchange rate. The main accounting books are:

Stock Book
Trial-Balance Book
Day-Book
Ledger
Wages and Salaries Payroll Book
Minute Book

For using the mentioned books, the certification by a Notary Public is required. The payroll book shall be certified with the Ministry of Labor and Social Promotion.

10. Profits

Dividends on shares can be paid only from real gained profits or free-availability reserves, provided that the asset value is not under the total share capital. Dividends allocation between the shareholders will be made in proportion to the amounts paid and the time of integration to the capital stock.

B. BRANCHES:

Foreign companies may freely set up branches in Peru, which shall be recorded with the register where these operate. For purposes of formalities, the registration must include the indicated address in Peru; capital appointed or assigned for the branch; appointment and powers of its legal representative in the country; branch's business line, including the business and operations it is engaged in; and the contract or equivalent document governing the branch in its main place. The certificate, proving the existence and force of the company, from the competent authority duly certified by the Peruvian Consular Representative; a document stating the power of the company to set up branches in other countries; and, the company's resolution to set up a branch in Peru shall be also included.

The legal representative appointed in Peru shall have enough powers to solve any matter related to the company's activities; to involve the company in transactions it carries out; to appear in court; and to answer to a claim.

II. JOINT VENTURE AND PARTNERSHIPS

Joint Ventures and Partnerships are contracts concluded by the parties, which do not require their registration with the Commercial Registry. These have no corporate existence, nor corporate's name. Resources destined to the aforementioned contracts shall be considered as Direct Foreign Investment,
provided that these grant foreign investors participation in the installed capacity, not involving necessarily capital contribution. Besides, these contracts shall correspond to contractual commercial transactions through which the foreign investor provides goods or services to the receiving enterprise in exchange of participation in the volume of the physical production, in the aggregate amount or in the net profits of the enterprise which receives the investment.

III.ADMINISTRATIVE FORMALITIES

In addition to the legal requirements mentioned above, certain formalities must be completed by foreign companies wishing to establish new companies or branches.

A. TAX CARD OR UNIQUE REGISTRY OF TAXPAYER (URT):

In accordance with the legislation thereon, the Superintendencia Nacional de Administración Tributaria - SUNAT - (National Superintendency of Tax Administration) has, among its duties, the taxpayers' registration providing them the respective certificate proving its registration with the Unique Registry of
Taxpayer.

The following papers must be submitted:

Incorporation Documents of the company, or branch, prior registered with the notary. Format given by the SUNAT.

B. REGISTRATION OF FOREIGN INVESTMENT

Foreign investment destined to the capital of a company shall be registered with the Comisión Nacional de Inversiones y Tecnologías Extranjeras - CONITE - (National Commission on Foreign Investments and Technologies).

Foreign investments contractually formalized with Peruvian enterprises, including joint ventures and any other form of partnerships, shall be also registered with CONITE.

For purposes of registration with CONITE, an application shall be submitted along with the following documents:

1) In freely convertible currency:

In cases of incorporation of companies; investments physically placed in the country; contracts of partnerships or similar, a copy of the document proving the entrance of foreign currency through the National Financial System must be enclosed. Such copy shall include the remitter's business name against an open account in a bank and/or financial entity abroad in the name of the receiving
enterprise. In case of contributions destined to the incorporation of enterprises, the remittance may be drawn in the name of the authorized representative or attorney of the investor, duly certified.

2) Contributions product of the capitalization of the private obligations with abroad:

The existence of outstanding obligations shall be proved by the submission of the copy of the respective accounting documents.

3) In physical or tangible goods:

Including the case of contracts of partnerships or similar, a copy of the commercial invoice, free of charge, and the customs import document issued by the corresponding Customs Administration shall be enclosed.

4) In technological intangible contributions:

A copy of the certificate of registry of the trademark, patent or any other element of industrial property, issued by the Instituto Nacional de Defensa de la Competencia y Proteccion a la Propiedad Intelectual (INDECOPI) proving the concession, in force, of the right in the investor's name and the copy of the
Minutes of the Board of Directors or Board of Shareholders, where states the confirmation of the valorization made, or copy of the corresponding contract, in case of associations in participations or similar.

5) In case of contributions in national currency with right of remittance, for the concept of profits, dividends, royalties or any other type of amounts due:

The availability of funds with right of remittance shall be proved with the copy of the respective accounting documents. Besides, in the case of royalties, the copy of the resolution of registration of the contract generating the obligation shall be submitted to the national competent agency.

For all the cases, the following papers shall be also enclosed:

Copy of the Incorporation Public Deed of the new company or branch, with the proof of registration in the respective Registry.
Copy of the capitalization bookkeeping entry.

In case of contracting joint ventures a copy of the corresponding contract shall be enclosed.

C. UNIFIED REGISTRY

Any person or corporate body, of any economic sector, proposing to engage in any commercial, industrial or any other activities shall be registered with the Unified Registry.

The following papers shall be submitted for the registration:

Format of the Unified Register, duly filled out (this format is available at the Banco de la Nación).
Copy of the Incorporation Public Deed with proof of its reception at the Notary's office.
Payroll Book.

D. MUNICIPAL LICENSE FOR OPERATION

It is required to operate commercially. It is applied for to the Municipality of the jurisdiction where the company is located

SELLING U.S. PRODUCTS AND SERVICES

USING AN AGENT OR DISTRIBUTOR

Peruvian law does not require the use of local distributors for private sector commercial sales. However, for sales to the government, it is recommended that U.S. companies contract and register a local agent. (See "Selling to the Government" later in this chapter.) Exporters to Peru often find it advantageous to have a representative on the ground to stay abreast of the latest opportunities and developments in the company's area of interest.

The Commercial Service in Lima recommends companies to be thorough when selecting an agent or representative in Peru. U.S. companies are encouraged to take advantage of U.S. Department of Commerce services by contacting the local Export Assistance Center (EAC) located in major cities throughout the United States, including Alaska and Hawaii. Services include the International Partner Search (IPS), which helps to pinpoint interested agents and distributors, the Gold Key Service (GKS), which arranges meetings in-country with potential company representatives (agents or distributors), and the International Company Profile (ICP), which reports on the credit and business history of individual local companies. For detailed information, refer to Chapter 10: Guide to Our Services.

ESTABLISHING AN OFFICE

It is essential for companies planning to operate in Peru to retain reputable legal counsel. Law firms are referred to as "Estudios" and attorneys as "Doctor" or "Doctora" followed by their last name. An attorney should be proficient in matters concerning taxes on corporate and branch income, corporate residence, value-added taxes, income determination, capital gains, inter-company dividends/pricing, stock dividends, depreciation and depletion, net operating losses (tax losses), and payments to foreign affiliates. Other significant issues to consider include workers' benefits, payroll and withholding taxes, municipal operating permits, and labor laws that will impact the business when it starts operations. Many U.S. companies retain the local representative of their U.S.-based auditor. A partial list of local lawyers and/or tax and audit firms can be found in this chapter.

Foreign corporations interested in doing business in Peru on a permanent basis must be formally incorporated and registered in the Peruvian Mercantile Registry (Registro Mercantil del Perú). Real estate may be acquired by any foreign entity without the need to establish an office. There are two main types of business organizations that can be used for these purposes: branch offices and incorporated subsidiaries. It is only necessary to vest a local individual with sufficient powers to conduct and close the sale.

Office space suitable for international companies has substantially increased in the last ten years in several neighborhoods of Lima. The price of rent for newly built offices has increased, partly the consequence of numerous foreign companies setting up shop in Peru. Because of the still ongoing housing boom, with fine dwellings built in Lima's residential areas, it is easier for foreign managerial staff to relocate to Peru. The situation in several other cities outside of the capital is more and more similar to that of Lima.

Industrial space is scarce in or close to Lima. New operations have thus had to accept areas in the southern and eastern outskirts of Lima.

ESTABLISHING A BRANCH

To establish a branch, the following documents will be required:

• Copy of the articles of incorporation of the parent company.

• Certificate of incorporation and good standing or other official document certifying the existence and continuous operation of the parent company. This certificate must state that the parent company is not prohibited, either by law or by its own by-laws, from establishing branches abroad. If such a statement cannot be included in the certificate, then a Notary Public may do so in a separate document.

• Copy of the minutes of the board of directors' meeting where the resolution to establish a branch in Peru appears. This resolution should specify:

o The domicile in Peru.

o Duration of the branch (may be indefinite) and the commencement of operations.

o The purpose of the branch, clearly specifying the business and operations that will be conducted in Peru, stating that said purpose is comprised in the parent company's purpose.

o Name of person(s) authorized to act in the registration of the branch and in its representation, and powers vested in him/her, which must include powers to resolve any issue related to the branch activities; to hold the corporation liable for its operations; to appear in court; and to respond to suits brought against it. The holder of the parent corporation's power of attorney, duly registered, directs the branch. The parent corporation can revoke such power anytime.

o There is no requirement for the parent company to submit its financial statements to Peruvian authorities.

A Notary Public or appropriate government official in the country of incorporation must legalize all documents granted abroad. A local Peruvian Consul must then authenticate the signatures of the Notary or the government official. The documents should be in Spanish, and if not, must be translated by an authorized translator. Upon receipt, the signature of the Peruvian consul must be legalized in the Ministry of Foreign Affairs (MFA).

Registration fees are as follows:

• Registration fee: approximately 0.3% of the assigned capital with a maximum of approximately US$1,400.

• Translation fees: between US$10 and US$12 per page.

• Legalization at the MFA: US$20 per document.

• Notary and legal fees: widely variable rates.

Once residence or domicile can be demonstrated, the foreign company must obtain a taxpayer number (Registro Unico del Contribuyente, "RUC"). The taxpayer will use its (or his or her personal) RUC number in all commercial transactions, similar to the federal tax identification number (EIN) in the United States.

INCORPORATING A SUBSIDIARY

The corporation is the most common form for establishing a business entity in Peru. A minimum of two shareholders is required. One hundred percent foreign ownership of an investment is allowed, except for a limited number of restricted activities (see "Chapter 6: Investment Climate, Openness to Foreign Investment").

To comply with the rules of incorporation of a subsidiary, various documents will be required.

If participating shareholders are foreign individuals, they need only present valid identification (passport), but for corporations participating as shareholders the following documents must be filed:

- Certificate of Good Standing
- Copy of the minutes of the board of directors' meeting where the resolution to participate in the incorporation of a Peruvian company appears. This resolution should indicate the name of the person appointed as representative to act on behalf of the shareholders in all the incorporation procedures.

No minimum capital is required.

The Business Corporation Law regulates three forms of corporation:

- Common corporation (SA: Sociedad Anónima)
- Closed corporation (SAC: Sociedad Anónima Cerrada)
- Open corporation (SAA: Sociedad Anónima Abierta)

CLOSED CORPORATION

The closed corporation (SAC) must have a minimum of two and a maximum of 20 shareholders. The shareholders and chief executive officer manage the SAC. Unlike a common corporation (SA), an SAC board of directors is optional. In case of transfer of shares, the law stipulates a right of first refusal for the existing shareholders, but company by-laws may eliminate this right.

OPEN CORPORATION

The open corporation (SAA) does not limit the maximum number of shareholders and is intended for companies making public offerings. No limitations are allowed for the transfer of shares. Peru's Exchange and Securities Supervisory agency (Superintendencia del Mercado de Valores, SMV) supervises open corporations.

The above types are limited liability corporations (LLC). Another LLC business structure is the Sociedad Comercial de Responsabilidad Limitada: a legal entity different from its owners, who can be either individuals or corporations. The liability of the partners is limited to the amount of their contribution. As with a typical closed corporation, the minimum number of partners is two and the maximum is 20. However, in this organization a transfer of shares to third parties is subject to approval by the existing partners—right of first refusal is mandatory—and must be registered in the Public Records Office. The name of the company must include the abbreviation "S.R. Ltda."

For more information on setting up a company in Peru, visit the following web pages of the Private Investment Promotion Agency of Peru (ProInversión) and the MFA.

http://www.investinperu.pe/modulos/JER/PlantillaStandard.aspx?are=1&prf=0&jer=5761&sec=17

http://www.rree.gob.pe/promocioneconomica/invierta/Paginas/Comience_a_Invertir.aspx (in Spanish)

http://www.rree.gob.pe/promocioneconomica/invierta/Documents/Peru_Business_and_Investment_Guide_2015_2016.pdf

All potential investors should contact an attorney and/or an accounting firm to understand the legal framework for investment protection established by the Foreign Investment Promotion Law, the Framework Law for Private Investment, the Law for the Promotion of Private Investment in State-Owned Companies, and the Law for the Promotion of Private Investment in Public Utility Facilities.

In the event of a commercial dispute, national or international arbitration may be used, but only if this is agreed to by the parties in an agreement or contract before the dispute arises. Arbitration cannot be imposed unilaterally after the fact as a means to resolve controversies or disputes. Please contact FCS Lima to discuss arbitration venue options. The American Chamber of Commerce in Peru (AmCham) and Lima Chamber of Commerce (CCL) maintain a fully staffed arbitration center open to members and non-members.

FRANCHISING

The franchise sector in Peru encompasses approximately 375 companies, primarily concentrated in food services. About 52% are foreign owned, mostly by U.S. companies (22%), and 48% are Peruvian. Experts report that the sector is growing and presently moves USD$ 1.2 million in one year.

There is no specific legislation to govern franchising, although franchises in Peru are subject to general commercial law, general antitrust law, and Decisions 486, 608, and 291 of the Andean Community. According to articles 162 through 164 of Decision 486, a written license agreement must be registered at the patents and trademarks office (INDECOPI: www.indecopi.gob.pe). Prospective franchisers need to be aware of a 30% income tax on royalties, 18% value added tax (paid by the local company), and import tariffs depending on the type of goods. Countries that have signed double taxation agreements with Peru have separate regimes for royalties and withholding income tax (the U.S. is not included).

Promising sectors apart from food services are:

• Aesthetics, beauty and health (beauty salons, spas, gyms)

• Clothing and accessories (clothing, footwear, jewelry, costume jewelry, gifts)

• Specialized services (entertainment, playgrounds, etc.)

• Education (high schools, universities)

DIRECT MARKETING

Direct marketing is well established in Peru in the services sector, especially among financial institutions and seminar organizers. A common practice is to hire personnel or to contract a company for telemarketing and mailing campaigns. Databases for direct marketing are kept private by its owners and thus are not freely available. Nevertheless, commercial information can be obtained through Peru's Chambers of Commerce and trade associations (See Chapter 10: Contacts, Market Research and Trade Events). Several call centers providing support to the U.S. or other Latin countries are operating in Peru as well.

Catalog sales for consumer goods in Peru remain small because consumers prefer to personally visit the retail location to determine the quality of the product and ease of obtaining warranty support. Additionally, consumers find parcel delivery through Peru's postal system unsatisfactory. Courier companies are taking advantage of this opportunity to promote their services.

JOINT VENTURES/LICENSING

Peruvian law allows for joint ventures and licensing agreements with a legally established local partner who will be accountable for all legal matters. The textile manufacturing industry in particular has attracted a great deal of licensing and joint venture activity.

SELLING TO THE GOVERNMENT

To sell to the Peruvian government, interested suppliers have to participate in a tender process, for which they must register with the National Registry of Suppliers (Registro Nacional de Proveedores, or RNP: http://portal.osce.gob.pe/osce/node/386 , in Spanish only). The RNP consists of the following chapters: construction firms, construction consultants, suppliers of goods and services, and unqualified suppliers to the government. An individual or a company can register in any of the first three chapters and can choose to register jointly as a goods and services provider.

To register, a company must follow several steps (Spanish, http://portal.osce.gob.pe/osce/content/guia-de-como-venderle-al-estado):

• Pay a fee (which is revised annually) at the Government Procurement Supervisory Agency (Organismo Supervisor de las Contrataciones del Estado, OSCE) of about $79 for suppliers of goods and/or services or about $124 for construction firms or construction consultants.

• After obtaining the User Kit provided by OSCE once the fee is paid, file the official form (available at www.osce.gob.pe) signed by the legal representative.

• The legal representative must have its powers registered with the Peruvian Public Registry. If the powers of the legal representative are not registered, this can be done within 15 working days. Provide a copy of the incorporation deed or documents that demonstrate the company's legal establishment/status, duly apostilled. The documents need to be translated into Spanish by an official Peruvian interpreter.

Peruvian law permits an independent distributor to pay commissions or fees to third parties in connection with sales to the government. For example, a company in Peru can purchase products from a company in the United States and then pay a third party fee to resell them to the Peruvian government. There are no Peruvian restrictions on commissions or mark-ups on sales to the government by either agents or distributors and the rates vary widely depending on product, client, and competition.

Government agencies must publish tender notices for all major purchases in the official gazette, while sometimes they also publish tenders in main local newspapers. The government, in an effort to ensure transparency for some government tenders, has been using the United Nations Office for Project Service (http://www.unops.org/) to notify potential suppliers or to handle some bids, but this method apparently does not allow screening by the General Controller Agency and has thus fielded criticism. Peru is not a signatory to the World Trade Organization (WTO) Agreement on Government Procurement. The United States-Peru Trade Promotion Agreement (PTPA) includes a specific chapter on Government Procurement ("Contratación Pública" in Spanish).

Selling to government agencies remains problematic in spite of PTPA's stipulations. In December 2007, the Garcia Administration requested Congressional authority to pass legislation on various matters in order to implement PTPA so that Peru could make the most of it, expressly including government purchases among those matters. Congress quickly consented to the request and Peru's Government passed Legislative Decree No. 1017 (LD 1017), Government Procurement Law (Ley de Contrataciones del Estado). This law requires public tenders for major purchases of goods, supplies and works by government agencies (including the Armed Forces and the National Police). On the other hand, the Peruvian armed forces and national police have long shown a preference to make deals directly, shunning open tenders. In July 2012, the Defense Ministry enlisted the support of OSCE which, with an implausible opinion, left out private companies from bidding for major purchases through a so called "government to government" procurement (i.e., purchases by a Peruvian government agency from a foreign government agency or government-owned company). The Defense and Interior Ministries used OSCE's opinion to pass a number of legal precepts on which they based several of their main procurement contracts since then. Further, an article hidden in the 2013 Budget Law (Thirty Final Supplementary Provision) specified that procurements of the Peruvian State from another State are not under the scope of LD 1017.

Among the reasons for its opinion (see Web Resources below), OSCE stated that government to government contracts due to their own character and the nature of the contracting parties (sovereign states) are different from the "administrative contracts" (those in which the parties are a government and a private party). OSCE implausibly argued that the government entity, acting in exercise of the administrative function and protecting public interest, can unilaterally modify contracts. This is in blatant contradiction with Peru's 1993 Constitution, Article 62, which establishes that "Contractual terms may not be modified by laws or any other provision whatsoever". Furthermore, even though the parties are sovereign states, OSCE acknowledged that "government-to-government procurement" is at least subject to each contracting State's public law rules, the rules of international law and the international trade rules.

In the last few years, local media have reported denunciations of overvalued prices in the case of several government-to-government purchases of goods for the police or the armed forces. Cases include purchases of a satellite, planes, and helicopters. Overvaluation has apparently occurred even in the case of open tenders as in the notorious recent case of the purchase of 591 binoculars by the Interior Ministry for the National Police in December 2013. The main local daily El Comercio denounced that the Interior Ministry bought the 591 binoculars at the grossly overvalued price of about

$1,736 each, whereas the daily found similar binoculars at about $121 each. In early February 2014, the Interior Ministry announced it had annulled the purchase, implying that it annulled the purchase before the daily's denouncement, but the daily proved that that was not the case. The preference of the Ministry of Defense and Ministry of Interior to pursue government-to-government deals continues to today, however the establishment of a new centralized procurement system by the Ministry of Defense for the Armed Forces should lead to positive changes in their purchasing practices.

DISTRIBUTION AND SALES CHANNELS

The population of Peru is highly centralized, with 30% of all inhabitants living in the capital city of Lima, 50% of GDP generated in and around Lima, and the national government being the main government buyer. As a result, a large portion of the sales activities of U.S. firms occurs in Lima. Sales opportunities do exist and are growing in other major population centers such as Arequipa, Chiclayo, and Trujillo. This could be a consideration for a U.S. company's overall marketing strategy. Representatives in Lima typically have sales agents in these cities, covering sales opportunities in the provinces. Sending letters via express delivery can take up to two weeks and for packages longer due to lengthy holding procedures by Peruvian customs.

The most common method of distribution is the appointment of a representative. Appointing an agent or distributor is advisable for companies seeking to develop a market on a sustained basis.

The Government of Peru has embarked upon an initiative to decentralize some elements of government authority and decision-making, including implementation of spending programs utilizing the "canon," a revenue-sharing scheme of taxes imposed on some extractive industries. This increase in regional authority is an important consideration when contemplating a local representative outside of Lima. Decentralization of government budgeting and spending authority can also make completing sales more challenging, especially in municipalities or provinces where government agencies may have limited experience in designing and implementing major projects or lack of financial and procurement expertise.

An alternative approach to distribution is to establish a local subsidiary or branch office. Companies with a complicated product or service use this method because it allows for effective after-sales service and more aggressive promotion of a product. Costs of commercial and industrial space are relatively high in the Lima area and in several main cities.

SELLING FACTORS/TECHNIQUES

Product pricing is a key selling factor in the Peruvian market. Products from Asian economies such as China, Taiwan, and Korea often outsell more expensive European or North American consumer products in the realm of consumer electronics, appliances and automobiles. Knockoffs and pirated goods are problematic as well. However, with investment in sales promotion and post-sales service infrastructure, U.S. goods can be competitive.

Equipment performance and efficiency influence the decision-maker when purchasing capital goods, notably advanced electronics and construction machinery. The customer often prefers more expensive U.S. or European products, which are highly rated for quality, durability, technology, customer support, and regional service.

Many of the larger representatives have regional offices in other cities outside of Lima. The rest of Peru is largely under-populated and underdeveloped and does not offer an attractive market for technical equipment, with certain exceptions, such as the large-scale mining operations located along Peru's Andes mountain range and petroleum operations in the Amazon jungle.

Payment for major purchases is generally on a net 30-day basis. For new market entrants or when dealing with new customers, it is advisable to request up-front payment or work on a confirmed, irrevocable letter of credit basis. Over the counter purchases are done in cash (U.S. dollars are widely accepted), wire transfer, or credit card. Most retailers use credit terms as a sales technique and major department stores issue their own credit cards. U.S. exporters are encouraged to explore the programs and services offered by the Export-Import Bank of the U.S. (www.exim.gov) to enhance the credit terms offered to Peruvian buyers.

ELECTRONIC COMMERCE

The Peruvian E-commerce market is small and developing slowly compared to international standards. Business-to-Business (B2B) commerce is mostly conducted between large enterprises with the percentage of transactions growing modestly. These companies use B2B as a commercial practice to cut operational costs. Many medium-size firms do not clearly understand the real importance of electronic B2B and Business-to-Consumers (B2C) solutions. They focus mostly on cost reduction instead of enhancing their distribution channels or developing new products or services that improve their overall reach.

The following is a list of successful firms considered to be local benchmarks in Peruvian E-commerce solutions:

a) http://peru.com/ A popular web portal.

b) http://www.rosatel.com/ Rosatel allows online orders of flowers and gift baskets.

c) All banks (e.g., http://www.viabcp.com, http://www.bbvabancocontinental.com) and most financial institutions have websites to provide clients with services such as paying utility bills, obtaining insurance coverage, internet shopping and information. Transactions are made with debit or credit cards such as Visa, Mastercard or American Express (Amex).

d) http://www.wong.com.pe Wong is Peru's largest supermarket chain. This website allows the company to receive and pay for orders via the internet from local and foreign-based consumers for local delivery.

e) Telecommunications industry firms have websites and portals to interact with the market in a variety of services, ranging from refilling pre-paid telephone cards to sending direct marketing SMS messages to target market segments (e.g., http://www.movistar.com.pe , http://www.claro.com.pe).

There have been interesting advances in the use of the internet in several Peruvian government institutions such as the tax collecting agency, SUNAT (http://www.sunat.gob.pe); the public registry, SUNARP (http://www.sunarp.gob.pe); and the Peruvian state-owned bank, Banco de la Nación, which handles the Treasury accounts (http://www.bn.com.pe). The National Elections Bureau, ONPE (http://www.onpe.gob.pe) is testing electronic voting and has also improved internet usage.

The Peruvian government has established a special task force under the name of E-Gob Peru managed by the National Office of E-Government and Information Technology (ONGEI: http://www.ongei.gob.pe/), under the President of the Council of Ministers. This office is seeking to continuously develop Gov2Citizens solutions for tax payment and information on customs and foreign trade (http://www.sunat.gob.pe/) as well as Gov2Gov transactions as a means to reduce expenses within the different agencies. Operational services include a citizens' IDs service portal (http://www.reniec.gob.pe/), and business-assistance services for small and medium-size companies (http://www.crecemype.pe/). The Peruvian government is also implementing an Electronic Procurement System (SEACE: Sistema Electrónico de Adquisiciones y Contrataciones del Estado). The principal stated objectives of this electronic system are to improve the transparency and the efficient operation of government purchases.

There is no Public Key Infrastructure (PKI) in Peru yet, but digital signatures are widely used for tax declarations (more than one million users). Transactions are made through electronic funds transfer and Banco de la Nación has created a secure platform for online transactions. The Antitrust, Unfair Competition, Intellectual Property Protection, Consumer Protection, Dumping, Standards and Elimination of Bureaucratic Barriers Agency (INDECOPI, http://www.indecopi.gob.pe/) is working to implement a PKI under the E-Gob Peru project. Peru is expected to use the U.S. PKI business model.

Development of the legal framework has proceeded as follows:

a) Protection of Personal Information: Complete.

b) Electronic Signature: Complete, but will be modified.

c) Electronic Commerce: Not explicit, but there is a bill that refers to concessions done electronically (Civil Code 141 and 141A.)

d) Validity for Procedures related to E-Gob Peru: Under development.

e) Electronic Governmental Hiring Process: Under development.

TRADE PROMOTION AND ADVERTISING

In 2014 Peruvian advertising expenditures are expected to reach USD$ 751 million. As in previous years, television advertisements account for the biggest expenditures, with USD$415 million. Newspapers and radio will claim an estimated USD$115 million and USD$83 million. Internet advertisements are expected to reach USD$ 40 million, up 14.3% from 2013.

Lima boasts 30 daily newspapers, a few of which strive for national coverage. Locally oriented newspapers can be found in most provincial capitals. First in terms of influence is *El Comercio,* the nation's second oldest paper with 175 years of continuous publication. Three major dailies, *Peru.21, Trome,* and business daily *Gestión,* belong to El Comercio Group. Other major dailies are *Correo, La República, La Razón, La Primera, Expreso,* tabloids *Ojo,* and *El Popular,* and the official gazette *El Peruano,* founded in 1825, which acts as the official

In August 2013, El Comercio Group acquired from the EPENSA Group the control over printing, circulation and publicity of *Correo, Ojo and El Bocón*. EPENSA retained control over the editorial line.

According to the Ministry of Transportation and Communications (MTC), as of February 2015 there were 5,325 radio and television stations in Peru. Lima boasts the most television stations (127), followed by Puno (121) and Junín (95). The Cajamarca region is the leader in radio stations (320), followed by Ancash (313) and Lima (304).

Radio reaches the largest audience of all communications media, reaching even the most isolated populations in Peru. It is often the first source of current news and is the principal vehicle in the regions outside Lima for transmitting information about local issues and events.

There are thousands of radio stations in Peru broadcasting on AM, FM, and short wave frequencies. Many of these stations are small storefront operations that serve relatively limited audiences. Radio's most influential source of news and information is "Radio Programas del Peru" (RPP). RPP is the only network with a national reach with transmitters and correspondents in virtually every important city in Peru. In most major cities, including Lima, RPP leads most AM and FM ratings and it boasts an influential listening audience, as well as a TV station for simulcast.

Television permeates the urban environment in Peru and has become increasingly available to rural audiences as well. As in the United States, television is often the primary source of news for a majority of those who have access to it.

The most important players in TV are the six major Lima-based television networks, along with a government-owned service, which for years was the only station available in many parts of Peru. These seven broadcasters use affiliates in the provinces much like their counterparts in the United States. In addition, there are numerous smaller independent stations that serve particular cities and regions.

Cable television is also a powerful player in the Peruvian market. A National Urban Study of Radio and TV Coverage conducted in May/July 2014 reported that as of 2014 57.7% of households use cable television (72.5% in Lima and 47.5% in the rest of the country). Canal N , a 24-hour cable news channel owned by *El Comercio,* is highly influential. The main cable service companies are Telefónica del Perú (Spain), offering "Movistar TV"; the America Móvil Group (Mexico), with its product "Claro TV"; the Caracol Group (Colombia), with its local product "Cablevision"; and the DirecTV Group (USA), offering its cable service "DirecTv." Their packages include CNN and programming from other Latin American, Asian and European countries. The remaining cable companies are small firms offering their services in concentrated areas surrounding Lima or in the provinces.

Major Lima-based networks maintain news websites that correspond to their print and broadcast outlets. The most popular are RPP, El Comercio, Andina, Peru.21, and La Republica news service.

According to a May 2015 poll reported in the daily Gestión, 30% of urban Peruvians use the Internet every day between one and three hours. The Penetration role of the Internet is 53% in Lima and 46% in the rest of Peru. Among youth between 18 and 24 years old, favorite internet tools are Facebook (96%), YouTube (63%), and Twitter (25%). The most popular websites include Google and YouTube. At the same time, 94% of internet users access news sites. Blogging is still not popular enough to be a source of independent income and most bloggers are affiliated journalists or academics. Although social media has not yet been used successfully in Peru to organize a large scale political movement, it has played a role in mobilizing public opinion and rallies on specific issues. The U.S. Embassy Lima Facebook page has over 205,000 fans and the Twitter account has over 40,000 followers including many of Peru's leading opinion makers.

PRICING

In general, Peru is an open market, with minimal trade restrictions. The imports-weighted average tariff is 1.8% and the simple average is 3.2%. Distributor mark-up varies according to type of product, but usually ranges between 12% and 25%. All imports are subject to an 18% value-added local sales tax, which can be used as a tax credit by the importer. There are some exceptions: enterprises established in industrial free zones and special treatment zones; companies that have their operations in the jungle regions of Loreto, Ucayali, Madre de Dios, Amazonas, and San Martin, in accordance with the Peruvian-Colombian Amazon Cooperation Treaty. Some luxury items have higher tariffs and some specific goods such as cigarettes, beer, wine, and liquors pay an excise tax according to the lists and rates included in Appendixes III and IV of Legislative Decree No. 821 (passed on April 23, 1996). In December 2007, the 10% excise tax for new automobiles was eliminated, and the excise tax applied to used cars was left at 30%. Imports from countries with which Peru has bilateral or regional agreements are covered by different, preferential tariff schedules.

SALES SERVICE/CUSTOMER SUPPORT

Peruvians consider service and support a critical factor in making the final purchasing decision, especially for products that require periodic servicing. It is important for the product to be sold through a reliable distributor that offers the quality and services that the client requires. For example, servicing and availability are currently the two perceived advantages that new Asian autos enjoy over their U.S. competitors in the Peruvian market. Another example would be mining equipment, where U.S. after-sales service enjoys a superior reputation to that of third-country competitors.

PROTECTING YOUR INTELLECTUAL PROPERTY IP RIGHTS CLIMATE IN PERU

While the legal framework for protection of intellectual property (IP) in Peru has improved over the past decade, enforcement mechanisms remain weak. Piracy remains a significant and endemic problem for legitimate owners of trademarks, copyrights, and patents in Peru. Peru has remained on USTR's Section 301 "Watch List" since 2001 due to continued high piracy rates and inadequate enforcement of IP laws. Weak or unenforced penalties for IP violators also contributed to the Watch List determination.

Under the U.S.-Peru Trade Promotion Agreement (PTPA), Peruvian law must provide the same protection for U.S. companies as Peruvian companies in all IP categories. The PTPA provides for improved IP protection on a broad range of IP rights. Such improvements include: protections for digital products (e.g., U.S. software, music, text, and video); protection for U.S. patents, trademarks and pharmaceutical and agrochemical test data; legal penalties to deter piracy; and an electronic system to register and maintain trademarks.

Despite PTPA implementation and recent changes in laws which create stricter penalties for some types of IP theft, egregious IP rights infringement persists. The judicial branch continues to fail in imposing sentences that adequately deter future IP theft. Prosecutors are not increasing the number of piracy cases they pursue through the entire process to final judgment. Furthermore, the Peruvian public knowingly and openly continues to purchase pirated software, CDs, DVDs, pharmaceutical products, books, and other products. Peruvians purchase pirated and counterfeit products from vendors who operate in the open, as neither party fears punishment by their government which has shown little will to prosecute these illegal actions. The Peruvian government has occasionally carried out raids against individual vendors of pirated goods, but few against criminal gangs that control the supply and distribution chains.

Peruvian government institutions, often with the support of the U.S. Embassy in Lima, sponsor public awareness campaigns about the damage that IP theft causes the Peruvian economy and personal health risks from counterfeit medicines to individuals. Peruvian newspapers highlight stories how piracy harms Peruvians, including counterfeited books by Peru's Nobel Laureate Mario Vargas Llosa.

The International Intellectual Property Alliance (IIPA) estimates that 98% of recorded music in Peru is pirated. The Business Software Alliance and the International Data Corporation (IDC) estimate that software piracy levels decreased from 71% in 2009 to 68% in 2012. While larger U.S. and foreign software companies have been able to provide heavily discounted or free cloud-based versions of their products, smaller software companies continue to struggle to prevent their products from being pirated. The majority of individually-owned motion pictures in Peru are pirated. Peru's piracy rate remains higher than the regional (61%) and global (42%) averages for software piracy.

U.S. pharmaceutical and agro-chemical industries claim that the Peruvian government fails to provide data exclusivity protection for their products. For instance, the Peruvian government does not provide patent linkage or "second use" medical patents. The pharmaceutical industry also claims the Peruvian government does not offer any extension of the patent term for pharmaceutical products to compensate for delays at the patent office. The agro-chemical industry has complained of government mechanisms that allow for the importation of generic copies that infringe on their registered patents.

The Peruvian government agency charged with promoting and defending intellectual property rights is the Institute for the Defense of Competition and Protection of Intellectual Property (INDECOPI, http://www.indecopi.gob.pe/), established in 1992. Peru belongs to the World Trade Organization (WTO) and the World Intellectual Property Organization (WIPO). Peru's legal framework provides for registration of trademarks, and inventors have been able to patent their inventions since 1994. Peru's 1996 Industrial Property Rights Law provides an effective term of protection for patents and prohibits devices that decode encrypted satellite signals. Peruvian law does not provide pipeline protection for patents or protection from parallel imports. Peru's Copyright Law is generally consistent with the World Trade Organization's Agreement on Trade-Related Aspects of Intellectual Property (TRIPS).

Protecting Your Intellectual Property in Peru:

Several general principles are important for effective management of intellectual property ("IP") rights in Peru. First, it is important to have an overall strategy to protect your IP. Second, IP may be protected differently in Peru than in the United States. Third, rights must be registered and enforced in Peru, under local laws. For example, your U.S. trademark and patent registrations will not protect you in Peru. There is no such thing as an "international copyright" that will automatically protect an author's writings throughout the entire world. Protection against unauthorized use in a particular country depends, basically, on the national laws of that country. However, most countries do offer copyright protection to foreign works under certain conditions, and these conditions have been greatly simplified by international copyright treaties and conventions.

Registration of patents and trademarks is on a first-in-time, first-in-right basis, so you should consider applying for trademark and patent protection even before selling your products or services in the Peru market. It is vital that companies understand that intellectual property is primarily a private right and that the U.S. government cannot enforce rights for private individuals in Peru. It is the responsibility of the rights' holders to register, protect, and enforce their rights where relevant, retaining their own counsel and advisors. Companies may wish to seek advice from local attorneys or IP consultants who are experts in Peruvian law. The U.S. Commercial Service can provide a list of local lawyers upon request.

While the U.S. Government stands ready to assist, there is little we can do if the rights holders have not taken these fundamental steps necessary to securing and enforcing their IP in a timely fashion. Moreover, in many countries, rights holders who delay enforcing their rights on a mistaken belief that the USG can provide a political resolution to a legal problem may find that their rights have been eroded or abrogated due to legal doctrines such as statutes of limitations, laches, estoppel, or unreasonable delay in prosecuting a law suit. In no instance should U.S. Government advice be seen as a substitute for the responsibility of a rights holder to promptly pursue its case.

It is always advisable to conduct due diligence on potential partners. A good partner is an important ally in protecting IP rights. Consider carefully, however, whether to permit your partner to register your IP rights on your behalf. Doing so may create a risk that your partner will list itself as the IP owner and fail to transfer the rights should the partnership end. Keep an eye on your cost structure and reduce the margins (and the incentive) of would-be bad actors. Projects and sales in Peru require constant attention.

Work with legal counsel familiar with Peruvian laws to create a solid contract that includes non-compete clauses, and confidentiality/non-disclosure provisions.

It is also recommended that small and medium-size companies understand the importance of working together with trade associations and organizations to support efforts to protect IP and stop counterfeiting. There are a number of these organizations, both Peruvian or U.S.-based. These include:

- The U.S. Chamber and local American Chambers of Commerce
- National Association of Manufacturers (NAM)
- International Intellectual Property Alliance (IIPA)
- International Trademark Association (INTA)
- The Coalition Against Counterfeiting and Piracy
- International Anti-Counterfeiting Coalition (IACC)

• Pharmaceutical Research and Manufacturers of America (PhRMA)

• Biotechnology Industry Organization (BIO)

IP Resources

A wealth of information on protecting IP is freely available to U.S. rights holders. Some excellent resources for companies regarding intellectual property include the following:

• For information about patent, trademark, or copyright issues -- including enforcement issues in the US and other countries -- call the STOP! Hotline: **1-866-999-HALT** or visit www.STOPfakes.gov .

• For more information about registering trademarks and patents (both in the U.S. as well as in foreign countries), contact the U.S. Patent and Trademark Office (USPTO) at: **1-800-786-9199**, or visit http://www.uspto.gov/.

• For more information about registering for copyright protection in the United States, contact the U.S. Copyright Office at: **1-202-707-5959**, or visit http://www.copyright.gov/.

• For more information about how to evaluate, protect, and enforce intellectual property rights and how these rights may be important for businesses, please visit the "Resources" section of the STOP fakes website at http://www.stopfakes.gov/resources .

• For information on obtaining and enforcing intellectual property rights and market-specific IP Toolkits visit: **www.stopfakes.gov**/businesss-tools/country-ipr-toolkits . The toolkits contain detailed information on protecting and enforcing IP in specific markets and also contain contact information for local IPR offices abroad and U.S. government officials available to assist SMEs.

• The U.S. Department of Commerce has positioned IP attachés in key markets around the world. The IP attaché who covers Peru is: Albert Keyack (based in Brazil) albert.keyack@trade.gov .

DUE DILIGENCE

U.S. businesses considering exporting to or investing in Peru should perform due diligence on their potential clients, associates, or partners. As a first step, the International Company Profile (ICP) program of the U.S. Commercial Service can provide a background check on the reliability of potential clients or partners. The ICP report includes information on a company's owners, year established, size, sales, financial information and reputation in the market. The Commercial Service and the Economic Section of the U.S. Embassy in Peru are also available to provide commercial and economic briefings to U.S. businesspersons traveling to Peru.

LOCAL PROFESSIONAL SERVICES

Private Banks

Banco Azteca: http://www.bancoazteca.com.pe
Banco Cencosud: http://www.bancocencosud.com.pe
Banco de Comercio: http://www.bancomercio.com.pe
Banco de Crédito: http://www.viabcp.com

Banco Falabella: http://www.bancofalabella.com.pe
Banco Financiero: http://financiero.com.pe
Banco GNB Peru: http://bancognb.com.pe
Banco Interamericano de Finanzas: http://www.bif.com.pe
Banco Internacional del Peru – Interbank: http://www.interbank.com.pe
Banco Ripley: http://www.bancoripley.com.pe
Banco Santander: http://www.santander.com.pe
BBVA Banco Continental: http://www.bbvabancocontinental.com.pe
Deutsche Bank: http://www.db.com.pe
Mibanco: http://www.mibanco.com.pe
Scotiabank: http://scotiabank.com.pe

Accounting/Business Consultants

Apoyo S.A.: economic studies, business consulting, market research, opinion surveys, multi-customer studies, strategic communication: Apoyo S.A.: economic studies, business consulting, market research, opinion surveys, multi-customer studies, strategic communication: Apoyo S.A.: economic studies, business consulting, market research, opinion surveys, multi-customer studies, strategic communication:

ConsultAndes: executive advisory, business development, public relations, community relations and public responsibility, crisis management, corporate communications, security: http://www.consultandes.com.pe (Bilingual)

DBM: outplacement consultant and career transition services: http://www.dbmperu.com

ERM: environmental consulting services: http://www.erm.com/en/Locations/Peru

Ernst & Young: accounting, auditing and tax advisory: http://www.ey.com

KPMG Caipo y Asociados: auditing, tax and financial advisory: http://www.pe.kpmg.com

LB&C Logistics Business & Consulting: supply chain security, international trade, legal services: http://www.lbcperu.com

Macroconsult: economic studies, business consulting, market research, infrastructure, regulation and competition, investment banking: http://www.macroconsult.com.pe (Bilingual)

Malaga - Webb & Asociados: business restructuring, continuous improvement, corporate finance: http://www.malaga-webb.com

Organizacion Cuanto: economic studies, social studies, polls, market research: http://www.cuanto.org

Pricewaterhouse Coopers SCRL: auditing, accounting, tax and legal services: http://www.pwc.com

Credit Rating Agencies

Coface Peru: http://www.coface.com.pe

Dun & Bradstreet S.A.C .: http://www.dnbperu.com.pe/eng_default.asp

Informa Peru S.A.: http://www.informadelperu.com

CREDIT REPORTING AGENCIES

Experian Peru: http://www.datacredito.com.pe

Infocorp/Equifax: http://www.equifax.com/home/es_pe

Sentinel: http://www.sentinelperu.com

Xchange Peru: http://www.xchange.com.pe

Executive Search

Amrop Hever: http://www.amrop.com
Boyden International: http://www.boyden.com/offices/lima
Korn/Ferry International: http://www.kornferry.com
Tasa Worldwide: http://www.tasaworldwide.com/index_en.html

LAW FIRMS

Barreda Moller: http://www.barredamoller.com/en (Bilingual)
Barrios, Fuentes, Urquiaga Abogados: http://www.bafur.com.pe (Bilingual)
Estudio Aurelio Garcia Sayan Abogados: http://www.garciasayan.com (Bilingual)
Estudio Echecopar: http://www.echecopar.com.pe (Bilingual)
Estudio Ferrero Abogados: http://www.ferrero.com.pe
Estudio Grau Abogados: http://www.estudiograu.com (Bilingual)
Estudio Olaechea: http://www.esola.com.pe (Bilingual)
Muniz, Ramirez, Perez-Taiman & Luna Victoria Abogados: http://www.munizlaw.com (Bilingual)
Payet, Rey, Cauvi Abogados: http://www.prc.com.pe (Bilingual)
Rey & de los Rios Abogados: http://www.reyrios.com/indexeng.htm (Bilingual)

Logistics

Maersk Sealand, ocean carrier: http://www.maerskline.com/peru (Multilingual)
Neptunia S.A.: http://www.neptunia.com.pe (Bilingual)
Ransa, logistics operator: http://www.agenciasransa.net (Spanish)
Scharff Logistica Integrada S.A.: http://www.scharff.com.pe (Bilingual)

MOVING

Atlas International Service S.A.: http://www.atlasperucorp.com (Bilingual)
Express Transports S.A.: http://www.express.com.pe (Bilingual)
Security International Moving S.A.C., national and international moving: http://www.simoving.com.pe (Bilingual)

Risk-Rating Agencies

Apoyo & Asociados Internacionales S.A.C. Clasificadora de Riesgo: http://www.aai.com.pe
Clasificadora de Riesgo Pacific Credit Rating S.A.C.: http://www.ratingspcr.com
Class & Asociados S.A. Clasificadora de Riesgo: http://www.classrating.com
Equilibrium Clasificadora de Riesgo S.A.: http://www.equilibrium.com.pe

TELECOMMUNICATIONS

Claro (Telmex Perú S.A.), telecommunications services: http://www.claro.com.pe
Movistar (Telefonica S.A.), telecommunications services: http://www.movistar.com.pe
Entel (Entel S.A.), telecommunications services: http://www.entel.pe/
Bitel (Bitel S.A.), telecommunications services: http://www.bitel.com.pe/

WEB RESOURCES

Antitrust, Unfair Competition Intellectual Property Protection, Consumer Protection, Dumping, Standards and Elimination of Bureaucratic Barriers Agency (INDECOPI): http://www.indecopi.gob.pe (Bilingual)
Central Bank: http://www.bcrp.com.pe (Bilingual reports and statistics)
Government Procurement Supervisory Agency: http://www.osce.gob.pe (Spanish)
InPERU, non-profit organization set up by Peru's main business organizations to promote foreign investments to Peru: http://inperu.pe (English)
Ministry of Energy and Mines: http://www.minem.gob.pe (Spanish with limited bilingual content)
Ministry of Foreign Affairs: http://rree.gob.pe/SitePages/home.aspx

National Interconnected System Operation (Comité de Operación Económica del Sistema Interconectado Nacional, COES-SINAC): http://www.coes.org.pe (Spanish)

OSCE's opinion on "government to government" procurement: http://portal.osce.gob.pe/osce/sites/default/files/Documentos/legislacion/Legislacion%20y%20Documentos%20Elaborados%20por%20el%20OSCE/Opiniones-2012/078-12%20-%20PRE%20-%20MINDEF%20-%20Ambito%20aplic.LCE%20contrat.gob.%20a%20gob.%20ver.final.doc (Spanish) Peru Export and Tourism Promotion Board, PromPeru: Peru Export and Tourism Promotion Board, PromPeru: Peru Export and Tourism Promotion Board, PromPeru:

Peru Travel, Peru Travel Information and Vacations Guide: http://www.peru.travel
Private Investment Promotion Agency – ProInversión: http://www.proinversion.gob.pe (Bilingual)
Public Registry (SUNARP): http://www.sunarp.gob.pe (Spanish)
Securities and Exchange Supervisory Agency (SMV): http://www.smv.gob.pe (Spanish)
SUNAT – Peruvian foreign trade statistics: http://www.aduanet.gob.pe/aduanas/informae/boleindi.htm
SUNAT - Information for Foreign Investors: http://inversionistaextranjero.sunat.gob.pe
Tax and Customs National Superintendence (SUNAT): http://www.sunat.gob.pe (Spanish)
United Nations Office for Project Service: http://www.unops.org (Bilingual)
U.S. Trade Representative (USTR): http://www.ustr.gov

LEADING SECTORS FOR U.S. EXPORT AND INVESTMENT

CONSTRUCTION EQUIPMENT

Unit: USD millions

	2013	2014	2015 (estimated)	2016 (estimated)
Total Market Size	2,338	2,222	2,288.6	2,345.2
Total Local Production	N/A	N/A	N/A	N/A
Total Exports	111	98	100.9	103.5
Total Imports	2,449	2,320	2,389.6	2,449.6
Imports from the U.S.	520	565	582	601

Exchange Rate: 1 USD	2.80	2.85	3.20	3.30

Total Market Size = (Total Local Production + Total Imports) – (Total Exports)

Data Sources: Global Trade Atlas

2014 Import Market Share (percent for U.S. and major competitors): United States 20.3; Brazil 18.2; China 14.1; Japan 10.6; Germany 5.4; South Korea 4.2.

The Peruvian construction sector has substantially upgraded itself by importing modern construction equipment like mixers, cranes, excavators, dump trucks, and other equipment, which led to a drastic reduction in construction times. This allowed the construction sector to begin work on several large mines, power generation plants, natural gas production facilities and transportation projects creating extensive growth. Modernizing the construction industry also aided the residential and office building boom, which increased overall infrastructure development.

Peru's past rapid economic growth created a large infrastructure gap, which some experts estimate surpasses USD$80 billion. The need for roads, ports, airports, water, sewage, telecommunications, and electrical lines is apparent. The Peruvian government has ambitious plans to bridge the infrastructure gap with massive projects that will contribute to the majority of the growth within the construction sector. Planned investments include the development of regional school infrastructure (USD$223.0 million), road projects in the Junín and Huallaga regions (USD$953.0 million), and infrastructure development of Huallaga region (USD$285.0 million). Business Monitor International estimates that the Peruvian construction sector will see a 2% real growth with a total industry value of USD$12.7 billion in 2015. The construction sector accounts for 5.0% of Peru's overall GDP.

Another significant change in the construction sector is the emergence of the Peruvian government as a partner to the private sector. In May of 2008, the government passed the Public-Private Partnerships (PPPs) legislative decree, which aims at facilitating the private investment promotion process through the creation, development, improvement, operation and maintenance of public infrastructure or the provision of public services, such as the Works for Taxes law (Obras por Impuestos). Under this initiative, a private company or a consortium is able to fund and execute government-approved public projects in lieu of the taxes they would have originally paid. The Works for Taxes law is a way to leverage the efficiency of private sector, while tackling Peru's infrastructure needs.

SUB-SECTOR BEST PROSPECTS

The figures below represent each product's share of Peru's 2014 total imports in this sector.

HTS Code	Description	%
842952	Mech Shovels Excavators Etc W 360 Degree Sprstruc	22.3
842951	Mech Front-End Shovel Loaders, Self-Propelled	15.4
843149	Parts And Attachments Nesoi For Derricks Etc.	9.2
847490	Parts Of Mach For Sorting Etc Earth Stone Ores Etc	6.1
847420	Crushing/Grinding Mach For Earth Stone Mnerl Subs	5.6
843049	Boring Or Sinking Mach Nesoi, Not Self-Propelled	5.4

843041	Boring Or Sinking Machinery, Nesoi, Self-Propelled	5.1
842959	Mech Shovels, Excavators And Shovel Loaders Nesoi	4.9
842911	Bulldozers And Angeldozers, Self-Prop, Track Lay	4.7
843139	Pts For Lifting, Hndlng, Loading/Unldng Mach Nesoi	3.8

Opportunities

Growth in the construction sector will be spurred by high demand in several areas. The need for transportation and communications infrastructure will contribute to growth of the construction sector, while the start/continuation of mining and energy projects and the continued demand for housing and office facilities will further boost the market.

Peru's housing deficit is estimated at 4 million homes and the government's plans to address this will contribute to the construction sector's growth. According to government estimates, only one third of all houses were built with a legal building permit. The Ministry of Housing, Construction and Sanitation is attempting to formalize the housing sector by creating affordable housing. According to a study released in April 2014 by the government's Fondo MiVivienda (MyHome Fund), over the next two years some 196,000 households plan to buy a home and approximately 276,000 families will improve or expand their homes. MiVivienda will promote 219,462 housing projects by offering favorable interest rates for 2016.

Peru's growing construction sector provides a wide variety of investment and business opportunities. While growth has slowed industry experts predict the sector to continue to grow around 4% per annum for the next couple of years. The need for construction equipment and materials will remain in demand because of ongoing and future projects.

Important projects requiring substantial capital investment include:

- Lima and Callao Metro line 2 and Av. Gambeta Branch, with an estimated investment of USD$5.7 billion and a construction period of just over five years. (Awarded April 2014)

- Cusco's Chinchero International Airport with an estimated investment of USD$ 658.0 million and the possibility of further expenditures on expansion. (Awarded April 2014)

- Southern Gas Pipeline, with an estimated investment of USD$4.0 billion. (Awarded July 2014)

Web Resources

Association for the Promotion of National Infrastructure - AFIN: http://www.afin.org.pe (Spanish)

Business Monitor International - Industry Trend Analysis - Ambitious Infrastructure Agenda To Fall Short

Fondo MiVivienda (MyHome Fund): http://www.mivivienda.com.pe/ (Spanish)

Global Trade Atlas: http://www.gtis.com/gta/

Peruvian Chamber of Construction – CAPECO: http://www.capeco.org/ (Spanish)

Private Investment Promotion Agency – ProInversión: http://www.proinversion.gob.pe/

(bilingual)

ProInversión Project Presentation - Projects portfolio 2014-2015 (April 2014, in English): http://www.proinversion.gob.pe/RepositorioAPS/1/2/JER/PROJECT_PRESENTATION/ppt%20de%20proyectos%20ingles_pptx%20.pdf

Ministry of Transportation and Communications: http://www.mtc.gob.pe/ (Spanish)

National Institute of Statistics and Informatics – INEI: http://www.inei.gob.pe/ (Spanish)

ELECTRONIC COMMERCE

Even though e-commerce transactions in Peru are still low, the growth in the last two years is meaningful. The number of credit card transactions in virtual stores grew from 2.2 million in 2012 to 4.1 million in 2014, representing an 89% increase in two years. Simultaneously, the dollar amount traded has increased 179%, growing from USD$ 668.0 million in 2012 to USD$ 1.868 billion in 2014.

By the end of 2014, the number of Internet users in Peru was estimated at 12,584,000 with a market penetration rate of 38%. This figure is still well below countries like Panama, Chile, Argentina, Mexico, Brazil, and Colombia, all of which exceed 50% market penetration. Furthermore, access to financing barely reached 30% (in other words, 30% of the population has at least one bank account), which is below the regional average of 50%.

However, internet access is expected to grow in the future through the deployment of cellular phones and broadband networks. In 2014, the mobile market expanded to 31.9 million lines, representing a high national density of 107% (more lines than population). In addition, the project of the "Red Dorsal de Fibra Optica" (Fiber optic network) is currently in execution. This project aims to reduce the cost of Internet access and is scheduled to begin operations in mid-2016.

SUB-SECTOR BEST PROSPECTS

Peruvian users spend 18.2 hours per month on the Internet, the second highest average in Latin America and surpassed only by Argentina. The vast majority of Internet users are men between the ages of 15-24 who account for 56% of total internet users. A Peruvian newspaper, El Comercio, reported that 19 million Peruvians will be able to access the Internet in 2019. Regarding the Business to Consumer (B2C) market, Peruvian consumers account for 7% of total online purchases and 2% (USD$ 1.250 billion) of the total Latin American market of online purchases. This is largely explained

by the low penetration rates, lack of confidence in online security, lack of financial means, and lack of education.

Out of Peru's 200 top private companies only 72% conducted electronic transactions through their own website or through a third party. On the regulatory side, SUNAT (Peru's tax authority) uses electronic means to exercise the detailed control of tax collection. Therefore, SUNAT has issued a regulation to establish the electronic invoice, "norma de la Factura Electronica" (Resolution No. 188-2010-SUNAT). However, in Peru there is no comprehensive state policy to promote the widespread growth of ICT including e-commerce, as in other countries.

In the case of B2B, businesses are beginning to use their own custom email domain servers instead of using an informal personal email address (like Hotmail or Gmail) to conduct business. The new trend of owning your own email domain allows Peruvian businesses to legitimize their companies and is becoming standard amongst Peruvian companies.

Since 2012, the Lima Chamber of Commerce of Lima has promoted Cyber Monday, which takes place on the Monday following the U.S. holiday "Thanksgiving." Cyber Monday usually occurs in late November or early December. Also since 2014, the Lima Chamber promotes CyberMami which was held on April 29 and 30 in 2015 right before the Peruvian mother's day holiday, which is traditionally held the second Sunday of May. Some companies, like the Saga Falabella department store, have also launched their own seasonal offers like Madrugo, which takes place when a new season arrives.

Opportunities

The Lima Chamber of Commerce predicts that in 2015 there will be a 50% increase in e-commerce sales. This favorable outlook is due to the expected number of sales related to food and entertainment industries. Lima continues to be the country's main economic hub, and other cities like Cusco, Trujillo, and Chiclayo are starting to make a positive economic impact.

A 2014 survey showed that 75% of the population owned a cellphone, with 16% being smartphone users. In addition, smartphones accounted for 49% (6.7 million units) of mobile equipment sold nationwide. The growth of smartphone users allows for better access to internet, which allows users to make purchases via mobile applications. It is estimated that food products, apparel, and utility bills (home phones) are the payments most conducted via mobile applications by consumers.

Web Resources

Peruvian Chamber of Electronic Commerce (CAPECE) http://www.capece.org.pe (Spanish only)

Lima Chamber of Commerce (CCL) http://www.camaralima.org.pe (Spanish only)

Peruvian Banks Association (ASBANC)
http://www.asbanc.pe/contenidoweb/Default.aspx?ref=8&cont=83 (Spanish only)

FOOD PROCESSING & PACKAGING EQUIPMENT

Unit: USD millions

	2013	2014	2015 (estimated)	2016 (estimated)
Total Market Size	359.3	438.1	451.2	462.5
Total Exports	16.6	15.8	16.3	16.7
Total Imports	375.9	453.9	467.5	479.2
Imports from the U.S.	55.4	111.9	115.3	118.2
Exchange Rate: 1 USD	2.80	2.85	3.20	3.30

Total Market Size = (Total Local Production + Total Imports) – (Total Exports)

Data Sources: Global Trade Atlas

2014 Import Market Share (percent for U.S. and major competitors): United States 24.7; Germany 22.0; Italy 14.9; China 7.2; Spain 4.2; Belgium 4.2; Brazil 3.4.

The ever-growing reputation of Peru's culinary culture has brought about a marked increase in locally produced packaged and non-perishable foods. This new trend is expanding the use of native Peruvian ingredients, such as fruits, peppers and Andean cereals, which increases the attraction and marketability of products for a variety of reasons. Consumers are slowly shifting towards packaged and prepared foods because of the items' decreased risk of contamination and increased lifespan. Peru's growing middle class is now willing to pay slightly higher prices for peace of mind. Products such as cheese, oils, fats, spreads, and baked goods are benefiting from the shift in consumers' preferences.

SUB-SECTOR BEST PROSPECTS

The figures below represent each product's share of Peru's 2014 total imports in this sector.

HTS Code	Description	%
843830	Machinery For Sugar Manufacture	44.36
842129	Filter/Purify Machine & Apparatus For Liquid Nesoi	11.98
841950	Heat Exchange Units, Industrial Type	7.96
841869	Refrigerating/Freezing Equipment, Nesoi	7.29
841989	Machine Etc For Mat'L Treatment By Temp Cont Nesoi	5.95
841940	Distilling Or Rectifying Plant	4.44
842230	Machinery For Filling, Closing Bottles, Etc	2.77
842290	Parts For Machines For Dishwashing, Packing, Etc	2.12
842240	Packing Or Wrapping Machinery, Nesoi	2.06
841981	Machinery Etc For Making Hot Drinks Cooking Heatng	1.51

Best prospects include fully integrated high technology equipment and machinery for processing and packaging purposes. This includes machinery for sugar manufacture; machinery for filling, closing, sealing, and labeling bottles, cans, bags or other containers; machinery for encapsulating bottles, jars, tubes and similar containers; machinery for aerating beverages; dairy machinery, heat exchange units; other packing or wrapping machinery. Peruvians prefer U.S. technologies for closing, sealing labeling equipment, and rigid containers

OPPORTUNITIES

EXPOALIMENTARIA PERU 2015 – International tradeshow of goods and services related to the food and beverages industry.

August 26 to 28, 2015 – Jockey Exhibitions Center, Lima

http://www.expoalimentariaperu.com/en /

WEB RESOURCES

Global Trade Atlas: http://www.gtis.com/gta/
Ministry of Production (Industry & Fisheries): http://www.produce.gob.pe (Spanish)
National Society of Industries: http://www.sni.org.pe/ (Spanish)

INDUSTRIAL CHEMICALS

Unit: USD millions

	2013	2014	2015 (estimated)	2016 (estimated)
Total Market Size	937.8	958.5	838.0	1,021.8
Total Local Production	N/A	N/A	N/A	N/A
Total Exports	424.3	408.7	434.1	328.1
Total Imports	1,362.1	1,337.2	1,272.1	1,338.1
Imports from the U.S.	368.0	359.0	308.56	316.3
Exchange Rate: 1 USD	2.80	2.85	3.20	3.30

Total Market Size = (Total Local Production + Total Imports) – (Total Exports)

Data Source: Global Trade Atlas

2014 Import Market Share (percent for U.S. and major competitors): United States 24.6; China 20.2; South Korea 8.5; Mexico 5.4; Brazil 4.8; Germany 4.7; Chile 4.1; India 3.4.

Peru has consistently depended on industrial chemical imports, owing to an increase in public and private investment in infrastructure development. The local demand for industrial chemicals is exceeding what can be produced locally, which is limited to acetylene, sulfuric acid, nitrogen, and oxygen. Plastics in primary forms such as polyethylene, polystyrene, polypropylene are imported from abroad.

Main U.S. exports to Peru are nitrile-function compounds, mixed alkybenzenes, saturated acyclic nonocarbox acid and anhydrous, halogon, coloring matter and carbonates. Industrial chemicals are an essential part in the following industries: textiles, cosmetics, plastics, paints, paper, detergents, and pharmaceuticals.

SUB-SECTOR BEST PROSPECTS

The figures below represent each product's share of Peru's 2014 total imports in this sector.

HTS Code	Description	%
2837	Cyanides, Cyanide Oxides And Complex Cyanides	6.33
3204	Syn Org Coloring Matter & Prep; Syn Org Brit Agent	5.76
3402	Organic Surf-Act Agents, Preps & Cleaning Preps	5.48
2926	Nitrile-Function Compounds	4.65
3817	Mixed Alkylbenzenes & Mixed Alklnaphthalenes, Nes	4.24
2835	Phosphinates, Phosphonates, Phosphates & Polyphosp	3.83
3206	Coloring Matter Nesoi; Coloring Prep Nesoi, Etc.	3.66
3506	Prepared Glues & Adhesives Nesoi; Glue Retail Pack	3.64
2915	Sat Acyclic Nonocarbox Acid & Anhyd, Halogon Etc	3.52
2905	Acyclic Alcohols & Halogenat, Sulfonatd Etc Derivs	3.48

OPPORTUNITIES

Peru's decade-long strong economic performance in the construction and mining sectors continues to increase demand for a variety of industrial chemicals. U.S. exporters would be smart to identify local representatives that can help them seize the opportunities of the increased demand.

WEB RESOURCES

Global Trade Atlas: http://www.gtis.com/gta/

Manufacturer's Society – Chemical Industry Committee:

http://comitedelaindustriaquimica-sni.com/l / (Spanish)

National Institute of Statistics and Informatics – INEI: http://www.inei.gob.pe/ (Spanish)

Private Investment Promotion Agency – ProInversión: http://www.proinversion.gob.pe/ (bilingual)

MEDICAL EQUIPMENT

Unit: USD millions

	2013	2014	2015 (estimated)	2016 (estimated)
Total Market Size	330.1	312.1	321.5	329.5
Total Local Production	N/A	N/A	N/A	N/A
Total Exports	9.7	10.8	11.1	11.4
Total Imports	339.8	322.9	332.6	340.9
Imports from the U.S.	76.8	69.0	71.1	72.9
Exchange Rate: 1 USD	2.80	2.76	3.20	3.30

Total Market Size = (Total Local Production + Total Imports) – (Total Exports)

Data Sources: Global Trade Atlas

2015 Import Market Share (percent for U.S. and major competitors): United States 21.4; China 17.8 Germany 13.5; Japan 7.2; South Korea 4.7; Brazil 3.5.

The Peruvian healthcare sector is composed of public sector entities such as Seguro Integral de Salud (government health insurance), Ministry of Health, EsSalud (social security), and military hospitals. The private healthcare sector is primarily composed of civil society organizations and insurance companies known as Entidades Prestadores de Salud (EPS) that have expanded their services to include the administration of private clinics and emergency centers in order to reduce their operating costs. A recent study shows that approximately 67% of the population has some type of health insurance, and Peruvians are becoming more conscious of their healthcare and the costs associated with maintaining it.

Peru is the eighth most populous country in the region with an average life expectancy of 75 years. According to the World Bank, Peru's annual health care expenditures in 2013 were 5.1% of the GDP, which points towards a promising future for the Peruvian healthcare sector. In July 2014, President Humala announced a USD$2.6 billion investment plan over the next two years

(2015-2016) to build and improve a variety of infrastructure projects, including upgrading and equipping several hospitals and healthcare centers with new equipment. Another initiative is the Works for Taxes law (Obras por Impuestos), which allows a private company or a consortium to fund and execute government approved public projects in lieu of the taxes they would have originally owed. The Works for Taxes law is a way to tackle Peru's infrastructure development with the quicker and more efficient response time that the private sector can offer.

The purchasing of medical equipment and devices is regulated under the Ministry of Health through the Direccion General de Medicamentos, Drogas e Insumos (DIGEMID). Under current regulations, the importation of preowned medical equipment is limited to individual physicians for their own personal use.

To become a medical equipment supplier, Peruvian law requires the local representative to register with the Peruvian Sanitary Registry, which is the list of government approved medical equipment and devices suppliers.

SUB-SECTOR BEST PROSPECTS

The figures below represent each product's share of Peru's 2014 total imports in this sector.

HTS Code	Description	%
901890	Instrument and appliances for medical, surgical, dental	22.42
901839	Needles, caterers and others	8.42
902139	Artificial Joints, parts and accessories	7.34
901850	Other ophthalmic instruments and appliances, parts	6.6
902214	Apparatus base on X-ray, medical, surgical, veterinary	5.23
901819	Electro-diagnostic apparatus and parts.	4.55
902131	Other artificial joints and parts and accessories thereof	4.27
300510	0Adhesive dressings and other articles having adhesive	3.77
902110	Orthopedic or fracture appliances, parts and accessories	3.44
901920	Ozone, oxygen, therapy, respiration apparatus and parts	3.42

Best prospects include diagnostic imaging equipment as the country invests in its radiology infrastructure. Other prospects are emergency room equipment and products, orthopedics, patient aids, and dental products.

OPPORTUNITIES

Peru's rising middle class and growth in disposable income is fueling the demand for improved healthcare services in and around Lima. Peruvians are spending more money on quality elderly care and treatment for cancer, cardiovascular diseases, and diabetes. Approximately 6.5% (2 million) of Peru's total population are 65 years old or older.

The government's forward approach on prioritizing and enhancing the country's healthcare system will yield opportunities for foreign medical equipment and device suppliers. The government announced it would invest in the health sector with plans including the construction of ten hospitals, 200 healthcare centers, blood banks, and a telemedicine system.

Peru's local healthcare-related manufacturing is limited to consumables, basic electro diagnostics and hospital furniture, which explains Peru's low export volumes. Regional governments and private companies look towards foreign medical equipment and device suppliers to fulfill the demand. This market trend creates vast opportunities for U.S. businesses that specialize in state of the art equipment such as computed tomography (CT) scanners, robotic radiosurgery system, and gamma knives.

Key Industry Events

Tecnosalud 2015 – International tradeshow of goods and services related to the healthcare sector

September 9-11, 2015, Jockey Exhibition Center, Lima

http://www.tecnosalud.com.pe

Web Resources

BMI-
https://bmo.bmiresearch.com/article/view?article=1054839&iso=PE&active_pillar=Daily%20Views
The Report – Peru 2015 by the Oxford Business Group
ProInversion - www.proinversion.gob.pe
DIGEMID - www.minsa.digemid.gob.pe

MINING INDUSTRY EQUIPMENT

Unit: USD millions

	2013	2014	2015 (estimated)	2016 (estimated)
Total Market Size	3,029.9	2,621.5	1,911.0	1,958.8
Total Local Production	N/A	N/A	N/A	N/A
Total Exports	172.7	192.6	215.7	221.1
Total Imports	3,202.6	2,814.1	2,126.7	2179.9
Imports from the U.S.	1,053.6	867.2	862.0	883.6
Exchange Rate: 1 USD	2.80	2.85	3.20	3.30

Total Market Size = (Total Local Production + Total Imports) – (Total Exports)

Data Sources: Global Trade Atlas

2014 Import Market Share (percent for U.S. and major competitors): United States 30.8; Brazil 11.4; Germany 10.9; China 10.8; Japan 5.0; Mexico 4.5; United Kingdom 2.8; Chile 2.5.

The mining industry has always been an essential part of the history and development of Peru and continues to play an important role in the Peruvian economy. The mining sector accounts for 52% of total exports making it Peru's top export sector. Much of this growth is driven by 54 Greenfield and expansion projects with a total investment value of USD$45.0 billion, accounting for most of the country's private investment.

In recent years, the mining industry has had to overcome many challenges, such as the negative press associated with increased illegal gold mining operations destroying the Amazon, causing the industry to become unfavorable in the public eye. As a result, regions like Piura, Cajamarca, Arequipa, Cuzco, Moquegua, and Puno experienced social conflicts and mass demonstrations. In some cases, protestors were motivated by legitimate fears of environmental degradation while others were motivated by false

information. However, progress has been made to create peace amongst the local people by both the public and private sectors investing in community development and relations. The Peruvian government has been working to expand major anti-poverty initiatives bringing social programs to isolated poor communities that overlap mineral-rich land.

Sub-Sector Best Prospects

The figures below represent each product's share of Peru's 2014 total imports in this sector.

HTS Code	Description	%
847490	Parts Of Mach For Sorting Etc Earth Stone Ores Etc	12.0
842952	Mech Shovels Excavators Etc W 360 Degree Sprstruc	11.3
870423	Truck, Diesel Eng, Gvw > 20 Metric Tons	7.8
870410	Dumpers Designed For Off-Highway Use	5.4
842951	Mech Front-End Shovel Loaders, Self-Propelled	5.4
843149	Parts And Attachments Nesoi For Derricks Etc.	4.0
392690	Articles Of Plastics, Nesoi	3.8
841480	Air/Gas Pumps, Compressors And Fans Etc, Nesoi	3.7
842959	Mech Shovels, Excavators And Shovel Loaders Nesoi	3.0
843041	Boring Or Sinking Machinery, Nesoi, Self-Propelled	2.9
842911	Bulldozers And Angeldozers, Self-Prop, Track Lay	2.8

When selling mining equipment to Peru it is important to offer post-sale services. Mining companies require assembly, maintenance, parts, and operational training.

Peru is ranked amongst the world's top producers of silver, copper, tin, and zinc thanks to the country's abundance in natural resources and a steady flow of private investments. Currently, 15% of the territory is designated to mining concessions with less than 2% under mining exploration or production. As of 2014, copper (42.4%) and gold (33.9%) represent the most profitable of the mining exports.

Opportunities

Peru is an attractive destination for mining investments due to its large mineral and metal reserves with major undiscovered deposits. The nation's legal framework is designed to attract private investment due to the availability of cadastral and geological information and the country's economic stability, which explains the presence of investors from the U.S., Canada, UK, Australia, Mexico, Brazil, and China. Investments in the sector have grown exponentially since 1992, reaching a record high of USD$9.7 billion in 2013.

Local officials predict Peru's mining sector will attract USD$43.9 billion in investments starting in 2014, a trend that will continue for the next five to ten years. The breakdown of the estimated expenditures include: expansion (USD$8.8 billion), Environmental

Impact Assessments (USD$21.0 billion) evaluation and construction (USD$2.1 billion), and exploration (USD$24.1 billion).

Key Industry Events

Peruvian Mining Convention and Trade Show: Perumin, September 21-25, 2015, Arequipa. Held every two years, this is the most important industry event in Peru.

http://www.convencionminera.com/perumin32/

U.S. Pavilion organizer: Kallman Worldwide, Inc.:

http://www.kallman.com/exhibitor-zone/forms.php?tradeshowID=182

MINPRO - V Meeting of Miners and Suppliers, November 25-26, 2015, Lima Grupo DIGAMMA - Rumbo Minero http://minproperu.com/index.html

WEB RESOURCES

Global Trade Atlas: http://www.gtis.com/gta/
Ministry of Energy and Mines: http://www.minem.gob.pe/ (limited English content)
Ministry of the Environment: http://www.minam.gob.pe (Spanish)
Ministry of Production: http://www.www.produce.gob.pe/ (Spanish)
National Institute of Statistics and Informatics – INEI: http://www.inei.gob.pe / (Spanish)
National Mining, Petroleum, and Energy Society: http://www.snmpe.org.pe/ (Spanish)
Private Investment Promotion Agency – ProInversión: http://www.proinversion.gob.pe/ (Bilingual)
Environmental Assessment and Control Agency – OEFA: http://www.oefa.gob.pe (Spanish)
Energy and Mining Regulatory Agency - Osinergmin: http://www.osinergmin.gob.pe (Spanish)

PLASTIC RESINS

Unit: USD millions

	2013	2014	2015 (estimated)	2016 (estimated)
Total Market Size	1,423.5	1,454.5	1,380.0	1,414.5
Total Local Production	N/A	N/A	N/A	N/A
Total Exports	312.5	372.6	352.1	360.9
Total Imports	1,736.2	1,827.2	1,732.1	1775.40
Imports from the U.S.	486.3	466.2	451.2	462.5
Exchange Rate: 1 USD	2.80	2.85	3.20	3.30

2014 Import Market Share (percent for U.S. and major competitors): United States 25.52; China 12.6; South Korea 9.9; Brazil 8.9; Saudi Arabia 8.5; Colombia 6.1; Taiwan 5.8; Mexico 3.8.

Peru does not have a domestic petrochemical industry; therefore, it relies on imported resins to support the recent surge in domestic manufacturers of pipes, bags, bottles, home and office articles, flexible packaging, containers, and toys. Plastic production has grown 5% in recent years. The industry's continued success is dependent on a steady stream of imported resins from foreign suppliers. The agro-export, food and beverages, textile, leather products, footwear, and chemical sectors rely on imported resins to continue to increase production and meet the local demand for finished plastic products.

SUB-SECTOR BEST PROSPECTS

The figures below represent each product's share of Peru's 2014 total imports in this sector.

HTS Code	Description	%
3901	Polymers Of Ethylene, In Primary Forms	26.1
3902	Polymers Of Propylene Or Other Olefins, Prim Forms	22.9
3907	Polyethers, Expoxides & Polyesters, Primary Forms	13.7
3904	Polymers Of Vinyl Chloride Etc., In Primary Forms	9.5
3920	Plates, Sheets, Film Etc No Ad, Non-Cel Etc, Plast	5.9
3906	Acrylic Polymers In Primary Forms	4.5
3921	Self-Adhesive Plates, Sheets, Film Etc Of Plastics	3.8
3903	Polymers Of Styrene, In Primary Forms	3.6
3919	Polymers Of Vinyl Acetate & Oth Vinyl Polym, Pr Fm	3.6
3909	Amino-Resins, Phenolics & Polyurethanes, Prim Form	1.9

The main sources of consumption and investments of plastic materials are from the following industries: packaging, beverages (bottles and containers), construction, food, home and office operations. Local demand continues to be attractive since consumption and investments continue to grow at promising rates.

OPPORTUNITIES

The U.S. is the main supplier of PVC resins for Peru, which are a key element in the production of PVC pipes. The demand for PVC resins is driven by the increase in use of PVC pipes in the local construction industry.

WEB RESOURCES

Global Trade Atlas: http://www.gtis.com/gta/
Manufacturer's Society – SNI; "Institute of Economic and Social Studies" Sector Report 2014: http://www.sni.org.pe/wp-content/uploads/2014/03/RE_Industria_Plasticos_Feb2014.pdf (Spanish)
National Institute of Statistics and Informatics – INEI: http://www.inei.gob.pe/ (Spanish)

SECURITY & SAFETY EQUIPMENT

Unit: USD millions

	2013	2014	2015 (estimated)	2016 (estimated)
Total Market Size	269.7	281.5	296.0	303.4
Total Exports	32.0	30.6	28.1	28.8

Total Imports	299.7	312.1	324.1	332.2
Imports from the U.S.	68.1	70.4	67.4	69.1
Exchange Rate: 1 USD	2.80	2.85	3.20	3.30

Total Market Size = (Total Local Production + Total Imports) – (Total Exports)

Data Sources: Global Trade Atlas

2014 Import Market Share (percent for U.S. and major competitors): China 36.8; United States 22.6; Germany 4.3; Mexico 4.0; Brazil Taiwan 3.8; Spain 3.2; Italy 2.4.

Demand for residential, industrial and office security equipment remains strong in Peru. Public opinion polls in Lima and other large Peruvian cities consistently find that inhabitants have a high sense of insecurity, with many people having been a victim of robberies or home break-ins.

Companies (headquarters and operation sites), government agencies, and households continuously invest in a wide range of security equipment designed to prevent break-ins and to aid security guards. Such instruments include surveillance cameras, alarms, lights, mesh netting, and barbed wire.

Pistols and revolvers are the most common self-defense weapons used in Peru. The Ministry of Interior's National Superintendence of Control of Security Services and Weapons, Ammunition and Explosives for Civilian Use (SUCAMEC) are in charge of regulating and enforcing applicable legislation, including issuing licenses to carry weapons.

In February 1997, the National Society of Mining, Petroleum and Energy (SNMPE) created an organization called SARCC . The objective of this organization is to support and coordinate security activities among its corporate members in the mining and energy sectors. SARCC provides emergency training resources and assist with emergency situations that threaten the safety of their corporate member's employees who are working in remote areas by providing services such as search and rescue operations, medical evacuation, etc.

SUB-SECTOR BEST PROSPECTS

The figures below represent each product's share of Peru's 2014 total imports in this sector.

HTS Code	Description	%
392690	Articles Of Plastics, Nesoi	34.5
630790	Made-Up Textile Articles, Nesoi	6.6
902000	Breathing Appliances & Gas Masks Nesoi; Parts Etc	5.7
830140	Locks Except Motor Vehicle Or Furniture, Base Metl	5.1
853110	Burglar Or Fire Alarms And Similar Apparatus	3.3
842489	Mechanical Appliance For Projecting Liquids Nesoi	3.2
853190	Parts Of Electric Sound Or Visual Signaling Aprts	2.8
842410	Fire Extinguishers, Whether Or Not Charged	2.2
650610	Safety (Incl Sports) Hdgr,Whether/Not Lined/Trimmed	2.2
730830	Drs, Wndws A Frms A Thrshlds Fr Drs, Iron Or Steel	3.6

Peruvian companies and organizations are beginning to develop strategies and procedures to protect critical information in the event of natural disaster or cyberattacks. Peruvian companies invest a large percentage of their budgets in physical security services and technologies, yet little is spent in cybersecurity.

OPPORTUNITIES

Companies and homeowners are demanding security equipment making the security and safety equipment sector in Peru very promising for U.S. exporters. Companies and private citizens continuously seek preventative equipment such as alarms, surveillance cameras, and lights. Steady growth in residential and corporate construction indicates that these products will continue to be in high demand.

WEB RESOURCES

Global Trade Atlas: http://www.gtis.com/gta/
Ministry of the Interior: http://www.mininter.gob.pe/
National Security Association: http://sociedadnacionaldeseguridad.org/

AGRICULTURAL SECTORS OPPORTUNITIES

HARD WHEAT (

1000 MT—*not US$*)

	2012	2013	2014
Total Market Size	1,927	2,038	1,879
Total Local Production	230	233	240
Total Imports	1,697	1,805	1,879
Total Imports from U.S.	246	648	351

Comments: Peru produces about 240,000 metric tons (MT) of soft wheat annually, which is used locally for traditional foods, and is not sold into processing channels. Most wheat is processed into flour for bread and pasta. The U.S. market share in 2014 was 19 percent. Other important suppliers are Argentina and Canada. Wheat imports into Peru are duty-free. An 18% value-added tax remains in place.

COTTON

(1000 MT)

	2012	2013	2014
Total Market Size	85	90	94
Total Local Production	38	32	35
Total Exports	2	0	1
Total Imports	49	58	60
Total Imports from U.S.	48	57	57

Comments: Peruvian textile and apparel exports are undergoing a severe crisis due to competition from other origins such as Vietnam. Exports are expected at US$2 billion in 2015. The U.S.-Peru Trade Promotion Agreement (PTPA) grants duty-free access to Peruvian textiles.

YELLOW CORN

(1000 MT)

	2012	2013	2014
Total Market Size	3,163	3,386	3,558
Total Local Production	1,324	1,365	1,225
Total Imports	1, 839	2,021	2,333
Total Imports from U.S.	1	220	1,699

Comments: Peru imports corn from Argentina and the United States. Corn from all origins is imported into Peru duty-free. However, due to the PTPA, Peru cannot assess the price band levy within our tariff-rate-quota (TRQ) U.S. corn. Yellow corn in Peru is used mainly for poultry production. At about 42 kilograms per capita, the consumption rate of poultry is one of the highest in the region. Another good export prospect is Dried Distillers

GRAIN.

Product Statistics & Data (PS&D) Code: Soybean Meal (1000 MT)

	2012	2013	2014
Total Market Size	1,055	1,022	1,100
Total Imports	1,055	1,022	1,100
Total Imports from U.S.	80	37	12

Comments: Peru imports soybean meal primarily for poultry feed. Bolivia was the leading soybean meal exporter to Peru in calendar year (CY) 2014 with a 68% market share. Soybean meal from all origins enters Peru duty-free.

DAIRY PRODUCTS

WHEY (MT)

	2012	2013	2014
Total Market Size	8,566	9,418	9,063
Total Imports	8,566	9,418	9,063
Total Imports from U.S.	2,013	3,822	1,727

Comments: Total whey imports into Peru slightly decreased (3.8 percent) in 2014, mainly driven by price advantage of substitute products. Imports from the United States decreased 55 percent compared to 2013 due to better prices from other competitors as Chile and Poland. The U.S. imports market share dropped to second position accounting for 19 percent of total imports in 2014.

CHEESE (MT)

	2012	2013	2014
Total Market Size	30,446	33,085	35,898
Total Local Production	26,790	28,613	31,516
Total Exports	38	50	12
Total Imports	3,694	4,522	4,394
Total Imports from U.S.	2,130	2,375	2,416

Comments: In 2014, imports from the United States accounted for 55 percent of the market. Argentina and Netherlands account for 24 and 5 percent, respectively, of Peru's cheese imports. The food processing and food service industries are two main destinations for this product. The PTPA provides a TRQ of 2,500 MT with a 12 percent increase per year. Currently the quota is 4,935 MT.

BEEF AND OFFAL

(MT)

	2012	2013	2014
Total Market Size	248,717	250,872	253,208
Total Local Production	229,785	231,299	235,450
Total Exports	74	47	260
Total Imports	19,006	19,620	18,018
Total Imports from U.S.	5,609	8,082	5,541

Comments: Peru´s beef and offal market size slightly increased 1 percent in 2014 with respect to previous year. An increment of local production supported the market growth. Nevertheless, U.S. beef and offal imports posted a 31 percent decrease during the same period. Higher prices forced importers to reduce orders, especially on the offal side. The U.S. Meat Export Federation has been actively involved in promotional activities within the region. Peru's stellar economic performance in years has been instrumental in driving consumer preferences towards high-quality products.

PET FOOD

(MT)

	2012	2013	2014
Total Market Size	40,336	44,722	49,310
Total Local Production	31,284	33,493	35,500
Total Exports	5,672	5,268	2,434
Total Imports	14,724	16,497	16,244
Total Imports from U.S.	2,972	3,260	3,008

Comments: An emerging middle-class, growing incomes and increasing urbanization all drive growth of Peruvian household pet owners. Four companies dominate the pet food sector, leading the category in order of appearance: RintiSA, Nestlé, Molitalia and Mars. Veterinary clinics and pet shops are important channels for premium, therapeutic and wet products that register interesting growing rates. In 2014, Argentina (51%), United States (22%) and Colombia (15%) dominated Peru's imported pet food market.

FOREST PRODUCTS

(US$ Millions)

	2012	2013	2014
Total Exports	160	154	165
Total Imports	193	238	264
Total Imports from U.S.	24	17	20

Comments: Mining projects slowing down and construction sector keeping its performance are driving the forest product market sustained growth. Peruvian imports are focused on coniferous - softwoods and engineered woods for furniture and structural purposes. We foresee and opportunity for poles, softwood lumber, OSB and engineered wood. In 2014, Chile (45%), Ecuador (39%), China (11%) and United States (8%) dominated Peru's imported forest products market.

BIOFUEL (ETHANOL)

(Liters-Millions)

	2012	2013	2014
Total Market Size Total Local Production	223.7 235	217.5 240	165.4 245
Total Exports	126	148	143
Total Imports	114.7	125.5	63.4
Total Imports from U.S.	114.7	113.0	57.1

Comments: Ethanol production for calendar year (CY) 2016 is forecast at 160 million liters, a 33% reduction from our CY 2015 estimate. This sharp decrease is attributable to the decommissioning of the Maple plant. We forecast domestic ethanol consumption at 172 million liters in CY 2016, up 7 million liters compared to our 2015 estimate. Peru is currently mandating a 7.8% ethanol blend rate with gasoline. We foresee Peruvian CY 2016 ethanol exports at about 69 million liters, a significant reduction from the 156 million liters estimated for 2015, up by 5 million liters or over 3% compared to our CY 2015 estimate of 160 million liters. Ethanol imports in 2016 are forecast at 80 million liters.

TRADE REGULATIONS, CUSTOMS AND STANDARDS

IMPORT TARIFFS

The entering into force of the Peru Trade Promotion Agreement eliminated duties on 80% of qualifying capital goods since February 1, 2009. The remaining dutiable items have a phase out schedule from 6 to 17 years. Peru imposes no duties on 56% of the items in its tariff schedule (4,224 codes covering some agricultural and intermediate goods, capital goods not produced locally, drip irrigation systems, some vehicles, books, some information technology items, cement, liquefied petroleum gas, some fuels, energy saving bulbs, and bank notes); 6% duties on 34% of the items (2,538 codes mainly regarding consumer goods and some intermediate goods); and 11% duties on 10% of the items (792 codes including rice, sugar, vegetables, dairy products, beef and beef products, chocolate, textiles, apparel, footwear, and other agricultural products). The non-weighted average tariff is 3.2% (including surcharge), down from over 60% in the mid-1990s.

Most imports (93% of codes) are also subject to an 18% value added tax (VAT), as are domestically produced goods. In addition, an excise tax (ISC) is applied to certain products such as tobacco and alcoholic beverages. There are no quantitative import restrictions.

TRADE BARRIERS

In March 1991, Peru introduced an import surcharge on a number of basic agricultural commodities; rice, corn, sugar and dairy products are still subject to potential surcharges. The government argues that the surcharges are necessary to offset exporting countries' subsidies. The surcharges were calculated on a weekly basis, according to prevailing international prices for each commodity. The government however began reducing the surcharges in increments in April 1994. In July 2001 this system was replaced by a "price band system" similar to that of the Andean Community. Thanks to the PTPA, U.S. agricultural goods are no longer subject to this price band

system. Due to decreasing international prices, the surcharge on agricultural imports to Peru under the price band system is currently in effect for non U.S. exporters. This situation benefits U.S.-origin agricultural exports, providing American exporters with an advantage over international competitors in the Peruvian market.

The Peruvian tax and customs agency, Superintendencia Nacional de Administracion Tributaria (SUNAT), implemented in recent years new systems for collecting taxes (VAT and income) in advance as a means to assure tax collection throughout the distribution channel and to increase revenues. This system may not cause much trouble to some sectors but others are being hurt because their margins are smaller than the advanced payments.

IMPORT REQUIREMENTS AND DOCUMENTATION

For imports, Customs (SUNAT) requires a Customs Merchandise Declaration (DAM – in Spanish), a commercial invoice, an airway bill or bill of lading, a packing list, and an insurance letter. If the product is imported from other Andean Community members (Colombia, Ecuador and Bolivia), a certificate of origin is required to qualify for tariff preferences. Several imports are subject to antidumping and countervailing duties. The list of products and countries is available at www.aladi.org . A certificate of origin is required for these products coming from other countries to avoid these duties. U.S. firms have experienced delays clearing products through Customs as a result of this requirement.

A food sanitary registry is required for processed food products (issued by DIGESA 's Food and Environmental Health Bureau or a Sanitary Certificate for animal, plants, or their by-products issued by SENASA).

Goods can be brought into the country and kept in a bonded warehouse without paying import duties for up to twelve months. During that period the importer can pay the duties on the goods kept in the warehouse and clear customs, or re-export them. This can be done for the entire shipment or it can be broken down according to the importer's needs.

Sanitary and Phytosanitary Regulations are drafted, implemented and enforced by SENASA. U.S. exporters are encouraged to request from SENASA an updated list of SPS requirements through the importer before shipping products to Peru.

For food and beverages, the importer must submit a sworn application to DIGESA accompanied by a Certificate of Free Trade and Use issued by the health authority of the country of origin, the future label, and the registration receipt. If the certificate is not available, the importer should present a document issued by the Peruvian Consulate in the country of origin. The sworn application includes the contact information of the importer's company and the manufacturer, taxpayer's identification (RUC), the list of products requested and for each product its content, the results of physical-chemical and microbiological analysis, lot code system, expiration date, packaging material, and storage conditions.

For imports of pharmaceuticals, cosmetics, biological and bio-chemical preparations as well as medical equipment and devices, a prior registration from the Direccion General de Medicamentos y Drogas-DIGEMID of the Ministry of Health is required. This sanitary

registry must be obtained before exporting the products to Peru. This procedure could take between six months to one year and must be performed by the local distributor or representative registered with DIGEMID. Imported products will appear under the name of the local registered company who fulfill the registration process as the representative of the U.S. company. Sanitary registrations must be renewed every five years. For more information contact: DIGEMID www.digemid.minsa.gob.pe

Business travelers who bring along a rather big quantity of samples; brochures; gifts (pens, desk weights, etc.), or similar articles, should be aware that SUNAT may deem those goods as merchandise and thus require the traveler to pay import duties upon entry or otherwise to re-export the goods.

For exports, a Customs Merchandise Declaration (DAM), a commercial invoice and an airway bill or bill of lading are required. Export licenses are required for cultural relics and antiques. In addition, end-user certificates are required for the export or re-export of items on the international munitions list, the international chemical/biological warfare (CBW) list and the missile technology control regime (MTCR) list. Such licenses cover a marginal portion of total Peruvian exports—less than 1%.

U.S. EXPORT CONTROLS

The U.S. government controls the export of weapons, ammunition, high technology machinery and equipment (e.g., certain high performance computers, precision industrial machinery, latest generation night vision equipment, polygraphs, etc.) and some chemicals (e.g., sodium cyanide).

A list that consolidates eleven export screening lists of the Departments of Commerce, State and the Treasury into a single search as an aid to industry in conducting electronic screens of potential parties to regulated transactions is available here: http://export.gov/ecr/eg_main_023148.asp .

TEMPORARY ENTRY

Some goods can be admitted into Peru temporarily for re-export within a year with a bond that guarantees the duties and taxes. The list with the 23 types of goods, Annex 1 to Resolucion Ministerial 287-98-EF/10 y modificatorias, is available at http://www.sunat.gob.pe/. Other documentation requirements are the same as those listed above.

LABELING AND MARKING REQUIREMENTS

Before reaching the point of sale, imported packaged foods must carry a separate adhesive label with a Spanish translation, including the importer/distributor's contact information and RUC (taxpayer number). Law 28405 (November 30, 2004) requires labeling for value-added products other than foods. If imported products do not comply with these requirements for customs clearance, importers are allowed to properly label them in private warehouses.

For food products, labeling requirements are relatively simple. Products normally retain their original labels, and the name and (RUC) of the manufacturer, importer, or distributor must be added to the packaging. The Ministry of Health, through its DIGESA bureau, is in charge of issuing the sanitary registration numbers for food products. The Consumer Protection Office of Peru's Consumer Defense Agency, INDECOPI is responsible for food and beverage labeling and advertising.

Food label contents must include the name of the product and country of manufacture. For perishable products, the following information must be included: expiration date, conservation instructions and warnings, ingredients, and net content of the product (by weight or volume). The label must also include information on dangerous ingredients. It is mandatory to include the name, address in Peru of the manufacturer, importer or distributor as well as the taxpayer number (RUC), sanitary registration number obtained from DIGESA, risk warning, and emergency treatment, when applicable. Perishable products must have the information clearly and visibly in Spanish.

On March 7, 2011, INDECOPI published a draft regulation to Article 37 of the Consumer Protection and Defense Code – Law 29571 (approved by Congress on September 2, 2010). The regulation entered into force through a Supreme Decree later that year and details the procedures and requirements for implementing mandatory labeling for genetically modified (GM) products.

Food packaging must be made of harmless material, free of substances that could affect food safety. Likewise, packages must be manufactured so as to preserve the product's sanitary quality and composition throughout its useful life according to the Ministry of Health's sanitary standards. Packaging with recycled paper, cardboard, or plastic is forbidden.

Materials and food additives for food and beverage manufacturing must meet the health quality requirements established in the sanitary standards issued by DIGESA. The use of food additives not included in the list of additives permitted by the *Codex alimentarius* is forbidden. Flavorings accepted by the U.S. Food and Drug Administration (FDA) and the Flavor and Extractive Manufacturing Association (FEMA) are permissible.

PROHIBITED AND RESTRICTED IMPORTS

The list of prohibited/restricted items from importation can be found on the following website: http://www.sunat.gob.pe/orientacionaduanera/mercanciasrestringidas includes flour potassium bromate, mercuric oxide, carbon tetrachloride, among other chemical products. Used tires, clothing and shoes are also prohibited. Only donations of used clothing and shoes are exempt from the prohibition. Donations provided to the private sector must obtain an authorization from the "Agencia Peruana de Cooperación Internacional", APCI (http://www.apci.gob.pe) before they arrive to Peru while donations to the public sector will require an authorization from the Peruvian Council of Ministers. Failure to meet these requirements may result in the shipper's or consignee's being assessed duties, fines, warehousing or other expenses before the donated goods can clear customs. Other products that are prohibited for import are some insecticides and fireworks. Toxic waste is also restricted. Imports of used cars older than five years and used buses and trucks older than two years old are prohibited, as are used tires.

U.S. imports of live cattle face technical barriers to trade; in 2013 the United States was declared at negligible risk for Bovine spongiform encephalopathy (BSE) by the OIE (World Organization for Animal Health). The Peruvian agency, SENASA, established strict regulations regarding BSE and other diseases. However, a deal was announced in April 2015 that SENASA approved the USDA Veterinary Health Certificate for the import of U.S. live cattle. This export certificate should be officially enacted in July of 2015.

CUSTOMS REGULATIONS AND CONTACT INFORMATION

Imports with an FOB value in 2014 higher than about US$ 4,070 (11,400 Nuevos Soles at the 2.80 exchange rate to the dollar, of three so-called tax reference units, Unidad Impositiva Tributaria-UIT) pay 89.30 Nuevos Soles fee (2.35% of one UIT) for the "valuation service". For 2014 one UIT is 3,800 Nuevos Soles (approx. US$1,360). In practice, Customs applies a US$34 flat valuation fee. Items imported under the U.S.-Peru Trade Promotion Act – PTPA, are exempt from this fee.

As stated above in the "Import Requirements and Documentation" section, Customs' priority is revenue generation rather than trade facilitation. Despite having signed the WTO customs valuation procedure, Peruvian customs uses a referential price verification system (Sistema de Verificación de Precios, SIVEP). Peru's custom agency Superintendence Nacional de Administración Tributaria(SUNAT), has a data base for price consultation of goods from each country, and from different suppliers. This allows for viewing and comparing declared values in commercial invoices and to make adjustments to identical or similar merchandise's prices that are less expensive than the average file.

SUNAT does accept discounts, as long as it appears on the bill and is unincorporated from the normal sales value, but the reason for the discount should be indicated to see if it is acceptable.

SUNNAT often request that the importer provide a Manufacturer's Price List. This document must be certified by Peru consulate in the country of purchase. This price list should not be addressed to the importer, but just with general information. This is very important in order to be accepted by SUNAT.

This system has prompted several complaints from local importers that SUNAT is assessing values above the real ones. One U.S. exporter has complained that SUNAT does not accept its invoices, valuing instead imports using price lists that do not consider distributor discounts. For SUNAT to accept the invoice value, it must be accompanied by a price list, and the discount must be described and detailed in the invoice. Payment terms must also be detailed. The SUNAT chapter of the US-PTPA addresses the referential pricing issue and is consistent with Peru's WTO obligations.

Contact Information for Peruvian Customs:

Superintendencia Nacional de Administración Tributaria

Av. Garcilaso de la Vega 1472, Lima, Peru

(511) 315-0730

Website: http://www.sunat.gob.pe/

Mr. Victor Martin Ramos, National Intendant of Tax Compliance (Intendente Nacional de Cumplimiento Tributario); vramos@sunat.gob.pe

Mr. Luis Enrique Narro, National Intendant of Taxpayer Service (Intendente Nacional de Servicios al Contribuyente); lnarro@sunat.gob.pe

Ms. Maria Ysabel Frassinetti, National Intendant of Customs Procedures (Intendente Nacional Tecnica Aduanera); mfrassinetti@sunat.gob.pe

TRADE AND CUSTOMES STANDARS

INDECOPI, the Defense of Competition and the Protection of Intellectual Property Agency (http://www.indecopi.gob.pe/) is the Peruvian standards development organization. Its Commission of Technical Regulations (CTR), created in 1992, addresses standards matters. The Commission has three functions:

• Approve technical standards and metrology regulations.

• Accreditation of the public or private institutions that may provide conformity assessments.

• Defense of free trade under World Trade Organization Technical Barriers to Trade (TBT) Agreement.

STANDARDS ORGANIZATIONS

The following is a list of the committees and directories inside the CTR working with standards issues:

• Committee for Testing Methodology
• Committee for Water Meters Testing
• Committee for Testing Laboratories
• Committee for Product Certifying Organizations
• Committee for Metrology Services
• Committee for Quality Management Accreditation
• Committee for International Standards Norms

NIST NOTIFY U.S. SERVICE

Member countries of the World Trade Organization (WTO) are required under the Agreement on Technical Barriers to Trade (TBT Agreement) to report to the WTO all proposed technical regulations that could affect trade with other Member countries. Notify U.S. is a free, web-based e-mail subscription service that offers

an opportunity to review and comment on proposed foreign technical regulations that can affect your access to international markets. Register online at http://www.nist.gov/notifyus/.

CONFORMITY ASSESSMENT

The following firms are certified by CTR to provide Conformity Assessment services:

• INASA- Phone: (511) 616-5200, http://www.inassagroup.com.pe/

• SGS del Perú: (511) 517-1900, http://www.pe.sgs.com/

• BSI Inspectorate Perú: (511) 613-8080, http://www.inspectorate.com/peru/

• EQUAS S.A.: (511) 349-4050, http://equas.com.pe/

• SG Nortek: (metrology services) (511) 572-2630, sgnortek@terra.com.pe

PRODUCT CERTIFICATION

Products coming from the U.S. will not have problems entering Peru if importers receive information in advance regarding the products' composition and/or ingredients. The Peruvian standards body's (CTR) regulatory framework is similar to that of the U.S. It is common to hold seminars sponsored by ANSI, ASTM, NEMA and others to encourage conformity with global standards.

ACCREDITATION

There are accreditation bodies for different industries.

http://www.digesa.sld.pe/

The laboratories that can provide assistance to U.S exporters can be found at: http://www.indecopi.gob.pe/repositorioaps/0/0/jer/acre01/Direct_Organ_Eva_Conf/LabDeEnsayo/RelacionLab(165).pdf

PUBLICATION OF TECHNICAL REGULATIONS

The office responsible for publishing standards and notifying private and public organizations is the National Information Service (SNI-CRT) under CTR. This office is also responsible for notifying the WTO-TBT Committee about changes related to standards issues in Peru. It is under that scheme that the U.S. and other countries may comment on modifications and propose new standards.

LABELING AND MARKING

In November 2004 Peru issued a new regulation on labeling and marking (Ley del Rotulado - Law 28405). This new law establishes that products exported to Peru should have a label with the following information:

• name of product

• country of origin

• address of exporter, importer, or distributor

• expiration date

• conservation method

• weight in metric system

• risks, if any, to use

International quality marks should be visible and easy to identify.

CONTACTS

The contact information at INDECOPI and CTR in Lima is:
(511) 224-7800 ext. 1261, fax (511) 224-7800 ext.1296.
The points of contact regarding standards issues at the U.S. Foreign Commercial Service in the Embassy Lima are:
Ricardo J. Peláez, Commercial Counselor
Gustavo Romero, Commercial Specialist
Phone: (511) 618-2442.

TRADE AGREEMENTS

Peruvians and Americans benefit from the PTPA, which entered into force on February 1, 2009.

Peru has been a member of the Andean Community (and its predecessor, the Andean Pact) since 1969. The Andean Community is currently comprised of Peru, Ecuador, Colombia, and Bolivia. In January 2002, the member countries of the Andean Community agreed to establish an Andean free trade zone, a common external tariff (CET), and a customs harmonization policy by January 2004. However, Andean Community members have not implemented these measures.

Peru is a member of the WTO and became a full member of the Asia-Pacific Economic Cooperation (APEC) forum in November 1998. Peru also has free trade agreements with the United States, Canada, Chile, the European Union, China, the European Free Trade Association (which includes Iceland, Liechtenstein, Norway and Switzerland), Honduras, Japan, Mexico, Panama, Singapore, South Korea, and Thailand. It has Framework Agreements with MERCOSUR countries (Argentina, Brazil, Uruguay, and Paraguay), the Andean Community of Nations (Bolivia, Ecuador, and Colombia), and a partial preferential agreement with Cuba. Agreements have been signed and are awaiting implementation with Costa Rica, Guatemala, and Venezuela.

Peru is participating in the negotiations of the Trans-Pacific Partnership (TPP), which aims to create a regional free trade agreement involving Australia, Brunei Darussalam, Chile, Canada, Japan, Malaysia, Mexico, New Zealand, Peru, Singapore, the United States, and Vietnam. The Peruvian government also is finalizing free trade agreements with El Salvador and negotiating free trade agreements with Turkey and India. Peru is a founding member of the Pacific Alliance, a new regional economic block with Mexico, Colombia, and Chile. It seeks the integration of the member countries and accounts for more than one third of Latin America's GDP.

Peru is currently the 32nd largest export market for U.S. goods. U.S. exports to Peru amounted to US$10.07 billion in 2014.

WEB RESOURCES

http://www.ustr.gov/trade-agreements/free-trade-agreements/peru-tpa/

TRADE AND PROJECT FINANCING

METHODS OF PAYMENT

According to Banco de Crédito del Perú, Peru's largest bank, 60% of payments for exports to Peru are via open accounts. Open account use has increased dramatically as Peru's economy has strengthened since 1990. Documentary collections are the second most common payment method, involving over 20% of total transactions. Letters of credit account for about 16% of transactions (down from close to 100% before 1990). Traders use other payment methods, including factoring, banker's acceptances, and cash in advance. Banks are the usual collectors for exports to Peru. Most credit cards are widely accepted with American Express, MasterCard, Visa and Diners Club being the most preferred.

The leading credit-rating agency in Peru is Dun & Bradstreet S.A.C. (www.dnbperu.com.pe dnb@dnbperu.com.pe), followed by Coface Peru (www.coface.com.pe ; coface.peru@coface.com.pe) and Informa Peru (www.informadelperu.com/english/index.html ; clientes@informadelperu.com)

There are two credit-reporting agencies in Peru, Infocorp/Equifax (www.infocorp.com.pe ; info@infocorp.com.pe), and CERTICOM (www.certicom.com.pe ; certicom@certicom.com.pe).

The Securities and Exchange Supervisory Agency (SMV, www.smv.gob.pe) lists the following four risk-rating agencies:

- Apoyo & Asociados Internacionales S.A.C. Clasificadora de Riesgo (www.aai.com.pe)
- Clasificadora de Riesgo Pacific Credit Rating SAC (www.ratingspcr.com)
- Class & Asociados S.A. Clasificadora de Riesgo (www.classrating.com)
- Equilibrium Clasificadora de Riesgo S.A. (www.equilibrium.com.pe).

BANKING SYSTEM

Peru's adherence to sound fiscal and monetary policies helped the country withstand the 2008-2009 global financial crisis, China's economic slowdown, and the ongoing situation in Europe. Peru's current economic situation is a far cry from that in the mid-to-late-1990s when its banks were heavily dependent on foreign credit lines (59% of the banks' credit sources in the first half of 1998 came from foreign credit lines). Before the 1990s

Peru suffered from chronic balance of payments and fiscal deficits, and from extremely low foreign reserves.

As of December 2014, Peru had over US$62.31 billion of net foreign reserves. Most banks' funding comes from domestic deposits. The local branches of foreign banks are strong. Private pension funds control large and growing assets. The financial system enjoys a low delinquency ratio. Additionally, the Ministry of Economy and Finance saved close to US$6 billion from fiscal surpluses in the 2006-2008 period. The Peruvian government used part of these savings to address the effects of the global financial crisis in 2008-2009 when Peru had a US$2.4 billion fiscal deficit. From 2009 to 2013, Peru again ran a fiscal surplus because of domestic demand, high commodity prices, exports, and foreign investment.

Trade financing is available to the Peruvian purchasers of U.S. goods and services through their local banks. The Export-Import Bank of the United States (Ex-Im Bank) offers loans and loan guarantees to U.S. exporters of goods and services and foreign purchasers. The Ex-Im Bank also provides credit insurance to U.S. businesses against non-payment by foreign buyers in the case of political or commercial risk. The Overseas Private Investment Corporation (OPIC), an independent U.S. government agency, offers medium- to long-term financing and political risk insurance.

Peru's financial system consists of 17 commercial banks, 33 municipal and rural savings banks and microfinance institutions, twelve specialized institutions ("financieras"), two leasing institutions, and four government-owned entities: the Central Bank (Banco Central de Reserva del Peru, or BCRP), the government's financial agent (Banco de la Nacion), development banks, the Corporación Financiera de Desarrollo (COFIDE) and Agrarian Bank. These institutions, along with five private pension fund administrators, 14 insurance companies, and 20 miscellaneous companies, are regulated by the Superintendence of Banks, Insurance, and Pension Funds Administrators, (Superintendencia de Banca y Seguros, SBS). SBS policy generally follows regulatory guidelines set by the Switzerland-based Bank for International Settlements (BIS). For example, regulators must audit bank financial statements in compliance with internationally accepted auditing standards. In cases not covered by BIS guidelines, regulators use standards set by the International Financial Reporting Standards (IFRS). In addition, SBS regulations require that at least two independent credit rating agencies, accredited by the SBS, conduct periodic compulsory assessments for all deposit-taking institutions. However, another 150 savings and loan corporations operate in an environment almost devoid of government oversight.

Financial institutions allocate credit on market terms. Observers consider the banking industry in Peru as competitive in serving customers. Private pension funds have competed in recent years for both private and public bonds issued locally by companies and the Peruvian government. These entities compete actively because the supply of domestic securities is insufficient given the small size of the local market. Foreign investors can obtain credit and float bonds on the local market. Several of them have done so in the last few years while terms remain more competitive than terms of usual international centers. Under the U.S.-Peru Trade Promotion Agreement (PTPA), U.S. financial service suppliers have full rights to establish subsidiaries or branches for banks and insurance companies.

The private sector has access to a variety of credit instruments. In 2014, primary issuance of bonds reached $1.17 billion, 33% below the previous year. Mutual funds managed US$6.29 billion in December 2014, a 6.5% increase from the December 2013 level. By December 2014, private pension funds managed a total of US$38.1 billion.

The banking system is considered generally sound, thanks to lessons learned during the 1997-1998 Asian Crisis. Since then, the SBS has progressively revamped operations, increased capitalization, and reduced costs. Using conservative criteria, SBS assessed that 2.4% of total loans were non-performing as of December 2014, down from a high of 11% in early 2001.

Customer deposits carry insurance financed by commercial bank contributions to an insurance fund (www.fsd.org.pe). The amount changes quarterly on the basis of the wholesale price index. For the December 2011-February 2012 period, the insurance fund insures accounts up to US$33,930. Peruvian law empowers the BCR to act as a "lender of last resort" in the case of a run on any commercial bank only up to the limit of the bank's net worth, since the SBS has set liquidity requirements on deposits and other short-term liabilities at relatively high levels. Banks must also meet liquidity requirements on all short-term liabilities, including amounts due to banks outside of Peru. Should the need arise (in cases of currency stress), the Central Bank has immediate access to US$662 million in credits from the Latin American Reserves Fund (Fondo Latinoamericano de Reservas, or FLAR), for up to one month or US$828 million for up to three years. The Central Bank can also access other credits for longer terms. U.S. Treasury instruments back FLAR's assets.

FOREIGN-EXCHANGE CONTROLS

The Peruvian government eliminated foreign-exchange controls in 1990. The BCR, however, has kept a tight lid on the amount that local private pension funds (AFP) can invest in foreign securities. In July 2011 a law increased this limit to 50%, but the BCR only raised the "operative" limit to 32% at the end of 2012. In recent years AFPs have protested this limit on grounds that the local securities market is still small and unable to absorb the increasing funds the AFPs manage. The BCR has signaled its readiness to increase the ceiling in response to these concerns. Companies and individuals are free to maintain and operate accounts in domestic and foreign currencies at local or foreign banks.

U.S. BANKS AND LOCAL CORRESPONDENT BANKS

Citibank is the only U.S. bank operating in Peru. In May 2015, Citibank sold its consumer retail division to Scotiabank and remains in Peru strictly working on commercial matters. Most U.S. companies select a correspondent bank by soliciting a recommendation from their U.S. bank. Most Peruvian banks have correspondent banking relationships with a U.S. bank or banks. As of June 2011, the commercial banks in Peru that had correspondent banking relationships with U.S. banks include (in alphabetical order):

Banco BBVA-Continental (http://www.bbvabancocontinental.com)
Banco de Comercio (http://www.bancomercio.com)
Banco de Crédito del Perú (http://www.viabcp.com)
Banco Financiero del Peru (http://www.financiero.com.pe)
Banco Interamericano de Finanzas (http://www.bif.com.pe)
Banco Santander (http://www.santander.com.pe
Citibank (http://www.citibank.com/peru)
HSBC Bank Peru (http://www.hsbc.com.pe)
Interbank (http://www.interbank.com.pe)
Scotiabank Peru (http://www.scotiabank.com.pe)

PROJECT FINANCING

Since the market reforms of the early 1990s, the private sector has carried out all major projects, though sometimes in a Public-Private Partnership with the government. Foreign companies have undertaken large projects with financing obtained in their countries of registration, from multilateral development banks, and/or from local lenders. In recent years, due to the Central Bank limit on the amount that Peruvian pension funds can invest abroad, there has been intense local competition for lending, interest rates have fallen below those in New York and London for creditworthy companies, and local banks have increased their sophistication. The number of projects totally or partly financed locally has grown since 1999. The three major banks involved in this area are Banco de Crédito del Peru, Banco BBVA-Continental, and Citibank. Some projects, such as the Camisea natural gas pipeline, have been partly financed by multilateral development banks, including the IDB, World Bank, and Andean Finance Corporation (CAF). Some projects have been structured with simultaneous or subsequent financing from the local capital market (e.g., corporate bonds). The U.S. Ex-Im Bank is an active market participant. There are 12 active Ex-Im Bank lenders/brokers operating in Peru. The U.S. Commercial Service Lima office offers a list of these companies.

WEB RESOURCES

Trade Finance Guide: A Quick Reference for U.S. Exporters, published by the International Trade Administration's Industry & Analysis team: http://www.export.gov/tradefinanceguide/index.asp

Export-Import Bank of the United States: http://www.exim.gov
Country Limitation Schedule: http://www.exim.gov/tools/country/country_limits.html
OPIC: http://www.opic.gov
Trade and Development Agency: http://www.tda.gov/
SBA's Office of International Trade: http://www.sba.gov/oit/
USDA Commodity Credit Corporation: http://www.fsa.usda.gov/ccc/default.htm
U.S. Agency for International Development: http://www.usaid.gov
Inter-American Development Bank: http://www.iadb.org
The World Bank Group: http://www.worldbank.org

BUSINESS TRAVEL

BUSINESS CUSTOMS

In Peru business dress is conservative, meaning suits and ties for men and dresses or suits for women are the norm. It is customary to exchange business cards at the outset of a meeting.

Business travelers to Peru seeking appointments with U.S. Embassy Lima officials should contact the Commercial Service in advance. The Commercial Service can be reached by telephone at (511) 618-2442 or 434-3040; by fax at (511) 434-3041, by email at: Office.Lima@trade.gov , or see the website at http://export.gov/peru/.

TRAVEL ADVISORY

International business travelers increasingly find a sufficient number of rooms in local hotels, several built in recent years. General travel information, including travel warnings and alerts, can be found at U.S. Department of State's webpage at http://travel.state.gov/ .

The Department of State issues Country Specific Information for all foreign countries, including Peru, with information including the location of the U.S. embassy or consulate, immigration requirements, health conditions, minor political disturbances, unusual currency and entry regulations, crime and security information, and drug penalties. Peru's Country Specific Information can be found at

http://travel.state.gov/content/passports/english/country/peru.html /.

The U.S. Embassy in Lima also maintains a website with a wealth of information for U.S. business travelers at http://lima.usembassy.gov/ .

The Department of State recommends that all U.S. citizens traveling overseas enroll their trip with the Smart Traveler Enrollment Program. Travelers may register their stay in Peru online at http://travel.state.gov/content/passports/english/go/step.html/ .

VISA REQUIREMENTS

A valid U.S. passport is required to enter Peru. Tourists staying less than 90 days do not require a visa. It is recommended that business travelers to Peru enter as tourists provided they are not reimbursed for their services while in Peru. However, if any compensation is earned and paid while in Peru, a business visa is required and an income tax declaration must be processed before departing Peru. This process takes approximately three days.

Travelers needing a business visa should contact the Peruvian Consulate General Office in Washington, D.C located at 1625 Massachusetts Avenue, N.W., 6th Floor, Washington, D.C. 20036; telephone number: (202) 462-1081; website: http://www.embassyofperu.org/ . There are also Peruvian consulates in Atlanta, Boston, Chicago, Dallas, Denver, Hartford, Houston, Los Angeles, Miami, New York, Paterson, and San Francisco.

U.S. Companies that require travel of foreign businesspersons to the United States should be advised that security evaluations are handled via an interagency process. Visa applicants should go to the following links.

State Department Visa Website: http://travel.state.gov/visa/

U.S. Embassy Lima Non-Immigrant and Immigrant Visas Section:
http://lima.usembassy.gov/visas.html

TELECOMMUNICATIONS

The telecommunications industry in Peru has been steadily modernized following the privatization of the national telephone company, which was bought by Telefónica de España (http://www.telefonica.com.pe) in 1994. Wireless internet access is available at many restaurants and cafes, as well as internet cafes. Telefónica has 55% of the mobile market and 81% of the landline market. Some companies and individuals have complained about Telefónica's customer service and slow installation rate. Competitors in the mobile market include Claro (http:// http://www.claro.com.pe) and Chilean-owned Entel, which acquired Nextel in April 2013. A new competitor that entered the market in 2014 is Viettel, a Vietnamese mobile operator. However, customers may use their U.S. providers while in Peru, since most U.S. providers offer international roaming services.

For travelers to Peru, a smartphone will function if it has GSM/GPRS service. For long distance calling there are a variety of pre-paid calling services. Long distance Direct Access through credit card numbers for AT&T, Sprint, and MCI WorldCom is also available. International calls can be made through Voice over Internet Protocol (VoIP) services such as Skype or Google Talk. Major U.S. long distance calling cards can be used at major hotels.

TRANSPORTATION

Airlines

There are eighteen international passenger airlines and six companies serving routes within Peru. Currently five U.S. airline companies offer 98 non-stop flights between the U.S. and Peru. American Airlines offers fourteen weekly flights Lima-Miami and seven weekly flights Lima-Dallas; Delta Airlines provides seven weekly flights Lima-Atlanta; United Airlines services seven weekly flights Lima-Newark and seven Lima-Houston. The low fare companies, Spirit Airlines and Jet Blue, provide seven weekly flights each Lima-Ft. Lauderdale. In addition, Avianca offers seven weekly flights to Miami while LAN Airlines services fourteen weekly non-stop flights from Lima to Miami, seven to New York, and fourteen to Los Angeles. Ninety-five percent of the international flights arrive at "Jorge Chavez International Airport" in Lima. Most of these airline companies also provide cargo transportation services.

Domestic flights between Lima and larger cities in Peru are provided by LAN Peru, Avianca, L.C. Peru, Star Peru, Peruvian Airlines, and ATSA (charter service.) Cusco is the second busiest commercial airport within Peru with more than twenty daily flights from Lima. Other international companies serving Peru and serving other countries are: Aerolineas Argentinas, Aeromexico, Air Canada, Air Europa, Air France, Copa Airlines, Iberia, KLM, LAN Airlines, Sky Airlines, Avianca, and TAM providing passenger and cargo services through the "Jorge Chavez International Airport" run by Lima Airport Partners (LAP).

Railways

The railway system in Peru is not well-developed and is limited to 1,928.8 kilometers formed by:

- Ferrocarril del Centro of 489.6 Km. Given in concession to Ferrovias Central Andina and operated by Ferrocarril Central Andino (FCCA). FCCA offers cargo services of minerals Huancayo-La Oroya-Callao and Cerro de Pasco-La Oroya-Callao and seasonal passenger services Lima-Huancayo.

- Ferrocarril Huancayo-Huancavelica of 128.7 Km. Run by the Ministry of Transport and Communications providing cargo and passenger services.

- Ferrocarril del Sur of 989.7 Km. Given in concession to Ferrocarril Transandino, operates Matarani-Arequipa-Puno, Juliaca-Cusco, Cusco-Machu Picchu, and Pacha-Urubamba. PeruRail and Inca Rai/1provide passenger roundtrip services from Cusco or the Sacred Valley to Machu Picchu in Aguas Calientes. PeruRail also offers passenger services between Cusco and Puno.

-Ferrocarril Tacna-Arica of 60 Km. Run and operated by the Regional Government of Tacna providing cargo and passenger services.

- Ferrocarril Toquepala-Ilo of 217.7 Km. Operated by the private mining company, Southern Peru Copper Corp. carries concentrates from the copper mines of Toquepala and Cuajone to the Ilo smelter, and the Ilo refinery to the port of Ilo.

-Ferrocarril Caripa-Condorcoha of 13.6 Km. Operated by the private cement company, Cemento Andino.

-Ferrocarril Santa-Clara-Cajamarquilla of 7.3 Km. Operated by the Brazilian company Votorantim Metais carries concentrates from the Cajamarquilla zinc plant.

Supreme Decree No. 059-2010-MTC approved Lima's basic metro system, the electric system of massive transportation of Lima and Callao, which includes 5 lines. Line 1,

already in operation, consists of two routes. The first one with a length of 22.2 Km., connecting Villa El Salvador with Estación Grau in Cercado de Lima (downtown Lima), and the second route recently inaugurated with 12.40 Km. long with ten stations, connecting Cercado de Lima to El Agustino and San Juan de Lurigancho.

The second Lima Metro line of 35 Km running east to west from Ate to Callao was recently awarded to the consortia Nuevo Metro de Lima formed by COSAPI (Peru), and European companies Impregilo, Iridium, Vialia, Ansaldo Breda and Ansaldo STS. Dragados, FCC and Iridium. This USD$5.6 billion investment will start its operation in June, 2014 and should be concluded in June 2019. It will have 35 stations and will travel underground through nine districts in Lima and three in Callao. Additionally a branch of 8 Km. will be built from Gambetta and Faucett avenues towards the Lima's Jorge Chavez International Airport.

Ground transportation

Public bus and mini-bus ("combi") ground urban and inter-city transportation is not recommended due to a high incidence of traffic accidents in Peru and, in the case of inter-city transportation, due to the high rate of highway bus robberies. Taxis are not metered, so fares must be negotiated before getting into the cab, with the caveat that few taxi drivers speak English. Taxis are plentiful and provide an inexpensive way to get around Lima and in major cities; however it is recommended to arrange these services with the hotels or call a radio taxi company. Non-contracted taxi services should only be used when other options are unavailable given numerous safety concerns related to the security and legitimacy of Peruvian taxi travel. Furthermore, given the increasingly congested traffic conditions and security concerns, it is advisable that business travelers contract hourly taxi service or hire cars with drivers instead of renting a vehicle. Tips are not expected on short rides. If you lease a car with a driver, a tip is common.

Airport Taxis

Transportation to and from the airport by radio taxi or taxi service is approximately US$25. The traveler can make transportation arrangements with the hotel before arrival or use one of the taxi services at the Lima International airport. The two taxi services that are considered safe and reliable are: MITSUI and CMV. These taxi services counters can be located in the baggage and customs area of the airport. The service counter is located on the left side before exiting the terminal glass doors. The domestic wing has similar taxi services.

LANGUAGE

Business is conducted in Spanish. Although a large number of executives in the Peruvian business community speak English, promotional literature should be translated into Spanish. Quechua and Aymara are spoken in the Andean highlands. High-tech companies like Microsoft and Claro promote their products in the traditional languages.

HEALTH

Peruvian medical facilities do not generally meet U.S. standards, although some private clinics do. If visitors take certain precautions about food and drink, the level of risk is manageable. Cholera, dengue, chikungunya and other infectious diseases such as hepatitis A, B and C are present in Peru. Travelers in Peru should always consume bottled beverages instead of potentially contaminated water. Avoid ice cubes. Fish, shellfish, and vegetables should not be eaten unless well cooked, and all food should be eaten while still hot. Peeled fruits are generally safe. Travelers to the jungle areas of Peru should have up-to-date yellow fever vaccinations and malaria prophylaxis. There are several clinics in the Lima area which have U.S.-trained personnel and up-to-date medical equipment. Since U.S. medical insurance is not always valid outside the United States, supplemental insurance is useful, especially to provide coverage for medical evacuation.

LOCAL TIME, BUSINESS HOURS, AND HOLIDAYS

Lima is situated directly south of New York and is in the Eastern Standard time zone (UTC minus 5), but Peru does not follow daylight savings time. Dates are written starting with the day of the month, followed by the month and finishing with the year.

Business hours in Peru are generally from 9:00 a.m. to 6:00 p.m. Breakfast meetings are becoming more common, and business lunches are normally scheduled between the hours of

1:00 to 3:30 p.m. Some shops and businesses operate from 10:00 a.m. to 1:00 p.m. and from 4:00 p.m. to 8:00 p.m., although continuous operation is increasingly common. Business offices, excluding banks, are closed on Saturdays. In the provinces, business hours are usually from 9:00 a.m. to 1:00 p.m. and from 4:00 p.m. to 7:00 p.m. "Peruvian time" refers to the fact that it is acceptable to arrive a half an hour late for social functions. However, punctuality is generally expected for business visitors for social and business functions.

Upcoming Peruvian official holidays are:

Saints Peter and Paul	June 29
Independence Day	July 28-29
Saint Rose of Lima	August 30
Battle of Angamos	October 8
All Saints' Day	November 1
Immaculate Conception	December 8
Christmas Day	December 25
New Year's Day	January 1
Holy Thursday	March 24
Good Friday	March 26
Labor Day	May 1

The U.S. Embassy is closed on these holidays and the following U.S. holidays:

Independence Day	July 3, 2015
Labor Day	September 7
Columbus Day	October 12
Veterans Day	November 11
Thanksgiving	November 26
Martin Luther King Day	January 18
President's Day	February 15
Memorial Day	May 30

TEMPORARY ENTRY OF MATERIALS AND PERSONAL BELONGINGS

Goods for registered trade fairs may temporarily enter Peru by paying a bond, but without paying duties, and following the normal documentation requirements mentioned in Chapter 5, Section "Import Requirements and Documentation." In addition to normal passenger baggage, a cellular phone (and its accessories) and a laptop are allowed without paying duties.

To access Peruvian customs information in English, refer to:

http://www.sunat.gob.pe/customsinformation/index.html

Customs Guide for Travelers:

http://www.sunat.gob.pe/customsinformation/passengerinformation/index.html

Customs Baggage Declaration Form, with the list of items that travelers can bring duty-free: http://www.sunat.gob.pe/orientacionaduanera/viajeros/formatos/DDJJ-Ingles.pdf

WEB RESOURCES

U.S. Department of State's Travel Website: http://travel.state.gov/
U.S. Department of State's Country Specific Information for Peru:
http://travel.state.gov/content/passports/english/country/peru.html
U.S. Department of State's Consular Information Sheet for Peru:
http://travel.state.gov/content/passports/english/country/peru.html
U.S. Embassy in Lima: http://lima.usembassy.gov /
U.S. Department of State's Smart Traveler Enrollment Program (STEP):
http://travel.state.gov/content/passports/english/go/step.html/
Embassy of Peru in Washington D.C.: http://www.embassyofperu.org/
U.S. Embassy in Lima, Lost and Stolen Passports: http://lima.usembassy.gov/lostpass.html/
U.S. Department of State, Visas: http://travel.state.gov/content/visas/english.html
U.S. Embassy in Lima, Visas: http://lima.usembassy.gov/visas.html/
Peruvian Customs Information in English: http://www.sunat.gob.pe/customsinformation/index.html

INPORTANT GOVERNMETN AND BUSINESS CONTACTS

U.S. GOVERNMENT

U.S. Department of Commerce (U.S. Embassy Lima, Peru)
U.S. Commercial Service Lima
3230 Lima Place
Washington, DC 20521
Ricardo J. Peláez, Commercial Counselor
Rachel Kreissl, Commercial Officer
Cesar Jochamowitz, Senior Commercial Specialist
Flora Muroi, Commercial Specialist
Gustavo Romero, Commercial Specialist
Jorge Prado, Commercial Specialist
Tel.: (511) 618-2442, 434-3040 Fax: (511) 434-3041
E-mail: Office.lima@trade.gov
Website: http://export.gov/peru/

Trade Information Center in Washington: 1-800-USA-TRADE
www.ita.doc.gov/td/tic/

U.S. Department of Commerce (Washington, D.C.)
14th & Constitution Avenue, N.W. Room Nr. C-300
Washington, D.C. 20230
Matthew Gaisford, Peru Desk Officer
Email: matthew.gaisford@trade.gov
Tel.: (202) 482-0052 Fax: (202) 482-1972
Website: http://www.commerce.gov/

U.S. Department of State (U.S. Embassy Lima, Peru)
Unit 3230
DPO AA 34031 - USA
Ambassador Brian A. Nichols
Mark Cullinane, Economic Counselor
Ernest Abisellan, Deputy Economic Counselor

Benjamin Yates, Economic Officer
Esteban Sandoval, Economic Specialist
Tel.: (511) 618-2410
Website: http://lima.usembassy.gov/econ.html

U.S. Department of State (Washington, D.C.)
2201 C Street N.W., Room 4915.
Washington, D.C. 20520
Shane Hough, Peru Desk Officer
Tel.: (202) 647-4177
Email: houghms@state.gov
Website: http://www.state.gov

U.S Department of Agriculture/ Foreign Agricultural Service (FAS)
(U.S. Embassy Lima, Peru)
Unit 3230, Box 381
DPO AA 34031
Tel: (511) 618-2491, 434-3042 I Fax: (511) 434-3043
Casey Bean, Regional Agricultural Counselor
Mariano J. Beillard, Regional Agricultural Attaché
Gaspar Nolte, Senior Agricultural Specialist
Alvaro Loza, Agricultural Marketing Specialist
Email: Aglima@fas.usda.gov
Websites: http://www.usda.gov and http://www.fas.usda.gov

Animal and Plant Health Inspection Service (APHIS)
Tel.: (511) 434-4202 Fax: (511) 434-0958
George "Andy" Ball, Senior Attaché for Chile, Ecuador, and Peru (resident in Lima)
Gladys Solano, APHIS Program Specialist
Email: gladys.solano@aphis.usda.gov
Tel: (511) 434-4202 I Fax: (511) 434-0958
Website: http://www.aphis.usda.gov
U.S. Department of Agriculture
1401 Independence Avenue, S.W. - MS 1071
Washington, D.C. 20250
Lisa Anderson, Western Hemisphere Area Director, Office of Foreign Service Operations
Email: lisa.anderson@fas.usda.gov
Tel: (202) 720-3221 I Fax: (202) 720-5183
Website: http://www.usda.gov and http:// www.fas.usda.gov

U.S. Department of Agriculture/ Foreign Agricultural Service
Trade Assistance and Promotion Office
Tel: (202) 720-7420
Fax: (703) 875-4009
Export-Import Bank of the United States (Ex-Im Bank)
811 Vermont Avenue, N.W.
Washington D.C. 20571
Tel.: Toll Free (800) 565-EXIM (3946), Business Development (202) 565-3900
Fax: (202) 565-3931
Email: info@exim.gov
Website: http://www.exim.gov
Xiomara Creque, Acting Regional Director-Americas
Email: Xiomara.creque@exim.gov
Tel.: (202) 565-3477 Fax: (202) 565-3931

Overseas Private Investment Corporation (OPIC)
1100 New York Avenue, N.W.
Washington, D.C. 20527
Tel.: InfoLine: (202) 336-8799 Fax: (202) 408-8959
Email: info@opic.gov
Website: http://www.opic.gov/
U.S. Trade and Development Agency (TDA)
1000 Wilson Boulevard, Suite 1600
Arlington, VA 22209-3901
Tel.: (703) 875-4357 Fax: (703) 875-4009
Email: lac@ustda.gov
Website: http://www.tda.gov
Isabel Sepulveda, Country Manager, Latin America and the Caribbean

GOVERNMENT OF PERU

Presidencia del Consejo de Ministros
(Presidency of the Council of Ministers)
Jr. Carabaya cdra 1, Lima
Lima – 1, Peru
Tel.: (511) 219-7000, 219-7012 Fax: (511) 219-7015
Website: http://www.pcm.gob.pe
Pedro Cateriano, President of the Council of Ministers

Ministry of Agriculture and Irrigation
Av. La Universidad 200, La Molina
Lima 12, Peru
Tel.: (511) 613-5800 Fax: (511) 432-0990, 431-0109
Website: http://www.minag.gob.pe

Juan Manuel Benites, Minister of Agriculture
Ministry of Agriculture/ Servicio Nacional de Sanidad Agraria (SENASA)
(Equivalent to APHIS)
Av. La Molina 1915, La Molina
Lima – 12, Peru
Tel.: (511) 313-3300, ext. 1800/1801 I Fax: (511) 313-3315
Website: http://www.senasa.gob.pe

Jorge Barrenechea, Director General
Ministerio de Comercio Exterior y Turismo
(Ministry of Foreign Trade and Tourism)
Calle Uno Oeste s/n Piso 17, Urb. Corpac, San Isidro
Lima 27, Peru
Tel.: (511) 513-6100 Fax: (511) 224-3362
Website: http://www.mincetur.gob.pe

Magali Silva, Minister
Ministerio de Economia y Finanzas
(Ministry of Economy and Finance)
Jr. Junin 319, Piso 4
Lima 1, Peru
Tel.: (511) 311-5930 Fax: (511) 311-9906
Website: http://www.mef.gob.pe

Alonso Segura, Minister
Ministerio de Energia y Minas
(Ministry of Energy and Mines)
Av. Las Artes 260
San Borja
Lima 41, Peru
Tel.: (511) 411-1100 Fax: (511) 224-4441
Website: http://www.minem.gob.pe

Rosa Maria Ortiz, Minister
Ministerio del Ambiente
(Ministry of the Environment)
Av. Javier Prado Oeste 1140, San Isidro
Lima 27, Peru
Tel.: (511) 611-6000
Fax: (511) 611-6000 Anx 1634
Website: http://www.minam.gob.pe

Manuel Pulgar-Vidal, Minister
Ministerio de la Producción
(Ministry of Production)
Calle Uno Oeste s/n, Piso 7
Urb. Corpac, San Isidro
Lima 27, Peru
Tel.: (511) 616-2222 Fax: (511) 616-2200 x705
Website: http://www.produce.gob.pe

Piero Ghezzi Solis, Minister
Ministerio del Interior
(Ministry of the Interior)
Plaza 30 de Agosto s/n - Piso 4, San Isidro
Lima 27, Peru
Tel.: (511) 225-0202 Fax: 224-2405
Website: http://www.mininter.gob.pe

Jose Luis Perez, Minister
Ministerio de Relaciones Exteriores
(Ministry of Foreign Affairs)
Palacio Torre Tagle, Ucayali 363
Lima 1, Peru
Tel.: (511) 623-2402 Fax: (511) 623-2410
Website: http://www.rree.gob.pe

Ana María Sánchez, Minister
Ministerio de Salud
(Ministry of Health)
Av. Salaverry Cdra. 8, Piso 4
Lima 1, Peru
Tel.: (511) 315-6649 Fax: (511) 431-0093
Website: http://www.minsa.gob.pe

Aníbal Velásquez, Minister
Dirección General de Salud Ambiental (DIGESA)

Las Amapolas 350, Urb. San Eugenio, Lince
Lima 14, Peru
Tel.: (511) 442-8353 Fax: (511) 422-6404
Website: http://www.digesa.sld.pe

Monica Saavedra, Director General
Ministerio de Transportes y Comunicaciones
(Ministry of Transport and Communications)
Calle Zorritos 1301
Lima 1, Peru
Tel.: (511) 615-7603 Fax: (511) 615-7578
Website: http://www.mtc.gob.pe

José Gallardo Ku, Minister
Ministerio de Vivienda, Construcción y Saneamiento
(Ministry of Housing, Construction and Sanitation)
Av. Paseo de la Republica 3661, San Isidro
Lima – 27, Peru
Tel.: (511) 211-7930, 211-7934 Fax: (511) 441-7761
Website: http://www.vivienda.gob.pe

Milton Von Hesse, Minister
ProInversión
(Private Investment Promotion Agency)
Av. Paseo de la Republica 3661, Piso 9
Lima – 27, Peru
Tel.: (511) 612-1200 Fax: (511) 221-2941, 221-2942
Website: http://www.proinversion.gob.pe/english

Carlos Herrera, Executive Director
Instituto Nacional de Defensa de la Competencia y de la Protección de la Propiedad Intelectual (INDECOPI)
(National Institute for the Defense of Competition and Protection of Intellectual Property)
La Prosa 138, San Borja
Lima – 41, Peru
Tel.: (511) 224-7800 / (511) 224 7777
Fax: (511) 224-0347 / (511) 224 7800 ext. 1715, Atención al Ciudadano
Website: http://www.indecopi.gob.pe

Hebert Tassano, President
Dirección General de Innovación, Transferencia Tecnológica y Servicios Empresariales
Calle Uno Oeste 060, Urb. Corpac, San Isidro
Tel: 616-2222 (x2484)
E-mail: abernaola@produce.gob.pe
Website: http://www.crecemype.pe

Alejandro Bernaola, Officer-in-Charge
Organismo Supervisor de la Inversión en Energía y Minería – OSINERGMIN
(Supervising Agency for Investment in Energy and Mining)
Bernardo Monteagudo 222, Magdalena
Lima – 17, Peru
Tel.: (511) 219-3400, 219-3410, 219-3411 Fax: (511) 264-0450 x.350
E-mail: osinerg@osinerg.gob.pe
Website: http://www.osinerg.gob.pe

Jesús Tamayo, President
Organismo Supervisor de la Inversión en Infraestructura de Transporte de Uso Público – OSITRAN
(Supervising Agency for Investment in Public Use Transport Infrastructure)
Av. Republica de Panama 3659, San Isidro
Lima – 27, Peru
Tel.: (511) 440-5115 Fax: (511) 421-4739
E-mail: info@ositran.gob.pe
Website: http://www.ositran.gob.pe

Patricia Benavente, President
Organismo Supervisor de la Inversión Privada en Telecomunicaciones – OSIPTEL
(Supervising Agency for Private Investment in Telecommunications)
La Prosa 136 , San Borja
Lima – 41, Peru
Tel.: (511) 225-1313, 225-2145 Fax: (511) 475-1816
Website: http://www.osiptel.gob.pe

Ruiz Gonzalo, President
Superintendencia Nacional de Servicios de Saneamiento - SUNASS
(National Superintendence of Sanitation Services)
Av. Bernardo Monteagudo 210 – 216 Magdalena del Mar
Lima – 17, Peru
Tel.: (511) 614-3180 Fax: (511) 614-3140
Website: http://www.sunass.gob.pe

Fernando Momiy Hada, President
Private Sector Associations
American Chamber of Commerce of Peru (AmCham)
Av. Victor Andres Belaunde 177, San Isidro
Lima – 27, Peru
Tel.: (511) 705-8000 Fax: (511) 705-8026
E-mail: amcham@amcham.org.pe

Website: http://www.amcham.org.pe
Federico Cuneo, President
Aldo Defilippi, Executive Director
Confederación Nacional de Instituciones Empresariales (CONFIEP)
(Confederation of Private Enterprise Institutions)
Av. Victor Andres Belaunde 147, Edificio Real 3, Piso 4 San Isidro
Lima – 27, Peru
Tel.: (511) 415-2555 Fax: (511) 415-2566
E-mail: postmaster@confiep.org.pe
Website: http://www.confiep.org.pe

Martin Pérez, President
Gabriel Amaro, General Manager
Sociedad Nacional de Industrias (SNI)
(National Society of Industries)
Los Laureles 365, San Isidro
Lima – 27, Peru
Tel.: (511) 616-4444 Fax: (511) 442-2573 / (511) 442-2570 / (511) 616-4433
E-mail: sni@sni.org.pe

Website: http://www.sni.org.pe

Andreas von Wedemeyer, President
Sociedad Nacional de Minería, Petróleo y Energía
(National Mining, Petroleum and Energy Society)
Francisco Graña 671, Magdalena del Mar
Lima - 17, Peru
Tel.: (511) 460-1600 Fax: (511) 460-1616
E-mail: postmaster@snmpe.org.pe
Website: http://www.snmpe.org.pe

Eva Arias, President
Caterina Podesta, General Manager
Asociación de Exportadores (ADEX)
(Exporters' Association)
Av. Javier Prado Este 2875 San Borja
Lima – 41, Peru
Tel.: (511) 618-3333, 346-2530 Fax: (511) 346-1879
Email: postmaster@adexperu.org.pe , cid@adexperu.org.pe
Website: http://www.adexperu.org.pe

Eduardo Amorrortu, President
Cámara de Comercio de Lima
(Lima Chamber of Commerce)
Gregorio Escobedo 398 Jesus Maria
Lima – 11, Peru
Tel.: (511) 463-3434, 261-4400 Fax: (511) 463-9864
E-mail: webmaster@camaralima.org.pe
Website: http://www.camaralima.org.pe
Jorge von Wedemeyer Knigge, President
José Rosas Bernedo, General Manager
Cámara de Comercio de Arequipa
(Arequipa Chamber of Commerce)
Quesada 102-104, Yanahuara
Arequipa, Peru
Tel: (5154) 380-505
E-mail: ccia@camara-arequipa.org.pe
Website: http://www.camara-arequipa.org.pe

Diego Muñoz-Najar, President
Cámara de Comercio y Producción de Lambayeque
(Lambayeque Chamber of Commerce)
Av. Balta 504-506
Chiclayo, Peru
Tel: (51-74) 23-8081, Fax: (51-74) 23-3040
E-mail: camara@cclam.org.pe
Website: http://www.cclam.org.pe

Otto Zoeger Navarro, President
Cámara Peruana de la Construcción (CAPECO)
(Chamber of Engineering and Construction Firms)
Víctor Andrés Belaúnde 147, Edificio Real 3, Of. 402,
San Isidro, Lima 27, Peru
Tel.: (511) 230-2700 / Fax: (511) 441-7028

E-mail: gerencia@capeco.org
Website: http://www.capeco.org

Carlos Vegas Quintana, General Manager
Asociación de Bancos
(Association of Banks)
Calle 41 #975, Urb. Corpac San Isidro
Lima – 27, Peru
Tel.: Direct: (511) 612-3303 / Switchboard: (511) 612-3333
Fax: (511) 612-3300
Email: estudioseconomicos@asbanc.com.pe
Website: http://www.asbanc.com.pe

Oscar Rivera, President
Julio Figueroa, General Manager
Asociación de Industriales Lácteos
(Dairy Product Producers Association)
Sociedad Nacional de Industrias
Los Laureles 365 San Isidro
Lima 27 - Peru
Tel.: (511) 616 4444, ext. 165 I Fax: (511) 441-1639
E-mail: adil@sni.org.pe

Rolando Piskulich, President
Asociación Peruana de Porcicultores
(Pork Producers Association)
Pomalca 327 Urb. Centro Comercial Monterrico, Surco
Lima – 33, Peru
Tel.: (511) 436-3729, 436-4168 I Fax: (511) 436-3729
E-mail: asoporci@terra.com.pe
Website: http://www.asoporci.org.pe

Guillermo Vidal, President
Ana Maria Trelles, General Manager
Asociación Peruana de Avicultura
(Poultry Producers Association)
Esmeralda 255 Chacarilla del Estanque
Lima – 33, Peru
Tel.: (511) 372-1551, 372-1540 I Fax: (511) 372-1538
E-mail: presidencia@apa.org.pe
Website: http://www.apa.org.pe
Jose Vera, President

Mario Berrocal, General Manager
Sociedad de Comercio Exterior del Perú (COMEXPERU)
Bartolomé Herrera 254, Miraflores
Lima-18, Peru
Tel (511) 625-7700 Fax: (511) 625-7701
E-mail: comexperu@comexperu.org.pe
Website: http://www.comexperu.org.pe

Guillermo Ferreyros, President
Jessica Luna, General Manager
Fongal Lima

(Dairy Producers Association)
Pumacahua No. 877, Of. 306 Jesus Maria
Lima – 11, Peru
Tel: (511) 431-0549 I Fax: (511) 423-4642
E-mail: fongallima@infonegocio.net.pe

Javier Valera, President
Comité de Molinos de Trigo
(Wheat Millers Committee)
Los Laureles 365 San Isidro
Lima – 27, Peru
Tel.: (511) 616 4444, ext. 131 and (511) 442-2460 I Fax: (511) 442-4351
E-mail: adaly@sni.org.pe
Alejandro Daly, President

COMPANY REGISTRATION[3]

No.	Procedure	Time to Complete	Associated Costs
1	Check the uniqueness of the proposed company name and reserve it online The entrepreneurs select a company name and conduct a search to verify that the name is unique in SUNARP website, (http://www.sunarp.gob.pe/ServiciosLinea.asp). The proposed name may be reserved or blocked for 30 days in the Public Registry so that no other company can register the same name during that time.	Less than one day (online procedure)	PEN 4 for search + PEN 18 for reservation
2	Prepare the deed of incorporation online with a notary The entrepreneur can access the system through the Portal de Servicios al Ciudadano y a las Empresas (http://www.serviciosalciudadano.gob.pe/). The entrepreneur selects a notary and sends him the necessary information for incorporation.	Less than one day (online procedure)	no charge
3	Sign the deed of incorporation before a notary public; file online the deed of incorporation with the Public Register of Commerce; obtain Certificate of Registration and obtain taxpayer identification number After the entrepreneur creates the public deed and the shareholders signature, it must file the deed with a Notary. Notary fees are up to 1% of capital, depending on the company size, the length of the public deed, and the initial capital contribution. The entrepreneur also pays the registration fees to the Notary. The Registrar receives the public deed and proceeds to register the company. The Registrar is also interconnected with the tax authority (SUNAT) to register the company as a taxpayer, where the entrepreneur will obtain the taxpayer identification number (Registro Unico del Contribuyente, RUC).	8 days	see procedure details

[3] The World Bank Materials

No.	Procedure	Time to Complete	Associated Costs
	The incorporation documents must include, at least: (a) the company name; (b) its purpose and duration; (c) the company domicile; (d) the initial capital contribution; (e) the shares nominal value and the total number of shares; (f) the classes of shares, if needed; (g) the name, nationality, marital status, occupation, and residence of any individual shareholder; (h) the names of the initial directors, managers, and agents; and the (i) the date of startup operations. Cost details: USD 200 notary fee (both fees depend on market conditions) plus registration fees which are composed by: 0.3% of capital + USD 15 for performing the registration + USD 8 per appointment of each director, manager or other representative, up to the limit of PEN 3,700 (equivalent to 1 UIT - Peruvian Tax Unit)		
4	Stamp accounting book and minute book The accounting book and the minute book need to be stamped by a notary.	1 day	USD 7 per book of no more than 100 pages. Most companies have between 5 and 9 of these books. Thus, the cost will range between USD 35 and USD 63.
5	Obtain municipal license from the City Council A municipal license, required to operate commercially, is obtained from the municipality of the jurisdiction where the company is located. Some district councils require a provisional license while the permanent license is being processed. In most cases, the district council requires a copy of the incorporation documents, the public deed, the distribution plan, property title documents (if applicable). Ordinance No. 857 simplified the license application process in the metropolitan municipality of Lima (Municipalidad Metropolitana de Lima). Law 28976 of 19 January 2007 on the operating license (Ley Marco de Licencia de Funcionamiento) has simplified the system by eliminating the need of a Certificate of Compatibility as a requisite and by replacing it by a simple verification that the new company meets zoning regulations. The requirements for the Certificate of INDECI have also been simplified. Categories I and II licenses (premises up to 500 m2) do not need to submit a Certificate of INDECI but the compliance with health and security requirements is now checked by the municipality with inspections after submitting	15 days	Fees vary depending on the District Council where the company's office is located. In San Isidro between PEN 391 and PEN 489.

No.	Procedure	Time to Complete	Associated Costs
	request for Municipal Operating License. This system is now operating in all Lima's District Councils.		

NEW COMPANIES OR BRANCHES:

Foreign investors and/or companies shall decide if they will operate either through new companies, branches or joint ventures.

Peruvian Legislation recognizes various entrepreneurial forms. Some of them are as follows: corporation, limited liability company, general partnership, noncommercial limited company, limited partnership issuing shares, partnerships and branches.

The Corporation and Branches of foreign companies are the most common form used in Peru, because of the advantages it grants.

A. CORPORATION:

1. Business Name

Corporations may adopt any name; nevertheless, they must include the terms Sociedad Anónima (Corporation) or the main letters S.A.

2. Capital

Capital stock is represented by registered stocks and formed by the shareholders' contributions, who do not support, by themselves, the corporation debts.

Incorporation requires that the capital stock be fully underwritten, and paid up, at least in 25%. There is no minimum capital amount.

3.Shareholders

Shareholders must be at least three individuals or juridical persons, residents or nonresidents.

4.Incorporation

There are two types of incorporation: By one action (Direct Creation) or by successive creation (Public Subscription). In both cases, a Notary is required. Also in both cases, the company's founder shareholders must supply the Notary with the documents necessary to start the incorporation (shareholder's identification documents and a deposit of the capital equity in a peruvian
bank)

a) Direct Creation:

The capital stock must be deposited in an account opened with a Peruvian Financial Institution. Once the money has been deposited, the shareholders will draw up the Incorporation Papers, which must be duly countersigned by an attorney; and then submit them to the Notary, who will make a Public Deed for
the registration thereof with the Commercial Registry corresponding to the place where it is incorporated.

b) Public Subscription:

The founder shareholders shall draw up a foundation program, which will be submitted to the notary, for the authentication of their signatures. Once the signatures have been certified, the program must be deposited in the Commercial Registry to be further published in order to find potential subscribers. A meeting of subscribers must be held within six months as from the date in which the program was deposited in the Commercial Registry. Within the thirty days following the meeting, the appointed person or persons shall provide for the company's Incorporation Public Deed, which shall be registered with the Commercial Registry where the company is addressed.

5. Setup Costs:

The expenditures involved in the incorporation are the following:

- Notary's expenses, calculated on the total capital stock and the length of the Public Deed.

- Registration Expenses, the rate to be paid is the 3/1000 of the capital stock.

- Other expenses, include the registration of the appointment of Directors and attorney's fees, etc.

6. Corporation's Term

Unless otherwise specified in the articles of association, the corporation term is unlimited.

7.Contributions

These can be made in national and/or foreign currency; or, in physical or tangible goods. It is also allowed intangible technological contributions, which can adopt the form of physical goods, technical papers and instructions, in order to be appraised. Non-money contribution shall be duly evaluated.

8. Company's Bodies:

8.1. General Meeting of Shareholders, is the meeting duly called to decide on inherent matters thereof. This body decides by majority, taking into consideration the proportion to the total capital equity. This is the maximum body of the company.

Meetings may be Special or Regular.

8.2. Board of Directors, it is elected by the General Meeting of Shareholders. This appointment must be registered with the Commercial Registry of the place where the company is domiciled. To become a Director, it is not necessary to be shareholder, unless the by-laws specify so. There is no residence or nationality requirement. The number of directors shall be fixed by the by-laws, or, otherwise, by the General Meeting. The Board of Directors is empowered with legal and management representation, necessary for the administration of the company, within its purpose.

The Board of Directors must prepare, in a maximum term of 180 days, counted as from the end of the fiscal year, the balance sheet with the profit and loss account, proposal of profit allocation and the annual report. The aforementioned documents shall establish, in a clear and exactly way, the partnership assets, gained profits or suffered losses and the state of its business.

8.3. Management: The manager is appointed by the Board of Directors, except the by-laws empower the General Meeting therefor. More than one manager may exist, if the by-laws or the General Meeting establish so. The term of post is unlimited, except the by-laws establish otherwise or the appointment has been made for specific term. Manager's duties are set forth in the by-laws, or at the time of the appointment; otherwise, it is assumed that the manager is empowered to perform acts and execute contracts inherent to the corporate business.

9. ACCOUNTING REQUIREMENTS

Companies shall keep accounting books, considered as main books, which shall be in Spanish and in national currency, unless the company is expressly authorized to keep it in foreign currency, because it receives or makes foreign investments; provided that the company contracts with the State or with Public
Enterprises or Institutions. The taxable base shall be determined in foreign currency; nevertheless, the payment of the corresponding taxes shall be made in national currency at the current exchange rate. The main accounting books are:

Stock Book
Trial-Balance Book
Day-Book
Ledger
Wages and Salaries Payroll Book
Minute Book

For using the mentioned books, the certification by a Notary Public is required. The payroll book shall be certified with the Ministry of Labor and Social Promotion.

10. PROFITS

Dividends on shares can be paid only from real gained profits or free-availability reserves, provided that the asset value is not under the total share capital. Dividends allocation between the shareholders will be made in proportion to the amounts paid and the time of integration to the capital stock.

B. BRANCHES:

Foreign companies may freely set up branches in Peru, which shall be recorded with the register where these operate. For purposes of formalities, the registration must include the indicated address in Peru; capital appointed or assigned for the branch; appointment and powers of its legal representative in the country; branch's business line, including the business and operations it is engaged in; and the contract or equivalent document governing the branch in its main place. The certificate, proving the existence and force of the company, from the competent authority duly certified by the Peruvian Consular Representative; a document stating the power of the company to set up branches in other countries; and, the company's resolution to set up a branch in Peru shall be also included.

The legal representative appointed in Peru shall have enough powers to solve any matter related to the company's activities; to involve the company in transactions it carries out; to appear in court; and to answer to a claim.

II. JOINT VENTURE AND PARTNERSHIPS

Joint Ventures and Partnerships are contracts concluded by the parties, which do not require their registration with the Commercial Registry. These have no corporate existence, nor corporate's name. Resources destined to the aforementioned contracts shall be considered as Direct Foreign Investment,
provided that these grant foreign investors participation in the installed capacity, not involving necessarily capital contribution. Besides, these contracts shall correspond to contractual commercial transactions through which the foreign investor provides goods or services to the receiving enterprise in exchange of participation in the volume of the physical production, in the aggregate amount or in the net profits of the enterprise which receives the investment.

III.ADMINISTRATIVE FORMALITIES

In addition to the legal requirements mentioned above, certain formalities must be completed by foreign companies wishing to establish new companies or branches.

A. TAX CARD OR UNIQUE REGISTRY OF TAXPAYER (URT):

In accordance with the legislation thereon, the Superintendencia Nacional de Administración Tributaria - SUNAT - (National Superintendency of Tax Administration) has, among its duties, the taxpayers' registration providing them the respective certificate proving its registration with the Unique Registry of
Taxpayer.

The following papers must be submitted:

Incorporation Documents of the company, or branch, prior registered with the notary. Format given by the SUNAT.

B. REGISTRATION OF FOREIGN INVESTMENT

Foreign investment destined to the capital of a company shall be registered with the Comisión Nacional de Inversiones y Tecnologías Extranjeras - CONITE - (National Commission on Foreign Investments and Technologies).

Foreign investments contractually formalized with Peruvian enterprises, including joint ventures and any other form of partnerships, shall be also registered with CONITE.

For purposes of registration with CONITE, an application shall be submitted along with the following documents:

1) In freely convertible currency:

In cases of incorporation of companies; investments physically placed in the country; contracts of partnerships or similar, a copy of the document proving the entrance of foreign currency through the National Financial System must be enclosed. Such copy shall include the remitter's business name against an open account in a bank and/or financial entity abroad in the name of the receiving enterprise. In case of contributions destined to the incorporation of enterprises, the remittance may be drawn in the name of the authorized representative or attorney of the investor, duly certified.

2) Contributions product of the capitalization of the private obligations with abroad:

The existence of outstanding obligations shall be proved by the submission of the copy of the respective accounting documents.

3) In physical or tangible goods:

Including the case of contracts of partnerships or similar, a copy of the commercial invoice, free of charge, and the customs import document issued by the corresponding Customs Administration shall be enclosed.

4) In technological intangible contributions:

A copy of the certificate of registry of the trademark, patent or any other element of industrial property, issued by the Instituto Nacional de Defensa de la Competencia y Proteccion a la Propiedad Intelectual (INDECOPI) proving the concession, in force, of the right in the investor's name and the copy of the Minutes of the Board of Directors or Board of Shareholders, where states the confirmation of the valorization made, or copy of the corresponding contract, in case of associations in participations or similar.

5) In case of contributions in national currency with right of remittance, for the concept of profits, dividends, royalties or any other type of amounts due:

The availability of funds with right of remittance shall be proved with the copy of the respective accounting documents. Besides, in the case of royalties, the copy of the resolution of registration of the contract generating the obligation shall be submitted to the national competent agency.

For all the cases, the following papers shall be also enclosed:

Copy of the Incorporation Public Deed of the new company or branch, with the proof of registration in the respective Registry.
Copy of the capitalization bookkeeping entry.

In case of contracting joint ventures a copy of the corresponding contract shall be enclosed.

C. UNIFIED REGISTRY

Any person or corporate body, of any economic sector, proposing to engage in any commercial, industrial or any other activities shall be registered with the Unified Registry.

The following papers shall be submitted for the registration:

Format of the Unified Register, duly filled out (this format is available at the Banco de la Nación).

Copy of the Incorporation Public Deed with proof of its reception at the Notary's office.
Payroll Book.

D. MUNICIPAL LICENSE FOR OPERATION

It is required to operate commercially. It is applied for to the Municipality of the jurisdiction where the company is located

LAW STABILITY SYSTEM - LEGISLATIVE DECREE 662 AGREEMENTS IN FORCE CONCLUDED WITH FOREIGN INVESTORS TO MAY 07, 1997

1. AGREEMENTS BY THE INVESTMENT ORIGIN COUNTRY

(In US$)

	INVESTMENT	**AGREEMENTS**
COUNTRY	ENGAGED	CONCLUDED 1/
	AMOUNT	NUMBER
ARGENTINA	51,667,500.00	4
AUSTRALIA	5,000,000.00	2
BAHAMAS	122,000,000.00	1
BARBADOS	28,992,200.00	3
BELGIQUE	57,000,000.00	1
BERMUDA	2,000,000.00	1
BRASIL	2,500,000.00	2
CANADA	71,609,369.52	3
CAYMAN I.	172,403,574.80	15
CHILE	207,559,896.67	42
CHINA	3,500,000.00	1
COLOMBIA	13,067,000.00	2
ECUADOR	6,500,000.00	3
FRANCE	17,961,046.96	5
GERMANY	631,210.00	1
IFC	4,100,000.00	2
JAPAN	1,659,000.00	2
KOREA	3,999,989.20	1

MEXICO	20,100,000.00	4
NETHERLANDS	346,910,133.95	9
NEW ZEALAND	3,500,000.00	1
PANAMA	303,010,721.90	12
SPAIN	2,343,175,304.38	17
SWITZERLAND	8,100,000.00	4
UNITED KINGDOM	64,000,000.00	4
URUGUAY	37,500,000.00	5
USA	813,610,440.53	30
VIRG. I. UK	26,750,000.00	7
TOTAL	4,738,807,387.91	184

1/ The total number of agreements concluded with foreign investors is 184; nevertheless, in two cases, investors from two different countries have signed one agreement.

2. AGREEMENTS CONCLUDED BY THE INVESTMENT DESTINATION SECTOR

(In US$)

	INVESTMENT	**AGREEMENTS**
SECTOR	ENGAGED	CONCLUDED 1/
	NUMBER	NUMBER
COMMERCE	130,901,480.00	19
COMMUNICATIONS	2,017,124,198.00	7
CONSTRUCTION	36,400,000.00	9
ENERGY	1,286,373,763.42	24
FINANCES	354,740,906.39	32
INDUSTRY	319,377,632.55	40
MINING	542,840,997.55	41
SERVICES	3,623,410.00	4
TRANSPORTATION	25,175,000.00	1
TOURISM	22,250,000.00	5
TOTAL	4,738,807,387.91	182

INVESTMENT ACTIVITY IN PERU

As a result of the existing investment opportunities and the confidence and security climate offered within Peru, this is the opinion of many investors of the international community. That opinion is supported by the significant foreign investment flows channeled to Peru during the last years in the context of the privatization process, and the plethora of important investments directed towards setting up new companies and in other cases to strengthen the already existing ones.

The solid and stable economic position earned by Peru in the last years, as result of the economic stabilization and structural reform process applied in the early '90s, was a determining factor for the creation of an appropriate climate for investment. Another factor was the implementation and execution of an adequate legal framework that strengthens the respect, guarantee and protection of investments and also includes a legal stability regime for the investor and his investments in the country. This regime is executed through the subscription of agreements directly with the State. In the external field, this legal framework is complemented with the access to bilateral and multilateral protection mechanisms, as well as to effective mechanisms with regard to dispute settlements.

The climate for the establishment of foreign investments has also been encouraged by the results of national pacification, in the domestic field; and, in the external field, by the recent Peace Agreement concluded with Ecuador. The recent peace reached between the both our countries will have a positive effect in the development of the corresponding border area and in the integration process with Andean countries, which will contribute to foster commerce and investment.

Notwithstanding, Peru was not excluded from the effects of the international financial crisis, though it was less vulnerable than other Latin American countries. According to some international entities, risk-rating agencies and investment banks the decision to keep the current macroeconomic policy will enable Peru to recover faster and reach dynamic growth again.

As we close the present decade, the actions taken by Peru as to openness and modernization of its economy enable the country to be considered as a trustworthy place for foreign investment. Facing the new millenium, Peru offers foreign investors: a stable economy that has largely liberalized its investment regime,clear rules, a skilled labor force and national entrepreneurs willing to share the challenge of developing within a market governed by modern competition policies, based on consumer protection laws and fulfillment of the WTO agreements.

Likewise, a pro-active attitude exists towards the participation within integration mechanisms that make it possible to access expanded markets. Thus, the investor established in Peru not only enjoys the benefits a highly deregulated economy, but also the country's capacity to reach a larger amount of potential consumers.

Peru is a member of the free trade area accorded amongst the Andean Community nations, which include Bolivia, Colombia, Ecuador and Venezuela and means a market of 106 million consumers. Additionally, Peru has concluded an agreement with Chile for a progressive establishment of a free trade zone. In a few years, we expect the Andean Community and MERCOSUR to agree on South American free trade zone.

With regard to the US market, the Andean Trade Preference Act (ATPA) benefits 6300 products which enter this competitive market with zero tariff. As to the European Union, the General System of Preferences for the Andean countries sets zero tariffs for fishing, agricultural and textile products for which Peru provides competitive advantages due to its natural resources. Finally, our country has become a member of the Asia Pacific Economic Cooperation (APEC) forum which comprises 50% of the world's trade, which makes us a natural link between the emerging economies of Asia and Latin America.

PRINCIPAL FOREIGN INVESTORS IN PERU

INVESTORS	COUNTRY
T.I. TELEFONICA DE SPAIN	SPAIN
SOUTHERN PERU LIMITED (ANTES SOUTHERN PERU COPPER CORP.)	USA
COMPAÑIA ELECTRICA CONO SUR S.A.	PANAMA
DOMINION ENERGY INC.	USA
ONTARIO-QUINTA A.V.V.	NETHERLANDS
GLOBAL BHP COPPER LTD.	UNITED KINGDOM
E.P. EDEGEL INC.	USA
BANCO BILBAO VIZCAYA S.A.	SPAIN
RAL CAYMAN INC.	UNITED KINGDOM
HOLBAH II LIMITED	UNITED KINGDOM
NORANDA ANTAMINA	CANADA
SHOUGANG CORPORATION	CHINA
REPSOL PERU B.V.	NETHERLANDS
THE COCA COLA EXPORT CORPORATION	USA
TECK BASE METALS LIMITED	UNITED KINGDOM
ENDESA DESARROLLO S.A. - ENDESAR	SPAIN
NESTLE S.A.	SWITZERLAND
YPF S.A.	ARGENTINA
THE SHELL PETROLEUM COMPANY LIMITED	UNITED KINGDOM
BELLSOUTH PERU BVI LIMITED	UNITED KINGDOM
DOMA B.V.	NETHERLANDS
INTERNATIONAL FINANCIAL HOLDINGS INC.	UNITED KINGDOM
INCHCAPE BOTTLING (CYPRUS) LTD.	CYPRUS
BHP COPPER INC.	USA

AGUAYTIA ENERGY, LLC	USA
DUKE ENERGY INTERNATIONAL PERU HOLDINGS Nº 2, LLC	USA
TRACTEBEL S.A.	BELGIUM
OCCIDENTAL PETROLEUM CORPORATION OF PERU	USA
THE PERU PRIVATISATION AND DEVELOPMENT FUND LIMITED	UNITED KINGDOM
EMPRESA NACIONAL DE ELECTRICIDAD S.A. ENDESA	SPAIN
ENERSIS S.A.	CHILE
COMINCO LTD.	CANADA
DELTA AIR LINES INC.	USA
CAMBIOR INTERNATIONAL INC.	UNITED KINGDOM
CHILECTRA S.A.	CHILE
EMPRESA MINERA DE MANTOS BLANCOS S.A.	CHILE
BANQUE SUDAMERIS	FRANCE
NEXTEL INTERNATIONAL (PERU) LLC.	UNITED KINGDOM
EMPRESAS LUCCHETTI S.A.	CHILE
PAN AMERICAN SILVER (BARBADOS) CORP.	UNITED KINGDOM
INCHCAPE OVERSEAS LIMITED	UNITED KINGDOM
CYPRUS CLIMAX METALS COMPANY	USA
COLOMBIANA KIMBERLY COLPAPEL S.A.	COLOMBIA
PEREZ COMPANC S.A.	ARGENTINA
MOBIL OIL DEL PERU (CIA. COMERCIAL) INC.	USA
THE PROCTER & GAMBLE INTERAMERICANAS INC.	USA
BANCO SANTANDER DE NEGOCIOS S.A.	SPAIN
MITSUBISHI CORPORATION	JAPAN
ARLABANK INTERNATIONAL E.C.	BAHRAIN
CHASE MANHATTAN INTERNATIONAL FINANCE LIMITED	USA
INVERSORA FALKEN S.A.	URUGUAY
LATIN AMERICAN HOLDING CORP.	CANADA
BANCO STANDARD CHARTERED (ANTES EXTEBANDES)	PERU

HYDRO QUEBEC INTERNATIONAL INC.	CANADA
HAC INVESTMENTS LTD.	USA
BANKBOSTON N.A.(ANTES THE FIRST NATIONAL BANK OF BOSTON)	USA
PHELPS DODGE CHAPI INC.	USA
J.P. MORGAN INTERNATIONAL CAPITAL CORPORATION	USA
MADECO S.A.	UNITED KINGDOM
MCDONALD'S RESTAURANT OPERATIONS INC.	USA
CITIBANK N.A.	USA
CAMBIOR INC.	CANADA
MANUELITA S.A.	COLOMBIA
GREAT YELLOWSTONE CORP.	PANAMA
LIMA HOTEL INC.	UNITED KINGDOM
FLEISCHMANN PERUANA INCORPORATED	USA
WIESE INVERSIONES FINANCIERAS S.A.	USA
GARRISON CORPORATION	UNITED KINGDOM
THE PROCTER & GAMBLE COMPANY	USA
BIMABEL INTERNATIONAL LLC.	USA
METALURGICA E INDUSTRIAL S.A.	CHILE
IBM WORLD TRADE CORPORATION	USA
INTERGAMA CORPORATION	UNITED KINGDOM
LUDLOW CORPORATION	UNITED KINGDOM
AEROVIAS DE MEXICO S.A.	MEXICO
MIRAMAR ASSOCIATES INC.	PANAMA
INTERNATIONAL FINANCE CORPORATION	NEUTRAL
MITIENWALD S.A.	URUGUAY
INCHCAPE (LATIN AMERICA) S.A.	PANAMA
MARUBENI CAJA INVESTMENT LIMITED	UNITED KINGDOM
THE BANK OF NOVA SCOTIA	CANADA
SHERATON INTERNATIONAL INC.	USA

MANAGEMENT SERVICES LTD.	UNITED KINGDOM
MONTROSE COMMERCIAL INC.	PANAMA
BIRMINGHAM MERCHANT S.A.	PANAMA
NUEVAS INICIATIVAS DEL SUR S.A. - NUINSA	SPAIN
UNELCO PARTICIPADAS S.A.	SPAIN
UPJOHN INTER-AMERICAN CORPORATION	USA
AMARANTE INVESTMENTS	NETHERLANDS
WHITE MARTINS GASES INDUSTRIAIS S.A.	BRAZIL
FRINT BEHEER XVII B.V.	NETHERLANDS
MOTOROLA INTERNATIONAL DEVELOPMENT CORPORATION	USA
MATSUSHITA ELECTRIC INDUSTRIAL CO. LTD.	JAPAN
MITSUI & CO. LTD.	JAPAN
COTE D'OR MANAGEMENT CORPORATION	PANAMA
INDUSTRIE BITOSSI S.P.A.	ITALY
THE GOODYEAR TIRE & RUBBER COMPANY	USA
EMPRESAS SANTA CAROLINA (CAYMAN) LTD.	UNITED KINGDOM
COMPAÑIA MINERA DEL MADRIGAL PRINCIPAL	USA
LANDY S.A.	URUGUAY

TAX SYSTEM FRAMEWORK

This document describes the principal taxes which apply to investors and the enterprises in which they participate. Taxes herein detailed are collected by the Central Administration.

PRINCIPAL TAXES:

1. Income Tax
2. Extraordinary Tax on Net Assets
3. General Sales Tax
4. Excise Tax
5. Customs Duties

1. INCOME TAX:

1.1 General Regime:

The Income Tax is applied annually to every income earned by domiciled or non-domiciled taxpayers, regardless of nationality, the place of incorporation, or location of the income source. Non-domiciled taxpayers are subject to income tax only with respect to their Peruvian-source income.

In the case of corporations, income tax applies to any gains or profits derived from transactions with third parties, as well as from the exposure to inflation calculated at the end of each financial year.

Income of irregular associations, consortia, partnerships and any contract of entrepreneurial collaboration shall keep bookkeeping independent from their partners or contracting parties.

For purposes of the income tax, taxable incomes are classified in categories as follows:

a. First: Incomes earned from real estate properties leasing, subleasing and transfer of goods.
b. Second: Other capital incomes (interests, royalties, etc.)
c. Third: Income from commerce, industry and other activities as provided by law.
d. Fourth: Incomes derived from personal independent services.
e. Fifth: Incomes earned from personal dependent work.

1.1.1. Income Tax Rates:

The tax rates are as follows:

Domiciled:

a. Tax payable by corporate bodies, partnerships and joint ventures on third-category income: 30% of net income.
b. Tax payable by individuals: 15% rate on annual aggregate net income (including earnings of first, second, fourth and fifth income categories). A 30% rate applies to income in excess of 54 UIT 1 .
Credits authorized by law shall be deducted from the tax calculated.

Non-domiciled:

The tax payable by corporations shall be determined applying the following schedule:

a. Interest coming from external credits: 1%, whenever they fulfill the following requirements:

- The loans cash will be proved with the entrance of the currency to the country
- The credit does not yield annual interest on the balance due superior to the preferential rate in the market where it comes from, plus 3 points.

The interests from external credits destined to financing imports are included, whenever they fulfill the legal provisions in force.
b. Interest paid abroad by banking and financial companies established in Peru, derived from their foreign lines of credit used in the country: 1%
c. Income earned by leasing of ships and aircrafts: 10%
d. Royalties: 30%
e. Other incomes, including interests derived from external credits that do not fulfill anyone of the requirements established in item a), and the interests paid abroad by companies of the country for credits granted by a foreign company with which is economically linked, except for that of item b): 30 %

Individuals shall calculate their tax applying a 30% rate on pension benefits or remunerations for personal services rendered in the country, royalties and other incomes.

1.1.2. Nontaxable incomes

Nontaxable incomes are:

a. Dividends and any other kind of profit distribution. Those persons who receive dividends or profits from other companies shall not include them when determining their taxable income.
b. Self-issued shares corresponding to the re-expression of capital that results from adjustment for inflation.

1.2. Principal exemptions

The following items are exempt from Income Tax until the year 2000:

a. Capital gains derived from:

a.1. The sale of securities registered with the Public Register of the Stock Exchange through negotiation mechanisms to which the Law of Securities Market referred.
a.2. Sale of securities at the Commodity Exchange authorized by CONASEV.
a.3. Redemption of registered and bearer securities, representative of debts issued through public offering in corformity with the Law of Securities Market, by corporate bodies, Investment Funds or
Trusteed Patrimony, formed or established in the country.
a.4. Redemption of Mutual Investment Funds in Securities certificates and representative securities of participation of Trustee Patrimony of Awarding Title Institutions issued through public offering under the Law of Securities Market.

b. Any type of fixed or floating interest rate in national or foreign currency, paid on deposit, under the General Law of Banking, Financing and Insurance Institutions, as well as interest accrued on deposits and investments in national or foreign currency originating Adjustable Certificates of Deposits. Any type of fixed or floating interest rate in national or foreign currency, as well as capital gains or capital readjustment as set forth in the Civil Code, paid to holders of

registered or bearer securities, representative of debts issued by Invetment Funds, Trustee Patrimony of Awarding Titles Institutions and corporate bodies, incorporated or to be incorporated in the country, provided that those are marketed through public offering, under Law of Securities Market. Likewise, any type of fixed or floating interest, in national or foreign currency, and capital increase, coming from Mortgage Certificates and Titles of Marketability Mortgage Credit, as well as Endorseable Mortgage Certificates to which the Law of Securities Market refers. Every profit earned from voluntary contributions with no previsional purpose is also herein included. Interests and capital adjustment, earned from Financial System companies authorized to operate by the Superintendency of Banking and Insurances for any of the concepts referred to herein, are not herein included.
c. Interest derived from development credits granted directly or through financial suppliers or intermediates, by international entities or foreign government institutions.
d. Royalties for technical, economical, financial or any other kind of advisory services rendered from abroad by government entities or international agencies.
e. Income from real estate owned by international entities and used as headquarters.
f. Wages earned, in the course of their duties in the country, by officers and employees so considered within the corporate structure of foreign governments, official institutions and international agencies, provided the articles of agreements so established.
g. Income resulting from the difference between the updated value of premium or shares paid by the insured and the amounts given by the insurance companies to the insured at the end of the term established in the contracts of life insurance and benefits or participations in lifeinsurance of the insured.
h. Compensation for lenght of service established by Law.
i. Interest and capital readjustment obtained from mortgage bills in accordance with applicable legislation.
j. The companies that are established or set up in the Centers of Export, Transformation, Industry, Commercialization and Services (CETICOS) of Ilo, Matarani and Tacna, and Paita until December 31, 2004, which annual operations correspond in not less than 92% to the export of goods produced, will be exempt from the Income Tax up to December 31, 2012.
k. Interests earned or paid by cooperatives of saving and credti for operations made with their associates.

1.3 Entry of Foreign citizens into the country:

Foreign citizens shall fulfill the following rules:

a. A foreigner who enters Peru temporarily with business visa and does not engage in activities which generate income from any Peruvian source must fill out an affidavit to hand to immigration authorities upon leaving the country.
b. A foreigner who enters Peru temporarily with a with business visa and engages in activities which generate income from Peruvian sources must fill out an affidavit to hand to immigration authorities upon leaving the country, which states that his or her taxes have been paid, or that any tax liability that may be attributable to said person shall be assumed by the entity or person signing the affidavit if it were to be necessary. In case the

income payers failed to retain the corresponding tax, because it is a non-domiciled corporation, it is obliged to pay directly and shall attach the corresponding receipt to the aforementioned affidavit.
c. A foreigner with business or non-immigrant resident visa and a labor contract approved or submitted to the labor authorities must deliver to the immigration authorities upon leaving the country a letter of guarantee issued by his or her employer or legal representative, certifying the retention of the applicable taxes and assuming the responsibility for any income taxes that may be owing.

Income obtained in the country of origin of a foreign citizen, who is not domiciled in Peru and who enters Peru temporarily to carry out activities prior to the execution of foreign investments or any other kind of business; including the supervision or control of the investment such as collection of data or information, meetings with persons of the public or private sectors; and the execution of agreements or similar acts is not considered to be Peruvian-source income.

1.4. Contractual Benefits

By means of the subscription of Law Stability Agreements the titleholders will be granted the following benefits for a ten-year period:

1.4.1. To the investors:
Stability of the Income Tax Regime effective at the moment of the subscription of the agreement, for the proportion corresponding to dividends and any other form of distribution of profits.
1.4.2. To the companies:
Stability of the Income Tax Regime effective at the moment of the subscription of the agreement.

1.5. Income Tax in the Amazon Region 2,3

1.5.1. The taxpayers located in the Amazon region, mainly engaged in the following activities: agrofarming, acquaculture, fishing, tourism; manufacturing activities related to the proecessing, transformation and commercialization of primary products derived from the before mentioned activities and forestry transformation, provided those products are produced in that zone; and, activities of forestry extraction, shall apply for purposes of Third Category Income Tax, a 10% (ten per cent) rate.

1.5.2 As exception, the taxpayers located in the departments of Loreto, Madre de Dios and the districts of Iparia and Masisea of the province of Coronel Portillo and provinces of Atalaya and Purus of the department of Ucayali, mainly engaged in the activities detailed in the foregoing paragraph, shall apply for the Third Category Income Tax purposes, a 5% (five per cent) rate.

1.5.3. The taxpayers of the Amazon Region who are mainly engaged in agrarian activities and/or transformation or processing of products considered as native and/alternate culture in such zone, shall be exempt from the Income Tax. For pusposes of the stated in the foregoing paragraph, products considered as native and/or alternate culture are yucca, soja, arracacha, uncucha, urena, palmito, pijuayo palmito, pijuayo, aguaje, anona, caimito, carambola, cocona, guanabano, guayabo, marañon, pomarosa, taperiba, tangerine, grapefruit, zapote, cami camu, cat's claw, annatto tree, rubber, pineapple, sesame seed, chestnut, jute and great mullein. In the case of oil palm, coffee and cacao, the exemption shall be applicable only to the agrarian production. Transformation or processing companies of those products shall apply a 10% (ten per cent) rate as Income Tax, provided they are located in the zone indicated in item 1.5.,; or, a 5% (five per cent) rate if they are located in the zone indicated in item 1.5.2.

1.5.4. Companies engaged in commerce activities in the Amazone Region that reinvest a minimum of 30% (thirty per cent) of their net income in the Investments Projects 4 may apply for purposes of the Third Category Income Tax, a 10% (ten per cent). As exception, those located in the departments of Loreto, Madre de Dios and the districts of Iparia and Masisea of the province of Coronel Portillo and the provinces of Atalaya and Purus of the department of Ucayali, shall apply a 5% (five per cent) rate.

2. EXTRAORDINARY TAX ON NET ASSETS

This tax, which rate is 0,5%, applies on taxpayers receiving third-category income (companies). Branches, agencies and other permanent establishments of non-domiciled companies are included.

Associations, partnerships, joint ventures, consortia and any other contract of business collaboration, which keep bookeeping independent from their parts, shall assess that tax and attribute it to each of their integrant parts regarding their equity participation. Each part, as the real taxpayer, shall add said amount to the tax to be paid, if the case may be.

2.1. Exemptions:

The following are exempt from this tax:

a. Taxpayers perceiving third-category income, who did not start production operations.
b. Companies that render electricity, drinking water and sewer system services.
c. Companies engaged in agrarian activities that develop cultivations and/or breeding, except for poultry, agroindustry and forestry industry.

d. Educational institutions, except the Academies preparing students for the entrance to universities.
e. Mutual Investment Funds in Securities
f. Companies that are incoporated or set up in the Centers of Export, Transformation, Industry, Commercialization and Services (CETICOS) of Ilo, Matarani and Tacna, and Paita up to December 31, 2004, which annual operations are higher than 92% of the export of goods produced, will be exempt up to December 31, 2012.
g. Entities non-burdened or exempt from the Income Tax according to law. (*)
h. Taxpayers, individuals and corporate bodies, that had subscribed Law Stability Agreements up to May 3, 1997, provided these agreements are in force as of January 01, 1999, and have included the tributary stability of the Income Tax as receiving companies. This benefit will apply whenever the taxpayers do not waive the Agreements referred during 1999.
i. Companies located in the Amazon region.

2.2. Taxable Basis

It is composed of the value of net assets consigned in the general adjusted balance sheet at December 31 of every year, depreciations and amortizations deducted.
In the cases in which the adjustment by inflation is not required, the taxable base will be composed of the assets at historical values.

The following are not taxable base:
a. Stocks, participations or equity rights of other companies, except those exempt.
b. The value of machinery and equipment acquired during 1997, whenever these do not have an antiquity over 3 years.
c. Companies of Multiple Operations (banks, financial institutions and cooperatives of saving and credit) will deduct legal reserve and specific provisions for credit risk made over 100% of the owing total amount. Further, they will calculate the Tax on 50% of net asset value.
d. Stocks accounts and outstanding debts derived from export operations in the case of exporting companies.
e. The participation certificates issued by Mutual Investment Funds in securities and Investment Funds.
f. Assests that support the mathematical reserves on life insurances, in the case of insurance companies.
g. Investments in bearer securities, deposits of financial instruments, certificates of participation of Mutual Investment Funds in Securities, derived intruments and swap operations.
h. Goods given in concession by the State to be used as public utilities, as well as the constructions made on them by the concessionaires.
i. Stocks, participations or equity rights of companies with Law Stability Agreements, that have stabilized the norms on the Minimum Income Tax prior to the validity of the law, except for the companies exempt from this tax.

The companies with Agreements subject to the Minimum Income Tax shall deduct from their Taxable Base, the stocks, participations or equity rights of companies burden with the Tax, except for the companies exempt therefrom. 5

3. GENERAL SALES TAX:

This tax applies to the following:

a. Domestic sale of goods and chattels
b. Domestic rendering or use of services
c. Construction contracts.
d. The first sale of real estate property made by its constructor, and the further sale made by enterprises economically linked with the constructor, whenever the real estate has been acquired directly from those enterprises economically linked with the constructor.
e. Importation of goods.

The general rate is 18%, which includes a 2% Municipal Promotion Tax.

The General Sales Tax stated in the Invoice that supports the acquisition of goods, services or construction contracts, or the GST paid for the importation of goods, may be taken as tax credit against the Gross Tax.

3.1. Non-Affected items:

The General Sales Tax does not apply to the following:

a. Export of goods.
b. Export of services detailed in Appendix V.
c. Leasing and any other form of cession for the use of real estate, provided that the income generated is qualified as First or Second Category Income to which sales tax applies.
d. Transfer of used goods made by individuals or corporate entities not engaged in business.
e. Transfer of goods as part of a business transfer.
f. The amount equivalent to the CIF value in the transfer of goods from abroad carried out before the importation into our country.
g. Importation of:
Goods or transfer of goods made free-of-charge in favor of entities and agencies of the public sector, except public companies; as well as, to religious organizations.
Personal goods and household furniture imported free from customs duties in accordance with legal provisions and up to the amount and term established therein, vehicles are excluded.
Goods acquired with donations from abroad, provided they are destined to public works projects in accordance with bilateral technical cooperation agreements between the Peruvian Government and other States or Governmental International Entities with bilateral or multilateral funds.
h. Gambling and bets, such as lotteries, bingo, raffle, slot machines and other electronic machines, casinos and horse race events.
i. Awarding at exclusive title to each contracting party of goods obtained from the execution of contracts of business collaboration that do not keep independent bookkeeping, base on the contractual proportion, provided they submit the SUNAT (National Superintendency of Tax Administration) the information required.
j. The allotment of funds, goods, services and construction contracts carried out by the contracting parties of associations, consortia, joint ventures or any other form of contract of business collaboration, which do not carry independent

accounting, for the execution of business or common work derived from an obligation expressed in the contract, provided the requirements and conditions established by SUNAT are fulfilled.
k. The competence of the operator of contracts of business collaboration, which do not carry independent accounting of the common goods, tangible or intangible, services and construction contracts, acquired for the execution of business or common work, subject matter of the contract, in the proportion corresponding to each contracting party, in accordance with that established by the Regulations.

3.2. Anticipated Recovery System:

The Anticipated Recovery System of the General Sales Tax consists on the refund of the tax paid in the imports and/or domestic acquisitions of capital assets carried out by individuals or corporate bodies engaged in productive activities of goods and services destined to be exported or which sale is burdened with the GST provided they have not even started their commercial activities.

The refund will be made by means of Negotiable Notes of Credit against the fiscal credit generated in the imports and/or domestic acquisitions of capital assets that had not been depleted during the 6 months following the date in which their capital goods were registered in the acquisition registry.

The minimum amount that shall be accumulated to request the refund shall be equivalent to 4 UIT in force at the moment of the application.

The regulations of the System establishes the types of machinery and equipment included therein, which should be registered as fixed assets of the company.

The following do not enjoy the present system:

a. Taxpayers that are formed by the merge or split of companies that have started productive activity.
b. Taxpayers that merge absorbing companies that have started productive activity.

On the other hand, companies that subscribe contracts with the State, under sectoral laws for the development, exploration and/or exploitation of natural resources, and those that conclude concession contracts with the State for the development of infrastructure works and public utilities are entitled to enjoy the Anticipated Recovery System of GST, related to imports and domestic acquisition of goods, services and construction contracts required for the execution of the project matter of the contract. Companies that fulfill the requirements 6 to enjoy this benefit shall be qualified by means of Supreme Resolution.

It is worth to mention that in these cases, the minimum amount that will be accumulated to request the refund will be 36 UIT.

The companies that have the referred Supreme Resolution shall be entittled to include in the Law Stability Agreements the stability of the anticipated recovery system, according to the norms in force at the date of subscription of the respective stability agreements.

3.3. Exemptions:

3.3.1. The following items are exempt from the General Sales Tax:

a. Operations listed in Appendix I and II until December 31, 1999
b. Those taxpayers whose line of business is the exclusive execution of exempt operations referred to in the foregoing item, when they sell goods acquired or produced to be used exclusively in said exempt operations.
c. Industrial enterprises located on the Peruvian border or in the jungle zones, as well as financial institutions in closing process, up to December 31, 1999.
d. Enterprises established in the jungle region up to 31.12.99 7
e. Companies that are incoporated or set up in the Centers of Export, Transformation, Industry, Commercialization and Services (CETICOS) of Ilo, Matarani and Tacna, and Paita until December 31, 2004, which annual operations correspond in not less than 92% to the export of goods produced, shall be exempt up to December 31, 2012.
f. Importation of goods for the Amazon region consumption.
g. Lodge and food services by lodge companies to touristic operators domiciled in the country, which transfer said services to touristic operators abroad to be used by persons non-domiciled in the country; in force up to 31.12.2003

3.3.2. Are exempt from the Tax, the taxpayers located in the Amazon 2 region for the execution of the following operations:

a. Sale of goods made in the zone for inner consumption
b. Services rendered in that zone; and,
c. Construction contracts or the first sale of real estates made by the constructors in the zone

The taxpayers shall apply the General Sales Tax to all their operations made out of the scope indicated in the foregoing paragraph, under the general regulations of the mentioned tax.

3.3.2.1. Sale of natural gas, oil and by-products made by the companies located in the departments of Loreto, Ucayali and Madre de Dios, provided those products are used in such departmants.

4. EXCISE TAX:

The excise tax is levied upon:

a. The domestic sale at producer level and importation of goods listed in Appendix III and IV.
b. The domestic sale made by the importer of goods listed in Appendix III and IV.8
c. Gambling and bets, such as lotteries, bingos, raffles, slot machines and other electronic machines, casinos and horse races.

4.1. Rates:

The Excise Tax Rate runs between 2% and 118%, according to the type of good or service detailed in Appendix III and IV. 9

The rates applicable to gambling and bets are:

a. Lotteries, bingo and raffles.......................... 10%
b. Casinos.. 5%
c. Horse races...................................... 2%
The fix monthly amounts applicable to each slot machine and other electronic machines are... 15 % UIT

4.2. Benefits: 10

a. Importation or sale of coal and/or natural gas up to December 31, 1999.
b. Companies incorporated or established in the CETICOS of Ilo, Matarani and Tacna, and Paita up to December 31, 2004, and which annual operations correspond to not less than 92% to export of goods produced, shall be exempt up to December 31, 2012.
c. Sale of natural gas, oil and by-products made by the companies located in the departmants of Loreto, Ucayali and Madre de Dios, provided those products are used in such departments.

5. CUSTOMS DUTIES:

The customs duties applied to the importation of supplies and/or products are:

a. Ad-valorem duties: Two rates:1 2% and 20% of CIF values listed in the Peruvian Schedule of Customs Duties.
b. Overrates:
b.1. Temporary additional overrate: 5% Ad-Valorem CIF.

The Overrate only applies 331 Tarif items (4,9% of total items) and aims at temporarily protect national agricultrue production, specifically:

• Products burdened with 17% (12% + 5%)
Meat and eatable leavings, milk and dairy products, potatoes, onion, garlic, fresh and refrigerated legumes, fruits, bark of citrous-trees and melon, tea, sausages, meat based foods and canned meat, legumes- and vegetables- based food, confectionary and cacao products, natural honey, durum wheat, cooked and frozen green peas and beans.

• Products burdened with 25% (20% + 5%)
Malt and extract of malt, black beer, wine of fresh grapes, other fermented beverages, ethylic alcohol not denaturalized with less than 80%, durum yellow wheat, sorgum, sugar cane and sugar beet.

5.1. Promotional mechanisms in productive sectors:

• Industry: Installments of customs duties on capital goods importation;
• Agroindustrial: The State assumes customs duties on importation on inputs and capital goods (seeds, equipment of technical irrigation, etc.)

6. COMMERCIAL AGREEMENTS

It is worth to mention that as part of its commercial policy, Peru has subscribed bilateral agreements within the ALADI framework. Those agreements establish tax reliefs for a list of products that can be periodically reviewed.

Within the subregional context, Peru has been reincorporated as full member country to the Andean Community of Nations (Bolivia, Colombia, Ecuador, Peru and Venezuela). The objective of this Community is the promotion of a balanced development of its members through the integration and economic cooperation with a view to gradual development of a common market. Nowadays, this entity is negotiating with MERCOSUR (Argentina, Brazil, Paraguay, Uruguay) the formation of Free Trade Zone that will enter into force in year 2000.

Likewise, Peru will participate at the next negotiations for the establishment of the Free Trade Area of the Americas that will entry into force in year 2005.

SELECTED LAWS AND REGULATIONS AFFECTING BUSINESS

FOREIGN INVESTMENT LAWS AND REGULATIONS FRAMEWORK

FOREIGN INVESTMENT PROMOTION LAW

The Foreign Investment Promotion Law, approved by Legislative Decree 662, 1991, is based on the equal treatment to national and foreign capital. Therefore, foreign investment is permitted to be established in any economic sector. No prior authorization is required due to its foreign status. Once made, the foreign investment shall be registered with the Comisión Nacional de Inversiones y Tecnologías Extranjeras - CONITE.

INVESTMENT COMMITMENT BY THE FOREIGN INVESTOR

The investor shall fulfill one of the following investment commitments:

- Direct Foreign Investment, as contribution to the capital stock.
- Contributions for the development of contractual joint ventures
- Investment in goods and properties located within the national land.
- Portfolio investments.

CAPITAL CONTRIBUTIONS

CONITE shall consider as foreign investment the contributions made under the following forms:

- Freely convertible currency, channeled through the national financial system.
- Goods and equipments
- Capitalization of debts
- Reinvestment of profits
- Intangible technological contributions
- Others contributing the development of the country

RIGHTS GRANTED BY THE LAW TO THE FOREIGN INVESTOR:

- Non-discriminating treatment against the national investor.
- Free remittance of profits or dividends
- Free re-exportation of his capital
- Unrestricted access to the domestic credit
- Free acquisition of technology and remittance of royalties
- Freedom to acquire shares owned by national investors
- Freedom to contract abroad insurances for his investment
- Possibility to conclude with the State Law Stability Agreements for his investment in the country

GUARANTEE AND SECURITY FOR THE INVESTMENT

With the purpose of complementing the new juridical framework to promote the private investment and create the right climate to encourage a bigger flow of foreign investments, foreign investors have been granted with some mechanisms of multilateral, bilateral and national nature granting guarantees and protection for their investment.

AGREEMENTS PROTECTING INVESTMENTS

In April 1991, the Congress ratified the subscription of the Convention Establishing the Multilateral Investment Guarantee Agency - MIGA, of the World Bank. Nowadays, important investments, mainly of the mining and financial sectors, are being executing under the covers granted by the MIGA.

In the same way, Peru has ratified the subscription of the Convention Establishing the International Center of Settlement of Investment Disputes - ICSID, thus, eventual disputes on investment matters with the State may be settled with this arbitrage tribunal.

In the bilateral field, Peru has concluded agreements for the promotion and protection of investments with more than 20 countries of Europe, Asia, and America, further detailed. Nowadays, negotiations to conclude these agreements with 23 countries more are under way.

With the same purpose, in December 1992, the Financial Agreement on Incentives to Investments was concluded with the United States. In conformity with such agreement, the Overseas Private Investment Corporation (OPIC) is issuing insurances, re-insurances or guarantees to cover American investments in Peru.

LAW STABILITY AGREEMENTS

Empowered by the Political Constitution, and under the Foreign Investment Promotion Law and the Framework Law for the Growth of the Private Investment, the State guarantees the law stability to foreign investors and to the enterprises where they invest, through the subscription of agreements with contract-law status, and abide by the general provisions on contracts established in the Civil Code.

Guarantees granted by the State to the Foreign Investor

- Equal treatment, by which the national legislation does not discriminate against investors participating in enterprises, due to their
- status of foreign person.
- Stability of the Income Tax System in force when the agreement is concluded.
- Stability of the system of free availability of foreign currency and remittance of profits, dividends and royalties.

Guarantees granted by the State to the Enterprise receiving the investment

- Stability of the systems of labor engagement in force when the agreement is concluded.
- Stability of the system of export promotion applicable when the agreement is concluded.
- Stability of the Income Tax System.

Who can conclude Law Stability Agreements?

Investors and enterprises receiving the investment, in the case of new enterprises or in the case of increasing the capital stock of the enterprises already established. Also in the case of investors participating in the privatization process and the enterprises involved in such process, which fulfill the following requirements:

Investment commitment by the foreign investor

The investor shall fulfill one of the following investment commitments:

- To make, in a two-year term, capital contribution's for an amount not under US$ 2 million.
- To make, in a two-year term, capital contributions under US$ 2 million, but over US$ 500 hundred; and additionally:
    1. To generate exports of over US$ 2 million worth; or,
    2. To generate more than twenty jobs
- To acquire more than 50% of the shares of an enterprise participating in the privatization process.

Requirements for the enterprise:

- One of its shareholders shall have concluded the corresponding Law Stability Agreement
- In case tax stability is required, the contributions shall account for 50% increase in relation with the total amount of capital and reserves, and shall be destined to the enlargement of the production capacity or to the technological development of the enterprise.
- The case of transfer of more than 50% of the shares of an enterprise participating in the privatization process.

INTELLECTUAL PROPERTY PROTECTION

The State protects the intellectual and industrial property rights, and therefore, foreign people's rights abide by the same conditions than those applied to the national ones. Contracts for the use of technology, patents, trademarks or any other element of the industrial property of foreign origin, as well as technical assistance, basic and detail engineering, management and franchising are freely negotiated between the parties and further registered with the National Institute of Defense of the Competence and Protection of the Intellectual Property - INDECOPI.

Royalties remittance is freely made through the national financial system, prior payment of the pertaining taxes. The corresponding financial entity shall further inform it to CONITE, only for statistical purposes.

BILATERAL INVESTMENT TREATIES SIGNED BY PERU

COUNTRY	STATUS
ARGENTINA	APPROVED
AUSTRALIA	SIGNED
BOLIVIA	IN FORCE
COLOMBIA	APPROVED
CZECH REPUBLIC	IN FORCE
DENMARK	IN FORCE

FINLAND	APPROVED
FRANCE	APPROVED
GERMANY	APPROVED
ITALY	IN FORCE
MALASYA	APPROVED
NETHERLANDS	IN FORCE
NORWAY	IN FORCE
PARAGUAY	IN FORCE
PEOPLE REPUBLIC OF CHINA	IN FORCE
PORTUGAL	IN FORCE
REPUBLIC OF KOREAO	IN FORCE
ROMANIA	IN FORCE
SPAIN	APPROVED
SWEDEN	IN FORCE
SWITZERLAND	IN FORCE
THAILAND	IN FORCE
UNITED KINGDOWN	IN FORCE
UNITES STATED /1	IN FORCE
VENEZUELA	SIGNED

/1 Investment Incentive and Financial Agreement signed with OPIC

INVESTMENT DECREE (N° 162-92-EF)

The Legislative Decrees N°. 662 and 757, Foreign Investment Promotion Law and Framework Law for the Private Investment Growth, respectively, include basic provisions for the growth of national and foreign private investment in all sectors of the economic activity;

Provisions on the granting of rights to investors, within the framework of the social market economy based on free competition, as well as rules oriented to guarantee said rights can be herein found;

Article 38 of Legislative Decree N° 757 disposes the application of said rights and guarantees in the same extent to national and foreign investors, as well as to enterprises where they participate;

A law stability system has been created in order to guarantee the investor's rights. This system will be implemented through the execution of Law Stability Agreements, which purpose is to enable the investors to plan their investments in a long-term;

Law Stability Agreements are internationally recognized as instruments which promote investments. Their main feature is that the execution of them does not imply benefits or tax exemptions, or privileges of other nature neither for the investors nor for the enterprises where they participate. which are those that are legally incorporated and pay the corresponding taxes;

The execution of such Agreements does not involve resources from the National Treasury. These Agreements only guarantee the investors and enterprises where they participate, the stability of the legislation, in force at the time of its signature, for a certain period, purely on matters included in the stability system;

It is necessary to enact the regulations required to guarantee the respect to the social market economy, free initiative and private investments, as well as those referred to the execution of Law Stability Agreements;

In accordance with Legislative Decree N° 560;

DECREES:

Article 1. Be approved the Regulations on the Private Investment Guarantee Systems, which contains one (1) Preliminary Title with four (04) articles; four (04) Titles with thirty-four (34) articles; nine (09) Complementary Provisions; and three (03) Annexes. These Regulations are contained in the present Supreme Decree.

Article 2. This Supreme Decree is countersigned by the chairman of the Cabinet and Minister of Foreign Affairs; Minister of Economy and Finance; Minister of Energy and Mines; Minister of Industry, Domestic Trade, Tourism and Integration; Minister of Agriculture; and, Ministry of Transport, Communications, Housing and Construction.

Article 3. The present Supreme Decree becomes effective the following day of its publication in the Official Gazette «El Peruano».

Given at the Government House, in Lima, on the ninth day of October, 1992.

ALBERTO FUJIMORI FUJIMORI
Constitutional President of the Republic

OSCAR DE LA PUENTE RAYGADA
Chairman of the Cabinet and Minister of Foreign Affairs

CARLOS BOLOÑA BEHR
Minister of Economy and Finances

DANIEL HOKAMA TOKASHIKI
Minister of Energy and Mines

JORGE CAMET DICKMANN
Minister of Industry, Domestic Trade, Tourism and Integration

ABSALON VASQUEZ VILLANUEVA
Minister of Agriculture

ALFREDO ROSS ANTEZANA
Minister of Transport, Communications, Housing and Construction

PRELIMINARY TITLE

Rule I. Every national or foreign investor, as well as the enterprises where they participate, are covered by the guarantees to private investments contained in article 38 of Legislative Decree N° 757 and in Chapter I of the Title II hereof. Said guarantees take the form of the following rights:

a. Non discrimination right among investors and enterprises, as to their nationality, sectors or economic activities they carry out, enterprises' geographic location, nor in the following matters:

• foreign exchange;

• pricing, rates or non-tariff duties;

• type of business;

• status of individuals or corporate bodies, nor

• any other reason of equivalent effects;

b. Nondiscrimination right among enterprises as to the State's participation;

c. Right of private property;

d. Right to carry out any economic activity;

e. Right of freedom for enterprise or industry;

f. Right of freedom for foreign trade;

g. Right of freedom for domestic trade;

h. Enterprises' right to freely decide the distribution of the full amount of profits or dividends generated;

i. Investors' right to receive the full amount of the corresponding profits or dividends;

j. Right to acquire shares, participations or similar rights; and,

k. Right to use the most favorable exchange rate existing at the exchange market.

Furthermore, investments made with resources coming from abroad enjoy the guarantees inherent in their nature of foreign capital, as to profit and capital remittances, including the right to use the most favorable exchange rate existing at the exchange market.

All guarantees referred to herein are granted in favor of national and foreign investors and enterprises where they participate. Consequently, the investors may demand the fulfillment thereof as from the date the Legislative Decree N° 757, Framework Law for Private Investment Growth, became effective.

Rule II. Investors may execute Law Stability Agreements with the State, provided they fulfill the conditions referred to in article 16 hereof, in order to guarantee the following rights for a ten-year period:

a. stability of the tax system regarding to Income Tax;

b. stability of the non discrimination right; and,

c. stability of the right to use the most favorable exchange rate existing at the exchange market.

Furthermore, investments made with resources coming from abroad may enjoy, by the execution of Law Stability Agreements for the same period, rights inherent in their foreign capital status included in the following guarantees:

a. stability of the system of free disposal of foreign currency; and,

b. stability of the right of free remittance of profits, dividends and capitals.

Rule III. The enterprises may conclude Law Stability Agreements with the State to guarantee the following rights for a ten-year period, provided they fulfill the conditions referred to in article 17 of the present Supreme Decree:

a. stability of the hiring systems in any of its forms; and,

b. stability of the export promotion systems.

Furthermore, enterprises may enjoy the stability of the tax system regarding Income Tax only when they fulfill the conditions referred to in the second paragraph of article 17 hereof.

Rule IV. Lesses of goods under financial leasing contracts may conclude Law Stability Agreements with the State, provided they fulfill the conditions referred to in article 18 hereof, to guarantee the stability right of the tax system governing said leasing contract, for a maximum term of ten years counted as from the execution date.

SCOPE

Article 1. The provisions required for the enforcement of the rules on juridical security for private investments, considered in Legislative Decree N° 662, as well as in Title II and in the First Chapter of Title V of Legislative Decree N° 757, are hereby enacted. These provisions are applicable to national and foreign investors.

For purposes of fulfillment of the provisions included herein:

a. Investors are national or foreign individuals or corporate bodies, titleholders of any type of investments made within the country, including the following modalities:

a.1. Contributions made to the enterprise's equity in any modality referred to in items a) to f) and i) of article 1 of Legislative Decree N° 662;

a.2. Portfolio investments, meaning those financial resources channeled through the National Financial System, destined to the acquisition of securities, financial documents and papers quoted in stock exchanges; or, bank deposit certificates in national or foreign currency; and,

a.3. Resources designated to joint ventures, that is, investments made by investors in goods or services, which are not capital contributions, but contractual commercial transactions, by which the investor receives a way of participation in production volumes, aggregate amount of sales or in the enterprise's net profits.

Those investments can also be made under the modality of association in participation referred to in the Sixth Section of the Third Book of the Amended Text of the General Corporate Law, approved by Supreme Decree N° 003-85-JUS.

b. Enterprises are those established or incorporated in the country under any corporate form included in the national legislation.

GUARANTEES TO INVESTMENTS AND INVESTORS INVESTORS' RIGHTS

Article 2. National and foreign investors, and the enterprises where they participate, enjoy all the rights referred to in the present Chapter, with no other exception than those herein included, in accordance with that established in the legal rules referred to in the first paragraph of the foregoing article.

Article 3. The nondiscrimination right among investments and enterprises means that the same treatment must be applied by the State, at any level, whether they are entities of the Central Government, Regional or Local Administrations, or enterprises owned by them. Therefore, investments and enterprises enjoy the same rights and obligations, with no other exceptions than those established because of national security in article 126 of the Constitution of 1979 and article 13 of Legislative Decree N° 757. Such exceptions are ruled by Title IV hereof.

The nondiscrimination referred to in this article means that no authority or enterprise of the Central Government, Regional or Local Administration, as the case may be, shall establish different treatment to investors or enterprises where they participate, because of their nationality, type or sector of the economic activity they carry out, or enterprises' geographic location. A discriminatory treatment can neither be established to investors nor enterprises where they participate, in the following matters:

a. Foreign Exchange: It includes all the rules and mechanisms oriented to the regulation of the exchange market applicable to operations and contracts made in foreign currency. This means that investors and enterprises have the right to acquire or sale foreign currency at the best exchange rate they may obtain. They cannot be compelled to make exchange operations under any system or mechanism involving a less favorable treatment than that applied to any individual or corporate body for the same type of operation;

b. Prices, rates or non-tariff duties: Different amounts or rates will not be applied, except for the case of prices of enterprises, which because of their geographic location, increase their corresponding costs.

For purposes of that established in this item, the points mentioned here must be understood as:

b.1. Prices: Those corresponding to goods and services delivered by State entities and enterprises directly or indirectly owned by the State;

b.2. Rates: Those corresponding to public services rendered by State entities and enterprises directly or indirectly owned by the State; and,

b.3. Non-tariff duties: Taxes charged by State's entities at all levels, for services inherent to the State or public works, other than taxes and import duties. Charges for administrative procedures are included herein.

c. Corporate form: Mechanism by which an enterprise is incorporated in the country under any modality considered in the national legislation, except for financial enterprises included in Legislative Decree N° 637, General Law of Banking, Financing and Insurance Institutions; Legislative Decree N° 755, Stock Market Law; and, other laws related to the Financing System;

d. The status of individuals or corporate bodies, except what is referred to the granting of concessions for the construction, repairing, maintenance and execution of public works, limited to corporate bodies in accordance with article 1 of Legislative Decree N° 758, Law of Private Investment Promotion in Public Works; nor

e. Any other cause of similar effects.

One reason of similar effects is the discrimination resulting from the mix of some factors described in the present article.

Different treatment in taxes or customs duties, because of sectors or types of economic activities, or geographic location of the enterprises, is not considered a reason of similar effects.

Article 4. The nondiscrimination right among enterprises as to the State's ownership of the capital involves that private enterprises must enjoy the same treatment than the given to enterprises which are directly or indirectly owned by the State, that carry out the same or similar activity.

Article 5. The right to private property has the following restrictions:

a. Those included in article 126 of the Constitution of 1979, ruled by that established in Title IV of the present Supreme Decree;

b. Special restraints and prohibitions for the acquisition, possession, working and transfer of certain goods because of national interest, stated by express law, according to the article 127 of the Constitution of 1979. For these purposes, reasons of national interest are those exclusively related to guarantee the external security and internal peace;

c. Expropriation of goods because of public necessity or utility or social interest, or in case of war or public disaster, in accordance with that established in article 125 of the Constitution of 1979, which is governed by Legislative Decree No. 313, General Law of Expropriation. For purposes of expropriations established by the Executive, public necessity or utility or social interest, reasons are understood as those exclusively related to the adoption of measures required for the execution of public works, following the definitions established in article 2 of Legislative Decree No. 758, Law for the Promotion of Private Investments in Public Works and Utilities; and,

d. Expropriation of cultural goods in risk to be lost for the Nation's Cultural Inheritance, due to abandonment, destruction, great damage or illegal exportation referred to in article 5 of Law N° 24047, General Law of Protection to the Nation's Cultural Inheritance, governed by Legislative Decree N° 313, General Law of Expropriation.

Article 6. The investor's right to carry out its preferred economic activity involves that any economic activity may be executed in the country, provided this is not considered as offense and fulfill the requirements established by the Constitution, treaties and laws. Are exempted hereof the reserves referred to protected natural areas and the production of war weapons, according to article 6 of Legislative Decree N° 757.

Certain activities may be reserved in behalf of the State, because of social interest or national security. These activities will be qualified in accordance with item c) of the foregoing article and article 32 hereof, respectively.

Economic activities made in protected natural areas will be governed by the corresponding Regulations.

War weapons can be fabricated by private enterprises only when they have concluded with the State an Agreement thereupon.

Article 7. The freedom right of an enterprise or industry, recognized by article 9 of Legislative Decree N° 757 and article 6 of Legislative Decree N° 662, implies that the State will not interfere in the way in which the enterprises carry out their productive activities, without detriment of the provisions related to hygiene, health, salubrity, environment preservation and industrial security.

Article 8. The freedom right of foreign trade has no other restraints than those established in article 12 of Legislative Decree N° 668 and article 55 of Legislative Decree N° 757. The following are the only restraints:

a. As to exports:

a.1. Prohibitions included in the list of Prohibited Export Products;

a.2. Those included in the Law N° 24047, General Law of Protection of the Nation's Cultural Inheritance;

a.3. Rights and duties derived from international agreements concluded with the State;

a.4. Temporary emergency measures required to guarantee the external security and internal peace; and,

a.5. Provisions destined to the preservation of native and improved Genetic Inheritance of cultivations and wildlife.

b. As to imports:

b.1. Rights and duties derived from international agreements concluded with the State;

b.2. Prohibitions established in the List of Prohibited Import Goods because of their condition of dangerous or radioactive residues or scraps;

b.3. Temporary emergency measures required to guarantee the external security, internal peace, and public health.

According to article 4 of Decree Law N° 25629, every provision which establish procedures or requirements, or that affect in any way the free foreign commercialization of goods or services, shall be approved by Supreme Decree countersigned by the Minister of Economy and Finances and by the Minister of the pertaining sector. In case of the temporary emergency measures, referred to in items a.4 and b.3 of the present article, the corresponding Supreme Decree shall additionally have the approving vote of the cabinet, as it is established in article 12 of the Legislative Decree N° 668.

Consequently, any other restraints for foreign commercialization of goods existing when the Legislative Decree N° 668 became effective, have been eliminated. Therefore, restraints or limitations other than those expressly listed in the present article cannot be established.

Article 9. The freedom right of domestic trade does not exempt from the fulfillment of the provisions on hygiene, health and environment preservation, as well as, rules to eliminate monopolistic, controlling and restrictive practices of free competition; those of defense against unfair competition; and, those of consumer protection. Provisions on pricing public utilities, which will continue to decided by administrative procedures are included within the scope hereof, up to they fit the Third Transitory Provision of Legislative Decree N° 757 and be governed by offer and demand.

In following that established in article 4 of Decree Law N° 25629, every provision establishing procedures or requirements, or affecting in any way the free domestic commercialization of goods or services, shall be approved by Supreme Decree countersigned by the Minister of Economy and Finances and by the Ministry of the pertaining sector.

Article 10. The right of enterprises to freely agree the distribution of the full amount of profits or dividends implies that the State cannot establish restraints to the distribution thereof, if they fulfill the pertinent legal obligations. The right of distribution of profits or dividends corresponding to the current year according to periodical balances, in accordance with that established in article 10 of Legislative Decree N° 757 is herein included.

The right referred to in this article does not exempt from the fulfillment of the following obligations:

a. Statement and payment of the corresponding Income Tax;

b. The legal binding reserve that corporations and limited partnership issuing shares must make, when during the financial year they receive after-tax net earnings over 7% of the paid equity; according to that established in articles 258 and 264 of the Amended Text of the General Corporate Law approved by Supreme Decree N° 003-85-JUS;

c. The Reserve Fund that banking and financial companies must generate, according to that established in the Chapter II of Title III of Legislative Decree N° 637, General Law of Banking, Financial and Insurance Institutions;

d. The responsibility of companies' directors and managers in the distribution of not really earned profits, or when loss of the capital stock exists, following that established in article 20 of the aforementioned Amended Text of the General Corporate Law, also that of banking and financial companies directors and managers in the same cases and relating the reserve fund, in accordance with article 72 of the Legislative Decree N° 637; and,

e. Those relating worker's participation in the enterprise's profits, under Legislative Decree N° 677.

Article 11. The investor's right to receive the full amount of profits and dividends does not exempt them from the fulfillment of the following obligations:

a. Those referred to the Income Tax, and

b. The obligation to repay the profits received from the distribution of profits not earned by the company according to the current final balance or when loss of capital stock exists, provided they act with malicious intent. The partners acting in good faith are compelled to repay the earned profits with their share corresponding to the following fiscal years or with the corresponding value share in case of liquidation, according to article 20 of the Amended Text of the General Corporate Law, approved by Supreme Decree N° 003-85-JUS.

In case profits have been distributed as the result of periodical trial balances made during the fiscal year, and, if by the current final balance, these have not been really earned by the company, the partners are compelled to pay the amounts unduly distributed by the company.

Article 12. The right of national and foreign investors to acquire shares, participations or similar rights, implies that the State will not restraint the transfer thereof, whether in or out Stock Exchange.

Shares, participations and equity rights of subregional investors are herein included. This right is extended to enterprises where national and foreign investors participate.

Article 13. The right to use the most favorable exchange rate means that the investor or enterprise has the right to accede to foreign currency at the exchange market at the most favorable rate. They cannot be compelled to make exchange transactions under systems or mechanisms involving a less favorable treatment than that applied to any individual or corporate body for any exchange operation, in accordance with:

a. In case of conversion of foreign currency into national currency: the investor may sell it to any individual or corporate body at the most favorable purchase rate he can obtain at the exchange market at the time of the exchange operation; and,

b. In case of conversion of national currency into foreign currency: the investor may buy it to any individual or corporate body at the best sale rate he can obtain at the exchange market at the time of the exchange operation.

GUARANTEES TO CAPITALS COMING FROM ABROAD

Article 14. Investments coming from abroad, according to the definition contained in article 1 of the Legislative Decree N° 662, whether of nationals or foreigners, enjoy the guarantees inherent in their nature of foreign capital included in this Chapter.

Investments coming from abroad must be channeled through the National Banking System and registered with the National Competent Agency in order to enjoy the guarantees referred to in the foregoing paragraph.

Article 15. The right of remittance of profits and capitals implies that these can be transferred abroad without restraints, in freely convertible currency, without prior authorization from the Central Government, Regional or Local Administrations, provided that the corresponding investment has been duly registered with the National Competent Agency and without detriment of the pertaining tax obligations. The following items may be remitted:

a. The full amount of capitals coming from abroad, including the capital resulting from the sale of shares, participations or rights over enterprises, reduction of capital and partial or total liquidation of enterprises;

b. The full amount of dividends or proved net profits resulting from the investment, or those obtained from the concept of payment for the use or benefit of goods physically located in the country; and,

c. The full amount of royalties and payments for the use or transfer of technology, including any other element of industrial property authorized by the National Competent Agency.

Royalties paid by local enterprises as affiliates of foreign enterprises to their main office or to other enterprises affiliate to the same main office, in accordance with the second paragraph of article 21 of Legislative Decree N° 662 are included in this item.

LAW STABILITY CONDITIONS TO ENJOY THE LAW STABILITY SYSTEM

Article 16. Only the investors who undertake the commitment to fulfill the following items may enjoy the system of law stability considered in article 19 hereof:

a. To make cash contributions to the capital of an enterprise already established or to be established under the Peruvian Laws in the country, provided the following requirements are fulfilled:

a.1 Contribution of non less than US$ 2 000 000 (Two million Dollars of the United States of America);

a.2 To be channeled through the National Financial System; and,

a.3 To be made in a maximum term of two years counted as from the execution of the stability agreement.

b. To make risk investments with third persons, provided the following requirements are fulfilled:

b.1 The amount must be at least US$ 2 000 000 (Two million Dollars of the United States of America);

b.2 It must be channeled through the National Financial System; and, b.3 It must be made in a maximum term of two years counted as from the execution of the stability agreement.

c. To make cash contributions to the capital of an enterprise already established or to be established under the Peruvian Laws in the country, provided the following requirements are fulfilled:

c.1 The corresponding amount must be at least US$ 500 000 (Five hundred thousand dollars of the United States of America);

c.2 It must be channeled through the National Financial System;

c.3 It must be made in a maximum term of two years counted as from the execution of the stability agreement.

c.4 It must direct generate more than twenty permanent jobs, or not less than US$ 2 000 000 (Two Million Dollars of the United State of America) in foreign currency as export proceeds during a three-year period as from the date of execution of the stability agreement.

d. To make risk investments with third persons, provided the following requirements are fulfilled:

d.1 The corresponding amount must be at least US$ 500 000 (Five hundred thousand dollars of the United States of America);

d.2 It must be channeled through the National Financial System;

d.3 It must be made in a maximum term of two years counted as from the execution of the stability agreement; and,

d.4 It must direct generate more than twenty permanent jobs, or not less than US$ 2,000,000.00 (Two million dollars of the United States of America) in foreign currency as export proceeds during a three-year period as from the date of execution of the stability agreement..

e. To acquire shares of enterprises directly or indirectly owned by the State, provided that the following requirements are fulfilled:

e.1 The corresponding amount must be at least US$ 2 000 000 (Two million dollars of the United States of America);

e.2 It must involve the transfer of more than 50% of the enterprise's shares;

e.3 The investment must be channeled through the National Financial System; and,

e.4 It must be made in a maximum term of two years as from the execution of the stability agreement.

f. To acquire shares of enterprises directly or indirectly owned by the State, provided the following requirements are fulfilled:

f.1 The corresponding amount must be at least US$ 500 000 (Five hundred thousand dollars of the United States of America);

f.2 It must involve the transfer of more than 50% of the enterprise's shares;

f.3 The investment must be channeled through the National Financial System;

f.4 It must be made in a maximum term of two years counted as from the execution of the stability agreement; and,

f.5 It must direct generate more than twenty permanent jobs, or not less than US$ 2,000,000.00 (Two million dollars of the United States of America) in foreign currency as export proceeds during a three-year period counted as from the execution date of the stability agreement.

Article 17. The law stability covers enterprises been established in the country, provided they receive or are incorporated with new contributions to the capital according to that stated in the foregoing article, or they invoke item b) of this article.

The law stability referred to in the foregoing paragraph includes tax stability for enterprises as to the Income Tax, only in the following cases:

a. When the new incorporated enterprises, or those already established in the country, receive new contributions for an amount over 50% of their capital and reserves, provided the contributions are assigned to the expansion of the production capacity or technological improvement, and have at least one investor, which make contributions under one of the modalities considered in items a) to d) of the last article, or

b. In the case of transfer of more than 50% of an State-owned enterprise's shares, with at least an investor who acquires these shares under one of the modalities considered in items e) and f) of the last article.

For purposes of item a) of the present article, the concept of production capacity includes all the enterprise's goods and services.

Article 18. Tax stability includes financial leasing contracts, provided that:

a. The worth of goods subject of the contract is not under US$ 2 000 000 (Two million dollars of the United States), or

b. The worth of goods subject of the contract is not under US$ 500 000 (Five hundred thousand dollars of the United States of America), provided the acquisition of said goods directly or indirectly generates more than twenty permanent jobs, or not less than US$ 2 000 000 (Two million dollars of the United States of America) in foreign currency as export proceeds during a three-year period from the date of execution of the stability agreement.

GUARANTEES GRANTED BY THE LAW STABILITY

Article 19. The law stability guarantees the investors and enterprises where they participate, as the case may be, the following rights:

a. Stability of the tax system on Income Tax in force at the execution time, in cases considered in item a) of article 10 of the Legislative Decree N° 662 and in articles 38, 40 and 41 of the Legislative Decree N° 757, in accordance with that established in article 23 hereof;

b. Stability of the system of free availability of foreign currencies, in accordance with that established in item b) of article 10 of Legislative Decree N° 662, applied under item a) of article 3 hereof;

c. Stability of the right of free remittance of profits, dividends, capitals and other earnings, in accordance with article 15 hereof;

d. Stability of the right to use the most favorable exchange rate at the exchange market, according to that established in article 13 hereof;

e. Stability of the right of nondiscrimination, according to article 3 hereof;

f. Stability of the system regarding hiring, in any of its forms, under that established in item a) of article 12 of Legislative Decree N° 662, specially in that related to systems covered by Legislative Decree N° 728, Work Promotion Law;

g. Stability of the export promotion system, in accordance with that established in item b) of article 12 of Legislative Decree N° 662, including the drawback system considered in article 8 of Legislative Decree N° 668, as well as the special systems contained in Legislative Decree N° 704, Law for Free Zones, Special Trade Treatment and Special Development Zones; and,

h. In the case of financial leasing contracts: total stability of the tax system.

Article 20. The stability mentioned in item c) of the last article implies that the investments made must be appraised and registered with the National Competent Agency, in freely convertible currency.

Capital earning is the difference between the amount in freely convertible currency in which the investment is transferred, and the registration value of it in the same currency; according to that established in the foregoing paragraph.

Article 21. In accordance with that stated in article 45 of Legislative Decree N° 757, rights, guarantees and insurances granted to the investors and enterprises, where they participate, under the rules referred to in Article 1 hereof, do not restraint in any way their right to enjoy other special systems considered in the national legislation.

Article 22. The law stability granted to investments made in mining enterprises, electricity public enterprises and in those engaged in working of hydrocarbons, are governed by that established hereby and by the special systems considered in Legislative Decree N° 708, Law of Promotion of Investments in the Mining Sector; Legislative Decree N° 693, Law of Promotion of Investments in the Electric Sector; and Legislative Decree N° 655, Law of Promotion of Investments in Hydrocarbons, respectively.

The execution of a Stability Agreement under one of the systems referred to in the foregoing paragraph does not prohibit the execution of other Stability Agreements under other systems, although these have the same subjects.

STABILITY OF THE TAX SYSTEM

Article 23.-The stability of the tax system involves the following:

a. For investors: they are guaranteed that, while the stability system is in force, the corresponding amounts will not be burden with an Income Tax higher than that in force at the time of execution of the agreement. Therefore, they shall receive said amounts in the same proportion for the following concepts:

a.1 Dividends agreed in their favor;

a.2 Profits granted;

a.3 Profits on their disposal; or,

a.4 Remittance of the corresponding amounts for any concept considered in the present item.

The stability system granted to investors under item a) of article 10 of Legislative Decree N° 662 implies that : if the Income Tax is modified during the term of the stability system, so the assessment base or aliquot affecting the enterprise generating the profits is altered; or new taxes burdening the enterprise´s income are created; or by any cause of similar effects, profits or dividends distributable or available for investors are percent reduced as to the before-tax profit, compare with that distributable or available by the time when the tax regime was guaranteed under the stability granted by the agreement ; aliquots of the tax on profits or dividends will be reduced, to make profits or dividends finally distributable or available, equal to those guaranteed, up to the limit chargeable to said tax.

b. For enterprises receiving investments included in items a) and b) of article 17 hereof: they are guaranteed that, while the stability agreement is in force the corresponding Income Tax will remains unmodified; and, the same terms, progress payment, deductions and scales for the calculation of the assessment base, at the time of execution of the agreement, will be applied.

The tax stability system granted to the enterprises under that established in article 40 of Legislative Decree N° 757 implies that, in case the Income Tax were modified during the term of the stability agreement, said modifications will not affect the enterprises receiving investments, which tax stability is guaranteed by the corresponding agreement, whether increasing or decreasing the aliquot; or, increasing or decreasing the assessment matter; or, by any other reason of equivalent effects.

c. For financial leasing contracts: it is guaranteed that, during the term of the stability agreement, the tax system applicable to said contracts will not be modified, and the same terms and benefits in force at the time of execution of the agreement will be applied. The tax stability system granted to financial leasing contracts under article 41 of Legislative Decree N° 757, implies that, in case the Income Tax or any other tax affecting them were modified during the term of the stability agreement, said modifications will not affect the financial leasing contracts, which tax stability is under the corresponding agreement, whether the aliquot or the assessment matter are increased or decreased, or by any other reason of equivalent effects.

Goods subject of financial leasing contracts referred to in this item will not be considered as capital contributions.

LAW STABILITY AGREEMENTS

Article 24. Pursuant to that established in the regulations referred to in article 1 of the present Supreme Decree, the stability of the legal system in force at the time of execution of the agreement, is given through Law Stability Agreements on matters over which the stability is granted.

The stability referred to in the foregoing paragraph implies that the same legislation in force at the time of execution of the agreement will continue be applying over every person protected by Law Stability Agreements; and, that modifications made to the legislation on matters and for the term considered in said agreement, included the repealing of regulations, whether fewer favorable or more favorable provisions, will not affect them.

Article 25. Law Stability Agreements grants the following guarantees:

a. For investors: those contained in item a) to e) of article 19 hereof;

b. For companies:

b.1. For those referred to in the first paragraph of article 17 hereof: those included in items f) and g) of article 19 hereof;

b.2. For those referred to in the second paragraph of article 17 hereof: those included in items a), f) and g) of article 19 hereof; and,

c. For financial leasing contracts: that contained in item h) of article 19 hereof.

Article 26. The Law Stability Agreements have the following features:

a. They are of civil nature, ruled by the Civil Code;

b. They have force of law between the parties, so the agreements may not be unilaterally amended for any reason while they are in force;

c. They are concluded with the State, represented by the National Competent Agency under that established in article 30 hereof, and;

c.1. Investors;

c.2. Companies receiving the investments; or

c.3. Leaseholder , in case of financial leasing contracts.

In case two or more investors invest in the same company, they may conclude, individually or as a whole, stability agreements with the State;

d. They must be executed before the investment and the corresponding registration with the National Competent Agency are made;

e. They have a ten-year term, count as from the date of execution, except in the case of financial leasing contracts where the agreements term may not exceed the term of said contract, with a maximum of ten years;

f. They may be subject of release by investors, companies or leaseholder , who in such a case, will be governed by the common legislation;

g. They may be subject of contractual position cession, provided that they have for that purpose prior authorization from the National Competent Agency, excepted those agreements granting law stability to companies receiving investments; and,

h. Modifications made thereto by common agreement of the parties cannot deal with the term, nor can reduce the investments under the minimum amounts considered in articles 16 to 18 hereof, according to the modality of the investment. In case the modification involves the increase of the original investment amount this will also be subject to the law stability in the same terms granted to the original investment, without considering the amount.

Article 27. The Law Stability Agreements must indicate at least the following data:

a. Identification of the contracting parties and their legal representatives, if applicable;

b. The total investment amount, valued in free convertible currency, and the modality in which the investment will be made;

c. Investment destination: project and corresponding company;

d. Term to make the investment;

e. Rights and guarantees granted by the law stability, specifying the legal norm on that matter at the time of execution of the agreement;

f. In case of tax stability, specification of the applicable legal norm, as well as the aliquot and the scale for the calculation of the assessment matter, if applicable, and the corresponding deductions and benefits;

g. Reasons for rescission or cancellation of the agreement;

h. Conditions for the modification of the agreement freely agreed by the parties;

i. Formalities for the renounce of the investor, company or leaseholder to the law stability system, in order to be governed by the common legislation;

j. Conditions for the national or international settlement under article 48 of Legislative Decree N° 757; and,

k. Conditions for the cession of the contractual position.

Article 28.- The following facts will cause the cancellation of Law Stability Agreements :

a. Failure to accomplish the contributions or acquisitions, which investors and companies agreed to do within the term established for this purpose in the respective stability agreement. This term may not exceed two years;

b. Failure to generate twenty permanent jobs, or the amount for export proceeds in foreign currency, which investors and companies have agreed to do within the term established in the respective stability agreement. This term may not exceed three years. The respective agreement will establish the way to prove the fulfillment of that established hereof;

c. Failure by investors or leaseholder to get the prior authorization for the assigment of their contractual position, if appropriate; and,

d. In case of financial leasing contracts: the rescission or cancellation of the respective financial leasing contract.

Investors, companies or leaseholder who fail under the aforementioned cause who, be meaning of the Law Stability Agreement have enjoyed a smaller tax burden than that corresponding if they would not sign the Law Stability Agreement, must reimburse the State the amount, updated or adjusted, of the taxes that would charge them if the agreement were not executed. Said updating or adjustment will be done following the regulations established by the Tax Code for nonpaid tax debt.

In the case referred to in the foregoing paragraph, if the investors, companies or leaseholder had held a higher tax burden because of the Law Stability Agreement, the State is not compelled to repay any amount.

PROCEDURE FOR THE EXECUTION OF LAW STABILITY AGREEMENTS

Article 29. An application for the execution of the respective agreement, according to the format of Annex II, shall be submitted to the National Competent Agency, in order to enjoy the law stability system referred to in the present Title.

The features and requirements of the application referred to in the foregoing paragraph shall be included in the corresponding Unique Text of Administrative Proceedings - TUPA, according to that established in Title IV of Legislative Decree N° 757.

(*)Article 30. The National Competent Agency for the execution of the law stability system referred to in the present Supreme Decree is:

a. For foreign and national investors investing with resources coming from abroad: the National Commission on Foreign Investments and Technologies - CONITE;

b. For national investors in the other cases: the Ministry of the corresponding Sector;

c. For national and foreign investors who wish to invest in the same company and submit simultaneously time the applications: the National Commission on Foreign Investments and Technologies - CONITE;

d. For companies receiving national and foreign investments: any of those considered in items a) and b) of the present article, at the company's choice; and,

e. For financial leasing contracts: the Ministry of the Sector where the company carries out its activity.

Article 31. Law Stability Agreements must be concluded following the model on Annex I, which is a constituent part hereof.

Local and Regional Administrations shall approve their corresponding models of Agreement-type for the execution of Law Stability Agreements on matters related to their exclusive field, appointing the competent authority in charge of executing them on their behalf.

RESTRAINTS TO OWNERSHIP AND POSSESSION BY FOREIGN INVESTORS

Article 32. Pursuant to that established in article 126 of the Constitution of 1979 and article 13 of Legislative Decree N° 757, the corresponding prior authorization, granted by Supreme Resolution countersigned by the Ministry Chairman of the Cabinet and the Ministry of the corresponding sector, is required for the exercise of the rights of ownership and possession of mines, lands, woods, waters, fuels or sources of energy by foreign investors, directly or indirectly, in areas within fifty kilometers from the borders of the country. Said authorization shall have the favorable opinion of the Comando Conjunto de las Fuerzas Armadas (United Command of the Army Forces), because of the reasons considered in the next paragraphs.

The conditions or limits for the exercise of the rights of ownership and possession, which can be restraint only because of national security reasons, must be established in the Supreme Resolution referred to in the foregoing paragraph.

National security reasons are understood as those required to guarantee the independence, sovereignty and land integrity of the Republic, as well as the internal peace, under that established in article 275 of the Constitution of 1979.

Article 33. Foreign investors or the enterprises where they participate shall submit an application to the Ministry of the Sector corresponding to the economic activity they want to carry out in order to get the prior authorization referred to in the foregoing article. Said application shall include the information indicated in Annex III of the present Supreme Decree, included herein.

Once made, the investment shall be registered in freely convertible currency with the pertaining National Competent Agency.

Article 34. The acquisition of goods referred to in article 32 hereof or the transfer of possession or ownership of said goods from foreign investors to other foreign investors, without the corresponding prior authorization, will be punished with the loss of the acquired rights by the investors in benefit of the State, under that established in article 126 of the Constitution of 1979.

In transfer of goods referred to in the foregoing article to national investors, the notification of it to the Ministry of the corresponding sector is sufficient.

COMPLEMENTARY PROVISIONS

First. In line with that established in article 3 of the present Supreme Decree, all discriminations against foreign investors included in the national legislation have been repealed as from the Legislative Decree N° 662 became effective, excepted those established because of national security. Therefore, foreign investors have full access to every economic activity carried out within the country, the privatization processes included.

Similarly, all discriminations against foreign investors included in article 1 of the Legislative Decree N° 730 are repealed as from the Legislative Decree N° 757 became effective. Therefore, the treatment to be applied to foregin investors will be the same than that applied to nationals.

Second. In line with that established in article 3 hereof, all discriminations against foreign investors included in the following legal provisions were repealed as from the Legislative Decree N° 757 became effective:

a. Article 23 of Legislative Decree N° 702, Promotion Law of Private Investment in Telecommunications;

b. Article 235 of Legislative Decree N° 722, General Customs Law; and,

c. Article 37 of Law N° 24882, Civil Aviation Law, according to the modification established in article 12 of Legislative Decree N° 670, without detriment of the legal domicile foreign enterprises shall have.

In the same way, discriminations because of the status of individual or corporate body contained in article 3 of Legislative Decree N° 698 have been repealed as from the indicated date.

Third. The mention to national shipping companies included in article 3 of Legislative Decree N° 683 shall be understood as shipping companies incorporated within the country.

Fourth. In accordance with that established in the last paragraph of article 8 hereof and article 20 of Legislative Decree N° 750, the Supreme Decree N° 035-91-TR has been repealed as from the latter became effective.

Fifth. In accordance with that established in article 14 of Legislative Decree N° 757, governing the principle of legality on tax matter, articles 67 and 77, as well as the third paragraph of article 58 of the Supreme Resolution N° 002-90-TR have been repealed.

Sixth. According to that established by Legislative Decree N° 625, the term of the tax system applicable to financial leasing included in articles 18, 19 and 21 of Legislative Decree N° 299, as well as articles 16 and 24 of the same Decree, except the benefits related to General Sales Tax and Excise Tax, have been extended up to December 31 of 2000.

Tax provisions contained in article 16 of Legislative Decree N° 299 applied to the leaseholder on import duties, transfer tax and other tributes which would replace them, affect the lessor only on goods subject of the financial leasing contract.

Seventh. For purposes of that established in the Seventh Complementary Provision of Legislative Decree N° 757, the guarantee granted to creditors of the company may be any of real nature referred to in Section Fourth of Book V of the Civil Code, or that considered in Title X of Section Second of Book VII of the same legal norm.

The guarantee referred to in the foregoing paragraph shall have the acceptance of the company's creditors. Said acceptance shall be valid if the following conditions are fulfilled:

a. More than the half of the total creditors is agreed; and,

b. Said creditors represent credits for an amount over 80% (eighty per cent) of the total amount.

For calculation of that stated in the foregoing items, credits under 1% (one per cent) of the total amount will be excluded from the total and from the creditors list.

Credits resulting from the payment of wages and social benefits, as well as from the tax payment, will be considered as one in each case, and will be represented according to that established in article 194 of Law N° 7566, Procedure Law of Bankruptcy.

Eighth.- For execution of that established in article 12 hereof, in the case of andean multinational enterprises, according to that established in item g) of article 1 of Decision N° 292 of the Cartagena Agreement Commission, their bylaws shall include mechanisms for the exercise of the preference right of subregional investors. Such mechanisms shall guarantee that the enterprise will not loose its status of andean multinational enterprise.

Exceptionally, andean multinational enterprises may acquire shares subject of the foregoing paragraph in order to avoid a big damage, under that established in the third paragraph of article 117 of the Arranged Text of the General Corporate Law, approved by Supreme Decree N° 003-85-JUS, subject to transfer them in the shortest term to investors of one of the Member Countries, fully respecting the approval percentages required to maintain the status of andean multinational enterprise.

Ninth. That established in the Fourth Complementary Provision of Legislative Decree N° 757 will be applied without detriment of that established in the Law N° 25327 because it is a specific norm.

LEGISLATIVE DECREE Nº 662

Whereas, the Congress of the Republic, in conformity with the provisions set forth in Article 188 of the Political Constitution of Peru, by means of Law Nº 25237, has delegated to the Executive the power to legislate on issues relating to the growth of private investments;

Whereas, the Congress of the Republic, by means of Legislative Resolution Nº 25312, has ratified the Agreement for the Constitution of the Multilateral Investment Guarantee Agency (MIGA) with the purpose of creating favorable conditions for foreign investments to contribute to the expansion of a free market economy in the country;

Whereas, foreign investment and the transfer of technology are essential to boost the country's economic development to complement national investment, as provided for in Article 137 of the Political Constitution of Peru;'

Whereas, the Government's objective is to remove the obstacles and restrictions on foreign investments in order to guarantee equal rights and obligations to foreign and national investors;

Whereas, the Government must provide Legal Stability to foreign investors by recognizing certain guaranties to assure them the continuity of the existing rules.

With the approving vote of the Cabinet Council;

Has given the following Legislative Decree:

FOREIGN INVESTMENT PROMOTION AND GUARANTIES

Article 1.- The State promotes and guarantees the foreign investments now or hereafter made in the country in all economic activities and in any corporate or contractual organizations permitted under national laws.

For these purposes, foreign investments will be considered to be any investments coming from abroad made in any income-generating activities under any of the following modalities:

a. Property contributions by foreign individuals or corporations, handled through the national financial system, to the capital of a new or existing company under any of the forms of incorporation stipulated in the General Corporate Law, in freely convertible currency or in physical or tangible goods, such as industrial plants, new and reconditioned machinery, new and reconditioned equipment, spare parts, parts, pieces, raw materials and intermediate goods;

b.Investments in national currency from resources authorized to be remitted abroad;

c.The conversion of foreign private obligations into shares;

d. Reinvestments made in conformity with the current laws;

e. Investments in goods physically located inside the territory of the Republic;

f. Intangible technological contributions, such as trademarks, industrial models, technical assistance and know-how, whether patented or not, in the form of physical goods, technical documents and instructions;

g. Investments assigned to the purchase of securities, financial documents and papers listed on the stock market or bank deposit certificates in national or foreign currency;

h . Resources assigned to joint venture contracts for similar contracts, whereby foreign investors are allowed to participate in the productive capacity of a company, if they do not imply a capital contribution and correspond to contractual commercial operations whereby foreign investors supply goods or services to the recipient company in exhange for a share in the physical production, overall sales or net profits of said recipient company;

The investments included in this item are subject to the respective tax laws; and,

i. Any other foreign investment modality contributing to the country's development.

Article 2. Foreign investors, and the companies in which they participate, shall have the same rights and obligations as those of national investors and companies, subject to no further exceptions as those stipulated in the Political Constitution of Peru and in the provisions set forth herein.

The national laws shall, in no event, discriminate against investors or companies on the basis of the national or foreign investors participating therein.

Article 3. Foreign investments made in the country shall be forthwith deemed approved. Once made, they must be registered with the National Competent Authority.

Article 4. The ownership right of foreign investors shall not be subject to any further limitations except those stipulated in the Political Constitution of Peru.

Article 5. Intangible property or copyrights of foreign investors shall abide by the same provisions as those applicable to national investors.

Article 6. Foreign investors shall have the right to freely conduct commercial and industrial activities and to perform any import and export operations.

Article 7. Foreign investors are hereby guaranteed the right to remit abroad in freely convertible currency, without requiring beforehand, for this purpose, an authorization from any central government authority, from decentralized public entities or from regional or municipal governments, after paying the taxes required by law, the following:

a. The full amount of their capital generated from the investments contemplated in Article 1 hereof registered with the national competent entity, including the sale of shares, participations or rights, capital reduction or partial or total wind-up of the companies; and,

b. The full amount of the verified dividends or net profits generated from their investments, as well as the payments for the use or usufruct of goods physically located in the country and registered with the national competent entity, and the royalties and payments for the use and transfer of technology, including any other element forming part of the intangible assets authorized by the national competent entity.

Article 8. Foreign investors, and the companies in which they participate, are hereby guaranteed their right to purchase shares, participations or rights owned by national or subregional investors. The payment thereof, handled through the national financial system, will be considered as a foreign investment for the purposes of this Legislative Decree.

Article 9. In all such cases in which foreign currency must be converted into national currency, foreign investors shall have the right to use the most favorable purchase rate of exchange to make such exchange operation. In the event of converting national currency into foreign currency, they shall be entitled to use the most favorable selling rate of exchange for such exchange operation.

LEGAL STABILITY OF FOREIGN INVESTMENTS

Article 10. The national competent entity, on behalf of the State, prior to making the investment and the corresponding registration, may enter into agreements with foreign investors in order to guarantee the following rights:

a. Stability of the taxation system in force on the date of signing the agreement.

By virtue of the guaranteed stability of the taxation system, the foreign investor shall not be subject to a rate higher that the one contemplated in the corresponding agreement for purposes of the income tax payable by the company receiving the investment and the tax assessing the profits attributed thereto and/or the dividends distributed in favor thereof; therefore, if the income tax payable by the company is increased, the rate applied to the foreign investor shall be reduced by the required amount so that the company profits freely available to it shall be at least equal to the guaranteed profits.

b. Stability of the regime on the free availability of foreign currency and rights contemplated in Articles 7 and 9 of this Legislative Decree.

c. Stability of the non-discriminating rights contemplated in Article 2 hereof.

Article 11. Only those foreign investors committing themselves to fulfill the obligations indicated below, within a maximum term of two years counted as from the date of execution of the respective agreement, will be allowed to resort to the regime set forth in the foregoing article.

a. To make cash contributions, through the national financial system, to the capital of a company now or hereafter organized subject to Peruvian laws, or to make risk investments, formalized with third parties, of at least US 2 000 000 (Two Million Dollars of the United States of America); or

b. To make cash contributions, through the national financial system, to the capital of a company now or hereafter organized subject to Peruvian laws, or to make risk investments, formalized with third parties, of at least US$ 500 000 (Five Hundred Thousand Dollars of the United States of America), provided :

i. The investment directly creates more than twenty stable job positions; or

ii. The investment directly generates an inflow of at least US$ 2 000 000 (Two Million Dollars of the United States of America) from exports during the three years following the date of execution of agreement.

The stability regime shall become effective on the date on which the agreement is signed and shall provide, under responsibility therefor, the express resolution that in case of failure to supply the amounts, or if these are reduced or transferred to third parties, said agreement will be invalidated subject to the relevant penalties and payment to the National Treasury of any outstanding tributes.

Article 12. Those companies to be organized or already existing in Peru with new foreign capital contributions made in conformity with the foregoing article shall be afforded the following rights:

a. Stability of the regimes for the hiring of workers under any modality; and

b. Stability of the special regimes exclusively designed for exports, such as temporary admissions, industrial, commercial and tourist free zones, special treatment zones and others to be created in the future.

Such rights shall remain in force to the extent the foreign investor does not commit the infringement contemplated in the last paragraph of the foregoing article, and to the extent the respective agreements entered into by the aforementioned companies, their foreign investors and the national competent entity, are not resolved or terminated in accordance with the provisions set forth in said paragraph.

Article 13. In order to enjoy the stability regime referred to in Article 10 hereof, foreign investors must file an application with the national competent entity in respect of any of the modalities stipulated in Article 11 hereof.

Article 14. The State obligates itself to keep in force the stability agreements entered into in conformity with the provisions contained in this Title until the expiration date thereof and shall not modify them at will by a Supreme Decree enacted under item 20 of Article 211 of the Political Constitution of Peru.

Article 15. The term of the stability agreements shall be ten years, counted as from the date of execution thereof.

Article 16. The State may submit the controversies arising from the stability agreements to the courts of arbitration established under international treaties in which Peru is a signatory country.

Article 17. The rights stipulated in this Title shall not affect or restrict the right of foreign investors to have access to the benefits granted now or hereafter by other laws or regulations.

Article 18. This Title shall become in force on January 1, 1992.

REGISTRATION OF INVESTMENTS AND FOREIGN TECHNOLOGY

Article 19. Once a foreign investment is made, it must be registered with the national competent entity.

Foreign investments formalized under a contract with a Peruvian company, including joint ventures and any other form of risk associations, shall also be registered with the national competent entity.

Article 20. Once a foreign investment is registered with the national competent entity, the holder thereof will be afforded the rights contemplated in Articles 7 and 9 hereof.

Article 21. The license agreements for the use of technology, patents, trademarks and other foreign intangible assets, as well as for technical assistance, basic and detail engineering, management and franchise stipulating the payment of royalties calculated on the basis of net sales percentages of a given product or other calculation system will be automatically understood as registered by merely presenting any such agreements to the national competent entity without any limitation as to the quantities or percentages and provided they satisfy the requirements set forth in Article 13 and in the last two paragraphs of Article 14 of Decision Nº 291 of the Andean Pact Commission.

Local companies considered as affiliates of foreign companies may enter into with their parent company or other affiliates of the same parent company the contracts stipulating the payment of royalties under the term set forth in this Legislative Decree, and such payment shall be expensed for income tax purposes.

The royalty payments stipulated in this article will be made after settling the taxes required by law.

Article 22. The contracts, once registered with the national competent entity, shall confer the licensee or recipient the right to transfer abroad the agreed royalties or payments, in freely convertible currency, after paying the taxes required by law, using the most favorable selling rate of exchange in force as of the date of the exchange transaction.

FORMULATION OF FOREIGN INVESTMENT PROMOTION POLICIES

Article 23. The national competent entity shall coordinate the promotion of foreign investments and shall centralize all foreign investment promotion activities carried out by the different public entities.

Article 24. The national competent entity shall coordinate with the Foreign Affairs Ministry the signing of agreements for the promotion and protection of investments as well as agreements to avoid double taxation.

Article 25. The entities or branch offices of the Public Sector are obliged to supply the technical information and assistance required by the national competent entity to fulfill its duties.

Article 26. The national competent entity shall coordinate with the Foreign Affairs Ministry the overseas promotion of investments in the country. The commercial and diplomatic representations abroad shall provide an active information and guidance support to investors.

COMPLEMENTARY PROVISIONS

Article 27. The provisions contained in this Legislative Decree shall apply to Andean subregional investors, in accordance with the integration treaties and the Decisions of the Andean Pact Commission.

Article 28. Any foreign individuals or corporations investing in Peru and who, as of the date of this Legislative Decree, have not registered them, will be allowed to register at any time with the national competent entity as foreign investors in order to conform to the provisions set forth in this Legislative Decree. For this purpose, they may use any preestablished probative documents authorized by law to certify the origin and destination of their investment.

Article 29. No government authority, nor any decentralized public entities, regional or municipal government companies or entities will be authorized, under responsibility therefor, to give a different treatment to national and foreign investors. This includes the following:

a. To establish conditions other than those stipulated in this Legislative Decree;

b. To grant a differentiating treatment to foreign and national investors; and,

c. To apply tributes, contributions or fees to foreign investors different from those applied to national investors.

Article 30. For purposes of the provisions set forth in this Legislative Decree, the national competent entity shall be understood to be the National Commission on Foreign Investment and Technology (CONITE).

Article 31. All laws limiting or restricting in any manner foreign investments in any economic activity are hereby revoked as from the effective date hereof.

Article 32. This Legislative Decree shall become in full force and effect thirty days after the date of publication hereof in the Official Gazette "El Peruano", in conformity with the provisions set forth in Law Nº 25327, except Title II, which shall become in force on the date stipulated in Article 18 hereof.

THEREFORE:

Be this published and enforced, notifying the Congress thereof.

Given at the House of Government, in Lima, August 29, 1991.

ALBERTO FUJIMORI FUJIMORI
Constitutional President of the Republic

CARLOS TORRES Y TORRES LARA
President of the Cabinet Council and Foreign Affairs Minister

CARLOS BOLOÑA BEHR
Minister of Economy and Finance

LEGISLATIVE DECREE Nº. 757

Whereas, the Congress of the Republic, in conformity with the provisions set forth in Article 188 of the Political Constitution of Peru, by means of Law Nº 25327, conferred to the Executive, inter alia, the faculty to promulgate Legislative Decrees in order to create the necessary conditions to promote private investment in various production sectors;

Whereas, it is necessary to consolidate the economic structural reform program launched by the Government; therefore, it is advisable to promulgate a framework law to stipulate the required provisions seeking to foster the growth of private investment in all sectors of the economy;

Whereas, in order to attain such objectives, it is imperative to eliminate all legal and administrative obstacles and distortions hampering the smooth conduct of economic activities and restraining free private initiative - a key element to a successful insertion into the international market- thus rendering private companies less competitive;

Whereas, the pertinent legal instruments must be promulgated in order to provide Legal Stability to investors and promote a development model to bring into harmony production investment and the conservation of the environment;

In conformity with the provisions set forth in item 10 of Article 211 of the Political Constitution of Peru;

With the approving vote of the Cabinet;

Has given the following Legislative Decree:

COPE OF THE LAW

Article 1. The object of this Law is to guarantee free initiative and private investment, now or hereafter existing, in all economic activities and under any corporate or contract form as authorized by the Constitution and the laws.

This Law creates rights, guaranties and obligations applicable to all national or foreign individuals or enterprises investing in the country. This Law shall be binding upon all Central, Regional or Local Government entities, of all tiers.

LEGAL STABILITY OF THE ECONOMIC REGIME

Article 2. The State guarantees free private initiative.

ocial market economy is based on free competition and free access to the economy.

Article 3. Free private initiative is understood to be the right that all individuals or enterprises have to engage in any economic activity they may elect, including the production or trade of goods and the supply of services, in accordance with the provisions set forth in the Constitution, international treaties signed by Peru, and the Laws.

Article 4. Free competition implies that prices are determined by the interaction of supply and demand, as stipulated in the Constitution and the Laws.

Only public utility service prices are subject to control, as expressly ordered by Congress Law.

Article 5. The State guarantees economic pluralism. Companies are authorized to adopt any of the corporate forms contemplated in the national laws.

Direct or indirect access to any specific economic activities shall be not restricted to investors, or to companies in which they invest, on the grounds of the corporate form adopted by the latter. Financial institutions are hereby excluded from this provision, in conformity with their governing Law, including other exceptions hereafter established by the Congress Law. All legal instruments contrary to the provisions contained in this Article are hereby revoked.

In the cases in which the Law provides that natural resources must be exploited or public utility services rendered under a concession or other awarding modalities to individuals, the provisions set forth in this Legislative Decree shall govern to the extent not contrary to the pertinent sectoral laws.

Article 6. All reserves in favor of the State are hereby revoked, whether in whole or in part, for the performance of economic activities or for the exploitation of natural resources, excepting protected natural areas. Such reserves shall solely operate due to social interest or national security reasons and must be expressly established by Congress Law or as provided for in Article 54 hereof.

In conformity with Article 285 of the Political Constitution, the fabrication of warfare weapons shall only authorized to private companies under agreements entered into with the State therefor.

Article 7. In the event an economic activity is performed both by the State and private companies, the same conditions shall be applied to both.

No state-owned company shall be assigned any dominant faculties or those pertaining to the Public Administration, except for the faculties specifically assigned by the State for coercive collection of taxes.

Article 8. The State guarantees private property, subject to no further limits except those stipulated in the Political Constitution.

In application of Article 131 of the Political Constitution, which endorses free enterprise, and in conformity with the provisions contemplated in this Chapter, the State shall not expropriate companies nor any shares or interests therein, except for the national interest, to be duly substantiated by a Congress Law.

Article 9. In conformity with the provisions set forth in Articles 130 and 131 of the Political Constitution, all companies are entitled to organize and carry out their activities as they may deem convenient.

All legal statutes providing for the production patterns or productivity levels prohibiting or imposing the use of consumables or application of technical processes and, in general, interfering with the production process of companies based on the type of economic activity performed by them, their installed capacity or any other similar economic factor, are hereby revoked, except those relating to industrial hygiene and sanitation, environmental protection and health.

Article 10. The State guarantees the rights of companies, regardless of their corporate form, to freely determine the distribution of all their profits or dividends, and the investors' rights to receive their total share in such profits or dividends, including those pertaining to the current year, based on periodic balance sheets, without prejudice to the obligations regarding the profit-sharing plan, legal reserves and the pertinent obligations stipulated in the General Corporate Law, provided the corresponding tax obligations are satisfied.

The distribution of the profits of financial institutions shall be governed by the specific laws on the subject.

Article 11. The State hereby guarantees the supply of basic public utility services, promoting the participation of the private sector, seeking to improve the quality of services.

Article 12. The State shall not create any discriminating or differentiating practices in relation to exchange provisions, prices, non-customs tariffs or duties, against investors or the companies in which they participate, or against any specific sectors or economic activity or geographic location of any such companies. The State shall neither establish any such practices making any distinction between national or foreign individuals or enterprises.

No Central, Regional or Local Government authorities, officials or employees, of all tiers, nor any state-owned companies shall establish or apply discriminating or differentiating practices, in conformity with the provisions set forth herein, and shall be answerable therefor.

Article 13. In conformity with the provisions set forth in the last paragraph of Article 126 of the Political Constitution, national or foreign private investment in production activities now or hereafter existing in the country's borderline areas, is hereby declared to be in the national interest. Consequently, foreign individuals and enterprises shall be authorized to obtain concessions and rights in relation to mines, land, forests, water, fuel, energy sources and other resources, for purposes of carrying their production activities within fifty kilometers off the country's borders, after obtaining authorization under a Supreme Resolution countersigned by the Minister acting as President of the Cabinet, and the Minister of the corresponding sector. Said Supreme Resolution shall provide for the terms to govern any such concessions or exploitation rights.

The competent sectoral authorities shall award concessions and other types of rights for the exploitation of natural resources located within fifty kilometers off the country's borders in favor of foreign individuals or enterprises applying for any such rights, after satisfying all applicable legal requirements and upon verification of the actual promulgation of the Supreme Resolution referred to in the foregoing paragraph.

TAX STABILITY FOR INVESTMENTS

Article 14. The constitutional principle of legality in relation to tax issues implies that the creation, modification or elimination of tributes, as well as the granting of exemptions and other tax benefits, determination of taxable matter, persons subject to tax, tax collectors and tax withholding agents, the corresponding tax quotas and the tax base, should be made under a Congress Law, in conformity with the provisions set forth herein.

The principle of legality is also applicable to the following cases:

a. In the event of Legislative Decrees promulgated under and within the limits of a law conferring legislative powers, such law must expressly determine the tax issue involved, the scope of the faculties to be conferred thereby and the term for excercising any such faculties;

b. In the event Regional Governments create, modify or eliminate tributes or grant exemptions therefrom, exercising the faculties conferred to them by a Congress Law, provided such Law fulfills the following requirements:

1. Determines the specific purpose for the delegation of faculties, the scope of such faculties, as well as the term for exercising such faculties; and,

2. Expressly stipulates, in the case of creating new tributes, the taxable matter, the tax-generating activities, persons subject to tax, exemptions and corresponding tax quotas, as well as the effective term of the new authorized tribute and, if applicable, the tax collectors or tax withholding agents. The same requirements must be satisfied for the modification of any tributes, to the extent applicable.

Exercising the tax faculties referred to herein, the tributes created by regional governments shall not conflict with the provisions of any national laws. Regional governments shall not be authorized to create tributes assessing any items already subject to national taxes;

c. In the event local governments create, modify or eliminate contributions, excise taxes or duties or grant exemptions therefrom, exercising the faculties conferred to them by a Congress Law, provided such law fulfills the following requirements:

1. Determines the specific purpose for the delegation of faculties, the scope of such faculties, as well as the term for exercising such faculties; and,

2. Expressly stipulates, in the event of creating new contributions, excise taxes or duties, the taxable matter, the tax-generating activities, persons subject to tax, exemptions and corresponding tax quotas, as well as the effective term of the new authorized tribute and, if applicable, the tax collectors or tax withholding agents. The same requirements must be satisfied for the modification of any tributes, to the extent applicable.

Contributions, excise taxes and duties are approved by a Municipal Ordinance, in conformity with the provisions set forth herein and subject to the following restrictions:

2.1. Improvement contributions are payments that taxpayers are obliged to make to municipal governments for any individual verifiable benefits derived from any new public works. Any such contributions shall be allocated to recover the investment made in such public works or to finance the corresponding maintenance expenses;

2.2. Excise taxes are taxes that taxpayers must pay to municipal governments for a public utility service supplied to them by the latter. The amount charged for this concept shall not exceed the total cost of such public utility service and such tax funds shall be solely assigned to finance such public utility services; and,

2.3. Duties are taxes that taxpayers must pay to municipal governments for any administrative services supplied to them by the latter. The amount charged for this concept shall not exceed the total cost of such administrative service and such tax funds shall be solely allocated to finance such administrative service.

Exercising the tax faculties referred to herein, the contributions, excise taxes and duties created by local governments shall not levy the entry, exit or transit of goods, merchandise, products and animals. Any tolls imposed by local governments shall only be applied to vehicles for the use of public roads or bridges built by municipal governments or maintained by them, provided such roads are not part of the national road system;

d. In the event tariffs are regulated by Supreme Decree; and,

e. In the event tax rates are modified by Supreme Decree.

Article 15. The principle of publication regarding taxes means that all tax laws and regulations must be published in the official gazette at least 5 calendar days prior to the date of maturity of the formal or substantive tax obligations, in order to enable taxpayers to comply with such obligations.

In the case of Legislative Decree, these must be published within the term contemplated for the fulfillment of the faculties conferred and with the anticipation indicated in the preceding paragraph.

Article 16. Companies and their investors shall be entitled to file an objection proceeding before the Tax Court or Customs Court, as the case may be, in relation to taxes, contributions, applicable rates, excise taxes, registration fees, tariffs, applicable rates and other duties charged for the handling of administrative procedures, strictly in accord with the law . The Tax Court or Customs Court, as the case may be, shall be the highest administrative authority.

ADMINISTRATIVE STABILITY FOR INVESTMENTS SCOPE OF APPLICATION

Article 17. This Title applies to all administrative paperwork and procedures followed by companies and investors before State authorities. Such procedures must secure due processing of the requests filed by any of the above and the procedures and corresponding requirements must be simple and clear.

Article 18. With the purpose of relieving the burdens and obligations imposed on companies and investors in their relationship with the Public Administration and in order to start an effective debureaucratization process in the country, administrative procedures or requirements shall only be established by Supreme Decree, Regional Executive Decree or Municipal Ordinance, whether by the Central, Regional or Local Government, respectively.

Article 19. Supreme Decree Nº 006-67-SC-Regulations on General Administrative Procedures- and Law Nº 25035- Administrative Simplification Law- shall apply in all cases not contrary to the provisions set forth in this Title.

REMOVAL OF ALL ADMINISTRATIVE RESTRICTIONS ON INVESTMENTS

Article 20. Ministries, public institutions and organizations, and any other Public Administration entities, whether of the Central, Regional or Local Government, shall be obligated to approve legal statutes aimed to unify, reduce and drastically simplify all administrative paperwork and procedures followed with the respective entity, in conformity with the provisions set forth in this Title.

Article 21. The entities referred to in the foregoing Article shall approve their corresponding Single Text of Administrative Procedures (TUPA), which must contain the following:

a. All the administrative procedures followed before the entity;

b. A clear and detailed description of all requirements necessary to complete each administrative procedure;

c. Classification of each procedure shall be governed as indicated below:

1. In the case of automatic approvals, in accordance with the provisions set forth in Article 24 of this Legislative Decree, or

2. If a preliminary evaluation by the Public Administration is required, the following must also be determined:

2.1. If a positive or negative administrative silences should follow after expiration of the corresponding term, in conformity with the provisions set forth in Articles 25 and 26 hereof; or,

2.2. If the application of the terms or the administrative silence do not operate for dealing with the administrative procedures referred to in Article 27 hereof;

d. The cases in which the payment of duties operates, as well as the amount thereof;

e. The branch office to which any requests must be addressed;

f. The competent authority in charge of approving each procedure; and,

g. The authorities or entities with jurisdiction to rule over any objection proceedings.

Article 22. The TUPA referred to in the foregoing Article shall be approved by Supreme Decree promulgated by the corresponding sector, in the case of branch offices of the Central Government; by a Regional Executive Decree, in the case of Regional Governments, and by Municipal Ordinance, in the case of Local Governments.

The legal statutes referred to in the first paragraph of this Article must be approved and published in the official gazette before June 30, 1992, under the responsibility of the competent authority of the sector or pertinent entity. Upon expiration of such term, any parties concerned shall not be required to fulfill any administrative procedures, requirements or payment of corresponding duties not included in the TUPA, to engage in any business activity.

All amendments to the administrative procedures followed with the entities referred to in art 20 hereof, involving the creation of new procedures, preliminary evaluation, operation of the negative administrative silence or the inclusion of additional requirements, must be based on the corresponding TUPA and shall require approval by Supreme Decree, Regional Executive Decree or Municipal Ordinance, whether dealing with entities of the Central, Regional or Local Government, respectively.

Without prejudice to the stipulations contained in the foregoing paragraph, any provisions relating to removal of procedures or requirements shall be approved by Ministerial Resolution, Regional Executive Resolution or Municipal Agreement, whether dealing with entities of the Central, Regional or Local Government, respectively. Any such provisions must be based on the corresponding TUPA.

The TUPA must be annually updated and published in the official gazette on or before June 30 of each year, under the responsibility of the competent authority of the sector or pertinent entity, unless the TUPA in force has not been modified, which must be informed to all those concerned by means of a notice published in the official gazette. Otherwise, the provisions set forth in the second paragraph of this article shall apply.

Article 23. The parties concerned shall only be required to fulfill the administrative procedures included in the corresponding TUPA. Consequently, no additional information, documentation or payment not expressly indicated therein shall be required, under the responsibility of the requiring officer.

Article 24. The requests filed with the different Public Administration entities referred to in Article 20 hereof shall be deemed forthwith approved on the date the corresponding request or form is filed, provided the requirements are fully satisfied and all documents required under the TUPA for each case are duly submitted.

For purposes of the provisions set forth in the preceding paragraph, a copy of the request or form filed by the party concerned containing the official receipt seal shall suffice as evidence of the automatic approval of the request.

Article 25. In exceptional cases, certain administrative procedures may require a preliminary evaluation; in which case, this must be expressly stated in the TUPA. In any such cases, the pertinent entity shall be afforded a maximum term of 30 calendar days to issue the corresponding ruling, counted as from the date of presentation of the request or form. If, upon expiration of such term, no such ruling has been issued, the procedure shall be deemed approved.

Article 26. Only in certain specific cases expressly stated in the TUPA, the request or form shall be deemed rejected upon expiration of the term referred to in the foregoing article, so the party concerned may file the pertinent administrative proceedings.

Article 27. The provisions set forth in Articles 24, 25, 26,28 and 32 hereof shall not be binding upon tax procedures, administrative procedures settling litigations between two or more individuals, procedures for the disposition or acquisition of goods and services by or on behalf of the State, or those pertaining to the awarding of concessions foreign infrastructure works.

Article 28. Any requests or forms filed in respect of any administrative procedures with different Public Administration entities, failing to fulfill the corresponding requirements, must be received on condition that any such defect or omission shall be rectified within 48 hours, expressly stating so in the original and copy of the corresponding request. If, upon expiration of the term in reference, such defect or omission has not been rectified, the request shall be deemed not filed and will be returned to the party concerned.

Article 29. All documents, requests or information submitted to the entities referred to in Article 33 hereof foreign administrative procedures shall be regarded as affidavits and must be countersigned by the party concerned or its representative, who shall be answerable for the truthfulness of the information and the authenticity of the documents filed; otherwise, they shall be held guilty or any of the offenses against public faith typified in Title XIX of the Criminal Code, as the case may be, and without dismissing the possibility of being subject to a later administrative inspection.

Article 30. The entities referred to in Article 22 hereof shall only charge the fees indicated on the TUPA to perform any administrative procedures. Such fees shall only be charged when such procedures are requested by the party concerned and to the extent the entity is required to provide a service inherent in such procedure. The amount of any such fees shall not exceed the actual cost of the service, which must be duly substantiated by the administrative department of the competent entity, and shall be answerable therefor.

In such cases in which the TUPA requires the filing of any forms, the Public Administration shall accept simple copies of the corresponding forms in lieu of the originals, unless the latter are distributed at no cost and are available to all parties concerned.

Article 31. The entities referred to in Article 20 hereof shall not require copies of documents issued by them nor any documents previously submitted to them by any party concerned and which are still fully valid, as indicated on any such documents.

Article 32. The copies of documents, whether or not authenticated by public notaries or by public officers or employees, shall be equally valid as the originals for fulfilling the corresponding requirements of the administrative procedures followed before any Public Administration entities, as referred to in Article 20 hereof. Any such entities shall not require official translations, and a simple translation shall suffice, the translator and the party concerned being jointly and severally answerable therefor.

Article 33. The presentation of documents or requests, the withdrawal of notices, certificates, rulings or documents, and the request of information by the parties concerned, as well as any other type of administrative procedure, shall take place during office hours. The Public Administration entities shall, in no event, reduce their office hours to devote part of their time to exclusively attend to certain issues.

Article 34. The Public Administration entities referred to in Article 20 hereof must establish only one office for the processing of documents, through which the parties concerned shall perform all procedures and obtain information required for any administrative procedures.

TRANSPARENT HANDLING OF ADMINISTRATIVE PROCEDURES

Article 35. Documents, background information, studies, rulings, statistical data and any other information held by public entities must be furnished to any person who so requests them. If any copies thereof are required, the parties concerned shall bear the corresponding expenses. Any documents and information which could jeopardize national security and foreign relations, those pertaining to Public Administration matters and for internal circulation and any confidential ones corresponding to any individuals, in conformity with any legal statues or referring to a trade or technological secrets, are hereby excepted.

Article 36. Any public officers and employees failing to fulfill the provisions contained in Article 23 hereof shall be held liable for infringement of discipline rules punishable in conformity with the provisions set forth in Article 26 of Legislative Decree Nº 276. Any parties concerned may file the complaint referred to in Article 108 of Supreme Decree Nº 006-67-SC and/or address the internal control body of the respective entity and/or file a complaint before the Attorney General referred to in Article 67 of Legislative Decree Nº 52, without dismissing the possibility of filing any civil or criminal actions, as applicable.

Article 37. Those persons from whom any public officers or employees request any grant, promise or any improper advantage in order to favor, perform or omit any procedure, whether in the fulfillment or in violation of their official duties, may report such facts to the internal control body of the respective entity and/or to the Public Ministry, in conformity with the provisions set forth in Articles 11,12 and 13 of Legislative Decree Nº 52, without dismissing the possibility of filing any civil or criminal actions, as applicable.

LAW STABILITY FOR INVESTMENTS LAW STABILITY AGREEMENTS

Article 38. This Chapter grants to national investors, and to the companies in which they invest, the same treatment granted under Title II of Legislative Decree Nº 662; therefore, all provisions therein contained, as well as those contained in this Chapter, shall be equally applicable to national and foreign investors and to the companies in which they invest.

Article 39. Law stability agreements shall be entered into under Article 1357 of the Civil Code and shall be deemed as legally binding; therefore, they cannot be modified or terminated at will by the State. Any such agreements shall be subject to civil and not to administrative law and shall be modified or terminated only by agreement between the parties.

Article 40. The object of the agreements entered into under Article 12 of Legislative Decree Nº 662 may also be to guarantee the stability of the taxation system applicable to investment recipient companies, solely in respect of taxes assessing the income of companies, provided that the total new investments received by a company exceed 50% of its capital and reserves and are destined to expand the production capacity or to obtain a technological improvement. Such agreements may also be signed in the event of transferring more than 50% of the shares of the companies managed by the State.

Article 41. The purpose of the stability agreements signed under Title II of Legislative Decree Nº 662 may also be to guarantee the stability of the taxation system applicable to leasing contracts, to the extent the value of the goods under such contracts is not less than US$ 2,000,000; or, if less, subject to a minimum limit of US$ 500,000, provided the acquisition of goods directly or indirectly generates more than twenty stable job positions or an inflow of at least US$ 2,000,000 from exports during the three years following the date of execution of the stability agreement, not providing for any capital contributions or minimum terms.

Article 42. The State shall approve the assignment of a contract position by an investor in favor of another investor in respect of the law stability agreement signed with the State.

Article 43. All procedures and paperwork relating to Law Stability agreements required from national investors shall be followed with the entity designated by the Ministry of the corresponding sector.

Article 44. Regional and Local Governments shall be authorized to enter into law stability agreements with investors investing in their respective jurisdictions and with companies now or hereafter established therein, solely in respect of matters within their competence.

Article 45. The stability, rights and guaranties contemplated in this Chapter do not limit in any manner the faculty of investors or companies to additionally resort to the regimes stipulated in other legal statutes.

PRIVATE INVESTMENT INSURANCE

Article 46. All investors shall be entitled to carry insurance, inside and outside the country, to protect their investment against commercial and non-commercial risk.

Article 47. The State shall facilitate to investors coverage for their investment through the World Bank's Multilateral Investment Guarantee Agency (MIGA) or other similar institutions of which Peru is member. Consequently, the State shall take all necessary actions and submit the documents required therefor. In the case of foreign investors, the State shall consent the coverage requested by investors.

SETTLEMENT OF INVESTMENT CONTROVERSIES

Article 48. The State, its branch offices, the Central, Regional and Municipal Governments, and other persons subject to public law, as well as the companies managed by the State, shall be authorized to submit to national or international arbitration all controversies relating to their goods and obligations, in conformity with national laws or international treaties, in which Peru is a signatory country, provided any such controversies arise from their relationship with a company subject to private law or under a contract.

LAW STABILITY FOR ENVIRONMENTAL PROTECTION

Article 49. The State encourages a rational balance between socioeconomic development, protection of the environment and the sustained use of natural resources, guaranteeing an adequate Legal Stability to investors by promulgating clear rules on environmental protection.

Consequently, the State promotes the participation of private companies or institutions in programs devised to protect the environment and mitigate pollution.

Article 50. The sectoral authorities competent to handle any issues relevant to the application of the Environment and Natural Resources Code are the Ministries with jurisdiction over the activities performed by the companies, without prejudice to the faculties of Regional and Local Governments, as provided for in the Political Constitution.

In the event a given company is engaged in two or more activities under the jurisdiction of several ministries, the competent sectoral authority will be determined depending upon the activity generating the highest annual gross income.

Article 51. The competent sectoral authority shall determine which activities are environmentally hazardous and so likely to surpass the permissible environmental pollution or damage standards or limits and so will necessarily require an environmental impact study prior to commencement of any such activities.

The environmental impact studies must provide assurance that the activities performed or supposed to be performed by any given company shall not surpass the limits or standards referred to in the foregoing paragraph. Such studies shall be submitted to the competent sectoral authority for registration and shall be borne by such companies.

The environmental impact studies shall be performed by public or private companies or institutions duly qualified and registered with the corresponding registry to be created by the competent sectoral authority, which authority shall establish the pertinent requirements therefor.

Article 52. In the event of an imminent serious peril to the environment, the competent sectoral authority shall order the companies in reference to adopt any of the following safety measures:

a. Measures to eliminate the risk or reduce it to permissible limits, establishing reasonable terms, depending on the intensity and imminence thereof, or

b. Measures to restrain the activities posing a serious and imminent risk on the environment, the life or health of people, the competent sectoral authority shall be authorized to suspend any permits, licenses or authorizations granted therefor.

In the event a given activity could potentially cause an irreparable damage, seriously endangering the environment.

Article 53. Companies providing drinking water and sewerage services shall be required to hold a certificate evidencing complained by them with the physical, chemical and bacteriological quality standards in the case of drinking water and with sewage treatment requirements prior to final disposal of sewage. Should any of such companies fail to obtain the quality certificates as regularly as required by the Health Ministry, the directors of such companies shall be held guilty of the offense contemplated in art 305 of the Criminal Code.

Public or private companies or institutions specialized in environmental sanitation shall monitor the quality of water for human consumption. They must be duly qualified and will be required to register with a special registry to be created by the Health Ministry therefor, and the latter shall establish the pertinent requirements and shall supervise the operations of the aforementioned companies or institutions.

Article 54. The status of protected natural area shall only be assigned by Supreme Decree, with the affirmative vote of the Cabinet. Protected natural areas can either be national, regional or local, depending upon the government in charge of the administration thereof, and this shall be expressly stipulated in the law creating them. Management policies applicable to such areas shall be determined by the National Government.

The creation of protected natural areas shall have no retroactive effect nor shall it affect any rights acquired prior to the creation of any such areas.

Article 55. No waste or refuse, regardless of the origin or material condition thereof, hazardous or radioactive due to the nature, use or purpose thereof, shall be allowed to enter the national territory. Such items shall be listed on a Supreme Decree, with the approving vote of the Cabinet.

Any other type of refuse or waste shall only be allowed to enter the country if it is to be recycled, reused or transformed.

Article 56. The State shall be empowered to lease or grant appropriation rights over land to individuals for ecology-tourism projects, upon presentation of the corresponding claim.

COMPLEMENTARY PROVISIONS

ONE. The exceptional measures which must be adopted in the country's own interest to reorganize companies, with the purpose of accommodating them to international evolution trends, and to take the necessary actions to increase the standard of the country's production sectors to be able to compete with international producers and particularly in response to international agreements signed with Latin American countries and with the Andean Pact member countries, shall be governed by the following principles:

- The country's fundamental economic principles contemplated in Article 110 of the Constitution;

- The requirements to engage in any business enterprise contained in Article 130 of the Political Constitution;

- Observance of treaties, particularly those relating to integration, referred to in Articles 100, 101 and 106 of the Political Constitution; and,

- The responsibility of all Peruvian people to contribute to a common good.

TWO. Any increase in prices and fees or compensation increases shall abide by the following rules:

a. The prices and fees which, by legal decree, must be regulated, shall be adjusted taking into consideration economic factors and not any automatic adjustment systems or methods based on price variation indexes; and,

b. Collective agreements shall not provide for any automatic compensation adjustment systems based on price variation indexes, or agreed upon or expressed in foreign currency. In conformity with Article 1355 of the Civil Code, companies and workers subject to the laws applicable to private enterprises governed in whole or in part by such rules, agreements or clauses, shall replace them by systems for determination of compensation seeking to enhance the production and productivity of each company.

THREE. With the purpose of promoting private investment in mutual fund management systems and guarantee their efficient operation, the Chattels Registry of the Mutual Fund Management System is hereby created and will be under the responsibility of the National Supervisory Commission of Companies and Securities (CONASEV).

The Registry Regulations referred to in the preceding paragraph shall be approved by Supreme Decree, countersigned by the Minister of Economy and Finance, within a term not to exceed 60 calendar days.

For purposes of calculating the duties referred to in Article 4 of Decree law Nº 23186, the capital contributions of mutual fund management companies shall not be taken into account as they do not constitute an actual income of such companies.

FOURTH. For purposes of registering the members of the Management Council of nonprofit corporations in the pertinent Registry, the presentation of a copy of the record of proceedings of the General Meeting of Members evidencing such agreement shall suffice. Likewise, in the case of managers and other representatives, the presentation of a copy of the record of proceedings of the competent corporate body shall suffice. This provision shall apply to all registrations after the effective date hereof, even though the agreements or appointments shall have taken place on an earlier date.

FIVE. It is hereby expressly stipulated that foreign entities shall be authorized to engage in business in the country through representatives, conferring to them special or general poweres of attorney, authorized to hire personnel and obtain labor and other registrations required to operate. The appointment of the representatives of such entities shall be registered with the Mercantile Registry, for which purpose, special entries shall be created for each case.

SIX. It is hereby agreed that all references to "minimum monthly wages" contained in Articles 1623, 1624 and 1625 of the Civil Code shall be understood as referring to Tax Units.

SEVEN. Item 3) of Article 359 of the General Corporate Law, the Single Revised Text of which was approved by Supreme Decree Nº 003-85-JUS, is hereby superseded by the following text:

"3. Losses which, as of the close of the business year, reduce the capital stock to an amount below one third of the capital unless restored or reduced, or if shareholders, directly or through third parties, furnish a guaranty in favor of the company's creditors, acceptable to the latter, in an amount equal to the capital reduction amount".

EIGHT. The following paragraph is hereby added to Article 8 of Law Nº 23323:

"The sum payable to a Mutual Fund under a contract shall, in no event, exceed 5 Tax Units."

NINE. All references to "authorities", "competent authority" or "environmental authority" contained in Legislative Decree Nº 613 -Environment and Natural Resources Code- shall be understood as referring to the competent sectoral authority; i.e., the Ministry of the corresponding sector.

Likewise, all provisions contained in the aforementioned decree to avoid polluting the environment shall be understood as referring to pollution above the permissible limits established for each effluent by the competent sectoral authority, taking into consideration the cumulative damage.

TEN. Article 137 of Legislative Decree Nº 613 is hereby replaced to read as follows:

"Article 137. All actions seeking to protect the environment, or the main subject of which is the protection of the environment, shall be filed with the court having jurisdiction over the area where such right was affected or at the defendant's place of domicile".

ELEVEN. In the event any action filed by any persons before the Judiciary, under the provisions set forth in the second paragraph of Article 3 of the preliminary title of Legislative Decree Nº 613, is dismissed, such persons shall be answerable for any damages caused.

TWELVE. The legal statutes establishing the Selective Consumption Tax assessing fuels are hereby excluded from the term stipulated in Article 15 hereof.

THIRTEEN. Prior to the release of any commercial advertisement produced abroad and broadcasted by any media in the country, the corresponding tributes must be settled. For purposes of the calculation and application of the corresponding customs tariffs, such advertisement shall abide by the provisions applicable to the motion pictures to be exhibited in Peru, to the extent applicable.

All communications media broadcasting commercial advertisement produced abroad shall require payment evidence of the corresponding tributes.

TRANSITORY PROVISIONS

ONE. Health authorities shall supervise and control pharmaceutical products, the assays and quality analyses of which must be consistent with the formula furnished by the manufacturer. The inspection and control of pharmaceutical products shall be commissioned to specialized private or public companies or institutions duly qualified and registered by the Health Ministry.

The manufacture, import, possession and transfer, by any reason, of polluted, adulterated, counterfeit or altered pharmaceutical products, is hereby prohibited.

This Article shall remain in full force until new provisions governing such issues are promulgated by Supreme Decree, which shall not provide for additional requirements than those contemplated in Article 12 of Legislative Decree Nº 668.

TWO. The effective force of the provisions contained in the last paragraph of Article 169, in the second paragraph of Article 222, and in item 3) of Article 359 of the General Corporate Law, the single revised text of which was approved by Supreme Decree Nº 003-85-JUS, is hereby suspended until December 31, 1994.

THREE. The provisions contained in laws and legislative decrees creating or regulating the systems for the calculation of public fees, in force as of the effective date hereof, shall subsist until conformed by Supreme Decree to the provisions set forth in the first paragraph of Article 4 hereof.

FOUR. Until approval of the respective TUPA, referred to in Chapter II of Title IV hereof, the Public Administration entities, whether from Central, Regional or Local Government, shall not be authorized to increase the fees charged for administrative procedures in force as of the effective date hereof.

FIVE. It is hereby agreed that the provisions contained in Articles 5 and 29 of Legislative Decree Nº 662 imply that the administrative duties, rates or tariffs charged to foreign investors must be reduced to the levels applied to nationals as of the effective date of Legislative Decree Nº 662.

FINAL PROVISIONS

ONE. The following legal statutes are hereby revoked:

a. Article V of the Preliminary Title, Articles 8, 17, 18, 56, 57,58,89,107 and 115 and Chapters XXI and XXII of Legislative Decree Nº 613;

b. Law Nº 25200, Article 19 of Law Nº 25185 and Supreme Decree Nº 014-89-PE;

c. Item 1) of Article 1599 and item 2) of Article 1913 of the Civil Code;

d. Supreme Decrees Nºs 020-90-TR,021-90-TR and item c) of Article 1 of Supreme Decree Nº 034-90-TR;

e. Supreme Decrees Nºs 399-86-EF, 400-86-EF, 226-90-EF, 254-90-EF and all complementary, amending and regulating provisions thereof; and,

f. All other legal statutes contrary to the provisions contained herein.

TWO. The Fifteenth Complementary Provision of Legislative Decree Nº 653 shall remain in full force and effect.

The provisions set forth in Article 12 hereof do not include any legal statutes defending the rights of agricultural producers, including specific rights, surcharges and hedge clauses.

THREE. This Legislative Decree shall be in full force and effect thirty days following publication it the official gazette "El Peruano".

BUSINESS TRAVEL

BUSINESS CUSTOMS

Business is conducted in Spanish. Although a great number of executives in the Peruvian business community speak English, it is advisable to have all promotional literature translated into Spanish. Peruvians are formal when engaged in business relations and suits and ties are the norm. Business hours in Peru are generally from 9:00 a.m. to 5:30 p.m. Breakfast meetings are becoming more common, and business lunches are normally scheduled between the hours of 1:00 to 3:30 p.m. Some shops and some businesses operate from 10:00 a.m. to 1:00 p.m. and from 4:00 p.m. to 8:00 p.m., although continuous operation is increasingly common. Business offices are closed on Saturdays. In the provinces, business hours are usually from 9:00 a.m. to 1:00 p.m. and from 4:00 p.m. to 7:00 p.m.

Lima is situated directly south of New York and is in the Eastern Standard time zone, but Peru does not follow daylight savings time. Dates are written starting with the day of the month, followed by the month and finishing with the year. The currency is the Nuevo Sol. As of July 2004, the exchange rate was 3.50 soles to one U.S. dollar. The metric system is used for weights, measures, and mathematical expression.

For further information, business travelers should note that the "Foreign Service Posts: Guide for Business Representatives" is available for sale by the Superintendent of Documents, U.S. Government Printing Office, Washington, D.C. 20402; tel. (202) 512-1800; fax (202) 512-2250. Business travelers to Peru seeking appointments with U.S. Embassy Lima officials should contact the Commercial Service in advance. The Commercial Service can be reached by telephone at (511) 434-3040 or 434-3000; by fax at (511) 434-3041 or by E-mail at: Lima.Office.Box@mail.doc.gov.

IMPORTANT INFORMATION

VISAS

The U.S. Department of State issues Consular Information Sheets for all foreign countries, including Peru. This document may be obtained via the Internet, at website "travel.state.gov", or from the Embassy website, http://usembassy.state.gov/peru; from the Consular Affairs Bureau, Office of Overseas Citizen Services, Department of State, Room 4817, Department of State, 2201 C. Street, N.W., Washington, D.C., 20520; or from the U.S. Embassy at the address noted in Chapter 11: U.S. AND COUNTRY CONTACTS. Travel information in general is also available at the telephone number (202) 647-5225, or fax (202) 647-3000. Useful information on guarding valuables and protecting personal security while traveling abroad is provided in the Department of State pamphlet "A Safe Trip Abroad." This publication, as well as others such as "Tips for Travelers to Central and South America," are available from the Superintendent of Documents, U.S. Government Printing Office, Washington, D.C., 20402.

A valid U.S. passport is required to enter Peru. Tourists staying less than 90 days do not require visa. It is recommended that business travelers to Peru travel on a tourist visa provided they are not reimbursed for their services while in Peru. However, if any compensation is earned and paid while in Peru, a business visa is required and a tax declaration must be processed before departing Peru. This process takes approximately three days. Travelers should contact the Embassy of Peru, 1700 Massachusetts Avenue, N.W., Washington, D.C., 20036, telephone number (202) 833-9860, or the nearest Peruvian consulate for visa information. There are Peruvian consulates in California, Florida, Illinois, New York, New Jersey, and Texas.

In general, the Department of State recommends that all U.S. citizens traveling overseas register with the American Citizen Services Unit, Consular Section, of the U.S. Embassy upon arrival. The U.S. Embassy in Peru is located on Avenida La Encalada, Block 17, Monterrico, Lima. The American Citizen Services Unit is open from 8:00 am to 12 noon on weekdays, except U.S. and Peruvian holidays. Registrants should bring their U.S. passport plus one photo. There is no fee for this service. Prior registration will facilitate the replacement of a lost or stolen U.S. passport. The loss or theft of a U.S. passport overseas should be reported immediately to the local police and the nearest U.S. Embassy or Consulate. The Embassy telephone number is (511) 434-3000. In case of an emergency after working hours, U.S. citizens should contact the Embassy at 434-3032.

There is a consular agent, Dra. Olga Villagarcia, in Cusco to assist U.S. citizens traveling in that area, including to Machu Picchu. Her office is located at Anda Tullumayu 125, Cusco, telephone number (51-84) 24-5102, fax numbers 23-3541, 23-9822, Internet address icpnacus@telser.com.pe.

HOLIDAYS

The Peruvian official holidays are:

Santa Rosa de Lima	August 30, 2004
Battle of Angamos	October 8, 2004
All Saints' Day	November 1, 2004
Immaculate Conception	December 8, 2004
Christmas Day	December 25, 2004
New Year's Day	January 1, 2002
Maundy Thursday	March 28, 2002
Good Friday	March 29, 2002
Labor Day	May 1, 2002
Saints Peter and Paul	June 29, 2002
Independence Day	July 28-29, 2002

BUSINESS INFRASTRUCTURE

The Ministry of Transport, Communication, Housing and Construction (MTC) estimates the total road network has 16,966 km: 8,140 km paved; 6,640 km unpaved; and 2,186 km of dirt roads. The Government of Peru aims to invest $175 million in the construction and rehabilitation for 2004. Approximately $55 million will come from the Public Treasury and $120 million from international institutions such as IDB, Corporacion Andina de Fomento (CAF), World Bank and Japan's Bank for International Cooperation (JBIC). These projects represent for Peru around 1,500 km of new road construction for 2004. The rehabilitation projects have also been increased. The budget projected for the rehabilitation of 9,711 km of roads is estimated at $40 million which is expected not to be sufficient. The government has plans to concession a significant portion of these paved highways in the coming years. The entering new government is planning for 2002 to keep with these projects. In the past Peru declared a $1.5 billion plan aimed at having 70% of the road infrastructure paved by the year 2005.

Operation of the railroad system was given in concession in July 1999, for 30 years, to two companies: Ferrovias Central Andina S. A. (central railway) and Ferrocarril Transandino S. A. (south and south-east railways). Two operators are currently running three railway systems. The 480 km. central railway servicing only cargo from the port of Callao to La Oroya-Huancayo run by Ferrocarril Central Andino S.A. and owned by six companies being one of these the U.S. firm Railroad Development Corporation. The 915 Km. Southern railway Matarani-Mollendo-Arequipa-Puno-Cuzco and the small South-eastern railway Cuzco-Quillabamba are run by Peru Rail S. A. (formed by the British/American Orient-Express and the Peruvian consortium Peruval).

There are a number of Peruvian airlines serving routes within Peru. Currently Peru's international airline is LanPeru, which flies to the U.S. (Miami). Lima is served by three U.S. airlines--American, Continental and Delta Airlines. International flights are available to most major cities in South America. Currently, the direct flights to the United States are to Atlanta, Dallas, Houston, Los Angeles, Miami and Newark. Flights between Peru and the United States have increased significantly since early 1995, and an "Open Skies" agreement was signed in 1998, which will allow unlimited frequencies by June 2002. There are also regular cargo flights to Miami on both U.S. and Peruvian carriers.

There is a high incidence of traffic accidents in Peru, frequently involving mini-buses and buses, for which reason public ground transportation is not recommended. Taxis are abundant and not metered, so fares must be negotiated before getting into the cab. More reliable radio-dispatched taxis are highly recommended. Transportation to and from the airport by radio taxi or taxi service is approximately U.S. $20. Tips are not expected on short rides. If you lease a car with a driver, a tip is common.

A number of new hotels have opened since 1992 and existing hotels have been renovated and expanded, so many business-class hotel rooms are currently available in Lima, and rates are highly competitive by regional standards. Reservations should be made at least two weeks in advance. The cost of rented residential space, apartments, or offices is relatively high, although declining demand during the last three years has increased supply and reduced prices.

The communications system is being modernized following the privatization of the telephone company in 1994. The cost of a call to the United States is approximately U.S. $0.60 per minute. The demand for better communications services has been notable, especially following many years of poor service and under-investment in technology. Cellular phones are very popular in Lima and other major cities and the number of wireless subscriptions should surpass the number of wire lines in 2002. Direct access to credit card number for AT&T, Sprint, and MCI Worldcom is also available.

Peruvian medical facilities do not generally meet U.S. standards, although some private clinics do. However, if visitors take certain precautions about food and drink, the level of risk is manageable. Cholera and other infectious diseases such as hepatitis are present in Peru. Travelers in Peru should always substitute bottled beverages for potentially contaminated water. Fish, shellfish and vegetables should not be eaten unless well cooked, and all food should be eaten while still hot. Peeled fruits should be safe. Travelers to the jungle areas of Peru should have up-to-date yellow fever vaccine and malaria prophylaxis. There are several clinics in the Lima area which have U.S. trained personnel and up-to-date medical equipment. Since U.S. medical insurance is not always valid outside the United States, supplemental insurance could prove useful, especially to provide coverage for medical evacuation.

TEMPORARY ENTRY OF GOODS

Goods for trade fairs may temporarily enter Peru by paying a bond - but without paying duties - and following the normal documentation requirements mentioned in Chapter 6, Section "Import Documentation." In addition to normal passenger baggage, a cellular phone (and its accessories) and a laptop are allowed without paying duties.

SUPPLEMENTS

SELECTED INVESTMENT CONTACTS

PUBLIC ENTITIES

CONAFRAN
Dirección: Calle 1 Oeste Nro. 050 Piso 16
Corpac - San Isidro Lima 27 – Perú
Phone: (51 1) 224-3244
Fax: (51 1) 224-3137
E–Mail: conafran@mitinci.gob.pe

CONASEV
Av. Santa Cruz Nº 315 Miraflores
Lima - Perú
Telf : (51 1) 441-6620 (51 1) 441-7815
E-Mail : postmast@conasevnet.gob.pe
URL: http://www/CONASEV/conasev1.htm

CONITE
Comisión Nacional de Inversiones y
Tecnologías Extranjeras – CONITE
Jr. Miro Quesada 320 – Piso 4 – Lima 1
Phone: (51 1) 428-9358 / 427-7696
Fax: (51 1) 427-7696
E-Mail : CONITE@mef.gob.pe
URL: http:\\www.mef.gob.pe/peruinv.htm

COPRI
Av. Las Artes 260 – San Borja – Lima 41
Phone: (51 1) 430-0660
Fax: (51 1) 475-0078
E-Mail :webmaster@copri.gob.pe
URL: http://www.copri.gob.pe/

INDECOPI
Av. Guardia Civil y Cuadra 15 de Av. Canada –
San Borja – Lima 41
Phone: (51 1) 224-7800
Fax: (51 1) 224-0348
E-Mail :postmaster@indecopi.gob.pe
URL: http://www.indecopi.gob.pe/

PROMPERU
Calle Uno Oeste S/N, Edificio MITINCI, Piso 13 ,
Urb. Corpac – San Isidro – Lima 27
Phone: (51 1) 224-3118 / 224-3271

Fax: (51 1) 224-3323
E-Mail : postmaster@promperu.gob.pe
URL: http://www.promperu.gob.pe/promperu/

MINISTRY OF TRANSPORT, COMMUNICATION, HOUSING AND CONSTRUCTION
Av. 28 de Julio 800 - Lima
Phone (51 1) 433-7800
Fax. (51 1) 432-9098
E-Mail :CSalazar@mtc.gob.pe
URL: http://www.mtc.gob.pe/

MINISTRY OF INDUSTRY, TOURISM, INTEGRATION AND INTERNATIONAL NEGOTIATIONS
Calle Uno Oeste S/N, Urb. Corpac (San Isidro)
Phone. (51 1) 224-3347
Fax. (51 1) 224-3264
E-Mail :webmaster@mitinci.gob.pe
URL: http://www.mitinci.gob.pe/

MINISTRY OF ENERGY AND MINES
Av. Las Artes 260 (San Borja)
Phones (51 1) 475-0206 - 4750278
E-Mail :postman@mem.gob.pe
URL: http://www.mem.gob.pe/

MINISTRY OF AGRICULTURE
Av. Salaverry S/N (Jesus Maria)
Phone (51 1) 433-3034
Fax. (51 1) 432-9098
E-Mail :postmast@oia.minag.gob.pe
URL: http://www.minag.gob.pe/

MINISTRY OF FISHING
Calle Uno Oeste S/N, Urb. Corpac (San Isidro)
Phones (51 1) 224-3336 - 224-3264
E-Mail :minpes-postmaster@minpes.gob.pe
URL: http://www.minpes.gob.pe/

MINISTRY OF FOREIGN AFFAIRS
Ucayali 363 - Piso 2 (Lima)
Phones (51 1) 427-3860 - 427-1992
E-Mail :webmaster@rree.gob.pe
URL: http://www.rree.gob.pe/

MINISTRY OF LABOR AND SOCIAL PROMOTION
Av. Salaverry 655 (Jesus Maria)
Phone. (51 1) 433-2512

OSIPTEL
Calle de La Prosa 136 Lima 41

Telf. 2251313 - Fax 4751816
E-Mail: sid@osiptel.gob.pe
URL: http://www.osiptel.gob.pe

PRIVATE ENTITIES
ASBANC
Calle 41 975 Urb. Córpac - San Isidro
Telf. : (51 1) 2241718
Fax : (51 1) 2241707
E-Mail : Asbanc@amauta.rcp.net.pe

Asociación de Exportadores del Perú – ADEX
Javier Prado Este 2875 – San Borja – Lima 41
Phone: (51 1) 346-2530
Fax: (51 1) 437-1879
URL : http://www.adexperu.org.pe/

Cámara de Comercio de Lima
Av. Gregorio Escobedo 389 – Jesús María- Lima
11
Phone: (51 1) 463-3434
Fax: (51 1) 463-9813
E-Mail : webmaster@camaralima.org.pe
URL : http://www.camaralima.org.pe/

CONFIEP
Confederacion Nacional de Instituciones
Empresariales Privadas
Av. V. Andrés Belaúnde 147 – Vía Principal 155-
Edif. Real 3, Piso 4 – San Isidro – Lima 27
Phone: (51 1) 221-7730 / 221-7694
Fax: (51 1) 440-7702

Sociedad Nacional de Exportadores –SNE
Bartolomé Herrera 254 – Miraflores – Lima 18
Phone: (51 1) 446-4394
Fax: (51 1) 446-4355
E-Mail : rguadal@amauta.rcp.net.pe
URL : http://www.rcp.net.pe/SNE/

Sociedad Nacional de Industrias – SNI
Los Laureles 365 – San Isidro – Lima 27
Phone: (51 1) 421-8830
Fax: (51 1) 421-8881

Sociedad Nacional de Minería y Petróleo
Fco. Graña 671 – Magdalena – Lima 17
Phone: (51 1) 460 – 1600 / 470-7819
Fax: (51 1) 460 – 1560
E-Mail : postmaster@snmpe.org.pe

Sociedad Nacional de Pesquería
Av. Javier Prado Oeste 2442 - San Isidro – Lima 27
Phone: (51 1) 261-2970 / 461-2003
Fax: (51 1) 261-7912
E-Mail: snpnet@protelsa.com.pe
URL: http://www.sea-world.com/snp

U.S. AND COUNTRY CONTACTS

U.S. GOVERNMENT

U.S. Department of Commerce (U.S. Embassy Lima, Peru)
U.S. Commercial Service Lima
Unit 3780
APO AA 34031
Margaret Hanson-Muse, Commercial Counselor
Cesar Jochamowitz, Senior Commercial Specialist
Flora Muroi, Commercial Specialist
Tel.: (511) 618-2442, 434-3040 Fax: (511) 434-3041
E-mail: Lima.Office.Box@mail.doc.gov
Website: http://www.buyusa.gov/peru/en/
www.export.gov

Trade Information Center in Washington: 1-800-USA-TRADE
http://www.ita.doc.gov/td/tic/

U.S. Department of Commerce (Washington, D.C.)
14th & Constitution Avenue, N.W. Room Nr. 3017
Washington, D.C. 20230
Maria Cameron, Desk Officer
Email: Maria_Cameron@ita.doc.gov
(Maria(underscore)Cameron@ita.doc.gov)
Tel.: (202) 482-0475 Fax: (202) 482-0464 or (202) 482-4726
Website: www.doc.gov/

U.S Department of State (U.S. Embassy Lima, Peru)
Unit 3730
APO AA 34031
Ambassador J. Curtis Struble
Adam Shub~~Timothy Stater~~, Economic Counselor
Hal Howard, Economic Officer
Marcos Mandojana~~Samantha Carl-Yoder~~, Economic Officer
Miguel Yepez, Economic Specialist
Tel.: (511) 434-3000 Fax: (511) 434-4095
Website:
http://usembassy.state.gov/lima/wwwhmain.html

U.S Department of State (Washington, D.C.)
2201 C Street N.W., Room 5906
Washington, D.C. 20520
Barbara Thomas~~Joaquin Monserrate~~, Peru Desk Officer
Email:
thomasbm@state.gov~~monserratejf@state.gov~~
Tel.: (202) 647-3338 Fax: (202) 647-2628
Website: www.state.gov

U.S Department of Agriculture (U.S. Embassy Lima, Peru)
Unit 3785
APO AA 34031
Foreign Agricultural Service (FAS)
Tel.: (511) 618-2491, 434-3042 Fax: (511) 434-3043
~~Melinda Sallyards~~Eugene Philhower, Regional Agricultural ~~Attachè~~Counselor
Email: aglima@usda.gov
Carlos Gonzalez, Agricultural Attaché
Email: Carlos.Gonzalez@usda.gov
Gaspar Nolte, Agricultural Specialist
Email: Gaspar.Nolte@usda.gov
Violeta Gutierrez, Agricultural Marketing Specialist
Email: Violeta.Gutierrez@usda.gov
Websites: www.fas.usda.gov (FAS), www.usdaperu.org.pe (Post)
Animal and Plant Health Inspection Service (APHIS)
Tel.: (511) 434-4202 Fax: (511) 434-0958
~~Carolin~~ Carolyn Cohen, Area Director for Chile, Peru, Bolivia (resident in Santiago)
Gladys Solano, APHIS Program Specialist
Email: gladys.solano@aphis.usda.gov
Tel.: (511) 434-4202 Fax: (511) 434-0958

Website: www.aphis.usda.gov

U.S. Department of Agriculture (Washington, D.C.)
14th & Independence Avenue, S.W.
Washington, D.C. 20250
Jeanne Bailey, Western Hemisphere Area Director, Office of Foreign Agricultural Service AffairsOperations
Email: Jeanne.Bailey@usda.gov
Tel.: (202) 720-3221 Fax: (202) 720-5183
Website: www.usda.gov

U.S. Department of Agriculture, Foreign Agricultural Service, Trade Assistance and Promotion Office:
Tel.: (202) 720-7420, Fax: (703) 875-4009

Export-Import Bank of the United States (Ex-Im Bank)
811 Vermont Avenue, N.W.
Washington D.C. 20571
Tel.: Toll Free (800) 565-EXIM (3946)
Business Development (202) 565-3900
Fax: (202) 565-3931
Email: info@exim.gov
Website: www.exim.gov
Xiomara Creque, Acting Regional Director-Americas
Tel.: (202) 565-3477 Fax: (202) 565-3931
Ken Vranich, Business Development Officer
Tel: (202) 565-3905, Fax: (202) 565-3961
ken.vranich.exim.gov

Overseas Private Investment Corporation (OPIC)
1100 New York Avenue, N.W.
Washington, D.C. 20527
Tel.: InfoLine: (202) 336-8799
FactsLine:(202) 336-8700
Fax: (202) 408-8959
Email: info@opic.gov
Website: www.opic.gov
Juan Carlos Rivera Montes, Manager – Small Business Center
Tel.: (202) 336-8685 Fax: (202) 408-5142 / 218-0182
Email: jrive@opic.gov
Deborah Moronese, Insurance Officer – Small Business Center
Email: Dmoro@opic.gov

U.S. Trade and Development Agency (TDA)
1000 Wilson Boulevard, Suite 1600
Arlington, VA 22209-3901
Tel.: (703) 875-4357 Fax: (703) 875-4009
Website: www.tda.gov
Anne McKinney, Regional Director
Keith Eischeid, Country Manager
Email: keischeid@tda.gov

United States Trade Representative (USTR)

600 17th Street, N.W.
Washington, DC 20508
Tel.: (202) 395-7360
Website: www.ustr.gov
Ambassador Susan C. Schwab, US Trade Representative
Everett Eissenstat, Assistant U.S.T.R. Americas
Email: contactustr@ustr.eop.gov

GOVERNMENT OF PERU

Presidencia del Consejo de Ministros
(Presidency of the Council of Ministers)
Av. 28 de Julio 878, Miraflores
Lima – 18, Peru
Tel.: (511) 447-0168, 447-1322 Fax: (511) 446-0469
Website: www.pcm.gob.pe
Jorge del Castillo, President of the Council of Ministers

Ministerio de Agricultura
(Ministry of Agriculture)
Psje. Francisco de Zela s/n, Jesus Maria
Lima 11, Peru
Tel.: (511) 613-5800 / 433-3034, 433-2219
Fax: (511) 432-0990, 431-0109
Website: www.minag.gob.pe
Juan Jose Salazar, Minister

Ministerio de Comercio Exterior y Turismo
(Ministry of Foreign Trade and Tourism)
Calle Uno Oeste s/n Piso 17, Urb. Corpac, San Isidro
Lima 27, Peru
Tel.: (511) 513-6100 Fax: (511) 224-3362
Website: www.mincetur.gob.pe
Mercedes Araoz, Minister

Ministerio de Economia y Finanzas
(Ministry of Economy and Finance)
Jr. Junin 319, Piso 4
Lima 1, Peru

Tel.: (511) 426-8495 Fax: (511) 428-2101
Website: www.mef.gob.pe
Luis Carranza, Minister

Ministerio de Energia y Minas
(Ministry of Energy and Mines)
Av. Las Artes 260
San Borja
Lima 41, Peru
Tel.: (511) 224-4301 Fax: (511) 224-4490
Website: www.minem.gob.pe
Juan Valdivia, Minister

Ministerio de la Produccion
(Ministry of Production)
Calle Uno Oeste s/n, Piso 7
Urb. Corpac, San Isidro
Lima 27, Peru
Tel.: (511) 616-2200 Fax: (511) 616-2200 x705
Website: www.produce.gob.pe
Rafael Rey, Minister

Ministerio del Interior
(Ministry of the Interior)
Plaza 30 de Agosto s/n - Piso 4, San Isidro
Lima 27, Peru
Tel.: (511) 225-0202 Fax: 224-2405
Website: www.mininter.gob.pe
Pilar Mazzetti, Minister

Ministerio de Relaciones Exteriores
(Ministry of Foreign Affairs)
Palacio Torre Tagle , Ucayali 363
Lima 1, Peru
Tel.: (511) 311-2402 Fax: (511) 311-2406
Website: www.rree.gob.pe
Ambassador Jose Antonio Garcia, Minister

Ministerio de Salud
(Ministry of Health)
Av. Salaverry Cdra. 8, Piso 4
Lima 1, Peru
Tel.: (511) 431-3331 Fax: (511) 431-0093
Website: www.minsa.gob.pe
Carlos Vallejo, Minister

Dirección General de Salud Ambiental (DIGESA)
Las Amapolas 350, Urb. San Eugenio, Lince
Lima 14, Peru
Tel.: (511) 442-8353 Fax: (511) 422-6404
Website: www.digesa.sld.pe

~~Jorge Alberto Albinagorta~~Dr. Maria del Carmen Gastañaga, Director

Ministerio de Transportes y Comunicaciones
(Ministry of Transport and Communications)
Calle Zorritos 1301
Lima 1, Peru
Tel.: (511) 315-7800 Fax: (511) 315-7618
Website: www.mtc.gob.pe
Veronica Zavala, Minister

Ministerio de Vivienda, Construccion y Saneamiento
(Ministry of Housing, Construction and Sanitation)
Av. Paseo de la Republica 3661, San Isidro
Lima – 27, Peru
Tel.: (511) 211-7930, 211-7934 Fax: (511) 441-7761
Website: www.vivienda.gob.pe
Hernan Garrido Lecca, Minister

ProInversion
(Private Investment Promotion Agency)
Av. Paseo de la Republica 3661, Piso 9
Lima – 27, Peru
Tel.: (511) 612-1200 Fax: (511) 221-2941, 221-2942
Website: www.proinversion.gob.pe/english/default.asp
Rene Cornejo, Executive Director

Instituto Nacional de Defensa de la Competencia y de la Protección de la Propiedad Intelectual (INDECOPI)
(National Institute for the Defense of Competition and Protection of Intellectual Property)
La Prosa 138, San Borja
Lima – 41, Peru
Tel.: (511) 224-7800 / (511) 224 7777
Fax: (511) 224-0347 / (511) 224 7800 ext. 1715, atención al ciudadano
Website: http://www.indecopi.gob.pe
Jaime Thorne, President
Ana Maria Capurro, General Manager

Comision de Promocion de la Pequeña y Micro Empresa (PROMPYME)
(Small and Micro-Enterprise Promotion Commission)
Av. Jose Faustino Sanchez Carrion 250, San Isidro

Lima – 27, Peru
Tel.: (511) 221- 0018 / (511) 221 1131
Fax: (511) 422-4063
E-mail: direccion@prompyme.gob.pe
Website: http://www.prompyme.gob.pe
Hugo Rodriguez, Executive Director

Servicio Nacional de Sanidad Agraria (SENASA)
Ministerio de Agricultura
(Equivalent to APHIS. Supervises sanitary conditions of imported agricultural commodities and animals)
Av. La Molina 1915, La Molina
Lima – 12, Peru
Tel.: (511) 313-3300 / anexos 1800 ó 1801
Fax: (511) 313-3315
Website: www.senasa.gob.pe
Dr. Victor PalmaJose Espinoza, National Chief a.i.

Instituto Nacional de Recursos Naturales (INRENA)
Ministerio de Agricultura
(Supervises matters related to use, exports, development, and preservation of land and natural resources such as wetlands, woodlands and wildlife)
Calle 17 No. 355
Urb. El Palomar, San Isidro
Lima – 27, Peru
Tel.: (511) 225-3287, 224-3298-, 225 1057 (directo de Jefatura Sr. AlvarezAngeles)
Fax: (511) 224-3218
Website: www.inrena.gob.pe
Leoncio AlvarezIsaac Roberto Angeles, Chief

ORGANISMO SUPERVISOR DE LA INVERSIÓN EN ENERGÍA Y MINERIA – OSINERGMIN

(Supervising Agency for Investment in Energy and Mining)
Bernardo Monteagudo 222, Magdalena
Lima – 17, Peru
Tel.: (511) 219-3400, 219-3410, 219-3411
Fax: (511) 264-0450 x.350
E-mail: osinerg@osinerg.gob.pe
Website: http://www.osinerg.gob.pe
Alfredo Dammert, President

Organismo Supervisor de la Inversión en Infraestructura de Transporte de Uso Público – OSITRAN
(Supervising Agency for Investment in Public Use Transport Infrastructure)
Av. Bolivia 144, Piso 19, Torre del Centro Cívico
Lima – 1, Peru
Tel.: (511) 330-7575 Fax: (511) 433-1944
E-mail: info@ositran.gob.pe
Website: http://www.ositran.gob.pe
Juan Carlos Zevallos, President

Organismo Supervisor de la Inversión Privada en Telecomunicaciones – OSIPTEL
(Supervising Agency for Private Investment in Telecommunications)
La Prosa 136 , San Borja
Lima – 41, Peru
Tel.: (511) 225-1313, 225-2145 Fax: (511) 475-1816
Website: http://www.osiptel.gob.pe
Guillermo Thornberry, President

SUPERINTENDENCIA NACIONAL DE SERVICIOS DE SANEAMIENTO - SUNASS

(National Superintendence of Sanitation Services)
Av. Bernardo Monteagudo 210 – 216
Magdalena del Mar
Lima – 17, Peru
Tel.: (511) 264-1440 Fax: (511) 264-4020
Website: http://www.sunass.gob.pe
Jose Salazar, President

PRIVATE SECTOR ASSOCIATIONS

American Chamber of Commerce of Peru (AmCham)
Av. Ricardo Palma 836, Miraflores
Lima – 18, Peru
Tel.: (511) 241-0708, 241-0710 Fax: (511) 241-0709
E-mail: amcham@amcham.org.pe
Website: www.amcham.org.pe
Fernando De la Flor, President
Aldo Defilippi, Executive Director

Confederacion Nacional de Instituciones Empresariales (CONFIEP)
(Confederation of Private Enterprise Institutions)
Av. Victor Andres Belaunde 147, Edificio Real 3, Piso 4 San Isidro
Lima – 27, Peru
Tel.: (511) 422-3311 Fax: (511) 422-1509
E-mail: postmaster@confiep.org.pe

Website: www.confiep.org.pe
Jose Miguel Morales, President
Ximena Zavala, General Manager

Sociedad Nacional de Industrias (SNI)
(National Society of Industries)
Los Laureles 365 San Isidro
Lima – 27, Peru
Tel.: (511) 616-4444 Fax: (511) 442-2573 / (511) 442-2570 / (511) 616-4433
E-mail: sni@sni.org.pe
Website: www.sni.org.pe
Eduardo Farah, President
Federico De Aparici, General Manager

Sociedad Nacional de Mineria, Petroleo y Energia
(National Mining, Petroleum and Energy Society)
Francisco Graña 671 Magdalena
Lima - 17, Peru
Tel.: (511) 460-1600 Fax: (511) 460-1616
E-mail: postmast@snmpe.org.pe
Website: www.snmpe.org.pe
Carlos del Solar, President
Katerina Podesta, General Manager

Asociacion de Exportadores (ADEX)
(Exporters' Association)
Av. Javier Prado Este 2875 San Borja
Lima – 41, Peru
Tel.: (511)618-3333, 346-2530 Fax: (511) 346-1879
Email: postmaster@adexperu.org.pe, cid@adexperu.org.pe
Website: www.adexperu.org.pe
Luis Vega Monteferri, President
Alvaro Barrenechea, General Manager

Camara de Comercio de Lima
(Lima Chamber of Commerce)
Gregorio Escobedo 398 Jesus Maria
Lima – 11, Peru
Tel.: (511) 463-3434, 261-4400 Fax: (511) 463-9864
E-mail: webmaster@camaralima.org.pe
Website: www.camaralima.org.pe
Samuel Gleiser, President
José Rosas Bernedo, General Manager

Camara de Comercio de Arequipa
(Arequipa Chamber of Commerce)
Quesada 102-104, Yanahuara
Arequipa, Peru
Tel: (5154) 25-4188
E-mail: ccia@camara-arequipa.org.pe
Website: www.camara-arequipa.org.pe
Mauricio Chirinos, President

Camara de Comercio de Lambayeque
(Lambayeque Chamber of Commerce)
Av. Balta 504-506
Chiclayo, Peru
Tel: (5174) 23-8081
E-mail: camara@cclam.org.pe
Website: www.cclam.org.pe
German Fernandez Castro, President

Camara Peruana de la Construccion (CAPECO)
(Chamber of Engineering and Construction Firms)
Victor Andres Belaunde 147, Edificio Real 3, Of. 402,
San Isidro, Lima 27, Peru
Tel.: (511) 441-7032/ Direct: (511) 422 5566
Fax: (511) 441-7028
E-mail: gerencia@capeco.org
Website: www.capeco.org
Lelio Balarezo, President
Carlos Vegas, General Manager

Asociacion de Bancos
(Association of Banks)
Calle 41 #975, Urb. Corpac San Isidro
Lima – 27, Peru
Tel.: (511) 224-1718 / Direct: (511) 612 3303 / Switchboard: (511) 612 3333
Fax: (511) 224-1707 / (511) 224 9512
Enrique Arroyo Rizo Patron – General Manager
Email: estudioseconomicos@asbanc.com.pe
Website: www.asbanc.com.pe
Ismael Benavides, President

Asociacion de Industriales Lacteos
(Dairy Association. Producers of dairy products)
Sociedad Nacional de Industrias
Los Laureles 365 San Isidro
Lima 27 - Peru
Tel.: (511) 616 4444 ext. 165
Fax (511) 441-1639
E-mail: adil@sni.org.pe
Rolando Piskulich, Manager

Asociacion Peruana de Porcicultores

(Pork Producers Association. Importers of animals, equipment and feed grain for pork production)
Pomalca 327 Urb. Centro Comercial Monterrico, Surco
Lima – 33, Peru
Tel.: (511) 436-3729, 436-4168 Fax: (511) 436-3729
E-mail: asoporci@terra.com.pe
Ana Maria Trelles, General Manager

Asociacion Peruana de Avicultura
(Poultry Producers Association. Importers of baby chicks, equipment and inputs for poultry and egg production)
Esmeralda 255 Chacarilla del Estanque
Lima – 33, Peru
Tel.: (511) 372-1551, 372-1540 Fax: (511) 372-1538
E-mail: apavic@apavic.com
Website: www.apavic.com
Pedro Mitma, President
Mario Berrocal, General Manager
Percy Separovich, Health Safety Manager

Fongal Lima
(Dairy Producers Association. Importers of inputs, equipment, and cattle for milk production)
Pumacahua No. 877, Of. 306 Jesus Maria
Lima – 11, Peru
Tel: (511) 431-0549 Fax: (511) 423-4642
E-mail: fongallima@infonegocio.net.pe
Javier Valera, President

Comite de Molinos de Trigo
(Wheat Millers Committee. Importers of wheat)
Los Laureles 365 San Isidro
Lima – 27, Peru
Tel.: (511) 616 4444 ext. 131 / (511) 442-2460 Fax: (511) 442-4351
E-mail: adaly@sni.org.pe
Alejandro Daly, Manager

CONSULTING FIRMS IN PERU

Apoyo S.A.
Gonzales Larranaga 265, Miraflores
Lima 18 - Peru
Tel: (511) 444-6262
Fax: (511) 445-881
Felipe Ortiz de Zevallos, Managing Director

Arthur Andersen (Medina, ZaldÁvar & Asocs.) (Andersen Worldwide SC)
Esq. Pardo y Aliaga y Camino Real, Piso 6, San Isidro
Lima - 27, Peru
Tel: (511) 222-1060
Fax: (511) 222-1060
Jorge Medina - Managing Partner

Booz-Allen & Hamilton del Per£ S.A.
Centro Empresarial Camino Real, Av. VÁctor Andrs Bela£nde 147,
Edif. Real 3, Piso 11, San Isidro
Lima - 27, Peru
Tel: (511) 215-1900
Fax: (511) 215-1911
Mark Hoffman - General Manager
Hugo Alegre - Advisor

Consultandes S.A.
Teruel 350, Miraflores
Lima 18 - Peru
Tel: (511) 221-4831, 222-5974
Fax: (511) 222-5977
E-mail: consultandes@amauta.rcp.net.pe
John Youle, President

Cuanto S.A.
Plaza del Ovalo 203 -San Isidro
Lima 27, Peru
Tel: (511) 442-3421, 422-4832
Fax: (511) 444-3421
Mr. Richard Webb, Director
Mr. Gilberto Moncada Vigo, General Manager

Deloitte & Touche, Gris, HernÊndez y Asociados (Deloitte Touche Tohmatsu International)
Paseo de la Rep£blica 3074, Piso 7, San Isidro
Lima - 27, Peru
Tel: (511) 442-3434, 442-7812, 221-4034
Fax: (511) 442-2861
Carlos AndÁa - Senior Partner

Dun & Bradstreet S. A.
Republica de Chile 388, Piso 2
Lima 1 - Peru
Tel: (511) 433-5533, 433-2989
Fax: (511) 433-2897
Florencio Kohata, Manager

Ernst & Young International
Pqe. QuiÛones 198, Jes£s MarÁa
Lima - 11, Peru
Tel: (511) 463-1818, 463-5616
Fax: (511) 463-4523

Hansen-Holm, Alonso & Co. Sociedad Civil (Coopers & Lybrand)
Juan de Arona 830 Piso 11, San isidro
Lima - 27, Peru
Tel: (511) 442-4248
Fax: (511) 442-2073
Humberto Allemant Salazar - Partner

Louis Berger International, Inc.
Av. Javier Prado Este 2875, Piso 5, San Borja
Lima 41, Peru
Tel: (511) 346-3000, 346-3020
Fax: (511) 346-2669
Rodrigo Carvajal - Director,
Internet[rcarvaja@msp.org.pe]

Macroconsult
Gral. BorgoÛo 1156, Miraflores
Lima - 18, Peru
Tel: (511) 221-2691, 221-2692
Fax: (511) 221-2696
Roger Espinosa - Director

Price Waterhouse
Las Begonias 441, Piso 14, San Isidro
Lima - 27, Peru
Tel: (511) 442-0555, 442-0567
Fax: (511) 442-6522
Luis A. Chinchilla - Partner

PRE-SHIPMENT INSPECTION FIRMS

Bureau Veritas S.A.
Republica de Panama 3030, Piso 14,
Edif.Banco del Nuevo Mundo,
San Isidro
Lima 27 - Peru
Tel: (511) 421-0101, 441-6765
Fax: (511) 441-0604, 441-0624
Rafael Fernandez Stoll - General Manager

Cotecna Inspection (PERU) S.A.
Camino Real 390, Torre Central Piso 10,
San Isidro
Lima 27 - Peru
Tel: (511) 421-1001, 440-6789
Fax: (511) 441-4191, 440-0577
Mercedes Castro de Rebagliati - General Manager

SGS Societe Generale de Surveillance S.A.
Republica de Panama 3050, San Isidro
Lima 27 - Peru
Tel: (511) 221-2140, 442-6900
Fax: (511) 442-5865
Alejandro Gomez de la Torre - General Manager

PROJECTED DIRECT FOREIGN INVESTMENT IN EXISTING COMPANIES/PROJECTS

Investing Company	US$ Million
Billiton Investment BV (mining, La Granja)	2,600
Lima Airport Partners (Lima airport)	1,037
Pluspetrol/Hunt/S.K. (Camisea, upstream)	800
Techint/Hunt/Pluspetrol/Sonatrach/S.K. (Camisea, downstream)	800
Cia. Minera Manhattan Sechura (mining, Tambo Grande)	600
Billiton (mining, Quellaveco)	515
BHP (mining, Tintaya)	369
Repsol (oil refining, La Pampilla)	320
Cominco/Marubeni (Cajamarquilla zinc refinery)	300
Doe Run Peru (mining, La Oroya, Cobriza)	300
Phelps Dodge (mining, Cerro Verde)	200
Other	1,500
TOTAL	9,341

BASIC TITLES FOR PERU

IMPORTANT!
All publications are updated annually!
Please contact IBP, Inc. at ibpusa3@gmail.com for the latest ISBNs and additional information

Title
Peru A "Spy" Guide - Strategic Information and Developments
Peru A Spy" Guide"
Peru Air Force Handbook
Peru Air Force Handbook
Peru Banking & Financial Market Handbook
Peru Banking & Financial Market Handbook
Peru Business and Investment Opportunities Yearbook
Peru Business and Investment Opportunities Yearbook
Peru Business and Investment Opportunities Yearbook Volume 1 Strategic Information and Opportunities
Peru Business Intelligence Report - Practical Information, Opportunities, Contacts
Peru Business Intelligence Report - Practical Information, Opportunities, Contacts
Peru Business Law Handbook Volume 1 Strategic Information and Basic Laws
Peru Business Law Handbook Volume 2 Investment and Trade Laws
Peru Business Law Handbook Volume 3 Export-Import and Trade Regulations
Peru Business Law Handbook Volume 4 Mining Industry Laws and Regulations
Peru Business Law Handbook Volume 5 Company and Business Formation
Peru Clothing & Textile Industry Handbook
Peru Company Laws and Regulations Handbook
Peru Constitution and Citizenship Laws Handbook - Strategic Information and Basic Laws
Peru Country Study Guide - Strategic Information and Developments
Peru Country Study Guide - Strategic Information and Developments
Peru Country Study Guide Volume 1 Strategic Information and Developments
Peru Customs, Trade Regulations and Procedures Handbook
Peru Customs, Trade Regulations and Procedures Handbook
Peru Diplomatic Handbook - Strategic Information and Developments
Peru Diplomatic Handbook - Strategic Information and Developments
Peru Ecology & Nature Protection Handbook
Peru Ecology & Nature Protection Handbook
Peru Ecology & Nature Protection Laws and Regulation Handbook
Peru Economic & Development Strategy Handbook
Peru Economic & Development Strategy Handbook
Peru Energy Policy, Laws and Regulation Handbook
Peru Energy Policy, Laws and Regulations Handbook
Peru Energy Policy, Laws and Regulations Handbook
Peru Export-Import Trade and Business Directory
Peru Export-Import Trade and Business Directory
Peru Foreign Policy and Government Guide
Peru Foreign Policy and Government Guide
Peru Government and Business Contacts Handbook
Peru Government and Business Contacts Handbook
Peru Immigration Laws and Regulations Handbook - Strategic Information and Basic Laws
Peru Industrial and Business Directory

Title
Peru Industrial and Business Directory
Peru Insolvency (Bankruptcy) Laws and Regulations Handbook - Strategic Information and Basic Laws
Peru Internet and E-Commerce Investment and Business Guide - Strategic and Practical Information: Regulations and Opportunities
Peru Internet and E-Commerce Investment and Business Guide - Strategic and Practical Information: Regulations and Opportunities
Peru Investment and Business Guide - Strategic and Practical Information
Peru Investment and Business Guide - Strategic and Practical Information
Peru Investment and Business Guide - Strategic and Practical Information
Peru Investment and Business Guide - Strategic and Practical Information
Peru Investment and Business Guide Volume 2 Business, Investment Opportunities and Incentives
Peru Investment and Trade Laws and Regulations Handbook
Peru Labor Laws and Regulations Handbook - Strategic Information and Basic Laws
Peru Land Ownership and Agriculture Laws Handbook
Peru Mineral & Mining Sector Investment and Business Guide - Strategic and Practical Information
Peru Mineral & Mining Sector Investment and Business Guide - Strategic and Practical Information
Peru Mining Laws and Regulations Handbook
Peru Oil & Gas Sector Business & Investment Opportunities Yearbook
Peru Oil & Gas Sector Business & Investment Opportunities Yearbook
Peru Oil and Gas Exploration Laws and Regulation Handbook
Peru Oil Potential, Exploration and Oil Blocks Handbook
Peru Privatization Programs and Regulations Handbook
Peru Privatization Programs and Regulations Handbook
Peru Recent Economic and Political Developments Yearbook
Peru Recent Economic and Political Developments Yearbook
Peru Recent Economic and Political Developments Yearbook
Peru Starting Business (Incorporating) in....Guide
Peru Taxation Laws and Regulations Handbook
Peru Telecom Laws and Regulations Handbook
Peru Telecommunication Industry Business Opportunities Handbook
Peru Telecommunication Industry Business Opportunities Handbook
Peru Transportation Policy and Regulations Handbook
Peru: How to Invest, Start and Run Profitable Business in Peru Guide - Practical Information, Opportunities, Contacts

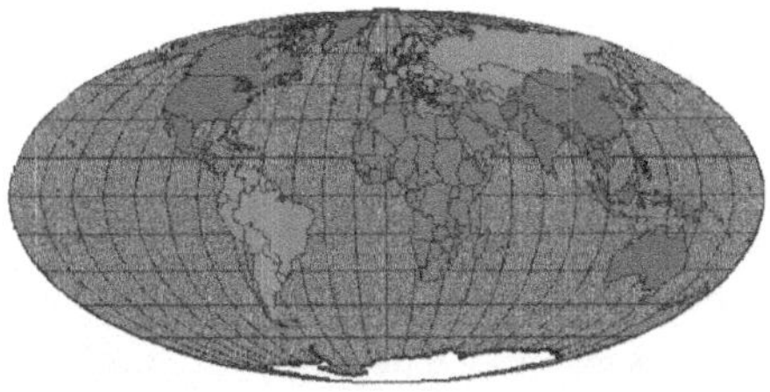

WORLD INVESTMENT AND BUSINESS LIBRARY

World Business Information Catalog, USA: http://www.ibpus.com
Email: ibpusa@comcast.net.

Price: $99.95 Each

TITLE
Abkhazia (Republic of Abkhazia) Investment and Business Guide Volume 1 Strategic and Practical Information
Afghanistan Investment and Business Guide Volume 1 Strategic and Practical Information
Aland Investment and Business Guide Volume 1 Strategic and Practical Information
Albania Investment and Business Guide Volume 1 Strategic and Practical Information
Algeria Investment and Business Guide Volume 1 Strategic and Practical Information
Andorra Investment and Business Guide Volume 1 Strategic and Practical Information
Angola Investment and Business Guide Volume 1 Strategic and Practical Information
Anguilla Investment and Business Guide Volume 1 Strategic and Practical Information
Antigua and Barbuda Investment and Business Guide Volume 1 Strategic and Practical Information
Antilles (Netherlands) Investment and Business Guide Volume 1 Strategic and Practical Information
Argentina Investment and Business Guide Volume 1 Strategic and Practical Information
Armenia Investment and Business Guide Volume 1 Strategic and Practical Information
Aruba Investment and Business Guide Volume 1 Strategic and Practical Information
Australia Investment and Business Guide Volume 1 Strategic and Practical Information
Austria Investment and Business Guide Volume 1 Strategic and Practical Information
Azerbaijan Investment and Business Guide Volume 1 Strategic and Practical Information
Bahamas Investment and Business Guide Volume 1 Strategic and Practical Information
Bahrain Investment and Business Guide Volume 1 Strategic and Practical Information
Bangladesh Investment and Business Guide Volume 1 Strategic and Practical Information
Barbados Investment and Business Guide Volume 1 Strategic and Practical Information
Belarus Investment and Business Guide Volume 1 Strategic and Practical Information
Belgium Investment and Business Guide Volume 1 Strategic and Practical Information
Belize Investment and Business Guide Volume 1 Strategic and Practical Information
Benin Investment and Business Guide Volume 1 Strategic and Practical Information
Bermuda Investment and Business Guide Volume 1 Strategic and Practical Information
Bhutan Investment and Business Guide Volume 1 Strategic and Practical Information
Bolivia Investment and Business Guide Volume 1 Strategic and Practical Information
Bosnia and Herzegovina Investment and Business Guide Volume 1 Strategic and Practical Information
Botswana Investment and Business Guide Volume 1 Strategic and Practical Information
Brazil Investment and Business Guide Volume 1 Strategic and Practical Information
Brunei Investment and Business Guide Volume 1 Strategic and Practical Information
Bulgaria Investment and Business Guide Volume 1 Strategic and Practical Information
Burkina Faso Investment and Business Guide Volume 1 Strategic and Practical Information
Burundi Investment and Business Guide Volume 1 Strategic and Practical Information
Cambodia Investment and Business Guide Volume 1 Strategic and Practical Information
Cameroon Investment and Business Guide Volume 1 Strategic and Practical Information
Canada Investment and Business Guide Volume 1 Strategic and Practical Information

For additional analytical, business and investment opportunities information,
Please contact Global Investment & Business Center, USA
at (202) 546-2103. Fax: (202) 546-3275. E-mail: rusric@erols.com

TITLE
Cape Verde Investment and Business Guide Volume 1 Strategic and Practical Information
Cayman Islands Investment and Business Guide Volume 1 Strategic and Practical Information
Central African Republic Investment and Business Guide Volume 1 Strategic and Practical Information
Chad Investment and Business Guide Volume 1 Strategic and Practical Information
Chile Investment and Business Guide Volume 1 Strategic and Practical Information
China Investment and Business Guide Volume 1 Strategic and Practical Information
Colombia Investment and Business Guide Volume 1 Strategic and Practical Information
Comoros Investment and Business Guide Volume 1 Strategic and Practical Information
Congo Investment and Business Guide Volume 1 Strategic and Practical Information
Congo, Democratic Republic Investment and Business Guide Volume 1 Strategic and Practical Information
Cook Islands Investment and Business Guide Volume 1 Strategic and Practical Information
Costa Rica Investment and Business Guide Volume 1 Strategic and Practical Information
Cote d'Ivoire Investment and Business Guide Volume 1 Strategic and Practical Information
Croatia Investment and Business Guide Volume 1 Strategic and Practical Information
Cuba Investment and Business Guide Volume 1 Strategic and Practical Information
Cyprus Investment and Business Guide Volume 1 Strategic and Practical Information
Czech Republic Investment and Business Guide Volume 1 Strategic and Practical Information
Denmark Investment and Business Guide Volume 1 Strategic and Practical Information
Djibouti Investment and Business Guide Volume 1 Strategic and Practical Information
Dominica Investment and Business Guide Volume 1 Strategic and Practical Information
Dominican Republic Investment and Business Guide Volume 1 Strategic and Practical Information
Ecuador Investment and Business Guide Volume 1 Strategic and Practical Information
Egypt Investment and Business Guide Volume 1 Strategic and Practical Information
El Salvador Investment and Business Guide Volume 1 Strategic and Practical Information
Equatorial Guinea Investment and Business Guide Volume 1 Strategic and Practical Information
Eritrea Investment and Business Guide Volume 1 Strategic and Practical Information
Estonia Investment and Business Guide Volume 1 Strategic and Practical Information
Ethiopia Investment and Business Guide Volume 1 Strategic and Practical Information
Falkland Islands Investment and Business Guide Volume 1 Strategic and Practical Information
Faroes Islands Investment and Business Guide Volume 1 Strategic and Practical Information
Fiji Investment and Business Guide Volume 1 Strategic and Practical Information
Finland Investment and Business Guide Volume 1 Strategic and Practical Information
France Investment and Business Guide Volume 1 Strategic and Practical Information
Gabon Investment and Business Guide Volume 1 Strategic and Practical Information
Gambia Investment and Business Guide Volume 1 Strategic and Practical Information
Georgia Investment and Business Guide Volume 1 Strategic and Practical Information
Germany Investment and Business Guide Volume 1 Strategic and Practical Information
Ghana Investment and Business Guide Volume 1 Strategic and Practical Information
Gibraltar Investment and Business Guide Volume 1 Strategic and Practical Information
Greece Investment and Business Guide Volume 1 Strategic and Practical Information
Greenland Investment and Business Guide Volume 1 Strategic and Practical Information
Grenada Investment and Business Guide Volume 1 Strategic and Practical Information
Guam Investment and Business Guide Volume 1 Strategic and Practical Information
Guatemala Investment and Business Guide Volume 1 Strategic and Practical Information
Guernsey Investment and Business Guide Volume 1 Strategic and Practical Information
Guinea Investment and Business Guide Volume 1 Strategic and Practical Information

TITLE
Guinea-Bissau Investment and Business Guide Volume 1 Strategic and Practical Information
Guyana Investment and Business Guide Volume 1 Strategic and Practical Information
Haiti Investment and Business Guide Volume 1 Strategic and Practical Information
Honduras Investment and Business Guide Volume 1 Strategic and Practical Information
Hungary Investment and Business Guide Volume 1 Strategic and Practical Information
Iceland Investment and Business Guide Volume 1 Strategic and Practical Information
India Investment and Business Guide Volume 1 Strategic and Practical Information
Indonesia Investment and Business Guide Volume 1 Strategic and Practical Information
Iran Investment and Business Guide Volume 1 Strategic and Practical Information
Iraq Investment and Business Guide Volume 1 Strategic and Practical Information
Ireland Investment and Business Guide Volume 1 Strategic and Practical Information
Israel Investment and Business Guide Volume 1 Strategic and Practical Information
Italy Investment and Business Guide Volume 1 Strategic and Practical Information
Jamaica Investment and Business Guide Volume 1 Strategic and Practical Information
Japan Investment and Business Guide Volume 1 Strategic and Practical Information
Jersey Investment and Business Guide Volume 1 Strategic and Practical Information
Jordan Investment and Business Guide Volume 1 Strategic and Practical Information
Kazakhstan Investment and Business Guide Volume 1 Strategic and Practical Information
Kenya Investment and Business Guide Volume 1 Strategic and Practical Information
Kiribati Investment and Business Guide Volume 1 Strategic and Practical Information
Korea, North Investment and Business Guide Volume 1 Strategic and Practical Information
Korea, South Investment and Business Guide Volume 1 Strategic and Practical Information
Kosovo Investment and Business Guide Volume 1 Strategic and Practical Information
Kurdistan Investment and Business Guide Volume 1 Strategic and Practical Information
Kuwait Investment and Business Guide Volume 1 Strategic and Practical Information
Kyrgyzstan Investment and Business Guide Volume 1 Strategic and Practical Information
Laos Investment and Business Guide Volume 1 Strategic and Practical Information
Latvia Investment and Business Guide Volume 1 Strategic and Practical Information
Lebanon Investment and Business Guide Volume 1 Strategic and Practical Information
Lesotho Investment and Business Guide Volume 1 Strategic and Practical Information
Liberia Investment and Business Guide Volume 1 Strategic and Practical Information
Libya Investment and Business Guide Volume 1 Strategic and Practical Information
Liechtenstein Investment and Business Guide Volume 1 Strategic and Practical Information
Lithuania Investment and Business Guide Volume 1 Strategic and Practical Information
Luxembourg Investment and Business Guide Volume 1 Strategic and Practical Information
Macao Investment and Business Guide Volume 1 Strategic and Practical Information
Macedonia Investment and Business Guide Volume 1 Strategic and Practical Information
Madagascar Investment and Business Guide Volume 1 Strategic and Practical Information
Madeira Investment and Business Guide Volume 1 Strategic and Practical Information
Malawi Investment and Business Guide Volume 1 Strategic and Practical Information
Malaysia Investment and Business Guide Volume 1 Strategic and Practical Information
Maldives Investment and Business Guide Volume 1 Strategic and Practical Information
Mali Investment and Business Guide Volume 1 Strategic and Practical Information
Malta Investment and Business Guide Volume 1 Strategic and Practical Information
Man Investment and Business Guide Volume 1 Strategic and Practical Information
Marshall Islands Investment and Business Guide Volume 1 Strategic and Practical Information

TITLE
Mauritania Investment and Business Guide Volume 1 Strategic and Practical Information
Mauritius Investment and Business Guide Volume 1 Strategic and Practical Information
Mayotte Investment and Business Guide Volume 1 Strategic and Practical Information
Mexico Investment and Business Guide Volume 1 Strategic and Practical Information
Micronesia Investment and Business Guide Volume 1 Strategic and Practical Information
Moldova Investment and Business Guide Volume 1 Strategic and Practical Information
Monaco Investment and Business Guide Volume 1 Strategic and Practical Information
Mongolia Investment and Business Guide Volume 1 Strategic and Practical Information
Montserrat Investment and Business Guide Volume 1 Strategic and Practical Information
Montenegro Investment and Business Guide Volume 1 Strategic and Practical Information
Morocco Investment and Business Guide Volume 1 Strategic and Practical Information
Mozambique Investment and Business Guide Volume 1 Strategic and Practical Information
Myanmar Investment and Business Guide Volume 1 Strategic and Practical Information
Nagorno-Karabakh Republic Investment and Business Guide Volume 1 Strategic and Practical Information
Namibia Investment and Business Guide Volume 1 Strategic and Practical Information
Nauru Investment and Business Guide Volume 1 Strategic and Practical Information
Nepal Investment and Business Guide Volume 1 Strategic and Practical Information
Netherlands Investment and Business Guide Volume 1 Strategic and Practical Information
New Caledonia Investment and Business Guide Volume 1 Strategic and Practical Information
New Zealand Investment and Business Guide Volume 1 Strategic and Practical Information
Nicaragua Investment and Business Guide Volume 1 Strategic and Practical Information
Niger Investment and Business Guide Volume 1 Strategic and Practical Information
Nigeria Investment and Business Guide Volume 1 Strategic and Practical Information
Niue Investment and Business Guide Volume 1 Strategic and Practical Information
Northern Cyprus (Turkish Republic of Northern Cyprus) Volume 1 Strategic Information and Developments
Northern Mariana Islands Investment and Business Guide Volume 1 Strategic and Practical Information
Norway Investment and Business Guide Volume 1 Strategic and Practical Information
Oman Investment and Business Guide Volume 1 Strategic and Practical Information
Pakistan Investment and Business Guide Volume 1 Strategic and Practical Information
Palau Investment and Business Guide Volume 1 Strategic and Practical Information
Palestine (West Bank & Gaza) Investment and Business Guide Volume 1 Strategic and Practical Information
Panama Investment and Business Guide Volume 1 Strategic and Practical Information
Papua New Guinea Investment and Business Guide Volume 1 Strategic and Practical Information
Paraguay Investment and Business Guide Volume 1 Strategic and Practical Information
Peru Investment and Business Guide Volume 1 Strategic and Practical Information
Philippines Investment and Business Guide Volume 1 Strategic and Practical Information
Pitcairn Islands Investment and Business Guide Volume 1 Strategic and Practical Information
Poland Investment and Business Guide Volume 1 Strategic and Practical Information
Polynesia French Investment and Business Guide Volume 1 Strategic and Practical Information
Portugal Investment and Business Guide Volume 1 Strategic and Practical Information
Qatar Investment and Business Guide Volume 1 Strategic and Practical Information
Romania Investment and Business Guide Volume 1 Strategic and Practical Information
Russia Investment and Business Guide Volume 1 Strategic and Practical Information
Rwanda Investment and Business Guide Volume 1 Strategic and Practical Information
Sahrawi Arab Democratic Republic Volume 1 Strategic Information and Developments
Saint Kitts and Nevis Investment and Business Guide Volume 1 Strategic and Practical Information

TITLE
Saint Lucia Investment and Business Guide Volume 1 Strategic and Practical Information
Saint Vincent and The Grenadines Investment and Business Guide Volume 1 Strategic and Practical Information
Samoa (American) A Investment and Business Guide Volume 1 Strategic and Practical Information
Samoa (Western) Investment and Business Guide Volume 1 Strategic and Practical Information
San Marino Investment and Business Guide Volume 1 Strategic and Practical Information
Sao Tome and Principe Investment and Business Guide Volume 1 Strategic and Practical Information
Saudi Arabia Investment and Business Guide Volume 1 Strategic and Practical Information
Scotland Investment and Business Guide Volume 1 Strategic and Practical Information
Senegal Investment and Business Guide Volume 1 Strategic and Practical Information
Serbia Investment and Business Guide Volume 1 Strategic and Practical Information
Seychelles Investment and Business Guide Volume 1 Strategic and Practical Information
Sierra Leone Investment and Business Guide Volume 1 Strategic and Practical Information
Singapore Investment and Business Guide Volume 1 Strategic and Practical Information
Slovakia Investment and Business Guide Volume 1 Strategic and Practical Information
Slovenia Investment and Business Guide Volume 1 Strategic and Practical Information
Solomon Islands Investment and Business Guide Volume 1 Strategic and Practical Information
Somalia Investment and Business Guide Volume 1 Strategic and Practical Information
South Africa Investment and Business Guide Volume 1 Strategic and Practical Information
Spain Investment and Business Guide Volume 1 Strategic and Practical Information
Sri Lanka Investment and Business Guide Volume 1 Strategic and Practical Information
St. Helena Investment and Business Guide Volume 1 Strategic and Practical Information
St. Pierre & Miquelon Investment and Business Guide Volume 1 Strategic and Practical Information
Sudan (Republic of the Sudan) Investment and Business Guide Volume 1 Strategic and Practical Information
Sudan South Investment and Business Guide Volume 1 Strategic and Practical Information
Suriname Investment and Business Guide Volume 1 Strategic and Practical Information
Swaziland Investment and Business Guide Volume 1 Strategic and Practical Information
Sweden Investment and Business Guide Volume 1 Strategic and Practical Information
Switzerland Investment and Business Guide Volume 1 Strategic and Practical Information
Syria Investment and Business Guide Volume 1 Strategic and Practical Information
Taiwan Investment and Business Guide Volume 1 Strategic and Practical Information
Tajikistan Investment and Business Guide Volume 1 Strategic and Practical Information
Tanzania Investment and Business Guide Volume 1 Strategic and Practical Information
Thailand Investment and Business Guide Volume 1 Strategic and Practical Information
Timor Leste (Democratic Republic of Timor-Leste) Investment and Business Guide Volume 1 Strategic and Practical Information
Togo Investment and Business Guide Volume 1 Strategic and Practical Information
Tonga Investment and Business Guide Volume 1 Strategic and Practical Information
Trinidad and Tobago Investment and Business Guide Volume 1 Strategic and Practical Information
Tunisia Investment and Business Guide Volume 1 Strategic and Practical Information
Turkey Investment and Business Guide Volume 1 Strategic and Practical Information
Turkmenistan Investment and Business Guide Volume 1 Strategic and Practical Information
Turks & Caicos Investment and Business Guide Volume 1 Strategic and Practical Information
Tuvalu Investment and Business Guide Volume 1 Strategic and Practical Information
Uganda Investment and Business Guide Volume 1 Strategic and Practical Information
Ukraine Investment and Business Guide Volume 1 Strategic and Practical Information
United Arab Emirates Investment and Business Guide Volume 1 Strategic and Practical Information

TITLE
United Kingdom Investment and Business Guide Volume 1 Strategic and Practical Information
United States Investment and Business Guide Volume 1 Strategic and Practical Information
Uruguay Investment and Business Guide Volume 1 Strategic and Practical Information
Uzbekistan Investment and Business Guide Volume 1 Strategic and Practical Information
Vanuatu Investment and Business Guide Volume 1 Strategic and Practical Information
Vatican City (Holy See) Investment and Business Guide Volume 1 Strategic and Practical Information
Venezuela Investment and Business Guide Volume 1 Strategic and Practical Information
Vietnam Investment and Business Guide Volume 1 Strategic and Practical Information
Virgin Islands, British Investment and Business Guide Volume 1 Strategic and Practical Information
Wake Atoll Investment and Business Guide Volume 1 Strategic and Practical Information
Wallis & Futuna Investment and Business Guide Volume 1 Strategic and Practical Information
Western Sahara Investment and Business Guide Volume 1 Strategic and Practical Information
Yemen Investment and Business Guide Volume 1 Strategic and Practical Information
Zambia Investment and Business Guide Volume 1 Strategic and Practical Information
Zimbabwe Investment and Business Guide Volume 1 Strategic and Practical Information

Made in United States
Cleveland, OH
04 November 2026

47644762R00160